# Automating Salesforce Marketing Cloud

Reap all the benefits of the SFMC platform
and increase your productivity with the help of
real-world examples

**Greg Gifford**

**Jason Hanshaw**

BIRMINGHAM—MUMBAI

# Automating Salesforce Marketing Cloud

**Group Product Manager**: Alok Dhuri

**Publishing Product Manager**: Richa Tripathi

**Senior Editor**: Nisha Cleetus

**Content Development Editor**: Nithya Sadanandan

**Technical Editor**: Pradeep Sahu

**Copy Editor**: Safis Editing

**Project Coordinator**: Deeksha Thakkar

**Proofreader**: Safis Editing

**Indexer**: Manju Arasan

**Production Designer**: Vijay Kamble

**Marketing Coordinator**: Deepak Kumar

First published: March 2022

Production reference: 3270622

Published by Packt Publishing Ltd.

Livery Place

35 Livery Street

Birmingham

B3 2PB, UK.

ISBN 978-1-80323-719-0

www.packt.com

# Foreword

I remember when I first saw the post from *Greg* about this book. It was big news. Very big news. I watched as the marketing community responded with excitement. *I* was excited. Finally, a book that goes deeper into the root of automation in Salesforce Marketing Cloud (SFMC).

While this is a technical book, calling it that does it a disservice. Sometimes the word *technical* can be pretty scary and off putting, especially a *technical book*. We think: stuffed with big words, convoluted examples that confuse you, and obscure terms that make you want to give up. Thankfully, that's not what you'll find in this book. The authors have conquered the difficult challenge of writing a book that clearly explains the intricacies of automation in Salesforce Marketing Cloud, which will make you want to challenge your original views on automation. The authors don't talk down to you. They haven't rushed through chapters. They haven't assumed you are an expert. They have written this book with one thing in mind - helping all practitioners who want to increase their knowledge of automation theory and the applications of SFMC.

Each page of this book will help you get there, one actionable step at a time. This book is full of tangible examples, new ideas, snippets of code, and practical tips to build your automation muscles. You can see the level of research coming through in the content. So powerful, so refined, so right on point, and so needed. This book doesn't rush through the concept. It's about forming and understanding a much deeper level the power of automation – what automation is, and how to approach it programmatically. Whether you're new to Salesforce Marketing Cloud, or are an experienced practitioner, you'll come away with fresh insights and effective guidance to help bring you right back on track, with added confidence.

*Guilda Hilaire*

*Director, Product Marketing*

*Salesforce, Inc.*

# Contributors

## About the authors

**Greg Gifford**, also known as *Gortonington* inside the Salesforce Marketing Cloud community, is a Salesforce MVP, Salesforce Marketing Champion, Trailblazer Community Group Leader, and a subject matter expert on the platform. As founder and managing director of `HowToSFMC.com`, Greg has made a large investment in the community and has striven to create a nurturing and learning-focused environment. Greg is also the owner and author of a blog, `gortonington.com`, where he posts interesting things he learns about Marketing Cloud or any other helpful tips or advice he can share. Greg is also very active on Salesforce Stack Exchange and is currently the top Marketing Cloud contributor of all time there under his alias, Gortonington. Greg is currently employed at Merkle as the director of SFMC engineering.

**Jason Hanshaw** is a Salesforce Marketing Cloud engineer with extensive experience in building solutions for the platform. A former web developer, he brings a background in web application development to Marketing Cloud in order to build innovative solutions that extend capabilities and meet complex needs. He is the author of the blog `InvokeCreate.dev` where he shares project-based examples for getting the most out of the platform. Jason is an avid contributor on Stack Exchange and within digital marketing communities, and is always seeking to grow his knowledge and share his own with others.

# About the reviewers

**Cameron Robert** is a marketing and automation subject matter expert from Australia. He is a Salesforce Certified Expert, Salesforce Marketing Champion 2020-2021, Trailblazer Community Group Leader, and a YouTube and blog content creator, as well as contributing to the Salesforce Marketing Cloud community wherever possible.

Specializing in implementation and enablement, Cameron has helped numerous businesses adopt Marketing Cloud and realize value from their projects. He is passionate about helping new users to onboard and unlock the full potential of Salesforce Marketing Cloud.

**Jason Cort** is a 4x Salesforce Certified CRM Technology specialist with 12+ years' experience across multiple platforms. With a primary focus on Salesforce Marketing Cloud, he has been a Salesforce Marketing Champion since 2020 and is one of the co-founders of HowToSFMC.com, where the community shares advice and tips for making the most of Salesforce Marketing Cloud and much more. Jason has presented webinars covering email deliverability and Salesforce Marketing Cloud functionality and has delivered presentations at email industry events including Litmus Live. He has worked in a range of industries, both on the brand side and as a consultant, and is a passionate advocate of making technology work harder to enable users to work smarter and more effectively.

**Shibu Abraham** is a Salesforce MVP and a Marketing Champion. Shibu currently heads the APAC Salesforce Practice for UST, a Crest Partner of Salesforce. He is also an Agile Champion and holds numerous certifications from both Salesforce and the Agile community. He also leads the Marketing Cloud Trailblazer Community Group in Malaysia. He is a big fan of Lightning Web Components (LWC), marketing automation, programming in SFMC, and content creation on SFMC topics. He believes in innovation, continuous learning, and sharing knowledge about Salesforce and promotes various events for the Salesforce Trailblazer Community.

# Table of Contents

# 3

# SFMC Automation Best Practices

# Section 2: Optimizing Automation inside of SFMC

## 4

## Automating Email Sends

## 5

## Automating Your ETL and Data

# 6

## The Magic of Script Activities

# 7

## The Power of In-Step APIs

# 8
## Creating Mini Web Apps

# Section 3: Optimizing the Automation of SFMC from External Sources

# 9
## Getting Started with Custom Integrations

# 10
# Exploring SFMC as a Piece of the Puzzle

# 11
# Exploring SDKs, APIs, and Specs

# 12
# Webhooks and Microservices

# 13

## Exploring Custom Journey Builder Activities

# Section 4: Conclusion

# 14

## Carpe Omnia

## Index

## Other Books You May Enjoy

# Preface

Are you a current user of **Salesforce Marketing Cloud (SFMC)**? Have you ever thought, *"There has to be an easier way to do this!"* or *"I am getting tired of copy and paste! I need more from my career"*? Then this book is for you.

We will dive into learning how to create new efficient and scalable solutions for the platform based on automation, both internally and externally. You will learn how to make your emails essentially send themselves and how to build applications and scripts to do monotonous tasks and help create shortcuts for your development needs.

Let's help you learn the theory, knowledge, skills, and more advanced use cases so that once you are done, you can go on to build your own automations and solutions to make your Marketing Cloud platform rise to the next level of efficiency!

## Who this book is for

This book is intended for those who are knowledgeable in SFMC and have a good grasp of both the platform and the tools inside of it. The purpose of this book is to help teach you how to *work smarter, not harder* inside of SFMC and get as much as possible out of the tools. Although not required, some development knowledge and skill is a plus to get the most out of this book.

## What this book covers

*Chapter 1, What Is Automation?*, takes you through the basic concepts of automation and why automation is important. It will go over what exactly automation is and the reason behind doing it. It will also go into detail on the best ways to implement and create solutions for automation. We will see high-level strategies as well as more intricate and technical tactics for automation implementation and maintenance.

*Chapter 2, SFMC Automation Tools*, is an overview of Automation Studio and Journey Builder. This chapter focuses on an overview of these two and how they work to help the internal automation of the platform.

*Chapter 3, SFMC Automation Best Practices*, dives into best practices for automation in SFMC with a major focus on things such as performance, efficiency, scalability, context, and preference.

*Chapter 4, Automating Email Sends*, covers the basics and some more in-depth knowledge of best practices and considerations for automation. With all this background under our belts, we start to explore real-life scenarios to put this knowledge into practice.

*Chapter 5, Automating Your ETL and Data*, moves to the bread and butter of what automation is made for – data! We discuss automating ETL via import/export/query activities as well as filter activities, and similar activities for segmentation and data staging.

*Chapter 6, The Magic of Script Activities*, takes the next step forward into developer-level solutions. This is a quick introduction to utilizing custom solutions using AMPscript or SSJS inside of script activities.

*Chapter 7, The Power of In-Step APIs*, explores the option of making API calls from inside SFMC. Through script activities, we can do API calls via WSProxy, native functions, and HTTP POST/GET to the internal endpoints. But we can also use Script.Util content syndication functions to make calls to external endpoints and add integration/interaction with external services.

*Chapter 8, Create Mini Web Apps*, introduces you to more advanced API implementation and uses. We will be diving into advanced development solutions that can essentially create mini web apps inside your automations!

*Chapter 9, Getting Started with Custom Integrations*, introduces you to proper planning methods as well as helping you understand the basic integration toolkits. This should serve as an introduction to the tooling, terminology, limitations, and basic setup necessary to begin building custom solutions.

*Chapter 10, Exploring SFMC as a Piece of the Puzzle*, dives into determining how to identify areas in your processes for automation as well as how to structure your project for success.

*Chapter 11, Exploring SDKs, APIs, and Specs*, covers the standard Marketing Cloud SDKs, including how to both read and extend the capabilities provided. Also, you will learn the major differences between the Marketing Cloud REST and SOAP APIs as well as how to create your own API gateway.

*Chapter 12, Webhooks and Microservices*, covers the basics of both webhooks and microservices as well as how to functionally incorporate these into your current business processes.

*Chapter 13*, *Exploring Custom Journey Builder Activities*, shows how to design, develop, test, and execute custom Journey Builder activities within Marketing Cloud. Special emphasis will be given to common component files as well as authentication and best practices.

*Chapter 14*, *Carpe Omnia*, is a basic recap and wrap-up of the book touching on the main points that we went over and the possibilities that are now open to us, as well as giving some last-minute tips and tricks based on this newly acquired knowledge.

# To get the most out of this book

The following is a list of software and languages covered inside this book. Although there are a lot of development aspects listed, not all are a requirement for understanding; rather, they are more a recommendation to get the most out of the book. The only major requirement is to have a licensed version of SFMC and have good general knowledge of the platform.

| Software/languages covered in the book | Requirements |
| --- | --- |
| Salesforce Marketing Cloud | Licensed version of Salesforce Marketing Cloud |
| AMPscript | Basic understanding of the purpose and syntax of the proprietary language |
| Server-side Javascript | Basic understanding of the purpose and syntax of the proprietary language |
| SQL Select Queries | Basic understanding of the purpose and syntax of SQL Select Queries |
| Heroku | A basic understanding of what Heroku is and how it is used |
| General Development | A basic understanding of development in general, with a focus on software development |

As you may notice, there are a few different languages and development capabilities listed here. These are not required beyond a very basic level. Most of it you can pick up inside the book or use the listed resources or general references on the internet to make sense of it.

> **Note**
>
> If you are using the digital version of this book, we advise you to type the code yourself or access the code from the book's GitHub repository (a link is available in the next section). Doing so will help you avoid any potential errors related to the copying and pasting of code.

# Download the example code files

You can download the example code files for this book from GitHub at `https://github.com/PacktPublishing/Automating-Salesforce-Marketing-Cloud`. If there's an update to the code, it will be updated in the GitHub repository.

We also have other code bundles from our rich catalog of books and videos available at `https://github.com/PacktPublishing/`. Check them out!

# Download the color images

We also provide a PDF file that has color images of the screenshots and diagrams used in this book. You can download it here: `https://static.packt-cdn.com/downloads/9781803237190_ColorImages.pdf`.

# Conventions used

There are a number of text conventions used throughout this book.

`Code in text`: Indicates code words in text, database table names, folder names, filenames, file extensions, pathnames, dummy URLs, user input, and Twitter handles. Here is an example: "PUT sends across an encrypted payload to interact with the target for overwrite update, but if that object does not exist, then PUT may create it instead."

A block of code is set as follows:

```
<script runat="server">
Platform.Load("Core","1.1.1")


var url = https://{{et_subdomain}}.rest.marketingcloudapis.com/
email/v1/rest
var req = new Script.Util.HttpGet(url);
var resp = req.send();</script>
```

When we wish to draw your attention to a particular part of a code block, the relevant lines or items are set in bold:

```
<script runat="server">
Platform.Load("Core","1.1.1")


var url = https://{{et_subdomain}}.rest.marketingcloudapis.com/
email/v1/rest
var req = new Script.Util.HttpGet(url);
var resp = req.send();</script>
```

Any command-line input or output is written as follows:

```
<script runat=server>
    Platform.Load("Core","1.1.1");
    var prox = new Script.Util.WSProxy();

    var name = "My Automation";
    var request = prox.retrieve("Automation", ["ProgramID"], {
        Property: "Name",
        SimpleOperator: "equals",
        Value: name
    });

    var objId = request.Results[0].ObjectID;
</script>
```

**Bold**: Indicates a new term, an important word, or words that you see onscreen. For instance, words in menus or dialog boxes appear in **bold**. Here is an example: "To do this, navigate to the **User Settings** menu and select **Developer Settings**."

> **Tips or Important Notes**
> Appear like this.

# Get in touch

Feedback from our readers is always welcome.

**General feedback**: If you have questions about any aspect of this book, email us at customercare@packtpub.com and mention the book title in the subject of your message.

**Errata**: Although we have taken every care to ensure the accuracy of our content, mistakes do happen. If you have found a mistake in this book, we would be grateful if you would report this to us. Please visit www.packtpub.com/support/errata and fill in the form.

**Piracy**: If you come across any illegal copies of our works in any form on the internet, we would be grateful if you would provide us with the location address or website name. Please contact us at copyright@packt.com with a link to the material.

**If you are interested in becoming an author**: If there is a topic that you have expertise in and you are interested in either writing or contributing to a book, please visit authors.packtpub.com.

# Share Your Thoughts

Once you've read *Automating Salesforce Marketing Cloud*, we'd love to hear your thoughts! Scan the QR code below to go straight to the Amazon review page for this book and share your feedback.

https://packt.link/r/1803237198

Your review is important to us and the tech community and will help us make sure we're delivering excellent quality content.

# Section 1: Automation Theory and Automations in SFMC

In this first section, you will get an understanding of the main ideas behind automation theory and the automation-related components inside of SFMC.

This section contains the following chapters:

- *Chapter 1, What Is Automation?*
- *Chapter 2, SFMC Automation Tools*
- *Chapter 3, SFMC Automation Best Practices*

# 1
# What Is Automation?

**Automation** is something that has become so ingrained in our society that we almost take it for granted. It is in our daily activities and helps us to achieve so many of our wonderful and innovative inventions. The odd thing though is that despite automation being such a day-to-day thing, not many people can actually explain what it means or where it came from. To help get us all in the right mindset, we first wanted to go over what exactly automation and **automation theory** are.

In this chapter, we will cover the following topics:

- *Automation theory*: A dive into the history of automation, the theory behind why automation is useful, and how it should be used

- *Defining automation*: Solidifying the meaning behind our focus in the book by defining exactly what an automation is

- *Automation opportunities and pitfalls*: A broad overview of the different benefits and potential risks that go along with automation

- *Concepts of automation*: Basic concepts related to automation and the areas they affect

- *Implementation best practices*: Some basic best practices related to automation when looking to implement it

- *Always Be Documenting (ABD)*: A case for why you should be documenting each automation and solution you create

With this knowledge, we will be prepared to move forward and fully digest the automation capabilities and possibilities related to Salesforce Marketing Cloud, as discussed further in this book.

# Automation theory

In some ways, automation theory is a self-feeding theory in that as each advancement happens, it will use that step as a building block to making further advances to larger and more significant feats. This means that before we dig into the exact meaning of what automation is, we should look at the history of automation and automation theory over the years. This rich history is what built the automation theory and capabilities that we know and love today, and will give great insight into the future of automation as well.

From the development of the first computer, all the way to recent advances in AI, automation theory has had a significant and life-altering impact on humanity and history. Each one of these developments and inventions has helped forge the way for further automation and efficiency in an exponential way. These advances have created a steady push forward to remove all the manual aspects of any activity or process to help improve the speed, efficiency, and possibilities of the results.

We could probably even go all the way back to the very beginnings of mankind's rise to find the roots of automation theory. The very first automation could have been something as simple as the repeating loop our roaming ancestors took when hunting and/or gathering or even utilizing a tool or their environment to remove repetitive actions in their day-to-day life. Automation does not need to involve technology as we view it today!

Without automation theory, the computer would never have existed, changing the entire world we live in today. And that is only the most recent example of how automation has changed our lives. Look at the world's first moving assembly line for mass production created by Henry Ford (`https://corporate.ford.com/articles/history/moving-assembly-line.html`). Without that innovation, our entire world would be irrevocably different.

Automation theory has helped advance and shape technology and theories throughout the years, including such recent advances as the following:

- **Control functions** (electronic digital computer)
- **Programming languages and capabilities** (computers and machines)
- **A vast array of sensor technology** (light, electromagnetic, kinetic, and so on)
- **Advanced mathematical theory of control systems** (evolved during WWII)
- **Artificial intelligence** (robotics and learning systems)

These advances have set the stage for the highly interconnected and digital world that we experience today. The simultaneous development and maturation of many technologies, in particular, information technologies, have enabled vast levels of interdependence and communication between previously disparate systems that were impossible before. While not a new feature of this development, automation has recently taken center stage in discussions about the future of business, communication, production, and many other aspects of our lives.

To help understand this, we wanted to provide a quick visual representation of automation theory as just described.

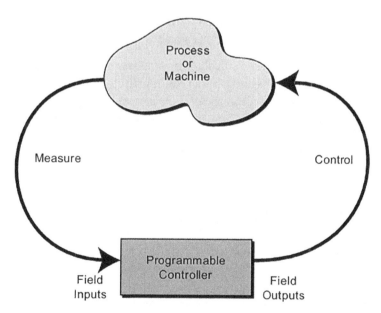

Figure 1.1 – Visual representation of automation theory

Now that we have a strong understanding of the history of automation and how it has affected our lives, let's figure out what exactly it is.

# Automation definition

The dictionary defines automation as *the technique of making an apparatus, a process, or a system operate automatically* (Merriam-Webster: `https://www.merriam-webster.com/dictionary/automation`). That's a bit generic for our purposes, so let's consider it in an IT context so that we can make that more applicable to this domain. Automation is the use of repeated instructions to create a process that replaces previously used human intervention in order to accomplish a task. There, that's a bit better, right?

It has become a buzzword in our modern era, and its application has re-shaped the ways that we interact and live within our world. From home appliances to robotic rovers on other worlds, automation has found its way into the fabric of our technical and social world. In a world driven by speed, connectivity, and efficiency, it's not hard to see why it's become such a central focus of many organizations and technologies today.

One of the more obvious consequences from this transformative concept, and one relevant to this book, has been the dramatic shift in the ways that both business and individuals communicate and interact with each other in emerging digital spaces. As the rate at which aspects of our lives occur within these spaces increases, so has the expectations for instantaneous communication and services tailored to the personalized needs of individuals.

This has presented challenges for sure, but has also created tremendous opportunities for organizations that have embraced this digital transformation and have sought to redefine their business and processes to operate in this space.

This digital transformation has been critical for businesses to meet emerging customer demands and expectations, and has become a requirement to compete in this new global, digital world. This does not come without cost, however, and businesses today must be more cognizant than ever before of how their organization uses technology, both internally and externally.

One of the key components and performance multipliers in digital transformation is automation. Incorporating automation as a central feature in business processes, aside from introducing an innovative mindset to an organization, introduces efficiency in costs and performance that can have dramatic impacts when well planned and thoughtfully applied. In that vein, let's move onward to learn about the different opportunities and pitfalls that come along with automation.

# Automation opportunities and pitfalls

Before diving further into the concept of automation, it's helpful to consider exactly why it can be such an important component of business processes and what risks are associated with its implementation.

First, automation is essential for reducing both financial and productivity costs associated with repetitive, time-consuming, and error-prone tasks. These could range from manual data-entry processes to complex monitoring or communication activities. In addition to its impact on these sorts of tasks, when well planned, it can introduce a single standard of quality that can be replicated and adhered to over time.

# Opportunities

Let's take a deeper look into the benefits that can be extracted from incorporating automation into your business processes. First, I wanted to start with a quick visual to show the benefits and then from there, we will dive deeper into each aspect.

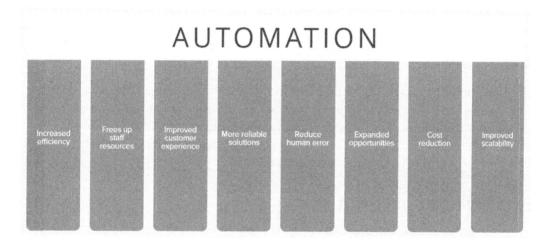

Figure 1.2 – Visualization of the benefits of automation

As you can see in each of the bars from the visual, there are a ton of great opportunities available. Now, let's take a deeper dive into these benefits.

## Increased efficiency

One of the simplest benefits of incorporating automation is that it increases the efficiency with which tasks or events can be completed. When repetitive or time-intensive tasks are eliminated, it frees up resources to do more innovative and impactful work. This provides an immediate cost benefit as resources can be allocated to other impactful projects while also *reducing the strain on employees*, all without a loss in productivity.

Its *impact in a customer-facing context* can be even more beneficial. As customers demand real-time engagement and services, being able to meet them in the moment is critical. Whether it's automated communication for a password reset request, or a one-click online checkout, creating sustainable automated processes that can deliver on customer requests immediately is a massive benefit and has become an expectation in our digital world.

## More reliable solutions

When it comes to any solution or project, consistent and reliable quality is an important factor for success. With manual solutions, where human input and decision making are ever-present and necessary for the completion of a task, there are risk factors that will inevitably impact the overall stability and reliability of the performance. *Humans, while our capacities for attention and skill are prodigious, are subject to factors that will reduce work quality and performance.* Whether it's a poor night's sleep, long periods of intense focus, or multi-tasking, attention to detail and performance will vary across individuals and circumstances.

This limitation provides an opportunity for automation. A well-defined, automated process suffers from no degradation of attention, nor experiences performance dips due to fatigue or distraction. In an interconnected global space, having an automated system that can operate 24 hours a day to meet challenges and complete tasks is important to a process that needs to be responsive on demand.

# Expanded opportunities

While not initially apparent, *automation can actually improve efficiency and productivity across teams* in an organization by exposing the nature of your current business processes. Before a system can be automated, those underlying processes must be thoroughly analyzed in order to both define opportunities where automation is feasible and to define what it's meant to accomplish.

By exposing these underlying procedures, it *encourages conversations about the current goals and future state of the program*, which can help improve the overall quality and foster innovation.

In addition to this, automation can work as a centralizing force for many disparate processes that may otherwise be isolated and poorly understood. By combining data and workflows into a centralized system that is capable of both producing and receiving input or completing a task, you can act on events automatically and extend the capabilities of your solutions while increasing productivity.

# Pitfalls

Now that we've covered just a few of the benefits that automation can bring to an organization, it's important to also consider the potential risks or downsides that can come from incorporating this as well.

## High initial investment

It has been said that nothing in life is free and automation, unfortunately, is no exception.

First, there are the obvious financial costs that come with implementing automation solutions. Whether it's purchasing cloud storage, training for teams to learn new skills and adjust to new workflows, or just the amount of planning and development needed to implement the solution, the decision to automate a process should not be taken lightly.

Secondly, it is important to consider the opportunity and productivity costs that take away from other current or planned initiatives. Attention is a finite resource and draining it for a new initiative comes at the expense of other priorities.

When you carefully consider the amount of planning, development, testing, documentation, and training that can go into proposed automation, it can become daunting to undertake for some, and perhaps impractical for others.

## Less ability to pivot quickly

We all know it's a perfect world, and all your solutions and initiatives are performing so well it's time to just set it and forget about it, right? Er, maybe not.

Even with the proper planning and strategies when developing automated solutions, unexpected shifts can leave your well-defined process at a disadvantage. Perhaps it's an urgent marketing need, or a new legal requirement that must be implemented to stay compliant, but automation can make you inflexible at an inopportune time.

By their nature, automated solutions are likely narrow and well-defined, which can leave them vulnerable to sudden shifts in goals that invalidate the existing implementation.

## You get out what you put in

It seems self-explanatory, but your solution is only as good as the strategy and the team behind it. Failing to adequately account for edge cases, resourcing, stable deployment processes, or any number of other factors in the project life cycle can have a significant impact on the overall performance of the automated solution.

While it's been noted that automation can increase the stability and quality of your workflows, it should be remembered that you get out what you put into it and poorly designed automation can cascade issues much more dramatically than a manual process.

Now that we've taken a look at some of the general advantages, and disadvantages, of automation, let's take a look at some select core concepts so we can get a better grasp of what automation looks like exactly.

## Concepts of automation

Many individual concepts within automation help define what it encompasses technically. In this section, let's focus on a few that are more applicable to common business scenarios or solutions within **Software as a Service (SaaS)**.

To help visualize these concepts, please reference the following diagram:

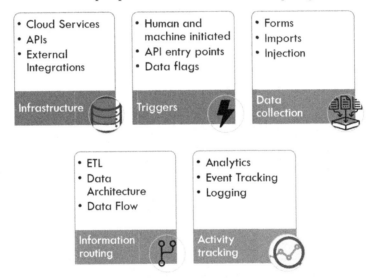

Figure 1.3 – Visualization of the concepts of automation

Now that we have seen the visualization, let's take a deeper dive into exactly what these concepts mean.

## Infrastructure

This is an important piece of the automation puzzle, and one not to be taken lightly. Thankfully, most SaaS will largely take care of this issue upfront. You begin provisioned with a powerful cloud solutions environment that can scale to your needs and contains robust APIs for interacting both internally and externally with the platform. Problem solved? Yes, but also no.

First, let's explore exactly what an API is. **API** is an acronym for **Application Programming Interface**, which is basically a middle software that allows two applications to talk to each other. APIs are essentially messengers for your two applications. I like to view it as if the API is a phone call between two friends. You can share information, receive information, make plans, cancel plans, and more via a phone call. Although you each have phones, voices, and so on, without the connection provided by the call, the API, you could not connect and communicate these messages without direct interaction. Now, back to the SaaS infrastructure.

While most SaaS platforms do resolve a lot of issues around provisioning and configuration, it may only be a piece in your larger workflow. Perhaps there is a business need for automating some communication with an external service at dynamic points in a customer life cycle? While some built-in tools can provide us with a way to track milestones in a customer journey, integrating custom services or solutions can require more complex solutions that require outside integrations.

Maybe you want to utilize your SaaS for individual functions within a larger automated workflow for your organization and not as a standalone product. Considering the road that your solutions run on is an important step in planning and designing a technical solution.

When selecting the environment that will house a given component of your solution, consider how well it integrates with the other platforms you've defined. Knowing how your systems are going to talk to each other is a key step of the planning phase and can drive the direction of your technical solution.

# Triggers

Triggers are the events that *flag* an activity or process from some response or action by your automated solution. These can be initiated by both humans and machines and are the primary method by which your automated solution is compelled to complete some tasks.

A common form of triggers in most SaaS platforms is API entry points. Usually, when you call an API into the platform, it comes in with information that is used once the call is received (the trigger to take an action) to create a new action or process, such as returning data from the platform to the requestor.

Another example might be a form hosted on a website, and integrated with an external service or custom solution. The user triggers the event by submitting the form on the website, and an automated solution is called by that event to take some action (say, send an email confirmation).

These types of events can take many forms and differ in both type and the complexity of the action being triggered. For a webhook, like our form submission scenario above, some event is triggered automatically when an event has taken place in our environment.

Using something like an API, for instance, requires data to be requested and for a response to be generated based on the validity of that request. The main takeaway here is that we need to keep in mind that there is a wide range of possible trigger events, but the core concept remains consistent.

## Data collection

Data collection often involves a form being completed, but it can also involve data being automatically extracted or received from a system. For most automated processes, the validity and robustness of your data store can define the scope or functionality of the solution.

While there are use cases where a method of data ingestion or collection is not needed, and the trigger itself is the only required source of action, most processes will require some form of data collection to generate an automated solution.

Planning how your data will be ingested and stored should be a priority when developing the flow of your automated solution. Ensuring your data store has a consistent structure and schema, and that the data you're storing is properly formatted and reliably populated, are both key to ensuring that you can retrieve it reliably when needed and that it will integrate well with your solution.

Important in this regard will be data validation, particularly when capturing or importing data from user-input or external services. Your solution will only be as good as the data you collect for it, so take care to make sure it's as clean and consistent as possible.

## Information routing

Information routing involves moving data between people or systems where business rules and logic dictate where data needs to travel next. This is a common concept that can be found in solutions both internal and external to most SaaS platforms. When implementing a solution that utilizes complex data flows, containing multiple sources or destinations, understanding the routing necessary to seamlessly pull it together into a final source requires careful consideration of both your individual components and of how they depend and interrelate with one another. Sequencing, timing, and monitoring are especially critical and can be the difference between a successful or failed program.

For external solutions or those that involve multiple systems integrating within the same core initiative, it becomes even more important to understand the information routing occurring with a solution. In this scenario, you're accounting for the flows across various services that are subject to failures, timing inconsistencies, and misconfigured trigger events, among others.

## Activity tracking

How can we define the success or failure of a program if we don't have a reliable way of tracking its performance against our defined goals? Tracking what happens from end to end in a process allows processes to be audited and measured in order to improve the solution or otherwise highlight points of failure that make it ill-suited for automation.

When integrating with external systems, this becomes even more critical, as there are more points for failure that must be accounted for and tracked reliably at the request level. Taking a proactive approach to logging, in addition to constructing your solution for ease in reporting and accountability, can help mitigate missed errors that propagate or obvious points for remediation and revision.

With these core concepts in hand, let's take a look at some common best practices to consider when building automated solutions.

# Implementation best practices

As we've indicated previously, while automation can be a powerful multiplier for efficiency and productivity, there are no guarantees. Poor planning or implementation can lead to solutions that fail to meet the need at hand or, worse, negatively impact your initiatives as a whole. While many important aspects of the automation development life cycle can dictate the overall success of the project, by far the most important step is planning and strategy.

Moving forward without a clear idea on both your objectives, and detailed solutions to meet them, can lead to runaway scope, poorly designed systems, and unnecessary complexity. Let's take a look at a few best practices to keep in mind during this crucial step of the automation process.

## Starting small

While it may be enticing to jump head-first into automating large and complex portions of your processes, the universally accepted best practice is to start small and target those items that will return the highest value for the lowest level of effort. Work with related teams to identify processes that are time-consuming or error-prone, particularly those that are both simple and repetitious.

Finding routine, manual processes that are low-risk and high-visibility ensures that you're both providing real value with your solution while not impacting your current initiatives in the event that something goes awry. Processes with low exception rates, that do not require human intervention, should be considered in this regard as well.

Ideally, you should consider those processes that are stable, well documented, and with well-defined risk and cost. Getting buy-in from internal teams is important as well, so looking for tasks where the savings from automation can be quantified and measured can drive support and adoption to get your solution into production.

Try and avoid the Rube Goldberg effect when an automated solution becomes so complex that no one but its creator has a hope of understanding its flow or intent. Processes that are atomic, reusable, and simple on their own are ideal.

## Understanding the process

The term *flying blind* has a negative connotation for a reason. Approaching your planning and strategy without an adequate understanding of the systems, or processes, that you will be automating is a recipe for failure. Understanding how a given process is structured end to end, including how it operates both internally as well as with external systems, is crucial to delivering a successful solution on time. A failure to account for some factor during your planning stage can derail a project, or kill it completely, if your solution no longer becomes viable or runs over the projected costs.

Understand the process well and why each of its steps is performed in its current sequence. It is important to know why things are performed in their current state as they might not be suitable for automation, or only partially suitable. It can be counter-intuitive to automate four tasks when only two of them make sense and the other two could potentially even increase workload via automation.

Rather than fully automating in bulk, automating *helpers* as part of a process can be vastly more efficient than forcing a full process to be automated. Sometimes, checks and balances are required that just simply cannot be automated. Trying to force this into an automated process could greatly increase the risk or increase the level of effort on other teams to do the manual checking amid the automation, and so on.

## Sticking to the objective

While automating data management, email deployment activities, or custom workflows and processes, you must always stick to the original objective outlined in your planning and strategy process. The introduction of a new business need or functionality, or new feature within the platform, can be alluring to attach to a project still in development, but it is important to stay focused on the initial needs and requirements outlined at the beginning.

By staying on track with your initial scope, you eliminate the possibilities of new additions either slowing down your implementation or derailing it altogether. Adding additional functionality in the middle of a project introduces unnecessary risks and has the potential to change the very objective of the solution you've previously outlined. So, while it might be tempting to turn your next data management process into a full-fledged machine learning solution, it's best to avoid this and to look for areas to enhance or branch for future projects.

These are just a few of the very important considerations and practices to take into account when getting started with the planning and strategy portion of the automation project life cycle. Obviously, there are other important practices to keep in mind during the development and testing phases of your project that have been touched on earlier in this chapter. One more that we should call out here is **testing**.

While you may think that your well-planned and developed project is immune to failure, you must identify likely exceptions and develop a testing strategy before you even begin your development. Having a solid testing plan and execution can reduce the error rate of your automation processes and can help drive more adoption and innovation across other processes in your organization.

Now, let's cover another best practice that is critical to the development and continued success of an automation project: **documentation**.

# ABD – Always Be Documenting

You've written well-thought-out and concise code, so you don't really need to document it right? Wrong. We're all familiar with the experience of reviewing the code comprising a feature, where the nature of its structure, or even its intent, isn't immediately obvious. Worse, we may not know how it integrates with other systems or parts of the solution. By not documenting your code and configuration, and how it integrates with other parts of your solution, you've isolated the group of people familiar with it to a single person, or small team, while introducing the risk that someone may unwittingly impact your solution or services it relies on.

The primary reason that documentation is ignored is because of time, and conflicting priorities. Development doesn't occur in a vacuum, and it's not often that we have the time to stop everything and focus on documentation for our solutions. Apart from designing and development, we also have to consider unit testing, user acceptance criteria and quality assurance, and code reviews (among others).

Documentation is easily pushed to the side for other priorities, and not considered essential. In reality, it can be one of the most important factors for the final, and continued, success of a solution.

Regardless of the task you are automating, it is very likely that you or your team will have to revisit the solution at some point in the future. The purpose of certain blocks of code, exceptions that need to be considered, or even the configuration itself might have faded with time in the minds of the author and those new to the project as a whole may be completely lost. By not documenting your process thoroughly, you incur additional costs in time and effort when revisiting your solution requires additional time to unravel its meaning or purpose. Worse still is the fact that you add additional risk by missing a key component that, while common knowledge during your development phase, has been forgotten.

As developers, when approached with a new system or project, our first inclination is to likely seek out and review the documentation. Next time someone wants to understand your solution, you can simply point them to your documentation. It saves time and effort for you and gives them a helpful reference so that they can self-learn without being dependent on your time and availability.

In addition to this, documentation can make you both a better developer and team member. When working on an automated solution, it can be very easy to get tunnel-vision with a specific configuration or block of code, and how that holistically fits in with the overall structure of the project may be lost. The process of creating documentation during development ensures that you're always keeping the purpose of your project in focus, and it shapes the way that you create the individual components of your solution. There is also an easy reference for yourself, or your colleagues, that can aid in collaboration among team members and increase both the stability and quality of your solution.

## Documentation best practices

Now that we understand some of the advantages of documentation, let's take a look at some best practices that will make it more useful to those reading it.

First, understand who the audience is for your documentation. Will it be other developers, or are you providing supplementary documentation for marketing or business teams? Including detailed code blocks and descriptions of their functionality may be critical for developers, but it's sure to drive away non-technical resources on your team. Structure your documentation to match the expectations of its intended audience in order for it to be both readable and effective.

Secondly, create a short, but descriptive, summary of your solution that explains the main purpose and intent of the project as a whole. This will help readers derive the purpose of the solution that you've automated as well as its relevance to their work or other business processes. Also, be sure to provide a description of the main components of your solution, noting any dependencies that may exist within your project. If your solution relies on APIs or third-party libraries, be sure to include their versions inside of your documentation as well.

Be generous with your coding examples when writing documentation for developers. Having a detailed explanation of what a given block is meant to accomplish, and how to both use and test its functionality, can save everyone time and effort when reviewing individual components in your solution. This will also make your code more readable as its intent will be clearly stated, and your solutions will rely less on inline-commenting or naming conventions to express their intent.

In summary, while it can be seen as a distraction or non-critical for a solution, documentation plays a key role in both the development and sustainability of your solution going forward. By empowering yourself and your team with a clear, and detailed, reference, you're incurring future savings of time and effort and ensuring that your solutions are more stable and of higher quality.

# Summary

We have now reached the end of our first chapter! This was a lot of fun so far, and we hope it was the same for you. You should now have a solid understanding of not only what exactly automation and the theory of automation *is*, but also the general concepts associated with these. After acquiring this knowledge, you should now have a general idea of the opportunities and pitfalls of automation and best practices for implementing it. After that, we wanted to emphasize the high importance of documentation on automation and the associated best practices.

With these new skills and knowledge gains, we are ready to move forward to the next chapter, where we will begin our journey into exploring Salesforce Marketing Cloud and the automation tools available inside it.

# 2
# SFMC Automation Tools

Every good SaaS worth its salt has automation capabilities. They have moved from being a cool feature to being necessary for success. Any good system will offer a variety of options to help optimize or create efficiencies in workflows. Whether they are baked-in and user-friendly or more developer-based and require technical skills and knowledge, there are almost always some automation capabilities. This could be a ton of different things, such as the following:

- A drag-and-drop scheduling tool
- A canvas-based pathing and logic tool
- Server scripting capabilities
- Widget functionality
- API capabilities

Each one of these gives you the ability to interact with the platform outside of general UI capabilities, allowing for efficiencies and automation. This statement is pretty much true regardless of whether those platforms focus on data, messaging, or one of the million other services that can be offered.

For this book though, we will be concentrating on automation in relation to just one specific platform – **Salesforce Marketing Cloud**. We will explore many aspects of this platform, such as the following:

- *Salesforce Marketing Cloud*: A brief history of the platform and details on what it is and what it does

- *Multi and cross-channel marketing*: Look at what multi-channel and cross-channel marketing is and how they are different

- *Automation tools in Marketing Cloud*: A dive into the built-in tools inside of Marketing Cloud

- *Journey Builder overview*: A broad overview of what Journey Builder is in regard to Salesforce Marketing Cloud

- *Automation Studio overview*: A broad overview of what Automation Studio is in regard to Salesforce Marketing Cloud

- *Comparing Automation Studio and Journey Builder*: A review and comparison between Journey Builder and Automation Studio

Learning about these tools and aspects will provide us with a strong base to build out our automations. The more we learn about where the platform came from, the history of the tools, and the details of how each tool works, functions, and interacts with others, as well as the platform itself, the more we can do in the future.

Let's not get too far ahead of ourselves yet though and instead of thinking about the future, let's dive a bit deeper into the past and learn about Salesforce Marketing Cloud and where it came from.

# Salesforce Marketing Cloud

**Salesforce Marketing Cloud** (**SFMC**) is a Salesforce platform that concentrates on multi-channel messaging and 1:1 customer journeys. Marketing Cloud originated back in December of 2000, then called ExactTarget. This tool was originally focused solely on email marketing messaging only and started fairly small and simple. From its beginning as ExactTarget down to the current Salesforce-owned iteration, Marketing Cloud has gone through many forms and changed direction more than once.

## The ExactTarget years

The platform slowly grew as time went on as it was a stable and versatile option with customer service that was above and beyond what was offered elsewhere. ExactTarget became a hit and continually grew and grew year by year. In late 2009, ExactTarget went international and established an office in London.

Through this powerful forward momentum, ExactTarget was able to purchase Pardot and iGoDigital among others in 2012 – increasing revenue and capabilities exponentially. These acquisitions gave ExactTarget more capabilities in multi-channel marketing and integrations. The platform shifted from just email to a more *marketing hub*-focused system, offering a lot of different capabilities and functionalities that placed them as a market leader.

This got ExactTarget a lot of attention and so the bigger companies started recognizing the potential. This is when Salesforce got involved and purchased ExactTarget in 2013. This was where the name Salesforce Marketing Cloud originated as the tool was rebranded and changed to fit within the Salesforce ecosystem. The official rebranding happened in 2014.

## Salesforce acquisition

As Salesforce worked to integrate the tool within its structure and model, there were a lot of shifts away from the way things were in ExactTarget. Through these changes, users gained capabilities such as a new pseudo-CMS capability via Content Builder, new capabilities with data extensions, and integrations with other Salesforce Clouds and products!

This platform grew from just a single focused email marketing messaging tool into a world-class, top-of-the-market platform for building and managing personalized multi-channel journeys and messaging. This included implementing SMS/MMS capabilities, mobile push notifications, social media, digital advertising, and more.

These changes led Marketing Cloud further and further from being just an email marketing platform and instead turned it into a full-service marketing tool that could effectively ingest, implement, execute, and report on all aspects of digital marketing. This vision and innovation have led SFMC to become a leader in the market and one of the most popular marketing tools available. Now that we know a brief history of the tool, let's move on to a look into multi-channel and cross-channel marketing inside the platform.

# Multi-channel and cross-channel marketing

Before digging into Marketing Cloud's foray into **multi-channel and cross-channel marketing**, our initial goal is to make sure we are all aware of what they are. Without knowledge of what multi-channel marketing or cross-channel marketing is, it doesn't really make as much sense or show the same level of impact, so we will give some quick insights into what they are.

# Multi-channel marketing

Multi-channel marketing leverages multiple communication channels and mediums, utilizing channels such as the following:

- Email marketing
- Mobile SMS/MMS and push
- Direct mail
- Social media

Leveraging multiple channels allows you to unify the numerous interactions your customer has with the marketing messaging they are receiving. Almost all messaging services are now multi-channel marketing, but even just a couple of years ago, this was a very strong selling point and something that only a few platforms had the capability to do (and do well). The following diagram gives a good visual representation of what we are talking about with regard to multi-channel marketing.

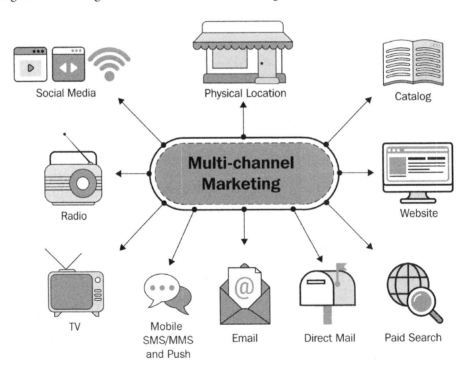

Figure 2.1 – Visualization of multi-channel marketing

Now that we have a good visualization, let's take a deeper dive into why you would want to use multi-channel marketing.

## Why use multi-channel marketing?

Now that we know what multi-channel marketing is, the question we need to ask is why is it important? What sort of value could you receive for all the added effort and organization required to utilize multiple different channels for your marketing campaigns?

Some of the major benefits are as follows:

- Expanded reach through the utilization of multiple channels.

- The ability to communicate with customers through their preferred channels.

- The combination of channels helps to unify messaging and perception.

- Increased engagement through broader reach with a unified strategy.

Now that we have a strong understanding of what multi-channel marketing is and why we would use it, let's move on to the very similar but also different cross-channel marketing.

# Cross-channel marketing

Cross-channel marketing is essentially people-based marketing. This is because it focuses on a combination of various marketing channels integrated together to form a more cohesive customer journey for your target audience. Through this integration and cross-pollination of messaging, you are able to let the customer control how they receive your messaging. This is basically the next step after multi-channel marketing as it takes that and further integrates and inter-connects messaging. Here is a good visualization of cross-channel marketing and it helps to differentiate multi-channel marketing from cross-channel marketing.

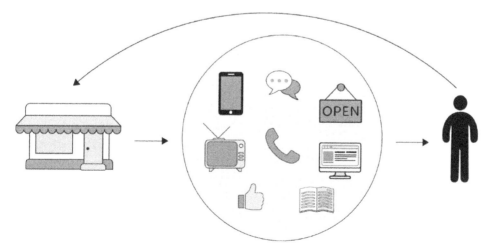

Figure 2.2 – Visualization of cross-channel marketing

As to how this visualization helps to show differentiation, you will notice that in multi-channel marketing, it all stems from the same place, but then sends the messages out across multiple mediums without them being connected in purpose, whereas the cross-channel marketing diagram shows that all the marketing mediums are being used collaboratively to engage the subscriber, rather than engaging separately. Now that we have learned what cross-channel marketing is, let's look at some of its uses.

## Why use cross-channel marketing?

So, we now get what cross-channel marketing is and how it is different from multi-channel marketing – but what does that mean for the benefits? What benefits does it offer and how are they different from what multi-channel marketing offers?

Here are the major benefits of cross-channel marketing:

- Optimized and holistic customer journeys
- Deeper personalization and customer preference for a 1:1 experience
- Increased engagement through more relevant messaging and touch points
- All messaging on one platform for easy access for your marketers
- Efficiencies and time saving for implementation and updating

With these benefits, we should now have a good understanding of cross-channel marketing and are ready to move forward with the story of Marketing Cloud as it evolves beyond just email.

## Marketing Cloud evolves beyond email

As with many companies in this market, Salesforce Marketing Cloud started as an **Email Service Provider** (**ESP**) to help with your email marketing needs. While email is a highly efficient and profitable messaging channel, there are other channels that can help capitalize and optimize customer communications beyond just email. By focusing just on email, you lose a ton of potential touch-points that may be preferable or more effective methods of connecting with some customers.

For these reasons, Marketing Cloud grew into multi-channel marketing through acquisitions and new services/improvements being developed, such as the following:

- Radian6
- Buddy Media
- IGoDigital
- CoTweet

This allows you to utilize the same platform for pretty much all of your marketing messaging needs. The issue is that these were still pretty siloed, and although you could create and use them on the same platform, it was still not fully integrated to utilize them easily in tandem.

After some further improvements to the platform, they were able to build a more cross-channel approach inside of their two built-in automation tools. Cross-channel marketing is very different than multi-channel marketing as it takes it a step beyond offering the service, into integrating each medium together to form a single, unified messaging journey/flow.

> **Times They Are A-Changing**
>
> As time goes on, the platform continues to grow. So, as the years go on, there is likely to be more and more added to it. At the time of writing this, we have no way of knowing what that will be. So, we highly recommend looking through Marketing Cloud release notes and official announcements for any changes or new features released after this book has been published to ensure you are working with the most recent and up-to-date information.

Now let's start to dig into the platform and see what makes it such an impressive tool.

# Automation tools in Marketing Cloud

Part of what helped Marketing Cloud to grow to be so powerful and so capable was the innovative ways they baked in **automation tools**. While most places preferred their automation capabilities to be more developer-friendly and less marketer-friendly, Marketing Cloud did both. They worked to allow marketers to have similar capabilities to the developers and technical experts without the high-level pre-requisite technical knowledge or skill necessary, while also further enabling the technical users' abilities to create custom solutions and integrations within the platform.

As these tools grew in capability and popularity, Marketing Cloud realized that these were items that needed to be bundled into every single enterprise, rather than having them as add-ons or optional. This way, companies could hit the ground running with some of the strongest and most capable automation tools available and not have to worry about further purchase orders or additional costs after the initial contract.

There are many different possible avenues that you can use to automate in SFMC. You can custom-build automation via different third-party integrations and connections, via raw API calls, internal scripting using proprietary languages, as well as marketer-focused internal automation tools. A good portion of the more customizable options are all developer-oriented, requiring a heavy technical skillset, but to counter this, Marketing Cloud also includes two very robust automation tools that are more marketer-friendly and require much less technical skill to utilize them well.

## Marketing Cloud tools

For this part, we will be keeping the focus on the baked-in automation capabilities of SFMC. Inside SFMC, there are two very distinct and powerful tools that can help us automate and make our lives easier with little to no technical skill required to efficiently operate. These tools are the following:

- **Journey Builder**: Focused on 1:1 journey mapping and custom interactions.
- **Automation Studio**: Batch-oriented activities to increase performance, efficiencies, and capabilities.

Each of these tools is pretty well renowned and extremely powerful in different ways. **Automation Studio** tends more towards the general idea behind automation, hence the name. Although it does not require a technical skillset to be utilized, the more technical knowledge you have, the more powerful **Automation Studio** becomes.

Journey Builder tends to be more trigger-based and 1:1 and focused more on pathways and the integration of multiple channels and activities. It also has a much lower technical knowledge and skill requirement to be utilized, making it less reliant on technical resources. This opens it up to non-technical marketers with little to no reduction in capabilities, allowing for a lower ramp-up and a lower-level pre-requisite skillset required.

In the next section, we will be going in-depth about what each of these tools is and will give further details on them. Each of these tools will greatly help to make your marketing more efficient and effective.

# Journey Builder overview

It's no surprise, in our current digital world, that customers both want and expect companies to respond in real time to their needs. Organizations that can deliver on these requests are at a significant advantage as they can build both brand loyalty and reputation while strengthening their own bottom line.

So, how can we provide customers with real-time responses and engagement in the moment? Enter **Journey Builder**. Journey Builder is an SFMC solution for providing complex 1-to-1 marketing experiences across channels that can both meet and anticipate customer needs so that organizations can deal with their customers individually in the moment.

So, just how does this solution enable 1-to-1 real-time marketing experiences? To understand that, we need to dive into the details of just what Journey Builder is and what it does. First, let's take a look at the types of journeys that are configurable within the Marketing Cloud.

# Single Send journeys

The first type of journey that can be configured in Marketing Cloud is the **Single Send journey**. This journey type allows for creating single, one-time, communications for email, SMS, and push marketing channels. The primary feature to note with this journey type is that it is limited only to a single instance of an activity, so repeated communications are not possible with this journey. Another consideration is the type of audience that can be utilized within this journey type. While email and SMS both allow only the data extension entry sources, push communications require an audience configured in Mobile Connect.

## Use cases

Single Send journeys can be a viable use case when data is already easily available or aggregated within Marketing Cloud and the needs for communication are both immediate and relatively simple. While there are other solutions that can provide this same functionality, such as **Automation Studio**, some users may find the centralization of the content, entry source, and scheduling options more intuitive with the Journey Builder interface.

# Transactional Send journeys

The **Transactional Send journey** type functions, more or less, as a UI implementation of the Transactional Messaging API. Unlike the API, which features no configuration or development settings with the UI, the Transactional Send journey type allows non-technical resources to set up the necessary API endpoints that developers can use to immediately send a transactional email message from the journey. While the entry source must be configured as a Transactional Messaging API endpoint, and only email messages are supported, there are some benefits of using this approach over more traditional Transactional Sends in Email Studio. First, the Transactional Messaging API executes a newer messaging system than traditional methods, which allows it to be both more performant and able to handle more throughput consistently compared to traditional triggered sends in the platform. A slight difference, due to this, is that the ability to select a priority for a message has become deprecated. With this new approach, all messages are deployed as soon as they are able, so you can be assured that every transactional journey is reaching your customer as fast as possible.

## Use cases

This journey type is ideal for any scenario where you need to enable real-time transactional messaging and want to utilize this capability with reduced need for technical knowledge to set it up. Within minutes, marketers can configure this journey to accept entries, and enable development teams to start integrating sends directly with the journey. Another added benefit is the inclusion of important metrics, integrated directly into the UI, which allows users to monitor important send metrics such as ongoing error counts and the depth of the current queue in the journey. Whether it's password reset requests or order confirmation email sends, marketers will find this to be an easy method to get their transactional real-time communications into production.

# Multi-Step journeys

The final journey type, and arguably the most powerful and important, is the **Multi-Step journey**. Unlike the previous two journey types, the Multi-Step journey allows for maximum flexibility and control in regards to both the entry and activity types that your journey implements. Journeys can be triggered from a variety of sources such as data extensions, API events, real-time changes in Sales and Service Cloud, among others. In addition to this flexibility in the entry source compared to the other journey types, Multi-Step journeys allow true cross-channel marketing capabilities rather than a more defined experience outlined in the other types. By allowing users to build journeys as complex as their business needs require, and in the channel their customers prefer, this has become the de facto journey type for most organizations and use cases.

## Use cases

Multi-Step journeys are particularly useful for complex or sequence journeys that need to perform actions across channels or time periods or require more advanced integration for entry or decision points across the journey. It allows for deep integration with the core Salesforce platform that isn't possible in the other journey types, with users able to read, create, and modify their CRM data in real time. This type also comes pre-configured with several templates that capture the most common use cases that organizations encounter, such as welcome series or abandoned cart journeys.

Now that we have some basic understanding of the various types of journeys that can be created and configured within the Marketing Cloud, let's take a look at some of the global configurations that aid marketers in both configuring and monitoring their lifecycles. It should be noted that while many of these configurations apply solely to the Multi-Step journey type, understanding their function can help inform both your selection of journey type as well as the flow of your customer experience.

# Journey Builder configuration overview

When building a multi-channel marketing journey, one of the most important distinctions to be aware of are the two types of data that can be actioned. This distinction can make or break your journey implementation and has a large impact on the decision-making as to how your flow is structured and any data dependencies are executed. Let's take a look at each data type and how they differ.

## Types of data

One of the most important considerations for marketers, and developers alike, is how and what data will drive their journey processes from entry to exit. Understanding exactly what data you need, and how your internal and external processes can support it, underlies every touchpoint in the journey lifecycle and can help drive strategy and technical discussions even in the planning phase of your projects. In Marketing Cloud, there are two data types that must be understood in order to effectively plan and build journeys: **contact data** and **journey data**.

## Journey data

When creating the entry source for your journey, you need to define the exact data fields and values that will be necessary to meet the criteria for entry. In addition to this, perhaps you have some immediate action that will occur, such as an email being sent, where some critical data is needed to effectively action some activity. With such a small window for an external integration or data process, to pass data to Marketing Cloud, it's important that we have a way of retrieving those values the moment a contact has been entered into the journey. This is where the concept of journey data is key.

Journey data is a snapshot of data that is captured upon journey entry and is available to be retrieved and compared at any stage within the journey. While you may access these values at any time, data will remain static for the contact throughout the experience in the journey and will reflect the values as they were captured on entry. This allows us to action activities immediately on journey entry as well as utilize these values for later touchpoints in the flow. Unfortunately, since these values are static, they aren't well suited to accommodate certain use cases. Let's say we want to exit a contact who made a purchase from our website after they had entered the journey. How can we action their purchase data when our journey data for their purchase history is no longer valid? For that, we'll turn to contact data.

## Contact data

Contact data differs significantly from journey data in that it can be evaluated in real time and is accessible across all journeys within Marketing Cloud. This is data that has been linked to a Data Designer attribute group. Data Designer is a tool within Marketing Cloud that allows you to organize and relate data within your Marketing Cloud instance that resides in lists or data extensions. This can then be used within tools such as Journey Builder as a real-time source for contact data in the platform. A possible use case is one where we want to determine whether a customer has decided to complete an abandoned cart purchase and thus might need to exit a journey built for that purpose. By linking our purchase data source to Contact Builder, we can action purchase data that has been altered since the customer's entry into the journey.

Understanding these two data types and their uses underlies much of what we can build within Journey Builder. Everything, from entry sources to our flow and exit criteria, is driven by one of these types of data, and knowing which to use in the correct circumstance is fundamental to a working journey. With the knowledge of this component in hand, let's take a look at **contact entry** configuration settings within Journey Builder.

## Contact entry

In addition to the type of data needed to act on in a journey, another important consideration is the possible flows that a subscriber can take during the journey lifecycle. Understanding your journey's purpose and both entry and exit flows is important in deciding the possible paths that a customer can take in your journey flow.

In some scenarios, a welcome journey, for instance, we might want our customer to enter our journey only a single time as the messaging and intent are no longer applicable to their needs after the journey has been completed. For another, where a single customer may meet your journey entry criteria multiple times during the lifecycle unintentionally, a system where we could prevent duplicate contacts from entering the journey is desirable. Finally, we may want to allow customers to enter and exit our journey flow at any stage and time. In this example, having no restrictions on our entry criteria is key.

To accomplish these scenarios, we can use the contact entry mode configuration within the Journey Builder settings. There are three possible selections for these configurations, and these three possibilities are as follows:

- **No re-entry**
- **Re-entry only after exiting**
- **Re-entry anytime**

Each one of these three possible selections correlates to a scenario described previously. We will now go into more detail about what each of these selections is.

## No re-entry

In this mode, once a contact has entered our journey for the first time, they will not be permitted to re-enter this journey again regardless of whether they meet the qualifying criteria for our journey or are present in our entry audience.

## Re-entry only after exiting

With this selection, a contact will be permitted to re-enter the journey flow, but only if that contact is not already within the current journey. This prevents a contact from being in multiple portions of the journey simultaneously, which might lead to a confusing and poor customer experience for some use cases.

## Re-entry anytime

This configuration removes any restrictions on the contact entry source. In this mode, a contact is eligible for entry at any time regardless of their past or current entry points into a journey. Due to this, it is possible for a customer to exit or enter at any time, and they can be in multiple spaces of the journey lifecycle simultaneously.

An errant configuration with these settings could lead to unfortunate circumstances that impact the overall health and customer experience of your journey. Knowing how your data integrates into your journey, and what the intent of your project is, can help inform which of these selections is the most appropriate for your use case.

On that note, let's take a look at some of the tracking and auditing processes built into Journey Builder that can help us stay informed and updated on the overall health and performance of our journey.

## Tracking and auditing

Another highly important part of Journey Builder is the capabilities it has around **tracking and auditing**. These capabilities retain the same smooth, user-friendly interface as the rest, allowing for dashboards and drag and drop utilization instead of technical heavy implementations and modifications.

## Goals

Using a journey goal can help you quantify the exact desired outcome that your journey is seeking to accomplish. This could be for the customer to make a purchase in a given period, engage with a specific set of product content, and any other metric that can be used to gauge the success or failure of your journey intent. In Journey Builder, this can be configured directly within the goal configuration module.

To configure a goal, ensure that your data source, which will determine the exact criteria that will trigger the completion or failure of a goal, is linked to the Data Designer attribute group and available for use as contact data in Journey Builder. On the primary configuration screen, simply enter your filtering criteria that define your goal, and select your target completion of this goal as a percentage of the total journey population or in absolute numbers.

In addition to defining the goal criteria and metric baseline, you can also configure this to automatically exit a contact once they have met your goal criteria. This ensures that you can stay focused on the intent of your messaging and allow the best possible customer experience once they have met the journey's intent.

## Exit criteria

Similar to the goal functionality, this feature allows marketers to define a set of criteria that defines when the journey is no longer viable for a contact and to exit them. This differs from goals in that it does not count towards your goal completion rate and allows you to accommodate a more robust set of scenarios where contacts may perform some action that, while it doesn't meet the stated intent of the journey, no longer provides meaningful value from the messaging and intent of the current flow. Exit criteria will be evaluated for each contact after they've exited a wait activity and, if they meet the criteria defined in your configuration, they will leave the journey at that point.

## Journey health

Journey health allows you to more closely monitor the status of your journey, both individually and globally, in order to gain a more comprehensive view of the overall performance and stability of your implementation. With this module, marketers are able to view the overall status of their goals, by seeing the performance data and goal criteria face-up in a convenient widget. In addition to this, users are also given visibility of the historical audience counts of the journey, including the number of contacts that are currently active within the journey at a given time. This is especially helpful during auditing when a rough snapshot of the current audience can indicate issues impacting customers before they are noticed retroactively. Additionally, there is a widget showing the current exit criteria of the journey, as well as the number of contacts that have met the journey exit criteria and have been removed.

There are two other important features within journey health that are very useful when assessing the current state of your implementation and to work quickly to mitigate issues. The first of these is the alerts widget, which contains data related to the number of contacts who have exceeded their defined wait times within a wait step in the journey. When a contact enters a wait step, Journey Builder calculates the appropriate end time and holds the contact until that limit has passed, after which they proceed to the next step of the journey. While this process has a reliable degree of stability, occasionally Journey Builder can encounter delays in processing contacts for the remainder of the journey and some may remain in the wait step longer than the pre-defined exit point. By using the alerts portion of journey health, we can gain visibility of the size of this group and assess the overall impact on the journey goal and performance.

The other feature available in journey health is the contact path, which allows marketers to search for the exact path taken in a journey for a given contact key. This is especially critical in journeys that use complex segmentation, multi-path customer flows, or A/B testing as it provides end users with a quantifiable way of viewing the path an individual customer has taken, which might be readily available or understood in a journey with sufficient complexity. In addition to this feature, it is also possible for users to remove a given contact from the journey directly from the UI. This ensures that marketers can respond quickly to customer complaints or errant miscues that might have an overall impact on their journey goals and performance.

## Journey analytics

In addition to journey health and goals, Journey Builder also comes equipped with a convenient dashboard to monitor the performance of the overall messaging effectiveness of your journey. With this widget, users can view important key metrics for their email messages such as open, click, and unsubscribe, both as a global count and as a percentage of the number delivered within your journey. Also, the global performance of SMS messages can be measured in regards to deliverability and click performance both globally and as a percentage.

While these are welcome additions to accurately assess the performance of a journey's content, it leaves out some key metrics that we might be interested in, such as conversion rate, related web traffic, or other engagement data that factors into a successful implementation. In addition to our base analytics dashboard, there are additional data views within Marketing Cloud that can be used to extract journey status information as well as providing a convenient method for tying together your customer data to provide a more comprehensive view of your performance beyond the standard capabilities within the analytics dashboard. Journey Builder also features a powerful integration with Google Analytics 360, which can directly integrate your journey messaging and reporting with Google Analytics in order to provide a complete view of the customer lifecycle across channels. While this feature is a premium service, there is also a free Google Analytics 360 integration that opens up some of these tracking and reporting features to all users with Journey Builder. Also important to note is the support for tagging and reporting on the GA4 property framework, which is available in both premium and free offerings on the platform. While GA4 parameters are generally configured within Parameter Manager, app events will need to utilize the Firebase SDK in order to be configured. Using these features, users are able to configure relevant parameters for tracking and can easily view conversion metrics, web engagement data driven from journey messaging, as well as other key metrics used to track the performance of the journey.

Now that we have a detailed idea of the overall configurations that are possible within Marketing Cloud journeys, let's take a look at the available event types and activities to really assess the capabilities of this tool.

## Journey entry events and activities

It goes without saying, but you can't generate real-time 1-to-1 marketing journeys for your customers if they have no method of getting into your lifecycle. As discussed in the preceding sections on journey types, the availability of certain methods of entry will be limited depending on the type of journey that meets your use case. Let's take a look at the entry sources for journeys in Journey Builder.

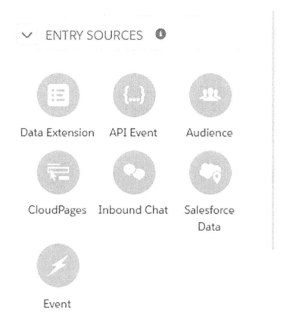

Figure 2.3 – Examples of the entry sources available in Journey Builder

As you can see in the screenshot, there are a few different types of entry sources available within the Marketing Cloud. While we won't analyze all possible journey entry types here, let's take a look at a few of the most commonly used ones in order to gain a clearer picture of how we can inject people into a customer journey.

## Data extension

The data extension entry source will certainly be a familiar concept to anyone who has used Marketing Cloud to prepare data or send communications in non-journey contexts. This entry source type allows marketers to use any sendable data extension in Marketing Cloud in order to inject contacts into the journey in a batched process. While the batched process does make this entry type less than ideal for use cases that require a real-time injection method, it is arguably the most powerful entry source in Journey Builder due to its ability to aggregate data across sources and channels for use within the journey. In some scenarios, having the data necessary to actively reach customers working in concert with each other at any given moment is not feasible. For those use cases, being able to aggregate all of these different sources in a timeframe that meets capabilities is critical and easily achieved by adding and segmenting them together in a single sendable data extension.

To use this entry source type, first set up a sendable data extension within Marketing Cloud that contains all of the necessary data attribute fields that you'll want to action as journey data within your flow. Then, set up your data processes to load the desired audience into this data extension. This can range from a simple ad hoc import into your data extension or complex API integrations and automations that manage the flow in and out of your process. After you've created your data extension, and have outlined your data processes, you're ready to configure your data extension source. Note that, in email and SMS Single Send journeys, this entry source activity is already included on the canvas but, for Multi-Step journeys, you need to drag the entry source from the menu and onto the journey canvas to begin the setup.

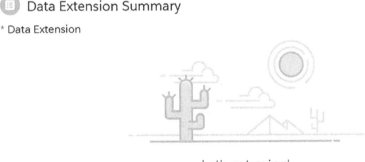

Figure 2.4 – View of the data extension entry source summary

Once you've got your entry source on the canvas, you'll need to identify the sendable data extension that you've set up with your journey data. Aside from simply selecting this within the source configuration, you'll also be presented with the (optional) ability to filter contacts. This allows you to utilize contact data on journey entry to further limit your entry criteria and apply the filter to your selected journey audience. Simply navigate to your appropriate data source linked to the Data Designer attribute groups and select any number of filtering conditions necessary to accomplish your use case.

With the journey data source configured, we now need to set the schedule to determine when the data extension should be evaluated to admit new contacts in the journey. First, there is the option to **Run Once**. This essentially mimics the functionality of the Single Send journey in the Multi-Step journey by allowing you to execute your journey audience as an ad hoc source into your flow. The second option is to set up your journey to evaluate the data extension audience for entry at a date-time-based interval. Similar to **Automation Studio** scheduling, this allows you to run your entry source at intervals that range from hourly to yearly. Finally, there is the **Automation Schedule Type**. This will only be enabled when your entry source data extension is being actively used within at least one automation in Marketing Cloud. To enable this feature, simply create a SQL Query, data filter, or any activity that targets and populates the source data extension of your journey as a step in your automation and save the configuration before returning to Journey Builder. After that, the schedule type will become enabled and you can now select your automation as the entry source for this journey. Once the journey has been activated, a **Journey Audience** activity will automatically be appended to your automation flow and, when run, will evaluate your data extension audience for entry into the journey.

If you've selected the **Automation** or **Recurring** schedule types for your journey, you will be required to configure the **Contact Evaluation** method as well. In this configuration, we'll need to let Journey Builder know how we want our contacts to be evaluated for journey entry. The first option is to evaluate only new records that have been added to the entry data extension since the last execution of our journey. This process is ideal for data processes that will add new rows to a data extension, rather than overwriting or deleting existing rows. Unless your data process to populate your entry source data extension uses methods that overwrite or delete the data source, this is the preferred **Contact Evaluation** method as it is more performant than the alternative. If your processes do overwrite the data extension source, then you'll need to select the other configuration option, **Evaluate all records**. With this evaluation type, all records in the data extension are evaluated for entry into the journey when your scheduling event is triggered. This will result in a slower processing speed compared to only evaluating net new records in your source, but it can accommodate use cases for an overwrite process, making the most sense.

## API event

For this entry event type, we're creating a configuration that developers can use to automatically inject contacts into our journey via the Marketing Cloud REST API in real-time rather than waiting for batched processes. This allows for use cases where some real-time action is desired to interact with a customer or perform some automated function within Journey Builder. It should be noted that this event differs in both functionality and configuration from the Transactional Send and Multi-Step journey types. Events created in one of these configurations cannot be applied to the other as they use different systems to manage the events and different API routes in order to trigger them. See the following for a screenshot of the API event entry source in Journey Builder.

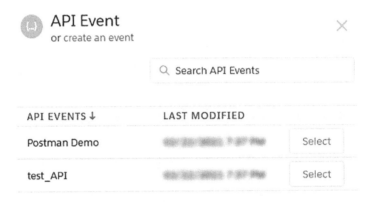

Figure 2.5 – Example of the API event entry source

Though these two API entry types do differ substantially in how they are integrated, they share several similarities with regard to their configuration. When configuring an API entry event source, you'll need to have a sendable data extension that will be the written source of the records that you qualify for injection into your journey. In the Multi-Step journey, you can select any configured sendable data extension while, with the Transactional Send journey, you can only select those data extensions that have been configured to be a **Triggered Send** type. These data extensions will contain the needed references for your journey data within the journey flow and can serve as historical records that can be utilized for quick visibility or error investigations.

In addition to the data extension source, you'll also need to configure an API event key. This key uniquely identifies your entry event into the journey and allows developers to integrate external systems to order to inject customers into the right journey with the right data structure. With this API key configured, you're now ready to start testing journey entry API calls to your entry source.

## Salesforce events

In addition to both data extension and API entry sources, another common and powerful source type is Salesforce data. Unlike the previous two, this configuration source requires Marketing Cloud users to have a Sales and Service Cloud instance connected to their Marketing Cloud business unit via Marketing Cloud Connect. Also, for those users that are connected to their Salesforce instance with the connector, only those users that have been integrated into Salesforce on their Marketing Cloud user record can create or edit Salesforce event sources. This can be easily done within the administrative menu under the **Salesforce Integration** option menu.

Figure 2.6 – Example screen for setting up the Salesforce event entry source

This event source is quite powerful in that it allows Journey Builder to immediately action events that happen in the core CRM system. Whether it's the addition of a new lead, an updated object record, or a community-based audience, this event type provides immense benefits for any organization that is well integrated with the Salesforce ecosystem. There are three primary distinctions within Salesforce entry sources that allow us to action different items on the platform:

1.  The first is the Salesforce Campaign event, which allows users to configure an event source that is triggered whenever a contact has been added to a Sales Cloud campaign.

2.  The second is the Salesforce Community event type, which can inject new members for a Salesforce Community into their journey when they are added in Salesforce, making it ideal for a welcome communication.

3.  The third, and most powerful, is the Salesforce Data event. This event gives users the ability to select a wide range of criteria, across objects, on data that exists within the Sales and Service Cloud platform.

Within the Salesforce Community and Salesforce Campaign event types, users can select either the campaign or community that they would like to inject and then configure the appropriate data fields from related objects that they will use to perform some action in the journey. In the Salesforce Data event, the configuration goes much deeper. Users will first select some object in Sales and Service Cloud that they want Journey Builder to evaluate for entry into the journey. It's important during this step to select the object on which most of your entry criteria are based or one that has a strong data relationship with all other objects used in your entry criteria. Once you've selected the object that you'd like to serve as the basis for your journey event, you'll be required to select the appropriate ID of the object that you will inject into the journey. This value will become the contact and subscriber key for your records in Marketing Cloud, so it is important that you select a value that is consistent with your other Marketing Cloud journeys and sending processes in order to prevent duplicate contact records or other impacts on your sending and reporting.

Next, we'll need to let Journey Builder know what event type it needs to listen for and the criteria that should drive the journey injection. Records can be evaluated when they are either created or updated and, while optional, specific criteria on who should be evaluated based on field values in the primary object record can also be included to further filter down the intended audience. After this has been configured, users also have the option to filter the journey entry audience by object field values that are related to the primary object selected for this event. This is separate from the previous step in which only values on that specific object record are available for defining further filters.

Finally, after users either skip or configure the filtering criteria widget, there is the ability to add any relevant data from related objects to inject as journey data whenever a record qualifies for the journey.

While there are other journey event types present in Marketing Cloud that may provide a more applicable solution for specific use cases, the three listed previously should encompass most of the scenarios that a business would encounter in order to inject customers into their journey lifecycle. With this knowledge in hand, and potential customers ready to inject into our journey, let's take a look at the actual journey building blocks you can use to reach customers.

## Journey Builder activities

While understanding how to inject contacts into our journeys is a critical component of developing within Journey Builder, what good is a journey if we don't have activities configured to interact with customers or automate business needs? An activity in Journey Builder is a configuration on the journey canvas that correlates to some specific function able to be applied to contacts within a journey. In Transactional Send and Single Send journeys, the type of activities that the journeys can contain is restricted only to those related to messaging and they cannot be deleted or removed from the canvas when selecting your messaging type. Multi-Step journeys, however, allow users to add and configure any collection of available activities for their account. This provides an excellent method of creating custom journey flows that meet specific business use cases and create additional value.

Activities within Journey Builder are grouped by their function type in the UI in order to generate a logical pairing for end users. These groups are classified as **Messages**, **Advertising**, **Flow Control**, **Customer Updates**, **Sales & Service Cloud**, and **Custom**. Let's take a look at each group in turn in order to gain a bit more insight into their functionality.

## Messaging

Unsurprisingly, messaging activities are a collection that focuses on capabilities for sending both transactional and commercial content to customers across channels. These channels include email, SMS, MobilePush, LINE, and in-app messaging (among others). These activities can be configured to action any user data within Marketing Cloud in order to deliver personalized content to contacts at any stage within the journey lifecycle.

## Advertising

Advertising activities allow you to automatically configure and deploy advertising campaigns across various sites and channels. Users can incorporate effective Facebook ad campaigns, adjusting for the audience and ad spend, to directly market to customers in the channel that they prefer. While this activity does require Advertising Studio, it's certainly a powerful form of communication for customers who may eschew traditional messaging channels for a more social environment.

## Flow control

**Flow Control** activities are those that allow custom routing or segmentation directly within the Journey Builder UI. Activities such as decision and engagement splits are critical for creating journeys that can adjust the given path for a contact based on their data or engagement behavior. For instance, perhaps we want our loyal customers to receive a different experience in the journey, or perhaps even a different set of activities. By utilizing splits, we can segment out our loyal customers to provide them with a more personalized journey flow that can lead to higher engagement and brand appreciation. Other examples of journey splits are random splits, which segment out contacts randomly into weighted percentages for each path, and Path Optimizer, which can allow users to conduct A/B/N tests on up to 10 variables on engagement that automatically encourage contacts to enter more highly-performing journey flows.

In addition to journey splits, wait activities are a key component of **Flow Control** and journey workflows generally. These activities essentially hold a contact in place until some given event or schedule has been completed. These can range from hardcoded date times to activities that wait for an API event to be triggered before contacts proceed with the remainder of the flow. When constructing multi-day journeys, or those where a special event requires exact communication touchpoints, wait activities are the preferred method of ensuring that customers reach your other activities exactly when they are meant to.

Finally, we have Einstein activities. These activities use aggregate, personalized data along with machine learning to allow users to target their customers by preference, affinity for the brand, and engagement history. With the Einstein Scoring and Frequency splits, marketers are able to send customers down varying paths within a journey based on metrics such as their personalized persona due to likelihood of engagement or their current email saturation status derived from their historical and current data trends. The **Einstein Send Time Optimization** (**STO**) activity is also a common implementation in Journey Builder and uses over 90 days of email or MobilePush data, and over 20 individual weighting factors, in order to generate an ideal send-time at the contact level. This greatly enhances the opportunities for marketers to anticipate customer interactions and deliver messages at a time that works for the individual customer.

## Customer updates

This group actually consists of only a single activity, called **Update Contact**. The **Update Contact** activity allows the user to update or modify any sendable data extension within Marketing Cloud when a user enters this step. After selecting the desired data extension, any field within it can be updated with a static value from the journey, making it ideal for logging and reporting purposes, among others.

## Sales and Service Cloud

The **Sales and Service Cloud** activities group allows for the functionality to create or update Sales and Service Cloud object records from either journey or contact data. This allows for the automation of several items within the platform, such as converting leads, closing, creating, or updating tasks and requests, creating journey logging records on custom objects, and many other scenarios that could be used to meet business use cases. For organizations that use the core Salesforce platform, having this functionality within Journey Builder can completely transform their marketing implementations and is one of the strongest use cases for Journey Builder.

## Custom

Finally, we have custom activities within Journey Builder. Unlike the previous groups, there is no pre-configured functionality or activity type that the user can automatically drag onto the journey canvas and utilize. Rather, this activity allows developers to extend the functionality of a journey by providing a platform of completely custom integrations and activities that are only limited by the external implementation itself. We will cover these more extensively in a later chapter, but their ability to extend Journey Builder to meet any use case makes them a powerful tool in the marketing toolkit.

Now that we've covered Journey Builder activities and the entry events that drive them, we're ready to start revolutionizing our marketing approach to customers, right? Well, not so fast. Before we can fully utilize the power and customization of Journey Builder, we need to be aware of some of the limitations and considerations when building a customer journey.

# Journey Builder considerations and best practices

There is much to consider when using Journey Builder. Just the range of capabilities and usage alone creates subsets of subsets of considerations and best practices. There are a few major considerations that need to be kept in mind about Journey Builder that are universal across each usage though. These considerations, combined with some basic best practices, will be listed in the following section.

## Considerations

Although, as stated, there are hundreds if not thousands of considerations for Journey Builder, we wanted to concentrate on just a few major ones that are considerations in almost every single usage of Journey Builder.

## Throughput

Journey Builder was built upon the trigger send definitions that existed previously in Marketing Cloud. This is great as it's a strong way to give 1:1 messaging to your audience. The drawback is that it does not allow for batching, so the greater the volume pushed in at once or at high frequency, the larger the queue and time delay until sending is. Journey Builder has been increasing its capabilities in this area over the last couple of years. It initially was absolutely terrible and near worthless for any sort of volume. With the introduction and push towards Single Send journeys, they increased the capabilities and got it to a point where it was strong enough for a good portion of email sends. That being said, if you plan to send emails out in the millions on a regular basis, expect major delays in email sends, spanning hours of difference. This can be a deal-breaker for some in utilizing Journey Builder for these campaigns.

## Scripting capabilities

Journey Builder does not offer a way for significant customization or scripting. There are no **SSJS Script** or **SQL Query** activity types that can be used. This limits Journey Builder in some ways and can wind up making it a less desirable tool for your automation. This is not to say that there are not any custom capabilities, the **Custom Journey** activity offers up a *ton* of capability and possibility that can help get you to where you need to be. The major issue with **Custom Journey** activities though is that they need to be hosted externally, are written in JavaScript, and require strong developer knowledge to implement. With these being hosted externally, it reduces the process draw on Marketing Cloud, keeping the system from being overwhelmed by the frequent runs of the same script for each subscriber that passes through.

## Tracking and analytics

Journey Builder does offer very beautiful dashboards and good basic tactical tracking and analytics data. It even offers information including goals, exits along with interaction, and performance-based metrics. What it does not offer though is logging capabilities or custom reporting. These are not necessary for every journey and may not be relevant for some usages, but this can be a major consideration on some complex or highly visible journeys that you need custom KPI tracking or monitoring of where people are in journeys, and so on. There are ways to implement these capabilities, but that implementation would mostly be through **Automation Studio** and utilization of some features of Journey Builder in ways they were not intended to be used, which requires a fairly high level of technical and development skill.

## Best practices

Now that we have looked at the considerations, we want to give a few best practice tips for the utilization of Journey Builder. These are broad and not specific because, similar to considerations, there are hundreds of different best practices depending on usage and context.

### Journey logging

Although, as stated earlier, this is not a native feature nor one that's easy to implement, it is highly recommended to implement it everywhere you can. Journey logging is something that if you do not have it and later need it, there is not really a good way to get that information after the fact. So, we always go by the philosophy: *I would rather have something I do not need than have a need and not have the information.*

### Pre-planning and heavy consideration

This is the bit that we see so many people fail on. Before implementing any journey, you should have a significant amount of time prior that is dedicated to just taking into account future needs and integrations to ensure what you set up will be able to be continually running for an extended period of time with few updates or edits. The more you edit and create new additions on top of your original journey, the more you create a risk of failure for the journey as well as the potential to unintentionally skew your historical data. The more consistent you can make your journey, the higher quality the output is.

### Journey monitoring

Although there are some built-in features or extra services to help with this process, these are far from comprehensive. we always recommend building an automation that looks at collecting the status, sent, opens, clicks, and queues for each of the email sends inside of your journeys to ensure these are running as expected. we also highly recommend keeping track of entry and exit numbers to ensure these are as expected and are filtering as expected. That is it for the overview of **Journey Builder**. Now, we will move on to an overview of the other major automation tool in Marketing Cloud, **Automation Studio**.

# Automation Studio overview

The general principle behind automation is to reduce manual actions and create efficiency within your processes and environment. Automation Studio therefore can interact and affect almost every part of Salesforce Marketing Cloud in some way, shape, or form. So, with that being said, what exactly is Automation Studio?

Automation Studio is a batch-driven performance enhancement platform. It allows you to utilize custom activities and actions in a highly performant and efficient manner. Automation Studio is very different from the 1:1 interaction focus of Journey Builder. But, an important thing to note is that different does not mean worse. They are both very powerful in what they do and are very complementary to each other.

This focus on bulk processing allows for more volume to be accomplished in a single run, which can help reduce the processing required and increase performance speeds, which reduces the total runtimes of actions. As a note though, bulk processing is not the only capability of Automation Studio, it also allows for server-side scripting and other types of integrations through automated exports/imports and similar custom solutions.

Inside of Automation Studio, there are two different types of automation triggers available – **Scheduled Automations** and **File Drop Automations**. The automations are separated based on the trigger type that is going to be used to initiate the **Automation** activities. These two types are very complementary to each other and cover almost every possible scenario you will face. These types involve a recurring, predictable option as well as a more real-time reactionary option.

## Scheduled automations

Scheduled automations are usually the type of automation that first pops into your mind when you think *automation*, using a recurring trigger type. Scheduled automations are repetitive tasks or sets of tasks that occur at specific times and/or recurrences while doing specific actions and activities. It is the bread-and-butter automation type and, honestly, most of the automations you work with will fall into this type.

These automations work off a trigger based on a specified schedule or recurrence where you can set them to run from yearly down to hourly, you can control the time period they run for, as well as the total number of times they can run. This trigger is a very clean, efficient, and predictable automation. By utilizing this, you can plan other activities and actions around these automations as you know the precise time it will run and what it will do.

A great benefit to the *predictability* and *clean* aspects is that this type is the most non-technical, resource-friendly automation type. These automations tend to be more intuitive and easier to pick up, understand, and use. For instance, the user interface wizard inside the system is very descriptive and it's easy to figure out the usage and how to set up each aspect. It is a drag-and-drop interface as well to help reduce needed user inputs or actions.

## Scheduled automation user interface

The main part that makes a scheduled automation unique is the setup or user interface. This offers many options and filters. The following screenshot is an example of this setup screen:

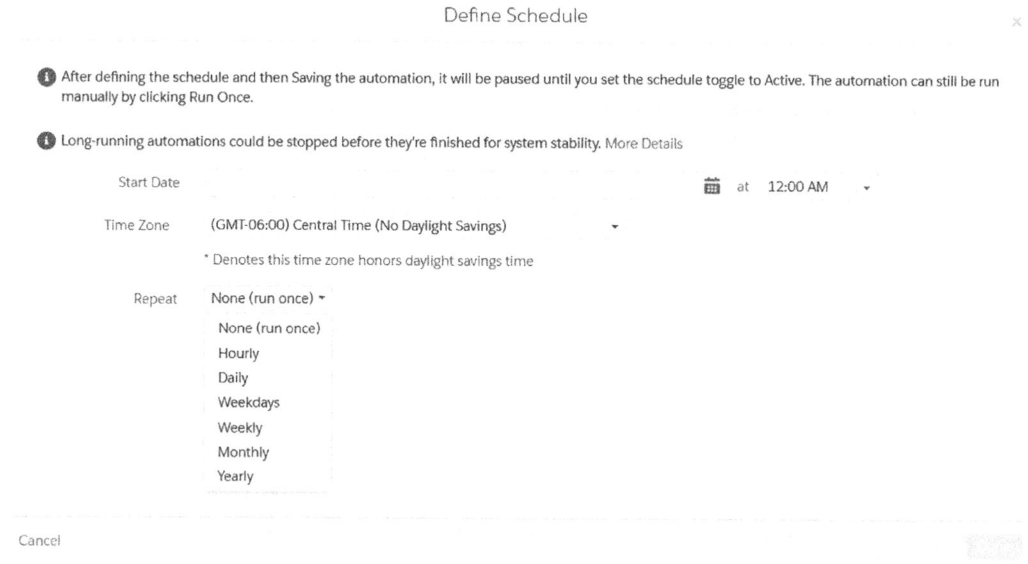

Define Schedule

ⓘ After defining the schedule and then Saving the automation, it will be paused until you set the schedule toggle to Active. The automation can still be run manually by clicking Run Once.

ⓘ Long-running automations could be stopped before they're finished for system stability. More Details

Start Date                                                                📅    at    12:00 AM    ▾

Time Zone       (GMT-06:00) Central Time (No Daylight Savings)              ▾

                * Denotes this time zone honors daylight savings time

Repeat          None (run once) ▾

                None (run once)
                Hourly
                Daily
                Weekdays
                Weekly
                Monthly
                Yearly

Cancel

Figure 2.7 – An example of the setup screen when creating a scheduled automation

As you can see from the preceding screenshot, there are a lot of options that can be used to set up your scheduled automation. The schedule options available are very easy to set. These are fairly self-explanatory in terms of how they work and what you need to implement or edit them. All of the available options are contained in dropdowns or date pickers that help you select what recurrence (repeat) type you want (if you want any recurrences) and then allow you to select the numeric value of that type. For example, you can choose **Hourly**, and then set the number to **2**, which means the automation will repeat every 2 hours. You can then also set an ending via **Date**, **Count**, or **No End Date**.

After you have set the schedule and saved it to the automation, this opens up quite a few other cool features:

- Two manual **Run Once** options:

  - One on the initial dashboard.

  - Another on the individual automation's canvas.

- **Active/Paused** options for your schedule:
  - **Active** – The schedule is running and recurring as dictated.
  - **Paused** – The schedule is not active so the automation is not running.
- **Easy Editing**, **Creating**, **Deleting**, and **Updating** (you need to pause to make edits):
  - **Editable Schedule**
  - **Automation Activities**
  - **Automation Name**
  - **Automation Properties**, and more

## Use cases

So now we know all the cool things about scheduled automations, why would we want to use them? The majority of use cases for scheduled automations are around data imports and manipulation or bulk campaign message sends, but that is certainly not all that they do! The following are a few examples of uses, but there are far too many possibilities for us to list them all here.

A good, solid example of a common use case for scheduled automations is to filter or query a master data extension to create a segmented sendable audience and then send an email for an annual anniversary, birthday, or reminder to take action.

Another common use case is for custom activities or programs where you use things such as **Script activities** or **SQL Query** activities to create custom solutions, reports, or capabilities. For instance, to use SQL queries on a schedule to create a Journey Builder log based on the corresponding data views and intermittent **Update Contact** activities inside the journey.

My final example of a scheduled automation use case is that it is very handy for creating custom reports and tracking/analytics data. By using *SQL queries*, data or tracking extracts, scripts, and similar activities, you can create and combine any sort of subscriber level and contextual data to fit your needs. An example of this is a report on your journey email sends that shows opens, clicks, bounces, and so on of each email send job.

## Considerations for scheduled automations

Along with all the good, there are a few limits or considerations that should be taken into account when dealing with scheduled automations. As with all things, there is contextual and quirky behavior that you will need to learn about through usage and research as it is not officially documented anywhere. In the following sections are a couple of caveats and benefits we have found over the years and wish that someone had told us when we first started.

## No queueing

Scheduled automations do not queue, so if you start the automation while another one is still running, the subsequent run will force the previous run to stop and the next automation will start or it will just error out/skip. The user interface has some security validations in place around **Run Once** options to help prevent this, but there are still a few instances where this can be an issue. For instance, if you schedule the automation to run every hour, and the automation takes over an hour to run, then you will never get the part of the automation beyond the 1-hour runtime to run as the next scheduled trigger will force it to stop and start over or it will miss every other run due to the overlap.

## No recurrence below hourly

As stated, Marketing Cloud and Automation Studio are not intended to be super-powered, highly capable ETL or automation tools, but instead, they are a messaging and communication platform that is focused on the enablement of custom capabilities and actions. This means that a lot of the higher-powered or process-heavy capabilities you can see on other tools are not here. One of those is the ability to have an automation with a high frequency (more than once an hour), continuous automation, or a listener. We defend this because the number of processes and amount of server power to enable this on top of everything else would sky-rocket the price for a tool that is already a big investment as well as potentially making the tool less intuitive and much more complex.

## Skip next occurrence

This is a very under-utilized and underrated ability. Through this button, you can automatically skip the next occurrence without needing to pause or stop the automation. This can be very helpful at times when you need to make a quick change to something and don't want to have to remember to come back and turn the automation back on after your changes are made. The number of times we have forgotten to switch an automation back to **Active** after pausing it for changes is staggering over my career and has led us to be very nervous people about ever pausing any existing and running automations.

## Bulk sending throughput

One of the major benefits of using an automation over a journey for bulk sends is the throughput available. What can take Automation Studio 20 minutes could take Journey Builder 2 hours or more. As time has gone on, this gap has shortened, but it is still something to consider. There are quite a few other considerations to determine which is the right tool to use to send your email, but this is one we like to make sure is mentioned as it can have a significant impact if not recognized.

## Snapshot of email at scheduling

The biggest benefit we have seen of using Automation Studio scheduled automations is the ability to take those bulk emails you have been scheduling out via the wizard in Email Studio and instead make a **Send Email** activity (also called **user-initiated email**) connecting the audience, properties, and email assets into a single object. You then pop that into an automation and schedule the automation.

How is this different? Well, when you directly schedule the email via the wizard, the email is preprocessed and a snapshot of all the content and scripting is made. Because of this, if you make any changes to the email after this but prior to sending, then those changes will *not* be reflected inside the send. You would need to cancel the scheduled email and reschedule it. If you use an **Email** activity inside of a scheduled automation, it will not snapshot the email until the **Email** activity is initiated inside the automation (at send time), allowing all content and scripting changes to be included.

# File drop automations

File drop automations were previously called **Triggered Automations** because they are *triggered* when a file (meeting certain criteria) is dropped onto the SFMC SFTP. The neat thing about this type of automation is that it can be in near real time (reliant on your data drop timing) and that the runs of this can be queued up to run after the initial run is completed.

File drop automations have a lot of unique and great features and capabilities that separate them out from scheduled automations. File drop automations not only allow for immediate *real-time* running capabilities but also offer flexibility and versatility on file naming convention and the usage of substitution strings are not available anywhere else.

As a note though, there are a few considerations and requirements that need to be taken into account when utilizing a file drop automation. They will help you to optimize your usage and make sure you create the most efficient and powerful solution for your needs.

## Salesforce Marketing Cloud SFTP

To utilize the file drop automation, you will need to have access to the Marketing Cloud Enhanced FTP, which is usually enabled by default in all new accounts, but you may need to talk with your account executive if you do not see it available in your enterprise. Although this is showing FTP in the name of the business rule, it is in fact an SFTP, providing that added level of security.

The reason you need this enabled and accessible is that file drop automations will only register file drops on the Marketing Cloud SFTP and not on any third-party FTP services. Even though you can use things such as imports and exports and file transfers to multiple third-party locations via file locations, this is not the case for file drop.

## Important considerations and tips

As with everything, there are certain contextual considerations and thoughtful approaches around the tool. They need to be weighed up when you are planning and building your strategy for your automation usage and structure. Most of them are not limitations or drawbacks but more along the lines of ways to optimize your usage of the platform and ensure it is future-facing.

### Default directories

It is not recommended to use the default `Import` or `Export` folders for this activity, but to instead create custom subdirectories. This is because the more listeners there are on a folder, or as they are also called, **directories**, the more complex they are and there is a higher risk of something breaking, failing, or otherwise working incorrectly.

By utilizing sub-folders instead, you are able to separate out and organize your triggers into separate locations, keeping them more focused and efficient. These folders are very easy to create and work with through any FTP tools, such as FileZilla, to access your Salesforce Marketing Cloud SFTP and interact with it.

### Multiple file drop listener events

Although with a naming convention defined, you can put multiple listener events in a single folder, only one automation can run per file. So even if your file meets all the criteria for each of the listener events, only the first one will be run; they cannot be triggered from the same file.

## Run Once

Inside of scheduled automations, there is the option to use **Run Once** on an automation to manually test it in its entirety or to test parts of it. Inside of file drop automations, there is no *Run Once* option nor any equivalent method. It instead uses **Active** and **Inactive**. To test an automation, you would need to drop a file while it is **Active** and run it the same as if it were live action.

## Use cases for file drop automations

Now, the use case for file drop automations usually stems from the immediacy and real-time capabilities they have. But this is not the only reason to use this type of automation. The file drop automation can also be used to run something at a rate more often than the scheduled automation limit of 1-hour recurrence. It can also queue up files, so that even if the automation takes 2 hours to run, if you drop files prior to that completing, it will not disrupt the running instance, but instead queue up the new one to run after that instance is complete.

A sample scenario for a use case of file drop automation is when you need to receive and import a compressed file upon drop so that SFMC is using the most up-to-date information that is possible via a file drop integration with another data platform. Through the file drop, you would be able to trigger it once the SFMC SFTP receives the file, which would then go through the correct **Activities**, such as **File Transfer** and **Import**, and so on to correctly manipulate the file and get it imported to the right place.

Another sample scenario for a use case of file drop automation is if you have a time-sensitive reminder or notice email that needs to go out once you drop the sendable data onto the SFMC SFTP. Basically, you would have the file drop with the correct settings in place. This would initiate the automation, which would then take that data and import it to the correct data extension and then run a user-initiated send that uses that **data extension** (**DE**) as the sendable audience to send out the email once the data is done being loaded in.

## Your file drop setup options

The file drop automation is focused solely on a file drop. This trigger can be honed or as broad as you like. Through different options such as selecting specific folders and naming conventions, you can make sure it will only run based on the exact file drop you want it to. This can be separated into two sections:

- **FileName Pattern**: You can set it to load specific filename patterns inside of a folder.
- **No FileName Pattern**: You set it to run on every file loaded into a specific folder.

Here is an example of what the **File Drop Setup** screen looks like:

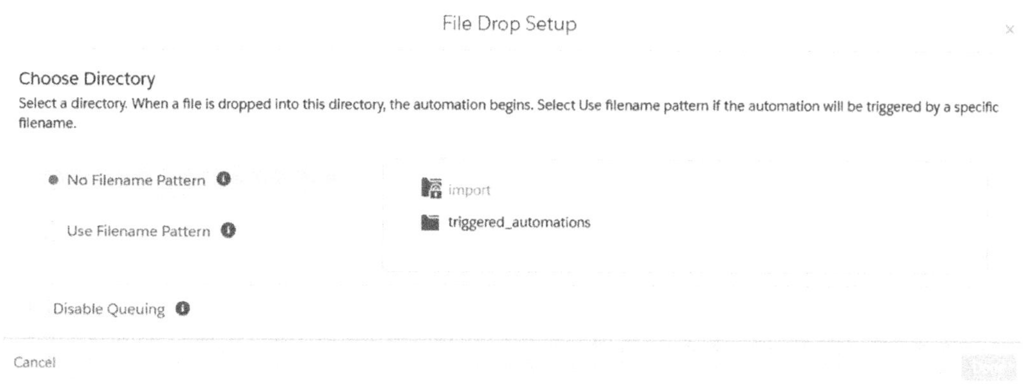

File Drop Setup                                                                    ×

**Choose Directory**
Select a directory. When a file is dropped into this directory, the automation begins. Select Use filename pattern if the automation will be triggered by a specific filename.

- No Filename Pattern ❶                          📁 import

  Use Filename Pattern ❶                          📁 triggered_automations

  Disable Queuing ❶

Cancel

Figure 2.8 – An example showing the setup window for a file drop automation

As you can see from the preceding screenshot, there is a clear selection that can be made from the options (**No Filename Pattern** or **Use Filename Pattern**) as well as a folder and subfolder visual pathway that you can use to select specific directory locations in your SFTP to target.

## Filename patterns

Filename patterns are used to set the filename `filter` or naming convention to be used to decide which files dropped to the corresponding folder will trigger your automation. Files that meet the filename requirements (case insensitive) are processed as Automation Studio parses them. This means that each file is loaded and read within the context of Automation Studio's file parser.

> **Note**
> The automation engine will not include any file extensions (anything after the dot, ., in the filename) so do not include this in your filter or it will fail.

## Operators available for filename patterns

To allow for versatility and to account for nearly every possible need when working with dynamically named files, the file drop automation filename pattern allows you to choose between three operators. Each of these three should cover your needs and let you make as complex or simple a solution as you need:

- **Contains** – Similar to `LIKE` in SQL and just looks to see if those characters exist in that order in any file (for example, `LIKE '%FNP%'`).

- **Begins With** – Similar to SQL's `LIKE` with no wildcard at the front (for example, `LIKE 'FNP%'`).

- **Ends With** – The reverse of **Begins With**. SQL's `LIKE` with no wildcard at the end (for example, `LIKE '%FNP'`).

Here is a screenshot of what is displayed on the platform for reference.

Figure 2.9 – Filename pattern options

> **Note on Wildcards in Filename Patterns**
>
> Wildcards that are available inside of the **Import** activities and **File Transfer** activities are *not* available inside of the file drop filenaming patterns. The field for file drop automations is a literal string, meaning that if you type in `myfile_%%month%%`, it will look for literally `myfile_%%month%%` and not `myfile_01` as it would inside the import of file transfer activities.
>
> There are no wildcards (that we are aware of) that work in this field, so you would need to account for this when setting up your naming convention. For example, if your files begin with `YYYYMMDD_myfile`, then you would need to do an **Ends With** `_myfile` as the variable part is not definable inside the file drop automation.

Now that we know how to create filenaming patterns, what happens when multiple files match the criteria?

## Multiple filename patterns in the same folder

We wanted to make a note on what will happen if you have two filename patterns in the same folder and the file drops match both patterns:

- Only a single automation will be triggered, not both.

- The filename pattern that is matched first is the one that will be triggered.

For example, say we have two filenaming patterns, CONTAINS Bootcamp and CONTAINS OrderDetails. These are both in the same folder. If we drop a file named Bootcamp_OrderDetails.csv, what would happen?

The answer is that the automation with the filename pattern of CONTAINS Bootcamp would be triggered and the other (CONTAINS OrderDetails) would be ignored despite matching on the filename because Bootcamp comes before OrderDetails.

## No filename pattern

If you choose to utilize the option to forgo a filename pattern, it basically creates a very broad stroke of possibilities to trigger the automation. To help contain this, each folder can only have one file drop associated with it that does not have a filename pattern assigned. By locking the folder for other listener events, you prevent issues like the ones we discussed when talking about multiple filename matches on the same folder.

This also means that any and every legitimate file dropped into this folder will cause your automation to run. Whether it is blank.txt or myRealFile.csv, it will trigger the listener and begin running your automation. Depending on the purpose of the automation, this can cause errors or the potential for unintended runs, and so on. You will need to account for this in your setup and planning.

## Benefits of file drop automations

When you mention file drop automation, there are a couple of big features that need to be considered outside of just the real-time capabilities. For instance, file drop automations can offer queueing and special substitution strings that are not available anywhere else. We'll explore these capabilities next.

## File queueing

File queueing is set up to verify if you want to create a queue of multiple triggers if a second file is dropped before the first run is completed. You can also turn this off if you do not want the triggers to queue:

- If you queue your runs, even if the previous run fails, it will still go through the queue until it is finished.

- The queue will run through the triggers in the order they were triggered, but it will use the most recent files.

- So, if you overwrite a file in a file drop for a later queued trigger, it will not use the original data, but the new data.

- If you turn off queueing, any triggers that happen during a currently running instance will cause that instance to stop and restart based on the new file trigger.

## File drop substitution strings

Inside file drop automations, there are custom substitution strings (similar to personalization strings) that can be used in **File Transfer** activities or **Import** activities. These strings allow you to reuse the name of the file that triggered the automation (via filename pattern or folder drop) in your activities in subsequent steps inside the automation as well as the option for date/time substitution strings. This should help ensure that your activities inside this automation type utilize exactly the right file.

## Overall features and capabilities of Automation Studio

One of the main features of Automation Studio is its data management capabilities. This includes **Extract, Transform, Load** (**ETL**) processes, such as segmentation or data manipulation, and its capabilities around relational database capabilities and object interaction.

One of the major uses of Automation Studio relates to its data manipulation and relational database capabilities. This can include the manipulation of sendable or relational data as well as the creation of custom reporting or tracking. You can also utilize Automation Studio for custom solutioning using **Script activities** and many of the other utility-type activities available.

## ETL processes

ETL is the commonly used operation of extracting data from one or more sources and transferring it to load into a destination system. This destination system would then represent the data differently from the original source(s) or inside of a different context. ETL also makes it possible to migrate data between a variety of sources, destinations, and analysis tools. This makes it a critical aspect in producing business intelligence and in the execution of broader data management strategies.

ETL allows you to do things such as segmenting your data in-platform from **Filter** activities, **SQL Query** activities, or even in **Script activities**. This can allow you to shape your audiences in ways that allow you to minutely target and effectively communicate your messaging. It also allows you to manipulate and form data for analytics and reporting.

That being said, SFMC is not designed to be an ETL system and is not to be utilized for major or frequent ETL needs. It is optimized for quick segmentation needs and more tactical-type manipulations, but once you get to transforming or otherwise interacting with large volumes of data or high-frequency interactions, it tends to fall flat. To this extent, there are limitations that need to be considered for these types of activities within the platform and you should consider doing these actions prior to bringing them into SFMC or inside of an external tool that is designed for these actions. This will make your process much more stable and efficient.

## Relational database capabilities and object interaction

Through actions such as the ETL capabilities described previously in **SQL Query** activities or **Script activities**, you can take data that are related via a foreign key and combine or otherwise interact with it. This can allow you to form a master marketing database if you want that pulls all relevant data into a single location to be used as sendable data. You would just utilize a **SQL Query** activity that *joins* the data based on these keys and then outputs the resulting data into your targeted marketing database data extension.

Automation Studio also allows you to manipulate and form custom relational objects that are completely separate from all other data in the platform. These are called data extensions. Now, through scripts, you can do a ton of things related to data extensions – including creating one, filling in the rows of a data extension, manipulating/adding/ deleting fields, and even copying or deleting. This can give you full access to automate container management in your enterprise. You can then link these relational objects for future needs via scripting and lookups based on the foreign keys.

What the heck is a foreign key, you may ask? We know what a primary key is, one of the unique identifiers for an object to define, add, or update capabilities, and like the key to a house – but a foreign key (*shrug*)? A foreign key is a field or column that provides a link between the data in each relational database table or object. This is what you match or *join on*, to utilize a SQL reference, to ensure that data is connected in the correct way.

## Custom reporting and tracking capabilities

Using a lot of the previously mentioned aspects, not only are you able to segment and prepare or massage your data prior to sending, but you are also able to do all this post-sending to create your own tracking and reporting objects.

By manipulating built-in objects, such as data views, you are able to get interaction and tracking data and utilize it inside of **SQL Query** activities to build your own reports based on your custom data, integrated and infused with the platform tracking information. You can also utilize **Data Extract** activities and **File Transfer** activities to do bulk drop integrations to an analytics platform. You also can utilize the APIs and scripting languages to build your own dashboards, reporting platforms, or other displays as well as further integrations of Marketing Cloud into other systems.

## Example custom solutions and capabilities

Outside of the data capabilities, there are a ton of other actions and activities that can be handled or built inside of Automation Studio. This is honestly our favorite aspect of Automation Studio – its ability to run custom solutions and actions. Now, the possibilities of these solutions and actions are much too far-reaching for us to list out here, but the following are some of our favorite aspects:

- **Script activities** that fully build out your email campaign needs (data extension creation, segmentation, suppression lists, emails, and user-initiated email sends (**Send Email** activity)) and then build and schedule the automation to run it

- **Script activities** that provide helpers such as an automation dashboard or data extension inventory report

- The ability to create, delete, update, schedule, pause, and stop other automations

- The ability to pre-assign coupon codes for campaigns

- Fire **Journey Builder** events or journey audiences

- Automating multi-channel sends

- Refreshing filtered lists and data extensions including mobile lists

Now that we have a strong understanding of Automation Studio and Journey Builder, let's dig into how they affect multi-channel benefits.

# Automation Studio activities

Let's take a quick look at the guts of Automation Studio and get a quick overview of some of the more prevalent activities available in it. These puzzle pieces are what we lock together, like a jigsaw puzzle, to form the beautiful image that is our completed automation.

Each one of these puzzle pieces is extremely powerful in its own right and deserves to have a detailed explanation, but for now, we are just going to give a brief overview of each and then go into details as we dive further into the book. We could probably sit here and write an entire book about the nuances of every one of these activities and the pros/cons and caveats/features of each.

## Popular activities

The following is a list of all the popular activities utilized in Automation Studio. These are not all of the activities as there are a ton, and some of them we joined together into groups as they all do similar or related actions:

- **Send Email activities**: Activities that execute a user-initiated email or Salesforce send

- **SQL Query activity**: Runs an SFMC SQL Query

- **Import File activity**: Imports a file into a data extension or list

- **File Transfer activity**: Manipulates a file in a defined file location

- **Script activity**: Runs an SSJS **Script activity**

- **Filter activity**: Executes a Filter Definition (lists and data extensions)

- **Data Extract activity**: Extracts data from multiple sources

- **Journey Builder activities**: Fires Events and Journey Audience

- **Refresh (Group/Mobile List) activities**: Refreshes a list or group that already exists

- **SMS/GroupConnect/Push activities**: Multi-channel options for messaging

- **Utility activities**: Activities such as **Verification** and **Wait**

This is a good general description of what activities are available in Automation Studio. These activities are instrumental in the strength and capabilities of Marketing Cloud Automation Studio. Later in the book, when we explore in-platform automation capabilities, we will learn more about how some of these activities can further enable automation capabilities. We now have a strong understanding of both Journey Builder and Automation Studio separately, but what about if we were to compare them?

# Comparing Automation Studio and Journey Builder

Now we know what both tools are and a good amount of detail on each of them, it's time to compare and contrast them. We know both tools are super-powerful and effective, but each is different and unique. There are strengths and weaknesses of each, as well as fun little nuances and unexpected behaviors.

This is true not just in general capability, but also in things such as planning, strategy, execution, tracking, and more! How you build a program or journey can have a great effect on the output, including things such as throughput, efficiency, integration, and capabilities.

Let's dive into these differences and see what we can find.

## The key differences

There are quite a few different discussions that can be had about the differences between the two tools. These differences do not necessarily mean weaknesses nor are otherwise negative. In many of these cases, there is no clear-cut winner, they just are different! Which one works best or best suits your needs fully depends on what your context and your goals are.

The following are a few of the key differences that we have noticed over the years dealing with both tools. Please do note that although the following key differences are definitively accurate, they are accurate as a general rule and not specific to your situation and context. With that factored in, there is always the potential that it may be different in some way. So please, always do your own testing and research prior to making any final decisions.

### Multi-channel mayhem

While both Journey Builder and Automation Studio offer multi-channel ways to send marketing messages, they each do so in different ways and at different levels. It is certainly not fair to directly compare them – think `apples` to `oranges` – but we can show the differences in usage, philosophy, capability, and so on that are inherent in each.

## Messaging strategy

Journey Builder provides a stronger messaging strategy benefit due to its 1:1 messaging focus. As each person will usually enter the journey individually, compared to large batches in Automation Studio, it enables you to better view and act on results and behavior in real time, instead of needing to wait for the bulk action to conclude. This includes Journey Builder providing more possibilities to test different strategies and optimize your messages based on engagement and interaction.

## Functionality and usability

Automation Studio is focused on bulk activities and ETL. Although Automation Studio is the more powerful tool, Journey Builder is much more *marketer friendly* with its drag-and-drop interface and functionality, so it requires much less technical knowledge and know-how to utilize. In Journey Builder, marketers can use the drag-and-drop functionality to pull in audience decision splits, create customized wait times, and configure firing events that allow customers to be injected from almost any data source.

## Segmentation stipulations

In Automation Studio, data filters and queries, using SQL, are built and leveraged to assist in segmentation needs, which can be much more confusing. For instance, building segmentation and A/B testing in Journey Builder would require dragging and dropping a split, such as a decision split, and then putting in the logic. To do this in Automation Studio, you would need to utilize **SQL Query** activities, which requires SQL language knowledge, among other activities, such as filters, user-initiated sends, and more in a much less intuitive way.

The user-friendly approach to segmentation and filtering is great for those who are not expecting large-volume or high-frequency interactions on the journey. The splits, filters, and segmentation in Journey Builder are limited and will greatly slow down the journey as the filter runs every single time on every single record. So, for instance, if you do a bulk import of 10,000 records to your journey, your segmentation will run 10,000 times, once for each record – whereas in Automation Studio, the SQL query or filter would only run once and affect all 10,000 records.

## Throughput and volume

Automation Studio offers a level of throughput and processing power that is well above and beyond what is available in Journey Builder. With this throughput and power, you can send millions of records in much less time than you could in Journey Builder. This can help ensure your audiences get the messaging you want within the timeframe you want to send it to them. Another thing of note is that the more complex a journey gets, the more this affects throughput and processing locally in the journey.

## Is mimicry really the best compliment?

Journey Builder is built on triggered email messages, which is great, but for the most part, this means that what you build in Journey Builder you can mimic in Automation Studio. So, with a lot more technical effort and planning/setup, you can build a better-performing version of pretty much any journey. Now, that comes with the caveat that Automation Studio would likely need a *lot* of duct tape and bubble gum coding and setup to fully mimic it, so the value of the performance is not likely to be worth the level of effort and risk to build it in Automation Studio.

## Reports and tracking

Lastly, is a comparison of reporting and analytics capabilities. Inside Journey Builder, you have a more real-time view of your analytics and tracking. This includes built-in goal reporting that does not exist in Automation Studio. This, combined with real-time tracking, such as what you see in triggered sends, gives insights in a very different and more agile way than what you get in Automation Studio.

That being said though, there is not really much you can do on custom reporting, automated exporting of your tracking data, or deep dives and analysis through micro-analysis. Journey Builder is very much just an out-of-the-box tool when it comes to reporting. The closest it can provide to allowing for custom reporting is the ability to *update contact* or send information to Sales or Service Cloud.

Automation Studio, on the other hand, provides all kinds of possibilities for custom reporting, extracts of data, and deep dives into data. Through **SQL Query** activities, you can build your own datasets and manipulate, join, or otherwise transform them to the form you want them to be. From there, you can even either put all this into an email or utilize it on a page and distribute that link via an email, all inside a single automation. There is the ability to also utilize tracking extracts to pull all the interaction data, subscriber data, and so on from Marketing Cloud and push it to an FTP to be digested externally.

# Which one should I use?

This is probably the question we hear the most whenever we talk to someone new to the platform. The question sounds simple enough and therefore should have a very simple answer, right? Well, kind of. The answer is: *it depends*.

The answer to this question is based completely on the context, personal preference, skill level, use case, business goals, environment, and integration considerations. With all these factors and more, finding which one is the best for your use case is a bit of an adventure in and of itself.

Now, in some cases, the answer is not really all that important and you can just go with personal preference and be done with it, but at other times, this decision can have a significant impact on your future capabilities and overall efficiency. To this extent, we always highly recommend putting in some cursory analysis prior to each build to see if you can find evidence that you need to do a deeper-dive pro and con list.

For that cursory analysis, we have a few questions we always recommend upfront and feel they are relevant regardless of context:

- Will your audience require real-time interaction?
- Is your audience entering your process via bulk imports or individually?
- Will the person building and managing this have technical knowledge or skill?
- Will this need to interact with Sales and Service Cloud?
- Is there going to be some complex multi-channel marketing?

From these questions, you can build a very basic analysis of which tool would be the better option. We highly recommend adding your own contextual questions to the preceding list as these are just very basic questions and although they're fairly simple, they do not always have simple answers.

# With our powers combined

Sure, there can be times where you have to make the choice of Automation Studio or Journey Builder for your needs, but we find that more often, of late, it is instead Automation Studio *and* Journey Builder that truly meet your requirements. Despite these two having the same general purpose, this does not mean they are exclusive or competitors of each other.

The different capabilities and strategies of these two tools actually dovetail together very well! All the weaknesses of Journey Builder are strengths in Automation Studio and vice versa. This allows for an extremely strong process across every aspect as one tool picks up the slack of the other through a combined effort. Is there a good analogy that could help explain this?

## The peanut butter and jelly sandwich

If you had peanut butter on your left and jelly on your right and were told to make a sandwich, would you only choose one or the other, or would you choose both? We can tell you that the more satisfying and delicious option is to use the combination of peanut butter and jelly – a staple in most households with young kids.

This is not to say that utilizing each individually or with other ingredients is wrong. You might have a peanut allergy and cannot have peanut butter. You might like Nutella better and use that instead of one or the other, and so on. But in general, if you have both ingredients, you would wind up with a peanut butter and jelly sandwich more often than not.

By utilizing both, you enable yourself to provide highly targeted and highly personalized messaging in a timely manner with efficient processing and throughput. Using the real-time capabilities of Journey Builder helps to make you more agile in your approach, where the bulk capabilities, powerful processing, and customization capabilities of Automation Studio provide a strong base to make Journey Builder effective and efficient.

# Automation Studio and Journey Builder interactions

Automation Studio is a great complement to Journey Builder and together they form a very powerful toolset. Both can slide records laterally or vertically across each tool and since they are fundamentally different in purpose, there is little overlap of capabilities that is not easily addressed and assigned.

For example, let's take a look at a few different use cases on how Automation Studio successfully interacts with Journey Builder.

## Entry events for Journey Builder

Automation Studio is a great way to prepare and manipulate data for entry events in Journey Builder, such as the following:

- Utilizing SQL queries, you can do most of the segmentation and filtering in bulk prior to the audience being uploaded to the entry source.
- You can bulk update relational data prior to entry to allow for journey data to be a more viable option and rely less on contact data, which slows down throughput.

## Custom actions or manipulations that are not possible in Journey Builder

Automation Studio is a great way to supplement journeys through **Script activities** to perform custom actions or manipulations on journey data that is not possible in Journey Builder, such as the following:

- Pre-assigning coupons
- Integrating and manipulating data for exit criteria
- Providing bulk manipulations of data for segmentation and splits
- Updating relational data for up-to-date contact data utilization

## Journey reporting

Automation Studio can be an effective reporting tool on journeys:

- SQL queries to combine tracking, custom, and subscriber data
- Data/tracking extracts to export data for use in third-party tools
- **Script activities** to build integrations or massage data for dashboards

## Entry source for Journey Builder

You can utilize Automation Studio as an entry source for Journey Builder:

- Through a few of the activities in Automation Studio, you can push records directly into a journey by firing an event.
- You also are able to utilize **Script activities** to hit the REST API entry point for Journey Builder if you need more custom conditions around it.

This enables you to have full control of the entry process and you can perform most bulk actions prior to entering a journey as they are combined into a single program and are not separate.

So, all in all, the answer to *Should I use Journey Builder or Automation Studio?* is simply *both*. The best solution is usually to utilize them both to create the most efficient and powerful solution for your needs. The power-up you get when you successfully integrate these two tools together for your solution is wonderful. We have seen campaigns go from fairly simple to highly personalized, dynamic, and powerful within a couple of months just by combining the two tools instead of concentrating on just one.

# Summary

You should now be very aware of not only where Salesforce Marketing Cloud came from, but its current capabilities and multiple channel usages. With the multi-channel and cross-channel options, Marketing Cloud has grown into a titan of the market and become one of the most popular and powerful platforms.

Along with general Marketing Cloud knowledge, you should also be well versed in the two existing, baked-in automation tools inside of Salesforce Marketing Cloud. Both Automation Studio and Journey Builder are very powerful in their own right, but each has weaknesses, specializations, and considerations. These can make a huge difference in your path forward in your automation adventure.

You can now better determine which tool fits better where, and all the caveats and considerations you need to take into account when implementing them. It is always better to utilize both where possible – rather than doing an *or* comparison, it should be an *and* consideration.

In the next chapter, we will begin exploring more of the best practices in automation in the Salesforce Marketing Cloud. This will include general automation best practices as well as insights into best practices for each of the tools we've discussed, as well as them both together.

# 3
# SFMC Automation Best Practices

Now that you know the basics of automation theory and the automation capabilities that are baked into **Salesforce Marketing Cloud** (**SFMC**), we will dive into the best practices for utilizing and building such automation. Whether you are using Automation Studio or Journey Builder or some combination of the two, following these practices should help you find the most efficient solutions for your needs.

*Best practice*, especially in Marketing Cloud, can be a broad term; so, for this chapter, we will be focusing on things such as performance, efficiency, scalability, contextual decision making, and personal preferences. That said, best practice is not always the best solution – so, take these as guidelines and not as gospel.

In this chapter, we will cover the following topics:

- *Best practices*: This section will provide a quick overview of what a best practice is and how we should apply it.

- *Creating high-quality testing*: In this section, we'll dive into testing, the sandbox options in Marketing Cloud, and our recommendations on it.

- *Is efficiency greater than performance?*: In this section, we will dive into efficiency and performance, as well as explore what makes a great solution.

- *Best practice is not always best*: Although best practices should be respected and considered, they are not always the best solution.

- *You (your preferences) matter*: The biggest gap most people have in designing solutions is personal context. You and your opinion are very important.

These topics will provide you with general tips and guidelines on creating, utilizing, and planning automation inside Salesforce Marketing Cloud. Through the basics, we can delve into testing, performance, and efficiency regarding the major considerations for automation in Marketing Cloud. Through this and some in-depth discussions on context and personal preference, we will be set to move forward and begin working in Marketing Cloud. Now, let's dive a bit deeper into **automation best practices** in Salesforce Marketing Cloud.

# Best practices

Before we get into the details around best practices, we need to become familiar with the basics and create a base to build upon. Without a strong foundation, you will find lots of gaps and faults in your creation and it will fail fairly easily. Think along the lines of a *house of cards on a windy day* sort of situation.

So, to help set you up for success, we will begin with the basics to ensure we pass valuable and usable information and skills across to you. When we say basic, we really mean basic. Let's begin at the very beginning. What exactly does *best practice* even mean?

> Best Practice
>
> **Best practice**, as defined by Merriam-Webster (`https://www.merriam-webster.com/dictionary/best%20practice`), is *a procedure that has been shown by research and experience to produce optimal results and that is established or proposed as a standard suitable for widespread adoption.* Or, in other words, through trial and error, this method has shown the best success and is the recommended approach to guide your action or usage.

Best practices focus on maintaining quality and are not a mandatory standard, especially as they can be based on self-assessment and/or benchmarking and not just internal dictation.

Best practice allows you to create templates or boilerplates to build off of that have proven to be effective, reducing the level of effort required to build your actions and activities.

A great example of a best practice that is used almost universally is creating a process for all of the data views inside Marketing Cloud to be saved to data extensions. Since the specifics, such as date range, what time remains in Marketing Cloud, and where it is stored, vary wildly depending on the context, please feel free to adjust these according to your context.

Usually, an automation process is created that targets a group of data extensions you created to mimic the data views. Then, it uses **SQL Query** activities to bring the data across. In our example, we are going to have it run daily and perform an *Update* action (add/update) for the corresponding data extension.

The following are some example steps:

1.  Build out the data views with fields, data types, and the maximum characters based on what is listed in the official documentation.

2.  Build out **SQL Query** activities that target the corresponding data extension while using the data view as the source.

3.  Create an automation process that is scheduled to run daily early in the morning.

4.  Add each of these **SQL Query** activities to different steps in the automation process.

5.  Bonus step: Add a data extract to take a snapshot of the data view each day for reference.

This process will allow for quicker interactions with the data views (with a maximum of a 24-hour delay in data) as querying and filtering a data extension is much faster than interacting with a data view. It can then be used inside of Journey Builder via attribute groups in Contact Builder. These benefits are all amazing, but the bonus of exporting the data views is that you can insert them into analytics platforms for even deeper and faster dives into your data. You will also have a snapshot point of reference if you are investigating or troubleshooting an issue.

Because of these benefits, this is considered a best practice that is universal for all who use the platform.

So, now that we know what best practices are, we have some questions. How does a best practice get established? What level of effort, information, or results is required to optimize them? Does a best practice ever expire or get too old to be useful? How often should it be investigated?

# Establishing a best practice

The level of effort and work that's necessary to deem a practice as the *best* is rarely done before the label is added. To this extent, we should be describing most of what we label as best practices as *smart* practices or *recommended* practices. For the sake of understanding, though, we will continue using best practice as the label for this book.

To establish a best practice, you need to tackle this in a similar way to proving a scientific theory. This can be done through things such as the following:

- **Published research**
- **Competitive research**
- **Think tanks**
- **Adoption of the practice over time**
- **Acceptance of the practice over time**
- **Proven methodology**
- **The achieved value being returned from utilizing the practice**

As you can see from the preceding list, proving a best practice takes a lot of time and effort to collect and verify. This is why it is fair to say that most things lauded as *best practices* are not likely proven to be so. But just because they haven't been proven to be best practices doesn't mean that they can't be considered as such by the community. Now that we have some level of understanding, let's look at the level of effort it takes to maintain best practices.

## Maintaining best practices

Benchmarking your processes and activities is your best bet to find and measure your best methodologies. Benchmarking is just the process of measuring your stuff against the leaders of your industry's *stuff* and comparing the results. Through repeated benchmarking and research, you can maintain the effectiveness of each of your practices and adjust and rewrite them when it's relevant.

So, we know how to maintain and review best practices, but how often should this be done? The answer is… it depends. There are a few things to consider when you're reviewing your current best practices and judging if you need to verify whether they are still the best options for you. You will need to review the following:

- How complex is the practice/methodology?
- How fast-paced or competitive is your context?
- Is the level of value declining compared to previous data?
- Are your competitors outperforming you?
- Is the increased efficiency/value higher than the cost to review and alter your current practice?

Your answers to these questions will determine the level of frequency and level of effort you will need to implement to maintain your best practices. The more questions that you answer *yes* to, the more often and more stringent you should make your investigations and research.

For example, let's say the following answers are provided for our currently considered best practice multi-channel automation solution. We have a new approach that involves more integrations and more capabilities for higher ROI, but is it worth it?

- *How complex is the practice/methodology?*

  The methodology we are using is highly complex as it has to touch multiple databases with different architecture – requiring multiple custom integrations.

- *How fast-paced or competitive is your context?*

  The context is fairly fast-paced, but not excessively so.

- *Is the level of value declining compared to previous data?*

  Yes, the effectiveness of our data is in a steady decline and becoming less valuable.

- *Are your competitors outperforming you?*

  Yes, they have a fully multi-channel marketing journey set up and running effectively.

- *Is the increased efficiency/value higher than the cost to review and alter your current practice?*

  No; our new approach will triple the ROI of each entry into the journey.

As you can see, although there is a high ROI, there is a lot of investigation that needs to be done due to all the *yes* answers. For the cost and level of risks that could be involved in such a solution, you should consider whether this is worth implementing. So, we would recommend you hold off for at least a couple of weeks to do some heavy investigation and testing before looking to implement or change anything officially.

## Keep it simple, stupid (KISS)

Although *keep it simple, stupid* is the way most people have heard it phrased, our favorite version of the acronym **KISS** is **keep it straight and simple**. We feel that this helps emphasize the ideal solution, which is not just the simplest but also the most linear solution. Sometimes, the simplest solution can also be the most convoluted solution in other ways. By keeping it straight *and* simple, you should align to the goal rather than just concentrating on simplicity. (Plus, by using this version, the acronym is not calling you mean names and demeaning your intelligence... the big bully!)

The strongest and most forward-facing solutions are the ones that act in the simplest and straightest path. Although complex and highly intensive solutions and automation can be hugely impressive, they also potentially open up significantly more risk since the more code you have, the more likely you are to have something go wrong. Just because someone makes this highly technical awe-inspiring code block does not mean it is elegant. It could just be needlessly complex.

## An example of KISS

A good example of the KISS theory is around over-engineering a solution. Sometimes, a developer will get so obsessed with the technical capabilities that they will forget about the simpler solution. For example, let's say that data is being imported into a data extension where some manipulations are being done by SQL; we need this data to be transferred from the data extension into **All Subscribers**.

As a developer, you may be in the technical mindset and thinking about utilizing SSJS and AMPscript, or maybe even the APIs or WSProxy to do this… but there is a much simpler solution. You extract the data on the data extension, and then import that data extension into **All Subscribers**. This would not only be simpler but likely also require less processing and incur less risk.

## Complex versus elegant

Many people have a misunderstanding of what the sought-after solution is. The most technologically advanced and innovative solution is not always the best solution. Most of the time, the level of knowledge, skill, and capability that's required for these solutions makes them very inefficient and adds massive resource costs. This does not mean that the best solution needs to be dumbed down or simple, just that it needs to be something accessible and agile. This is then the beginning of considering what is deemed elegant versus what is deemed complex.

### Complex

More complex solutions tend to have more points of failure than those that utilize a more minimalistic approach. This is because complex solutions usually have more points of action or activity that are susceptible to human error or other risks of failure. The more moving parts something has, the more places that it can break. Now, complexity does not necessarily require additional code executions – it could also refer to things such as overly complicated instructions or overtly confusing or difficult to read coding syntax and structure.

**Example of a complex solution**

Utilizing something like the following is a possible solution:

```
var arr = []
arr[0] = "First";
arr[1] = "Second";
arr[2] = "Third";
arr[3] = "Fourth";
```

However, this is much more complex and explicit than just doing the following:

```
var arr = ["First","Second","Third","Fourth"]
```

The reason we are confident in saying this is because it is utilizing constant or *hardcoded* values and not dynamic or variable values. There is no reason to separate each value like that to build the array when the second example provides the same information in a much more efficient and understandable way.

## Elegant

This is not to say that you should not explore creative and highly technical solutions; you just need to make sure they remain straightforward. The best word, in our opinion, to explain this concept is *elegant*.

Elegant solutions are those that provide precision and simplicity that are unmatched. To achieve precision, you need in-depth technical knowledge and understanding to find the absolute most efficient way to accomplish your tasks and activities. The more elegant your automation is, the more power and return you will get from your solution. By keeping things precise and succinct, you free up more processing to be used in other areas, allowing for even more possibilities.

**An example of elegant processing**

Let's build on the complex solution example we shared previously. In this example, let's say that instead of a numerical order, we need to sort the array in alphabetical order. There are some ways in which you could utilize a `for` loop or build multiple comparison conditionals, and you could even use the more elegant built-in `array.sort` function:

```
var arr = ["First","Second","Third","Fourth"]
arr.sort(function(x, y) {
  if (x < y) {
    return -1;
  }
  if (x > y) {
    return 1;
  }
  return 0;
});
//returns ["First","Fourth","Second","Third"]
```

Now you may be wondering why this is not listed as simply `arr.sort()` and instead has a function inside. This is because inside of SSJS in Marketing Cloud, it will toss an error without the function. In normal JavaScript, you would not need the function as this function represents default behavior. As this book is focused on Marketing Cloud though, we wanted to present an example that would work directly in the platform.

## The circle of development

All this talk on best practices, elegance, and complexity reminds us of a mantra that we have heard over and over again throughout our careers that has helped us grow to the level we are at today:

- **How can you tell a junior developer from a developer?**

  - A junior developer uses very basic and simple code to achieve the solution.

  - A developer uses highly complex and technical code to achieve the solution.

- **How can you tell a developer from a senior developer?**

  - A developer uses highly complex and technical code to achieve the solution.

  - A senior developer uses very basic and simple code to achieve the solution.

To help clarify the meaning of this circle, take a look at the following diagram:

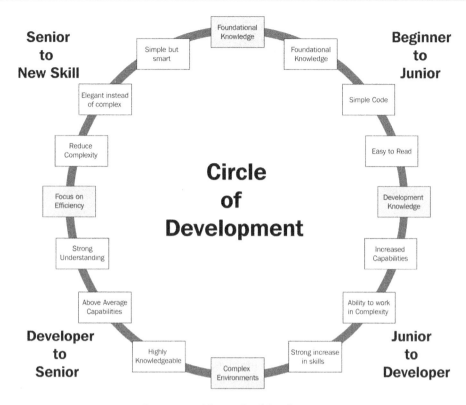

Figure 3.1 – The circle of development

This is saying that you, as a developer, go in a circle of complexity as you grow. You start at the basics in a super simple way, but as you grow, things become more and more complex until you start to become a more experienced developer. Then, you can start reverting to finding the most linear and simplest solutions again to ensure elegance. This relates to automation as you may find these crazy awesome scripts that you can use to do amazing things but find that just using a native activity or two instead would be more elegant and effective.

## Less does not always mean more (elegant)

One point to keep in mind is that less code, processes, or activities does not mean your code is elegant. Through some shortcuts and *hacks*, you can greatly reduce the amount of code or activities needed, but this can also greatly increase the required technical knowledge, as well as the processing requirements of the code. This will make it more likely for performance degradation to occur, as well as points of failure to increase. Elegance includes precision and not just compaction and reduction. So, if you jump through hoops and utilize some hacky behaviors to reduce your code base and character count, you may be making your solution worse, not better.

For example, you could write a script that utilizes dynamic variable creation to shorten your script from 90 lines of code to 40 lines of code, but this will introduce highly complex syntax, theories, and development theories. This limits those who can utilize and understand this code. This also introduces risk as there is likely only a very specific way it can be set up or it will fail – meaning that only those who are highly skilled and well informed on the solution can edit, utilize, or maintain this code without great risk of error. This is not how an elegant solution would be defined, despite being less than half the code.

Now that we have covered the basic best practices in Marketing Cloud regarding automation, let's start exploring some more specific aspects. The first stop is going to be learning how hugely important testing is for ensuring accurate and effective automation.

# Creating high-quality testing

No matter how great you think your solution is based on the self-created test data and reviewing you have done, without high-quality testing data, you can miss giant gaps in your process. Testing and testing data are instrumental to releasing a high-quality and performant solution.

There is no place that testing, especially high-quality testing, is more important than building automation. To confidently *set it and forget it*, you need to know it is going to work as you expect and that there are no unturned stones.

Unfortunately, there are some things inside of Marketing Cloud that make this a bit more difficult than what you may experience in other platforms. Let's explore a few of those woes next.

## Testing woes in Salesforce Marketing Cloud

Inside of Salesforce Marketing Cloud, it is usually much harder to carry out **quality assurance (QA)** and test your automation or processes due to everything being in a live environment. This can lead to requiring you to publish and make your solution go live to test it. This then opens the risk that the people outside of your organization or testing group can access it before it is officially launched and finalized.

> **Quality Assurance**
>
> Quality assurance is a process in which a group or individual will review all the aspects of a project or solution to validate that it is a high level of quality before the solution or project moves forward.

There are different roadblocks or filters you can put in place to help dissuade this possibility, but this also alters your test results from what would exist in a live environment. So, how do we handle this?

Well, we have seen the following two methods being utilized the most to help provide a testing environment before production implementation/launch:

- **Creating test versions in your production business unit**
- **Creating a new *sandbox* business unit**

Neither of these is a perfect solution and each has some drawbacks. But out of all the solutions, we would say one or the other should fit your business need and help guide you to your solution for testing. Now, let's explore these two options in more detail to share the positives and negatives of each.

## Creating test versions in your production business unit

We have found that utilizing some *test* automation that is separate from the *live* automation you are looking to use helps remove any accidental actions during testing that can provide production actions before the go-live date. For instance, this would require us to shift the following aspects for our test version:

- **File Drop naming pattern**
- **File Drop folder location**
- **Target data extensions**
- **Script target and source data extension or content**
- **Email and content**

My usual *go-to* in these situations is to duplicate the existing content, data extensions, and so on. Then, we would just prepend it with *DEV-*. So, if your data extension name is MyDE, you would create your test data extension with the name DEV-MyDE. This prepending allows you to easily see that this is a development data extension and not a live one. It also provides the full name of what is used in production for easy reference, but differentiates to remove any potential issues and risks associated with testing and development.

Now, although this is our recommendation, it can very easily bog down your business unit with a ton of assets that may no longer be relevant and cause some confusion due to there being multiple versions. The best way we have seen this handled is to create a good, solid folder structure to account for this.

A good example of this folder structure is to have a DEV folder inside your main project folder that will store all the corresponding assets. Also, make sure that you mimic this structure across each studio – for example, Email Studio, Content Builder, and Automation Studio. From there, once you have all the assets, everything has been pushed live into the correct folders, and once you have testing finalized, you can delete all the development assets in those DEV folders.

Why would you delete it? Well, reducing the files that all share the same name will greatly increase your capability to search for assets within the UI. It also cuts down greatly on clutter and unnecessary file storage. Finally, it also removes the confusion of working in DEV and Live and seeing which one has updated versions of what. The reason this works so well is that it will also force you to copy off of the *live* version each time you need a new dev version, meaning there is no possibility of old or otherwise incorrect content being inside it. To help explain this, we will go through an example of this process.

## Example of a test version versus a live version

Let's say we are working on creating a piece of automation that imports and manipulates, via SQL Query, our customer information. Before creating the final production (or live) version, we must create a **development** (**dev**) version to test with. So, for the test version, we would start with the following:

- **Automation**: DEV-CustomerImport_Auto
- **Data Extension**: DEV-CustomerDE
- **Import**: DEV-CustomerImport_Import
- **Query**: DEV-CustomerImport_SQL

Then, we would do the following for the live version (once development is done):

- **Automation**: CustomerImport_Auto
- **Data Extension**: CustomerDE
- **Import**: CustomerImport_Import
- **Query**: CustomerImport_SQL

This would cause you to have eight different objects compared to the four that you need for production. However, this would create a separate environment for you to work with the code without affecting anything that's live. This offers a completely clean slate for when you begin production, without any of the development history potentially causing issues.

# Creating a sandbox business unit

Another popular option is to build solutions and automation inside a separate *sandbox* business unit for all the testing and then port it over to the live environment once it's been fully tested and approved. This is how most development processes build and it's tried and true. However, in Marketing Cloud, it comes with caveats:

- **The sandbox is just another normal business unit**:

  - It still has access to All Subscribers and *production* data via Contacts.

  - It still costs the same amount of super messages that your *production* business unit has in terms of emails, web page views, and mobile messages. This means that Marketing Cloud will not differentiate your test sends from your live sends, so it will charge you the same amount per send. This can add up quickly.

  - There is a potential added cost by requiring an additional business unit on your account.

- **There is no easy way to lift and shift your automation or build where there is no risk of corruption or error**:

  - Deployment Manager and Package Manager is an option, but see the *Deployment Manager and Package Manager* section for more details on that.

  - The level of effort for implementation and maintenance can be doubled.

  - QA and troubleshooting timelines will be doubled due to the two environments.

  - It increases the risk of potential failures when you're shifting across due to human error.

  - This also entails risk as you have two places to keep updated or risk having an *old* version overwriting the current, correct content/action.

- **Effort is duplicated in terms of setup, data management, and administration**:

  - You will need to update the data architecture across both accounts in unison.

  - You must create all the APIs and similar packages across both and store each for reference.

  - You must create test data for your sandbox that is identical to your current live data to allow for the highest level of success in testing.

Now, that is not to say in any way this is not a viable option – we just wanted to share the differences from the *normal* sandbox methods compared to how it works in Marketing Cloud. We have seen many major companies that utilize this methodology in their Marketing Cloud environments. It is a secure way to ensure the separation of test and development away from live production environments; it just comes with a heavy cost increase if utilized.

## Deployment Manager and Package Manager

These two applications exist inside Marketing Cloud, with the idea of being able to duplicate certain builds, such as automation, emails, and data groupings, between business units or enterprises. Although this sounds great, these tools have their limitations and, in our opinion, they have more problems than benefits. This is not to say they cannot be used or are not a solution for certain things – but like many aspects, it all depends on your circumstances and a little bit of luck. Before we get too far into that, let's look at what exactly each of these applications is:

- **Package Manager**: Package Manager is a fully supported native feature of Marketing Cloud that is used to bundle items such as journeys, automation processes, content assets, data extensions, and attribute groups. These bundles can then be deployed to other business units or enterprise accounts.

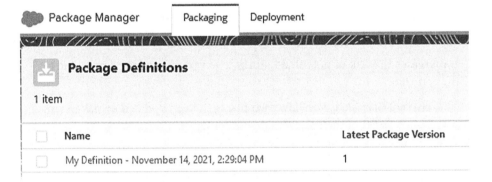

Figure 3.2 – The Package Manager interface

- **Deployment Manager**: Deployment Manager is a Salesforce Labs application that is not supported by Salesforce and is instead a *use at your own risk* application. Deployment Manager is the precursor to Package Manager and does nearly the same things, including bundling objects and deploying them across other business units or enterprises.

Figure 3.3 – The Deployment Manager interface

The major issue that we find with both of these applications is that the deployment part appears to be somewhat fickle, to the point that even if you do not manipulate the bundle that's created, it will still fail to deploy, which can then create more work and effort for you to manually create a part of the packaged deployment. This can have a domino effect on other objects.

We are sure that since Marketing Cloud works on Package Manager and gets it to be a bit more stable and robust, it will be an amazing application, but until then, we would recommend you to be cautious to plan around it being successful and instead ensure you plan backups for if it fails.

Now that we have explored the two major options inside Marketing Cloud, we will begin exploring the development and testing that occurs outside Marketing Cloud, which is then brought in.

# Developing and testing outside Marketing Cloud

This one is the hardest to do, but if you have the tools and capabilities to do it, it can be one of the best options. Essentially, to provide the best **quality testing environment**, you must build an environment outside of Marketing Cloud that utilizes the APIs and other integrations to mimic capabilities you would normally need from within the user interface, such as email previews and running automation processes.

By utilizing an outside environment, you can store your tests locally, giving version control that does not weigh down your instance, and you can do most of the testing without even requiring anything to be hosted on the platform. This sounds quite amazing, right? Seriously, why isn't this the go-to for everyone?

Well, the main reason is that the public APIs capabilities are limited. Without building your tool to perform some *hacky* behavior on the user interface to utilize the *internal* endpoints or functions of the UI, your environment will be super limited. There is also the fact that you and your team would be required to utilize this tool and do nothing directly inside of Marketing Cloud; otherwise, it could cause inconsistencies or misalignments. This is on top of the huge development time to build it, plus the maintenance and training/onboarding required for someone to utilize it, which can make the awesome value it can add seem a lot less valuable.

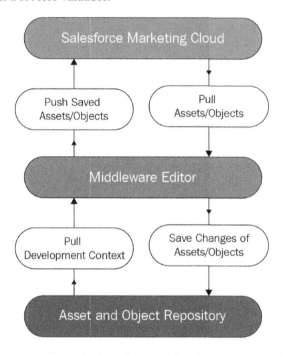

Figure 3.4 – Example flow of external development and testing

We have seen some awesome tools that utilize this process, and they are very impressive. It's hard to find a good use case that lets them provide the full value they should. This is a shame, but a lot of the cool possibilities for integration via powerful API endpoints do not seem to be a priority to Salesforce Marketing Cloud.

Now that we have covered the basics of best practices, including best practices around testing, we should start investigating some of the larger topics surrounding automation that need to be taken into account when you're building anything. Next, we will explore performance and efficiency considerations.

# Performance and efficiency in your architecture

*Effective performance is preceded by painstaking preparation.*

*– Brian Tracy*

We feel this statement is a great mantra to have whenever you work with any automation in Salesforce Marketing Cloud. Without the proper planning and preparation, your automation is not going to perform at peak levels, especially as your needs and capabilities grow. We usually look to have equal parts planning and development to ensure that what we are looking to build is the solution we need. We would ask ourselves the following questions about every project or automation we work on:

- Will the solution solve the problem?
- Is the solution your best path forward to meet your needs?
- Does this solution consider all future scenarios?
- Can the solution handle triple the volume and frequency that's currently expected?
- Is the solution fully planned out and developmentally sound?

Now, these are not the only things to consider in your planning, but we find them to be the most helpful questions to help get you moving down the right path. In this section, we will look at each of these questions and dig into performance considerations in general.

## Will the solution solve the problem?

You would be surprised how many times while planning that we get distracted by all the bells and whistles and all the innovative solutions that are available that we stray from the original need. The solution you build is amazing at doing quite a few things, but it does not do what you originally needed, making it significantly less valuable – which means you have to go back and replan and redevelop it. This can lead to very terrible final forms as you will need to get out massive amounts of duct tape and bubble gum to make it work, or just simply rebuild it from scratch.

By keeping your need or problem inside your planning phase, you can build a strong base solution that provides you with the flexibility to build all those cool and innovative possibilities on top of it. This allows you to retain the highest value return by ensuring you *keep your eyes on the prize* and solve the issue that needs solving.

# Is the solution your best path forward to meet your needs?

Just because a solution can resolve your need does not mean it is the solution you should pursue. Context is highly important to the solution, and although you should ensure the problem is solved, you cannot focus simply on that as the only priority.

By resolving an issue with a solution that does not fully consider the context, you leave yourself with a siloed solution, creating gaps and disconnects from your other processes and solutions. These gaps can then lead to a significantly increased risk when you're implementing your solution. This added risk then decreases the viability of the solution, meaning it may not be a solution at all. Let's explore the considerations around integrations and interactions to help reduce this risk and ensure you have a forward-facing solution.

## Integrations and interactions

When you're building your solution, you need to consider how much interaction there will be with existing systems. With these integrations and interactions, there will likely be restrictions or certain requirements that need to be considered to ensure effectiveness.

Some of these restrictions can be things such as corporate policies. You will always need to consider things such as network security, data limitations, and encryption, and certain permissions or user restrictions will be required. This, along with the technological limitations, such as governor limitations and the direction/flow of solutions, can have a significant impact on your solution.

For instance, if you have specific naming conventions, this can limit your options by reducing the options you have in terms of interacting with the names of each activity or aspect of your automation. There could also be huge limitations if an integrated system can only accept 100 records per second; you would need to account for this when you're building your automation to ensure it never goes above that and prevents overloading. Next, we will dive into how skill level and training play a huge factor in your solution.

## Skill levels and required training/onboarding

Not only do you need to consider the capabilities and restrictions on the existing systems and processes, but also on the personnel and their capabilities and capacity. Just because a solution is available and is possible doesn't mean that you can build it, nor that your team can use it properly.

By assessing your team's skill level, you can get a good feel for the level of effort it would take to bring them up to speed on using the solution and the required level of effort for onboarding any new users into this solution. For instance, having a command-line tool built for a bunch of non-tech savvy marketers to use is likely to be a very long training and ramp-up period that will require a ton of training sessions and support. This can greatly reduce the value of the solution. Now, let's look at the effects that time and monetary costs can have on your solution.

## Time, cost, and effort to build and maintain your solution

So, now that we know it will work with our existing tools and that our team can use it, we need to start making sure it's something that we can either build ourselves or whether the cost of having someone else build it makes sense with the value it will provide. As a previous mentor and friend always liked to say to me, *You want to build something? You have three options: fast, cheap, or good. But you can only pick two of them for any project.*

Sometimes, building a solution internally makes the most sense as you can fully customize and plan it out to fit exactly what you need. But along with this comes the time, cost, and effort that's needed upfront to build it, as well as the time, cost, and effort to maintain and support it. These costs can add up very quickly and, depending on your available resources, this can take an extremely long time to get done.

So, by exploring this cost compared to the available vendors or agencies to complete the solution for you, you can find which solution makes the most sense and adds the most value to your organization. It is always worth considering all the building options when you're planning on creating a tool because building it yourself, just because you can, will sometimes make a solution turn from a good solution into a bad solution. To make a good solution, we need to keep future scenarios in mind; otherwise, they could quickly become outdated or need to be replaced.

# Does this solution consider all future scenarios?

You should always consider the future state when you're making your plans. This means that you need to consider things that you have not built yet and account for other needs or issues that do not currently exist. If you do not prepare for the future, you will limit your capabilities and require rework or coming up with more solutions at a later date. In the next few subsections, we will dive into a few of the major considerations to keep in mind while you're validating that your automation/solution has future possibilities in mind.

## Future integration possibilities

When you're building a solution, you should always keep in mind that it will likely have to interact or integrate with other systems – potentially, systems that do not even exist yet. To that extent, you need to create some sort of service or connector that can accept and handle these new systems.

Probably the most important part to consider is that if the service or language is old or antiquated now, it will be completely useless in the future. So, when you create things, you need to build them with newer services in mind. For instance, nowadays, you would not build a service that utilizes a SOAP API connection instead of a REST one. Sure, SOAP can still get the job done and many places do use it, but it is on its way out and to build something on it is to put a definitive expiration date on it.

## Handling capability growth and new additions

One thing to always keep in mind is that no matter how *perfect* or well thought out your final solution is, there is going to need to be new updates or additions to it in the future. This is inevitable and should be a major consideration in your architecture. Setting up your solution to account for the ability to easily build on top of it will allow the solution to handle future needs and updates better.

Also, by considering platform and capability growths in the build, you can provide visibility for your solution. This versatility will increase the lifetime of your solution and help it to be much more valuable.

## Data analytics and reporting

This is one part that tends to be left on the back burner when it comes to solutions. Without good analytics, logging, or reporting, the value of a solution significantly drops. Most of the time, you will notice that solutions will be implemented. Then, there will be a half thought out solution to handle reporting and logging the solution that was added at the end when it was already mostly done.

Logging is especially important for solutions. There is no better way to debug and troubleshoot a solution than to review the logs and find where the solution *fell over*. Without a log, it can easily take 10 to 20 times longer to resolve these solutions, making logs an invaluable resource.

# Can your solution handle triple the volume and frequency that's currently expected?

When you are building a tool, you need to go in with the idea that what volume and frequency you see now is just a drop in the water of what the future will hold. If you do not approach it this way, your tool will very quickly reach peak capacity and will need a new solution to be built out, greatly reducing the efficiency and value of your solution.

My general rule of thumb for this calculation is to look at three times the currently expected volumes. Not the current volume, but the expected volume you are getting from your research for the future. Times that by three and you should get your solution into a better place to ensure future capacity against future demand.

So, for instance, say that your current flow is around 1 million records per day into this process. With the efficiencies of the tool and the increase in productivity and capability, you can see it growing to 10 million over the next couple of years. At that point, our recommendation is to take that 10 million and times that by 3. This means that the capacity of your tool should sit at around 30 million per day.

The reason is that we have always found that the expected capability and capacity are almost always going to be much lower than the actual need, no matter how much you over-estimate. This is because, as things move forward, new variables are introduced, new programs and marketing strategies come into play, contextual sales changes, and more that can greatly change and affect the volume.

Using these along with just general technological updates and capability increases can significantly increase flow beyond anything you could have believed in the initial plan. Also, we have always found that having the extra processing power and not needing it is much less impactful to value than needing more capacity and not having it.

# Is the solution fully planned out and developmentally sound?

This may sound like it should be common sense, and in many ways, it is, but it is something we find is most often a problem when we are creating a solution. The issue is that with so many possibilities, considerations, contextual roadblocks, and integration variances, you can easily lose track of the core of your solution.

We have found ourselves getting lost in the details very easily and without someone to remind us to focus and keep things on the right path instead of in the stars, our solutions would have greatly suffered. To that extent, in any and every project we work on, we have checks written in every step that simply say something such as the following:

- *Check to make sure this makes sense*

- *Don't forget to build the ship before you design the deck*

It just needs to be something to draw our attention outside of our own blinders and let us step back and evaluate the solution along the way. Without this reminder, we could have become distracted and completely missed some very important details.

A great example of this is that we wanted to build a simple import logging automation/ script inside Salesforce Marketing Cloud. Now, anyone who has looked into this will likely be laughing at us for our usage of *simple* there. This process is far from simple.

Multiple REST API endpoints are needed to log every import and file from import activities. To that extent, we went down a deep rabbit hole around **File Drop** automation and imports and wound up creating a big process on logging **File Drop** automation and their interactions with the FTP, instead of anything related to the initial solution. We spent nearly a week on a solution that there was no real problem to solve for, instead of working on the requested solution. If we had put in our checks and notes to remind us to evaluate whether this makes sense, we could have redirected all that time and effort and got the solution built much quicker than we did.

The method you implement to do these checks is not nearly as important as the checks themselves. Choose the method that works best for you. We have seen people use post-it notes, checklists, digital assistant reminders, calendar reminders, and to-do lists. Our favorite is to grab a teammate or someone who is not a major part of the project and ask them for 10 minutes of their time to go through all the current highlights and forward paths you are working on. This gives you an outside opinion and by forcing you to say it out loud, you can catch gaps or unintentional fallacies in your path. To help give more context on this, we will go through an *answered* example of this process.

## Example of performance evaluation

The automation in question is built on Marketing Cloud, but is pulling data from a segmentation that's been made on the company's data lake. It's sending the messaging, followed by immediate reporting and analytics being sent back to the analytics platform via an API.

Let's look at the questions we went over for this example:

- *Will the solution solve the problem?*

  Yes. Through this, we can get the target audience we want to send into Marketing Cloud, send the dynamic messaging to the audience, and then pass that information to our analytics system.

- *Is the solution your best path forward to meet your needs?*

  Since the segmentation solutions inside Marketing Cloud are not optimized for this level of segmentation and data preparation, it is more efficient and effective to use a data lake. This, coupled with Marketing Cloud's capabilities with dynamic messaging and the integration with our analytics platform, supports this as the best path forward.

- *Does this solution consider all future scenarios?*

  This solution accounts for all audience sizes and for capabilities to adjust the integrations as needed. There should not be a future scenario that cannot be accounted for.

- *Can the solution handle triple the volume and frequency that's currently expected?*

  With the power of data lakes and the power of the dynamic messaging throughput of Marketing Cloud, we can handle volume and frequency well above our current needs.

- *Is the solution fully planned out and developmentally sound?*

  We have implemented similar solutions previously with high success and this solution has been fully mapped out and developed.

# Is efficiency greater than performance?

Now, let's look at a question that does not have an answer – some don't even feel like they make any sense. The first thing we should do is evaluate exactly what efficiency and performance mean. If you look up the two literal definitions, you will notice that they are quite similar. Does this mean they are the same thing, though? A few people we know would vehemently say 100% yes, but we are not so certain.

# Why are we not certain?

Are they related to each other? Very much so. Are they, at the core, identical? No! There is a fairly big difference between these two that is pretty well hidden in the language that's used to define them. In our opinion, efficiency and performance can be defined as follows:

- **Efficiency** mostly focuses on reducing waste and optimizing how resources are used. It is aligned to find the best way to create a solution with minimal impact or resource allocation.

- **Performance** focuses almost exclusively on the output. It is based on how much you can get out of the resources you have. It is less concerned with waste and more about the potential power you can get from your resources.

These are our definitions of these words. Through these definitions, we feel there is a better understanding of the difference between these words. Using this understanding, let's take a look at a solution that is performant, but not efficient:

*Joe has a cabin in the woods and it gets extremely cold there during the night. He has to come up with a solution to help keep him warm that is fairly easy to accomplish and effective. As his cabin is in the woods and he has access to a ton of wood, he decides that the solution will involve fire. With woodcutters, an ax, and a fireplace, it becomes obvious as to what his solution should be.*

*His solution is to go out and chop down a lot of firewood and use that firewood in his fireplace in his cabin. This will let him burn the wood inside his house, which will then be able to retain the great amount of heat that's put out by the fire. All the waste (smoke and ash) will go out through the chimney.*

Pretty smart, right? Well, it is certainly a performant solution that outputs a lot of heat in a way that can help keep Joe more than warm enough across each chilly night he is there. With his abundant resources, he does not need to worry much about running out of fuel. But this is not the most efficient way to resolve this.

By burning through at least a couple of wood blocks each night, he is burning through his fuel at a fairly high rate – it is only the abundance of the fuel source that makes this efficient. If he wanted an efficient solution, he would look to call in someone to insulate and seal his home first. Even then, he could look up things such as geothermal heating or other potential solutions that offer up to 70 or 80% higher efficiency of resources than a wood fireplace could offer.

# Is efficiency better than performance?

Yes, but also no. The answer to this question depends on what you need your solution to do. If you, like Joe, have an abundance of the necessary resource and are not worried too much about making sure that you get the most out of every piece, then performance would likely be your priority. However, if resources are scarce, it would make more sense to make sure that you get every last bit of productivity and value from your resources, regardless of whether it causes a slowdown in output.

There is no definitive answer to this question, but we would say more often than not that most people tend to place a higher value on performance than efficiency. This is best seen in the preceding example story – Joe did not want to spend those extra days, dollars, and effort getting all that work done upfront for a highly efficient solution; he went with performance to get his solution up and running at a quicker and lower upfront cost.

Finding efficiency is a significant effort upfront as it usually requires quite a bit of preparation, research, and investigation. It can also have the largest impact on the current process and methodology. Although it may be a *better* solution in the long run, the substantial costs and risks upfront can be far greater than the long-term values it can offer.

I do want to emphasize that a lot of the time, this determination is not people being *lazy* or *rushing* to just get something in. The decision is based on a ton of calculations and risk analysis. Sometimes, there is an obvious solution that is by and large the best one in the long term, but it comes with a lot of requirements. The following are some examples:

- **It could take up to a year for it to be up and running and begin creating any value**:

  - Increasing risks, due to the length of time to implement compared to the possibility of changing the environment or need.

  - Increasing the starting costs exponentially due to the high cost for the first year of work with no returned revenue counters this.

- **It could require you to restructure the current methodologies and processes before they're implemented**:

  - Increases risks as this restructuring could cause other issues that can incur more costs or effort

  - Potentially high costs for rebuilding and training these new methods

  - Lower efficiency during the implementation of these new methods due to unfamiliarity

- **There is an increase in cost for other partner systems to implement**:

  - If it requires other *partner* technologies, you could be looking at having to buy or build solutions for things you already have solutions for, thereby increasing cost and risk.

With all these added to the calculation, that gap between solutions can substantially decrease. We have seen cases where the most optimal and efficient solution would take nearly 10 years of running to just pay off the costs and *catch up* if we had just implemented the other solution. We can tell you that in 10 years, if not before that, the solution would likely be outdated and need to be re-evaluated. This means that it would be the less valuable option.

Now that we have a strong background and have taken a deep dive into best practices and the best practices in Salesforce Marketing Cloud around automation, We want to start investigating how to use them. There are many considerations around utilizing a best practice beyond just implementing it as-is.

# Best practice is not always best

We have a ton of background and strong knowledge in the dos and don'ts of Marketing Cloud automation. Great! Progress! But now, we want you to put all that to the side so that we can make this very important note around all that information.

These best practices are not the be-all solutions for every automation process. Sometimes, you need to toss out *best* and use *your* solution. You will find that what works for 9 out of 10 people is not the best solution for your needs. There are a ton of things that go into a solution and due to all these variables, best practices cannot account for them all.

Think of best practice solutions to be more of guidelines or boilerplates for you to use. From these, you can get a head start on building your solution and then just adjust, add, and subtract as necessary to meld it to fit your unique situation. To that extent, we want to recommend the following things you should keep in mind whenever you build from a best practice solution:

- **The context of your problem and solution is paramount to a good solution.**
- **The smartest person in the room is not always right.**
- **Always test and research everything yourself – don't trust external results.**

By remembering these three key topics, you should be able to build out and strategically build a solution that best fits your needs. Best practice does not mean it is always the best solution, just that it is the best general method to get these general results.

Let's look at those three topics in more detail.

# Context matters

One of the many things you hear tossed about is that *No matter what you do, someone else has already done it*. I always hate this saying. Sure, something similar has happened before, but it was not right here, right now, in this very specific way. Just because it is very closely related does not mean it is identical.

Context is one of the most important things to consider in nearly everything. Even something as simple as sitting a foot away from where you are can completely change the context and understanding of a situation. Let us explain.

**Story 1 – John's point of view**

John is sitting down next to Jenny and Sam is sitting on Jenny's other side. John is watching a fireworks display and Jenny leans over and blocks his view as she digs into her purse. John missed the big finale, so he was not happy with the fireworks show since the rest was pretty boring.

From *Story 1*, we can see that John was not happy with the fireworks show since it was pretty boring for the most part. He did miss the big finale though because Jenny was leaning over in front of him to dig into her purse for something. Because he only missed a little bit of the fireworks show, he assumed that he likely did not miss much and concluded the show was bad.

**Story 2 – Sam's point of view**

John is sitting down next to Jenny and Sam is sitting on Jenny's other side. Sam is watching a fireworks display and he doesn't even notice when Jenny leans over in front of John to dig into her purse as the big finale begins. Despite the rest of the show being mediocre, the finale was the best Sam had ever seen and he left the show amazed with how great it was.

From *Story 2*, we can see that Sam agreed that the show was not going great for the most part, but that the finale was amazing. After seeing such an amazing couple of minutes, Sam left the show feeling very positive about his experience and the show in general.

This is a great example of how the context of a couple of feet can completely alter the information and understanding you have of a situation. Due to these differing contexts, John may never come to this show again and never see the amazing finale; he may potentially even poke fun at Sam for how much he loved it. On the other hand, Sam will see it every year and not understand how John could think so poorly of it.

Now, we can see how important context is. What may be the best solution in the world to others can be a John and Jenny moment for you, where the amazing ending cannot be watched, so the solution is not for you. That does not make you wrong and the others right. It just means that in your situation, it does not make sense to use that solution.

The story of your needs and your solution is as important – if not more so – than any recommendation or best practice documentation you can find.  Just because someone is a master in their field or highly respected does not mean that they know the entire situation and that you should trust them more than yourself.

# Subject matter experts don't know everything

One thing that most successful automation campaigns need is subject matter experts. These are people that are intimately knowledgeable about the subject matter at hand. In this case, it would be experts in Salesforce Marketing Cloud and automation within it.

Subject matter experts are a valuable asset and a great resource for platform knowledge, but they are not infallible. Just because an expert tells you to do something in a specific way does not mean that is the best or only way to get it done. The level of intelligence, skill, and experience in a platform, while impressive, does not give you a card that means everything you say is accurate no matter what.

My main focus in this section is to make sure you keep in mind that when you call in an expert, them being the smartest person in the room does not mean they are always right. That being said, though, you shouldn't completely ignore any expert. They got that status for a reason and probably have some valuable insights that you can use.

The focus here is to ensure you fully explore what is being said by the export and verify that it is something that works for you and your needs, instead of blindly accepting best practices. This extra due diligence exploration can wind up saving you tons of money and time that could be lost due to *bad advice* from an expert.

## Smart does not mean right

There are plenty of times where we have worked with a client or helped consult someone in one of the many forums we frequent where we have been recommending one approach, only to find out that the way their data feed is set up, their systems are built, or the way their company policies dictate make our solution impossible or more difficult. This means there's more of an upfront cost than they may be willing to take on, which means my *best practice* solution sucks.

So, despite being pretty smart people with a lot of experience in Marketing Cloud and similar platforms, we were wrong in what was recommended! Best practice and platform knowledge can get you most of the way there, but without the full view of the situation and the nuances of the context, we will only get so far. Think of best practice as more of a great starting place that you fill in the blanks of with your data and shift it to best fit your needs.

We are sure everyone here can commiserate with this. That *smartest person in the room* has to show off how much more intelligent, talented, and skilled they are than everyone else. These people are fairly rampant in the technology world and unfortunately, they tend to be the ones that make a name for themselves. Luckily, in the Marketing Cloud community, it seems like this is less prominent than in most other technology communities.

This self-proclaimed *smart person* will fight tooth and nail to prove that whatever they said is right and best, even if it requires them to make stuff up, bully you, or attack you personally. As soon as someone starts doggedly fighting you about which solution is better and is not just discussing or arguing, then you know you can stop the conversation and look elsewhere. An expert is someone smart enough to know a lot, but also smart enough to realize that they also don't know everything. There are tons of people out there that know more about those things than they do.

## Do not ignore the actual smart people

We are certainly not telling you that subject matter experts are not to be respected and listened to – far from it! We just are saying to take what they share as the advice and guidance it is, and not as a complete or singular solution. Combine that advice with your knowledge and understanding to find the best solution for your needs.

Subject matter experts are great collaborators and consultants as well! The more you work with them and discuss the context, the more they can get a feel for your needs and help guide you to the correct solution. We have known tons of companies that will pay very smart people a bunch of money to sit and give them best practice advice for a few months on big projects or initiatives they want to implement. We can tell you that almost every single company has come back to say the cost was well worth it. Most of those that say it was not either hired the wrong person or refused to partner with the consultant properly.

As mentioned previously, bringing in an expert as a consultant is something that is going to take a lot of time as they will need to fully digest the entire context and situation of your organization. There is usually a lot of things that need to be considered, researched, and tested before you can align with a suggested solution.

# Do research and testing

So, there is a ton of information out there on nearly any and every topic you can think of. This information is all at our fingertips and can mostly be accessed for free or at a fairly reasonable price thanks to the internet. We live in an information age that helps make research and investigation easier than it ever was before.

If that is true, then why would we tell you to do research and testing? Well, because despite there being a ton of information, not all of it is relevant or related to *you* and *your situation*. Some of it may look related, but it can give contradictory information to your actual situation, causing massive confusion and potentially causing future issues or a reduction in quality.

In the infamous words of Thanos, *Fine. I will do it myself.* However, here, we are not aiming to collect Infinity Stones or talk about the failings of our subordinates – we are talking about doing first-person data analysis and research. Plus, we would say that most of us are not purple and gigantic. Other than that, we are all very similar.

## Benefits of doing research

There is a level of understanding and comprehension that's gained from doing research and testing to find a solution that just cannot be matched with grabbing data from other resources. Knowing how your company and its existing solutions work and taking that into account can take a good solution and make it great!

Not only does your understanding and comprehension grow by doing research and testing, but you can get different viewpoints and perspectives through your knowledge gains. By doing some legwork, you get exposure to many things you may not have seen otherwise and can dig up hidden *landmines* or opportunities to help guide your solution to an even better and smoother outcome.

## Test yourself before you wreck yourself

Testing on your own, whether through proof of concepts or actual solution testing, is a great way to ensure the optimal solution is in place. We have found that even if you are going to hire an agency or contractor to build your solution, it is best to build a small proof of concept yourself first to get a feel for what is needed.

When you're building this concept, it will help you gather insights into the systems that will need to be included or integrated, all the associated data and company policies, and so on that would need to be considered in your solution. The more information and guidance you can provide for the build team, the better the results will be. This, combined with end-to-end testing, will get you a level of scrutiny and familiarity that can lead to not just a strong solution but a much better maintenance and upkeep methodology.

Doing testing once the solution is completed is paramount as well. It not only ensures that the solution was correctly built and works as expected, but also gives your team much-needed familiarity and experience with the tool. This is especially important when you're utilizing contractors or agencies for solutions. If the people that built the solution will not be around in 6 months or so when something will most likely go wrong, you need to have the knowledge and familiarity with it to be able to resolve it yourself.

# You (your preferences) matter

Two things that are probably the most important thing to be considered when you're planning and building are your preferences and insights. It is so easy to be distracted or lost in the millions of different references, resources, and investigations. You need to keep your head above water and always remember that when push comes to shove, this is something that you and your team will need to build, maintain, and use. So, *you* need to be considered in the solution to make sure it's optimal for you and your team.

This can be a tough thing, especially for someone who may not have the confidence or outgoing personality to speak up, but you need to speak up for yourself and make sure you are included in the solution. The biggest roadblock to this is the dreaded **imposter syndrome**.

## Imposter syndrome

**Imposter syndrome** is the state in which someone believes that they do not deserve to be where they are. In this situation, you may feel that those around you are more accomplished and realize how out of your league you are and shun you. It is something that is rampant for many people and it is something that needs to be addressed.

One key to success is knowing yourself and recognizing your weaknesses, but the other key is to not let those weaknesses hold you back. It is fine to feel insecure at times and feel scared or nervous, but it is when you let those feelings stop you from stepping up and doing the thing that you want to do that it becomes an issue.

This requires a certain level of maturity and confidence. The best way we have found to reach this level is to take a deep look at yourself and learn to trust yourself, let others tell you *no*, and not to pre-emptively limit yourself. By freeing yourself from your limits, you open up more possibilities and solutions for your automation due to a reduction in self-doubt.

# Trust yourself

This one always sounds like it's so easy, but it is a very difficult thing to do. There are all kinds of self-help books, classes, and philosophies dedicated to just this. To that extent, we know it is far from easy and requires a lot of work. By trusting yourself, you also allow yourself to make decisions faster. You allow yourself to follow your *gut instinct* instead of potentially overthinking things and slowing down a process. Overthinking can also lead to over-complicated solutions or talking yourself out of the best solution just because you felt like your decision could not be right.

You also won't be able to fully digest and understand the current state situation you are in without being able to trust the information and research you have gathered. You need to have confidence in your abilities to fully assess your situation, which is one of the major factors that's required to build an optimized solution.

# Your situation matters

An amazing gift in many circumstances can be a complete insult in another situation. Where you are, what you are giving or doing, and who you are giving it to can greatly alter the value of the gift. There are times when the same item and the same place but different people could drastically alter the value, where one is an amazingly heartfelt gift and the other is a very hurtful insult.

For instance, to many people in America or England, getting a new watch can be a wonderful and thoughtful gift, but if you were to give that same gift to someone in China, it could hold an ominous meaning and would be considered insulting. In China, the gift of a watch or a clock can be perceived as telling someone that *their time is running out* and can be considered a grave insult. This is an example of how vastly important context and situations are.

By putting in the time and effort to fully assess the situation and utilize that knowledge in your solution, you can greatly optimize your results. Through this effort, you can easily discern which options make sense and which ones, such as the watch, are a bad idea.

Although many people mention *due diligence* as a good measure of the level of investigation you should do before you create a solution, we disagree. We think that is the bare minimum amount that needs to be done. You need to not only know the situation but also fully understand it to succeed. To do this, you need to go beyond just the surface and dig into what everything is and what that means. With an in-depth understanding, you will be able to find many different things that can greatly affect or alter your initial solutions. For instance, you could find things such as hidden land mines, roadblocks, and shortcuts that could greatly reduce or increase the level of effort necessary.

The other benefits you get from your understanding of the situation is that you learn places where you can use existing structures or processes to build upon, reduce the requirements of your solution, and recognize weak points inside your infrastructure that you can include when you're planning your solution.

Using knowledge of your systems, platforms, policies, and more will get you more access to ways in which you can solve using existing processes. For instance, one time Greg built an entire email library UI based on using the Marketing Cloud API, Cloud Pages, and data extensions, as well as utilizing an in-house data platform and content system to take on some of the heavy lifting and retain version control beyond just the current version. Without this knowledge to use the existing data platform and content system, the solution would not have been nearly as smooth and may not have even been possible due to the heavy processing required.

## Summary

Wow! We made it through the setup and the best practices section! Congratulations! Through the past few chapters, we have learned so much, starting with talking about automation and then the best practices in automation for Salesforce Marketing Cloud. Throughout this chapter, we have learned about many things concerning automation in Marketing Cloud, including the building-block best practices of automation in Marketing Cloud; how to create high-quality testing to maximize your solutions; figuring out the difference between efficiency and performance; learning that best practice does not always mean the best solution; and that your preference, context, and opinions are major considerations.

With these topics under our belt, we can confidently close this section of this book. These topics will guide us in our future endeavors in automation by creating a strong understanding and building block that will form a strong base in our capabilities within Marketing Cloud. From here, we will start investigating automation capabilities inside Salesforce Marketing Cloud and how best to utilize them.

In the next chapter, we will begin diving deeper into building and utilizing automation inside Salesforce Marketing Cloud. This includes use cases and examples, as well as in-depth explanations and analyses. First, we will dive deep into automating email sends inside Salesforce Marketing Cloud. This topic is a staple in marketing automation tools and is a good starting point.

# Section 2: Optimizing Automation inside of SFMC

Now that we know the basics of automation and how to use automation in SFMC, we will explore more details on best practices, implementation options, optimizations, and advanced usages, all within the platform.

This section contains the following chapters:

# 4
# Automating Email Sends

Automation best practices are always a great place to start from, and now we have a lot of understanding of these general best practices and how to use them. Even though best practices are not infallible or ultimate solutions, they are great ways for pointing you in the right direction or for having a boilerplate solution to build off of.

To build off that strong base, we are now going to start exploring more in-depth and detailed information on specific topics of automation in Marketing Cloud. Our first stop in exploring automation in Marketing Cloud is **email messaging automation**. In this chapter, we will dive deep into what email messaging automation is and how to use it to your advantage.

Email messaging automation is almost universally the most popular automated activity across all messaging platforms. Who wants to have to go through the weekly process of setting up a message, validating it is set up correctly, and then sending it over and over again when you can just do it once and then *set it and forget it*? Certainly not the majority of people, that is for sure.

Our focus is going to be on email in this chapter as it is a staple for messaging software and the base on which Salesforce Marketing Cloud and Exact-Target were built, but most of the following principles and actions can be applied to other messaging mediums. In this chapter, we will explore the following:

- Email marketing automation overview

- Real-time versus scheduled

- 1:1 messaging versus batch sends

- Analytics-powered insights

- Considerations regarding email automation

Now, as mentioned precedingly, there are a couple of places where we dive deep into theories on messaging automation strategy as well as some general considerations you should keep in mind while automating your messages. This is because a lot of automation is contextual, so that can mean subjective opinions and outside influences will affect each automation and need to be included in your solution.

At the other end of the scale, however, there is also a section talking about the utilization of analytics and tracking information to provide more scientific insights. Through a combination of *science* and *art*, we usually find effective marketing automation.

As a note, this chapter starts with the assumption that you have some basic background in email marketing and the capabilities and functionality of Salesforce Marketing Cloud in relation to email messaging. If you feel you are missing some aspects, We would recommend checking out Trailhead, by Salesforce, or one of the many blogs or communities out there to get some background concerning Marketing Cloud.

First, let's dive into the basics of email marketing automation and the benefits it provides.

# Email marketing automation overview

**Email marketing** is one of the oldest and strongest relationship marketing strategies available. With the right cadence, elements, and targets, your campaigns can provide amazing returns on your efforts.

That brings us to the question of what is **email marketing automation**? It is the act of fully preparing and sending out email campaigns programmatically based on triggers, categories, and/or schedules that are set by you.

Automating your promotional campaigns is useful as it saves marketers from needing to create and send email jobs each time a need arises. By creating an automated process, you greatly reduce the need for manual action every time an email is ready to be sent thereby reducing the draw on your staffing resources and a drop in the time it takes to get each email campaign created.

Next, we will go into detail about how email automation is very different from **email blasts** or **batch and blast** methods. These are more one-off email broadcasts that are sent manually to all of your subscribers. Email marketing automations are more aligned, with a smarter, permission-based marketing strategy, and have vastly increased performance and return.

The main benefits of email automation are as follows:

- Reduced manual effort/wasted time: By automating aspects of your process, you reduce the number of tasks that your team needs to accomplish or validate manually, thereby reducing the draw on your team to complete tasks manually and freeing them up for other tasks.

- Personalized content: Because of the automation capabilities, you are able to personalize and dynamically fill in each individual email through scripting while retaining the singular build and send approach, making each email personal without the added efforts.

- Improved scalability of your marketing strategy: As your campaigns grow, so too does the cost and level of effort required to execute them. By automating, you can spend the same time sending an email to 10 people as you would to 10 million. It also can allow you to loop messaging together in linear or journey pathing options.

- Reduced costs and time to deployment of your campaigns: Through automation, you reduce the level of effort and the number of resources needed to deploy your campaigns. This allows you to save costs on resourcing and reduce the time required to execute the campaign.

Through these benefits, you can greatly increase the ROI of your email campaigns and be able to take them to the next level.

Now that we have the basics of email marketing automation covered, let's explore the different opportunities we have for email message automation inside Marketing Cloud. One of the first places we see multiple opportunities is around the execution type and timeline of messages. This then begs the question: *What is the difference between* **real-time** *and* **scheduled** *messaging strategies?*

# Real-time versus scheduled

As you will likely consider as you read on, this could also be phrased similar to a section in *Chapter 2, SFMC Automation Tools*, as *Comparing Journey Builder and Automation Studio*. But even that is not fully accurate as there are ways to do both strategies in each tool. For instance, there are ways to do scheduled email sends inside Journey Builder through different **Wait Activities** and **Entry Events** and you can use **File Drop** automations in Automation Studio or even **Triggered Sends** and **Transactional Sends** (from Email Studio) to perform real-time messaging.

Although both strategies are available in both tools, each tool is explicitly designed to specialize in one or the other. Journey Builder can most definitely do scheduled sends through different entry event or wait options, but it is specifically designed to be a real-time marketing strategy tool. Similar to that, Automation Studio has options for real-time delivery/action, but it is most definitely optimized to run more with a scheduled or recurring marketing strategy.

Before we dive too much deeper, let's explore what exactly real time is.

# Real time

Merriam Webster's dictionary defines **real time** as the actual time during which something takes place. Now, this is great as a general definition, but this is not what we would say is a real-world definition of real time in relation to email marketing or even marketing in general. Usually, there is a certain *gray area* that exists around this definition as real time is not always immediate. Even if a couple of hours have passed since the trigger, that can still be considered real time in some contexts. Odd, right?

Well, the difference revolves around the path the person takes to get there inside the automation. For instance, it could be considered real time because prior to that, it had to go through a bunch of different data systems and warehouses where it was validated, cleansed, transformed, and filtered prior to reaching the send activity. So, although the actual send was delayed, the process was initiated and was run in real time.

Another option is to include a purposeful delay prior to the messaging being released. We know that for things such as abandoned carts or similar *reminder*-type messages, there is usually a well-curated waiting period within the path used so that although they enter the path in real time, the message is not sent until a pre-determined wait period afterward.

Now that you have a good idea of what real time means in relation to email marketing, let's take a look at learning what options you have in utilizing this strategy.

## Real-time messaging options

As stated earlier, this capability is not limited to just one tool or the other, but there is definitely one that is optimized for this specific type of execution – Journey Builder. Journey Builder is a tool designed to optimize the handling of real-time, 1:1 messaging needs.

Outside of this, other options sit outside of the two tools that can be used, such as API interaction triggered sends and transactional sends. Each option that is capable of being real time are the following:

- **Journey email activity**
- **Triggered sends**
- **Transactional sends**
- **Journey Builder transactional journeys**
- **Automation Studio Send Email activity**

Now that you have the list, which we must admit is not exhaustive, let's dig more into each option and get a better feel for it. We will start at the top and explore the Journey email activity.

### Journey email activity

Journey Builder, by default, utilizes a form of **triggered send** as its email activity, meaning it is triggered immediately per individual and not stored and sent later. This setup allows it to be more agile in terms of the speed when a message is executed, creating fewer hurdles to getting the email out the door.

These messages are triggered by an action that then makes the system send the message out to the corresponding data source. In Journey Builder, the trigger is made via the journey path as it moves through – pushing each record individually onto this activity at the time of activation. This is slightly different and a less technical approach than what you would find in the regular triggered sends.

### Triggered sends

A triggered send is something that has been around in Marketing Cloud since when it was still ExactTarget. This was the original way in which the platform could offer real-time messaging. Triggered sends require an API call to be made that contains all the relevant information in its payload. This allows it to align the sendable data with the correct email definition, and so on, so that it can immediately send the email out.

These are very developer-heavy options as there is no UI attached to execute these (as we are separating out triggered sends from Journey Email activities). So, it requires you to develop an outside service to make an API call to a specific endpoint with a specific payload in order to have it execute. This can make it a bit unwieldy for some.

Next, there is the **transactional send**, which is basically the triggered send's younger brother.

## Transactional sends

The **transactional send** is a newer version of the triggered send. It is basically Marketing Cloud's response to **SMTP (Simple Mail Transfer Protocol)**-based email services that are streamlined for speed of execution and delivery. According to Salesforce, these offer much faster processing, higher priority, and reduced queueing services compared to triggered sends.

Despite all this, much of the usage and perceived execution is the same. You still need to trigger this via an API call and it needs to contain specific information to connect it to the sendable data and the email definition. After this API call, it still appears very similar in the process as triggered sends as it creates a new record in the corresponding data extension.

Figure 4.1 – Example of workflow for the transactional email API

The main difference comes in through setup and execution. The email definition and other setup needs have to be done via API, not the UI. This means that you cannot use the UI to identify what existing transactional emails you have created, or that are running or paused. You will need to review all of this as well as interact with them via API only. This can be very burdensome and may require building an external tool to interact with this through its own custom UI to allow for fewer technical resources to be required to do this.

This can be a huge task that potentially could be looking at a significant effort to implement. To make life easier for non-technical resources, Salesforce created the **transactional journey**.

## Journey Builder transactional journeys

Journey Builder **transactional journeys** basically just use Journey Builder as a UI for the transactional send APIs. It provides all the same results and benefits of the transactional sends, but with a UI so non-technical resources can use it.

That does not mean that it is a 1:1 comparison though. There are a lot of capabilities and customization that are available via the API that are just not possible inside of the journey. The API also has a stronger throughput due to the streamlined approach. Now, the advantage to the journey, outside of the UI, is that tracking and analytics are available on the journey, and this is not easily available via the API version. Next, we move to a more batch-oriented, but still potentially real-time, messaging option.

## Automation Studio Send Email activity

Admittedly, nine times out of ten, this activity would be used in a scheduled environment, not real-time, but it is possible to use it that way. For instance, if you use a File Drop automation to drop an audience, this activity will send the email upon dropping/ importing, instead of waiting for a scheduled time/date.

You would set this up as a fully defined object prior to creating the automation; for instance, selecting the sendable data extension, the email creative, the subject line, and the sender profile. After this, you just slide this into a *File Drop* automation after an import to grab the most recent information that was dropped, and then your email will be sent within minutes of the file landing on the SFTP.

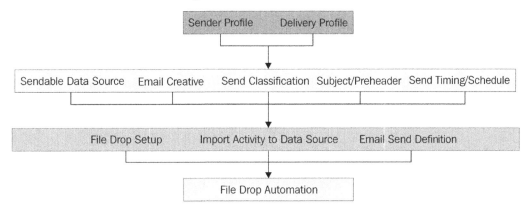

Figure 4.2 – Diagram of each of the pieces of a File Drop Automation email send

Now that you have a pretty good handle on real time and the messaging options associated with it, let's explore what exactly *scheduled* means.

# Scheduled

Merriam Webster defines **scheduled** as a procedural plan that indicates the time and sequence of each operation, essentially saying that it was set aside until it hit a pre-planned time and date where it was then executed and sent. Now, this might sound similar to what we mentioned earlier about real time, but it is actually quite different.

For instance, the idea of real-time pathing with a waiting period can sound like scheduled messaging, but it is not. It is different because each message is entered in real time, and therefore, the time the message is actually sent out is different, just the waiting period on each is the same. In a scheduled send, the audience is usually created prior to the send and the email is usually sent in batches.

You may recall that we mentioned in the beginning that scheduled messaging was possible with a Wait activity, but now we are saying that it isn't possible? Huh? How can it be both? Well, if you set a specific date for everything to be released, then it is scheduled, but just putting a waiting period of *2 days* would just be a delay in a real-time message, not a scheduled send.

Something scheduled is also usually a more repeatable task, similar to that weekly email send example at the beginning of the chapter. Sure, there are times that the email might have changes to the content and sure, the audience might have some subscription changes, but in general, it is nearly identical from run to run. This consistency and repetition are the major key features and defining factors in scheduled messaging.

## Scheduled messaging options

Similar to real time, this is not limited to just one tool or the other but is definitely one that is optimized for this specific type of execution – Automation Studio. Automation Studio was created with the idea of creating automated solutions for repeatable, procedural tasks, which, as you can see, is very much the definition of scheduled.

Each option capable of being scheduled is as follows:

- Journey Builder email activity
- Triggered sends/Transactional sends (kind of)
- Automation Studio Send Email activity
- Email Studio Send Wizard
- User-initiated send definitions

This list, much like the real-time one, is not exhaustive, so you may find other possible options that can be used as scheduled. This is just a list of the majority of the options and the ones that are easiest to implement.

## Journey Builder email activity

The Journey Builder email activity has three major ways in which you can accomplish scheduled messaging in Journey Builder. Well, to be fair, there are other ways, but they are far outside of best practice and mainstream needs. The first one we will be going over is utilizing an automation from Automation Studio as the entry point.

This entry source is actually part of the **Data Extension Entry Source**. Inside this entry source, you would have three choices, one of which is **Automation**. Upon selecting this, contacts will be admitted based on the schedule of the automation from Automation Studio. This automation would require an import, filter, or query activity to apply so that it can correctly adjust the data prior to execution. You would also need to establish whether you want this to evaluate new records only or all records each time.

The data extension entry source using automation is very similar to utilizing a **Send Email** activity in Automation Studio, which we will go over later in the chapter. Next, we are going to be focusing on the same entry source, but in a different way.

Sticking to the **Data Extension Entry Source**, next, instead of **Automation**, we will be exploring the **Recurring** option. This can be used to set a scheduled send by including a column with a send date in it. From there, you would just set the entry filter to be something like *SendDate equals Today* and as it is recurring, you can then later update this data and with it being recurring, the emails can send again at a later date. This is especially useful for dynamic weekly emails. Next up, we will be exploring an option that is a tad more out of the box.

Basically, you would have everything ingested into the journey through the normal real-time entry point (API, Data Extension, and others) but, prior to any email messaging send, you have a wait event. This wait event is a specific rolling range date/time so that it will only send all those queued in the journey during that specifically scheduled time period.

Now there are two ways you can do this. You can have a wait period where you manually set the specific date and time on each send via a Wait until Date activity. Or, with a bit of fancy footwork, you can make this date dynamic by using a *data extension* to hold the date of sending. You would map that data extension to an attribute group used by that journey and then update the date in that data extension to the next time you want the email sent, after each send.

The cool thing about this approach is that if you use *contact data* for this **Wait By Attribute** activity, whatever date is the value when the subscriber hits that activity is the date used. So, if you need to change it a bunch of times throughout the journey, up until they hit the **Wait By Attribute** activity, those other values won't matter. That being said though, once it hits that activity and begins the queue/waiting period, it can no longer be changed or adjusted even if you alter the value in the data extension. Basically, what this means is that when a subscriber enters the journey, they might have October 11th as the date value in the contact data that is used by the **Wait By Attribute** step, but they are still around 3 days away from hitting that step. Inside those 3 days, the date they want to send this out has been pushed back a couple of times and now, as it enters the step, it is the date of October 24. As it has now entered the queue for the **Wait By Attribute** step though, no changes to the contact data in the data extension will affect the date in this step.

---

**Wait By Attribute and Contact Data Notes**

We know that the previous statement may be hard to follow abstractly, so we wanted to try and give it a bit more of an explanation of what we mean.

**Contact data**: Data that is pulled live from the contact object in Marketing Cloud, unlike Journey Data, which is a snapshot at entry.

**Wait By Attribute**: An activity inside Journey Builder that will wait until the criteria you set around a specific attribute in the associated data is met.

So, by using a Wait By Attribute activity and the attribute is associated with contact data, this value can change multiple times prior to when it will hit that activity. This will adjust the *schedule* of the email send, right up until the Wait by Attribute activity. Once it enters the activity, the data value is then locked in and cannot be adjusted.

---

This is a roundabout way to turn a real-time tool into a scheduled automation tool. Not exactly best practice, nor does it make a strong case to use this instead of a more optimized tool. The great part about this though is that Marketing Cloud gives you options to follow defined best practices or to customize the solution to meet your specific business needs.

Next, we will explore another unconventional way of turning something real time into a scheduled process. This one is a bit more straightforward though, but only by a little bit.

## Triggered sends/transactional sends (kind of)

We will be honest; this one is not innovative, or elegant, or in any way creative. It is simply taking one thing and putting it into another and through that, controlling how the first thing behaves. Not exactly rocket science and it can be a bit clunky.

Basically, you take a **Script activity** from Automation Studio and, in that activity, you write up an API call that iterates through your source sendable data and then writes an API call to either the trigger or transactional endpoint. You then loop through each record so it will make the call once for each record.

Let's break it down:

- You would create a **Triggered Send Definition** email inside of Marketing Cloud. This would include an email, sending profiles, and an attached data extension.

- You would create a **Script activity** in Automation Studio.

- Inside this **Script activity**, you would use SSJS to take the data in the source of your choice and push that, via the Core Library, an API, or WSProxy, to the **Triggered Send Definition**, sending the email.

- You then take that **Script activity** and push it to a scheduled automation.

This then means that although the trigger or transactional email will be running in real time, it will only be running in real time at specific times. Now, after you run it, it likely would make sense to clear or otherwise flag those you have already sent to and ensure you are not spamming every time the automation runs.

OK, we promise most of the workaround or custom solutions are done now and we can focus more on best practice usage. Now the focus is mostly on Automation Studio and Email Studio scheduled email capabilities.

## Automation Studio Send Email activity

As far as scheduled automated sends go, this is pretty much what you would see if you looked it up in a dictionary. Before you go grab a dictionary, we can promise it is not actually there; we were just speaking figuratively to make a point. Although, how cool would that be? Open up a dictionary and then bam, right there on the page is an image of the **Send Email** activity from Salesforce Marketing Cloud Automation Studio!

Alright, back to the activity. So, basically what this is a defined object that holds each of the related objects required for an email to send. You can reference *Figure 4.2* or see the following list for this information:

- Email creative
- Audience
- Subject line/Preheader
- Sender profile
- Delivery profile
- Sender policy
- Exclusion scripts

Each of these objects would be combined into a single object that would be the **Email Send Definition**. This definition would then be pulled in via the **Send Email** activity, which is activated when the automation runs, which is set via a schedule.

As previously stated, this is the epitome of automated scheduled email messaging sends. Now, if you need it all together as an object, but don't want to create an automation, but schedule it out yourself ad hoc, then you need to check the next part out.

## User-Initiated send definitions

So, if you go into the **Interactions** tab in **Email Studio**, you will notice something called **User-Initiated Sends**. This is basically the exact thing listed earlier, but prior to the creation of the **Send Email** activity.

It is the combination of each of the required objects to form an email send. These objects are combined into a single definition that you can then interact with to edit or execute the send. This definition can then be pushed into **Automation Studio** via a **Send Email** activity, or it can be manually scheduled. This manual scheduling is very similar to if you schedule an email via the send wizard in **Email Studio**, in that you set a time and day and then it creates a send job.

To note though, if you schedule it this way instead of via **Automation Studio**, Marketing Cloud will take a *snapshot* of the email creative at that point in time and use that for sending. The email creative will not update (outside data-dependent personalization) on any changes made to the creative.

> **What is a Snapshot?**
>
> Inside of Salesforce Marketing Cloud, there is an occurrence that happens when an email is published (**Triggered Send Definition** or Journey) or an email job is scheduled (Email Wizard, Simple Send, or Schedule an Email Send Definition), or otherwise enters the send queue.
>
> Basically, what happens is that the email code and content are compiled at a general level (excluding anything related to data) and are then stored inside the job object. This means that after you have scheduled or published the email, any content changes you do inside of Content Builder or Email Studio will be ignored. You will need to either cancel the send and reschedule, pause, republish, and restart the triggers, or edit and save inside Journey Builder to get the new content.
>
> For scheduled sends, you can get around this by utilizing a scheduled automation with an Email Send Definition activity inside of Automation Studio, as scheduling the automation does not snapshot the email.

The data (sendable and relational) will not be locked in, however, until it hits the **send queue**, also known as **at time of send**. This means you can adjust your data easily to where you want it prior to it sending out. This comes with the caveat that if you are using throttling and mess with the data after the initial send queue, you can cause the rest of the send to error out.

We usually recommend pushing all scheduled sends into **Automation Studio** as a best practice as it gives you the most options and flexibility as it removes most of the issues with this snapshot. Next, we move on to another platform sending solution – the send wizard.

## Email Studio Send Wizard

This one is basically combining the creation of the **Email Send Definition** with scheduling into one wizard-led setup. The wizard guides you through each aspect, attaching the correct objects you need for the email definition, and then, at the end, asks you to define the date/time you want it sent at.

It is a pretty simple capability and is one that is regularly used by marketers, but we still recommend utilizing Automation Studio's **Send Email** activity for the same reason as with user-initiated send definitions – the snapshot of email content. So many options and so many possibilities...what is the best choice?

# Real time or scheduled – which is the right choice?

This question depends on what is the top priority for you. Do you need the message to be out as soon as possible right up in the subscriber's face, or is it better for this to be a more planned and repeatable process?

For instance, if you have a monthly newsletter that you send out, it would make much more sense to have this be a scheduled send, rather than real time. Setting a recurring schedule where there are minimal updates to content and data lets you hit that optimal send time and burst capabilities that real time cannot offer.

Whereas, if it's a receipt or shipping notification email, the amount of time before the email is sent is hugely important. In that case, you need to have it be real time. Scheduling it to be sent out *every 30 minutes* is not a viable option as most people will expect these emails within seconds of finalizing the action/transaction.

There are a ton of places where this choice honestly doesn't even matter. However, whether it's scheduled out or it's a real-time message will play little to no significant value in the success or failure of the campaign. So, although this can be a majorly important choice, it also can be fairly insignificant as well in relation to other options.

Realizing there are other questions leads us into a very similar, but also very different, option. Should you do custom messages in a 1:1 context, or is dynamic, personalized batch sends a better choice?

# 1:1 messaging versus batch sends

Very similar to real time versus scheduled, 1:1 messaging versus batch sends are a very contextual choice. Usually, both of these options correlate together, so if real time is needed, it usually means that it is best sent as a 1:1 message, while scheduled sends tend to be better as batch sends.

Before digging too much further into this, we should dig into exactly what each of these sends is and how they are used. Let's start by taking a look at 1:1 messaging.

## 1:1 messaging

As defined by Merriam Webster's dictionary, *1:1* means *pairing each element of a set uniquely with an element of another set*, and *messaging* is defined as *a communication in writing, in speech, or by signals*. Combining these two, you get a definition of 1:1 messaging as *a communication that pairs each element of itself to an element in a dataset to ensure a fully personalized experience*.

1:1 messaging is usually synonymous with real-time messaging, which are the two major elements that make up Journey Builder. To that extent, most of your needs relating to 1:1 messaging will be handled inside of Journey Builder. As stated previously, Journey Builder is built upon the triggered send definitions of Email Studio, so there are most definitely other options out there to do 1:1 messaging outside of Journey Builder.

## 1:1 messaging options

Now, the following list is going to be strikingly familiar to the one you just read through from the discussion regarding real-time sends. This is because 1:1 messaging options are nearly identical to the scheduled messaging options, just with a twist.. There is one major exclusion from this though in that the Automation Studio **Send Email** activity is not included:

- Journey Builder email activity
- Triggered sends
- Transactional sends
- Journey Builder transactional journeys

Although this list seems smaller, the multiple facets of each of these options are significant. As we have already gone over the basics of these earlier, next we will just dive into how each of these relate to 1:1 messaging.

## Journey Builder email activity

This is the easiest, least technical, option you have for 1:1 messaging. Here you can set up the entire message inside the UI, including the email, the data, and the different segmentation and splits associated with it. This can be utilized inside a multi-step journey or a single send journey depending on your needs, but the behavior of the activity is the same in each context.

## Triggered sends

Previously, we would say that triggered sends were the most popular way to make 1:1 messaging in real time. Journey Builder's upgrades have taken it to a level where the ease of use and simplicity have led to it taking the top spot. The following is a quick workflow example:

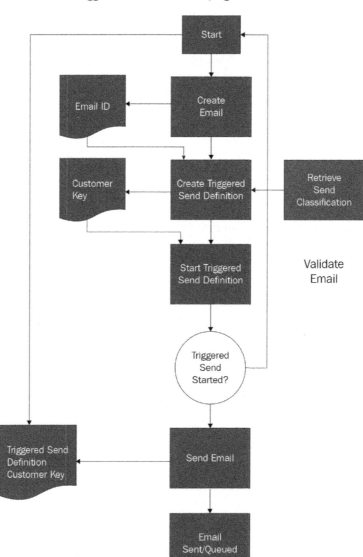

Figure 4.3 – Representation of the triggered send workflow

That being said, triggered sends are still a very powerful and very efficient option. They require a bit more technical knowledge, but outside of that are pretty easy to implement and, depending on your needs, they may not require the level of setup that a journey does by default.

## Transactional sends

This is basically a more efficient version of the triggered send. There are a lot more technical hurdles to it as it requires most of the setup and tracking to be done via the API, hence it can be more inhibitive and require much more outside of the platform.

To this extent though, it offers things such as webhooks to check the status and tracking information on individual sends in real time as well as a ton of other very customizable options to help make your transactional emails as efficient and effective as possible. Here is a good visual taken directly from the Marketing Cloud website displaying the steps and capabilities of the transactional messaging API:

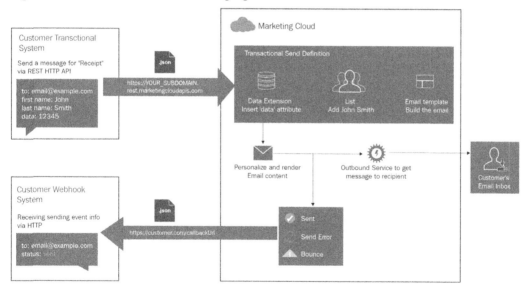

Figure 4.4 – Representation of the Transactional API capabilities

To help make life easier for those who want to utilize transactional messaging, but do not have the technical skills or resources to set up the APIs and automation necessary for it, Marketing Cloud created a new Journey type that combines the two.

## Journey Builder transactional journeys

This still requires some technical skills to work as you need to have an API event to initiate, but it allows you to build out almost every other aspect within the UI, making the process much easier for the average marketer. The following is a brief sample of what a transactional journey looks like in Marketing Cloud:

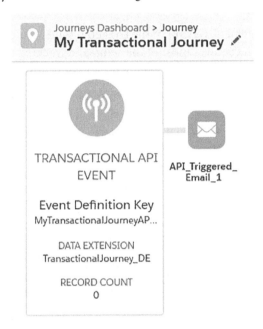

Figure 4.5 – Sample of transactional journey in Journey Builder

Next up, we will dig into the unexpected 1:1 capability of Automation Studio and Email Studio. These two studios are usually associated more with batch-type email sends. Now that we know about 1:1 messaging, next, let's explore the alternative – **batch messaging**.

# Batch messaging

This type of messaging has been used in email marketing for years and is usually the way people think of when they think about marketing emails. Batch, as defined by Merriam Webster, is *the quantity produced at one operation*. Basically, this means that through the one send, we are producing a larger volume rather than a single message.

A common misconception with batch messaging is the old adage of *Batch and Blast*. This phrase came about years ago to explain the shotgun approach email marketers used to take where they would create a single message and then, quite literally, blast it to each and every person they knew the email address of. It was invasive, annoying, and caused major disgruntlement with everyone.

This type of behavior is what brought about the legal movements to protect email address owners, such as the CAN-SPAM Act. Through this, email marketers had to realize that email was not just another form of *junk mail* and that they had to actually spend the time to build the medium out as a unique marketing channel.

Now, batch messaging done wrong can still be ineffective and invasive, but if it is done right, it can be invaluable and a highly efficient and faster way to get your message out there. Batch messaging is more aligned with a repetitive or scheduled messaging strategy, along with things such as reminder emails, newsletters, weekly promotions, and others. It also can help to get out an urgent mass message or deal with your audience.

## Batch messaging options

So, due to the recent concentration in 1:1 messaging as the preferred method and the simplicity of what is needed for it, batch messaging options are fairly limited. In the following, you will see our list of the three current options for sending batch messaging:

- **Automation Studio Send Email activity**
- **Email Studio Send Wizard**
- **User-initiated send definitions**

One major thing to note is that we left off **Journey Builder email activity** from this list even though batch-esque options are now available in Journey Builder. Next, we will dig into why it was left off.

## Why not Journey Builder email activity?

With the creation of the single send journey and the capability of utilizing automations and data extensions for entry sources, Journey Builder allows you to do batch entry into a journey. The issue is that as the system was not designed for this intended purpose, what it is actually doing is just processing each in a 1:1 environment one after the other. This is not actually a batch send, so we did not include it as an option.

That being said, if you are not as into semantics as we are, it is still a very viable option to send your message out in a batch context; it just actually isn't a batch send, technically speaking, just a batch entry. The only other thing to consider around this is things like throughput and such that we explored in the previous chapters. As a refresher, this is about the fact that Journey Builder has a more limited batching capability, limited to its throughput per hour. As it is built to do 1:1 messaging, the speed it can send is affected. This has been a major focus of Marketing Cloud and they have made great strides forward in bridging this gap, but it is still worth noting if you are looking to send a high volume of messages.

## Automation Studio and Email Studio

So, the three messaging options are actually nearly identical. As most of what was involved and required was stated in the *Scheduled* section, we are going to combine these three into a single section to discuss. The following is a sample of what the send screen looks like inside the Send Wizard in Email Studio:

Figure 4.6 – Example view of the Email Studio Send Wizard

These three options are the epitome of what batch email is. This process has not changed much over the years; it has just been optimized and streamlined. You still need to take an email and the related elements/objects and attach it to data that is then sent in batches to a **Mail Transfer Agent** (**MTA**), which then pushes it to the send queue where it is then sent out to the corresponding email address.

## How does batch now differ from the 'bad batch' of yesteryear?

So, the previous batch philosophy was to get the same idea out to as many people as possible as quickly as possible. With email marketing being so cheap, there was no need to put significant effort into strategy or optimization since, if you got even just one person to buy at times, it paid for the whole campaign right there. This cheap cost is how the **return on investment** (**ROI**) of email marketing usually sits at something crazy, like 4200% ROI, which means you get $42 per $1 you spend, as per the DMA in 2019: `https://dma.org.uk/uploads/misc/marketers-email-tracker-2019.pdf`.

Although this worked for a while, new restrictions and laws were implemented to help save the medium from what would potentially be the end of its use due to the frustration and overwhelming amount of spam that would come from utilizing email. These laws actually had an amazing effect on marketing in the medium since, instead of people being lazy and just copying their direct mail pieces into a digital format and blasting it out, they had to actually strategize and build campaigns that were specialized for the medium and the audience in that medium.

This is what saved email marketing from dying, although at first, the extra effort made people believe that the ROI would decrease and that the channel would die out. But with the increased relevancy and targeting, the ROI gathered actually stayed the same and, in some cases, actually increased due to the more positive customer perception of the channel. This is because when email marketing is done right, it is highly effective and has many easy lead-ins to a call to action that most other mediums do not have.

So, what made that difference? The difference was that people realized that marketing to people who actually wanted to hear your message instead of sending messages out for people to delete or have a bad connotation associated with your name greatly increased efficiency. And so, from this, permission-based marketing was born.

Although batch sends are not personalized to the level of 1:1 messaging usually, it is best practice to include at least some custom aspects in them and show the subscriber that you know who they are and respect their preferences.

## Batch or 1:1? Why not both?

As noted earlier, there are great rationales to each option, and even the opportunity to combine both. Simply put, the following are good general rules of thumb to follow in deciding what to use:

- **1:1 messaging**: Use this when you want an individual to do a specific action that is unique to them or send a unique message based on data to push them to a specific action.

- **Batch messaging**: Use this when you have a very specific message you want to send out to a large audience. It is very intuitively aligned with scheduled automation.

- **1:1 batch messaging**: Use this when you want to give unique messaging to multiple subscribers based on data and preferences but need them all out at the same time. It is more aligned to being used with scheduled automation, but is also possible via real-time sends.

Next, let's jump into how to utilize analytics and tracking data to level up your email messaging and strategies.

# Analytics-powered insights

Any marketing campaign worth its salt is based on a ton of data and analytics. Analytics is based on the action of analysis, which, as defined by Merriam Webster, means *a detailed examination of anything complex in order to understand its nature or to determine its essential features*.

Essentially, that means the marketer takes all the data and insights and applies those to the different pieces of the campaign, and works to maximize and optimize it for the best effect. Although this adds a lot more work and effort to each campaign you send, the results and added benefits far outweigh that cost.

To that extent, we wanted to bring your attention to where you can grab analytics from in Marketing Cloud.

## Analytics in Marketing Cloud

Most analytics in Marketing Cloud come from external sources or via built-in reporting. Due to some recent purchases at the time of writing, these potential built-in analytics capabilities offer some highly valuable analytics platforms. Some of the platforms listed here are not exclusively analytics but can offer insights and relevant data on the subscriber to help or support analytics.

Here are some examples of Salesforce owned and highly popular options for Marketing Cloud:

- **Tableau**
- **Datorama**
- **Analytics Builder**
- **Interaction Studio**
- **Salesforce CDP**
- **Customer 360**
- **Google Analytics Connecter**

Rather than go into each of these options, we are going to be exploring how best to use the built-in data and capabilities of analytics to power up your email marketing.

## Tracking data

Ever wonder which email version has the most conversions or is the most popular? When is the time people usually open or interact with your emails? Inside Marketing Cloud, you can use the data views inside Email Studio, Tracking Extract options, and even some native reports to gather all this information.

### Data views

Data views are available for the user to interact with via SQL in Automation Studio or via Measures in Email Studio Filters. We would never recommend Measures since, in our experience, they are unreliable and very confusing. Avoid these if possible.

Data views offer information on many different aspects. Much of the focus of this is centered on email and subscriber interaction with email sends, but there are other options, such as SMS and push, that are unrelated to email. Here are a few examples of data view tables available to query:

- **Sent (_Sent)**
- **Open (_Open)**
- **Bounce (_Bounce)**
- **Click (_Click)**
- **Unsubscribe (_Unsubscribe)**
- **Complaint (_Complaint)**

- **Business Unit Unsubscribe (_BusinessUnitUnsubscribe)**
- **Job (_Job)**
- **Subscribers (_Subscribers)**
- **List Subscribers (_ListSubscribers)**
- **Enterprise Attribute (_EnterpriseAttribute)**
- **Journey (_Journey)**
- **Journey Activity (_JourneyActivity)**

As you can see from these options, there is a lot of different relational points of information you can use to build your own custom reporting and analytical discoveries. This option requires a lot more technical knowledge and outside interaction to be able to find the required information you need. A less customized and detailed option is the built-in reporting and tracking capabilities of Marketing Cloud.

### Built-in reporting and tracking

Inside Marketing Cloud, there is a studio that is dedicated to this exact thing – **Analytics Builder**. This suite of tools offers insights into both **Datorama Reporting** as well as **Web and Mobile Analytics**. Previously there were some other built-in reports called **Discover reports**, but these have been discontinued and are no longer in use, or are only available for a limited time.

As we are focusing on email, the part of this we will be concentrating on is Datorama Reports. So, although Datorama reporting is built in, there are also some tiers to the level of capability this reporting can offer. The basic reports provide pretty strong insights similar to what was available in Discover reports, but the higher tier you pay for, the more information and insights you can get. The final tier of this offer is basically a full implementation of Datorama integration with Marketing Cloud. The following is a sample of the dashboard of Datorama Reports:

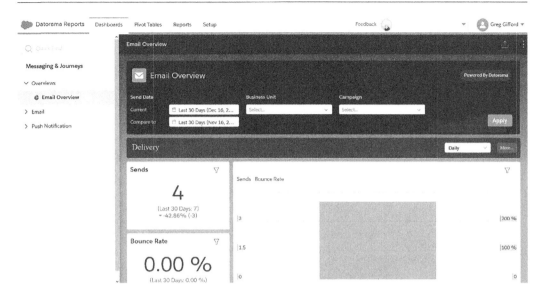

Figure 4.7 – Example view of the Datorama Reports overview screen

Datorama Reports will give you access to analyze your data and receive intuitive dashboard views to visualize your aggregated data. These dashboards and reports can be interacted with and manipulated via elements such as filters, sorting, summation, and organization.

The next part that is built-in is the **Tracking** tab inside **Email Studio**. This tab offers a few different options, but honestly, the only one to pay attention to is the **My Tracking** section as the rest are more legacy options and will likely be disappearing in the near future. The tracking section holds a list of all the send jobs you have pushed out and all the tracking data (opens, clicks, and bounces) that are associated with that job. Refer to the following screenshot for an example of this in the UI:

| Job ID | Name | Date/Time Sent | Status | Emails Sent | Unique Click-Through |
|---|---|---|---|---|---|
| 1031329 | ImpressionRegionTesting | 1/6/2022 12:22 PM | Complete | 4 | 0 |
| 891056 | uuu_test | 7/26/2021 5:49 PM | Complete | 3 | 0 |
| 535715 | TestEmail1 | 4/23/2020 2:26 PM | Canceled | 0 | 0 |
| 535712 | TestEmail1 | 4/23/2020 2:08 PM | Complete | 0 | 0 |
| 535701 | TestEmail1 | 4/23/2020 2:00 PM | Complete | 2 | 0 |
| 534369 | Trigger_Test | 4/22/2020 8:15 AM | Complete | 4 | 25 |
| 513219 | TestEmail1 | 3/31/2020 11:43 AM | Complete | 4 | 0 |
| 493559 | Example-Email | 3/12/2020 10:42 AM | Complete | 4 | 25 |
| 493556 | Example-Email | 3/12/2020 10:40 AM | Complete | 4 | 50 |
| 493502 | Example-Email | 3/12/2020 9:56 AM | Complete | 4 | 50 |

Figure 4.8 – Example of the Tracking tab inside Salesforce Marketing Cloud

Then, when you open up a specific send job on this screen, you will see be taken to a dashboard like this:

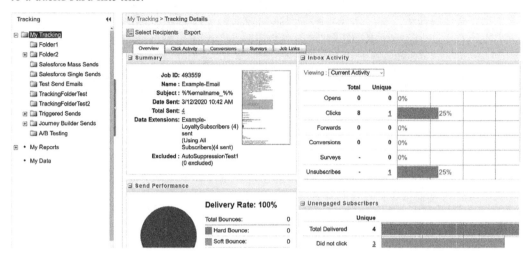

Figure 4.9 – Tracking information for a send job inside the Tracking tab

This offers a ton of information aggregated together for a simple review of a single send job. It is great for a specific review, but when looking beyond a single send context, this is very limiting and could require a ton of manual effort to utilize.

Next up is the Journey Analytics capabilities. There are some limitations to this, including a limited date range (around 90-day range) and no way to drill down beyond the high-level engagement metrics. This includes total sent, delivery rate, unique opens, unique clicks, and unsubscribes only. This is good for a quick overview, but is only designed for the overall journey and will not display per email.

To view an email, you can open the journey and click on the email you want to view and there will be a more focused version called **Email Analytics** that gives essentially the same info as you saw in Journey Analytics, but only in relation to that single email.

If you happen to already own or have an existing analytics platform and do not need to use anything built in or purchase anything new, you will need to find a way to push all this data into the platform. This is where **Tracking Extracts** comes into play.

## Tracking Extracts

To get the information from Marketing Cloud to your external analytics tool, you will need to extract it from the platform and then push it to a location that can allow that tool to ingest it. The most popular way to do this is by using *Marketing Cloud Tracking Extracts*.

This is a built-in export process that will output a ZIP file containing CSV files. In turn, these CSV files contain relational files that contain all the data you requested when you built the extract. The ZIP file can be pushed to any file location you have listed in your file locations in Marketing Cloud, allowing you to push it to an external FTP for your analytics tool to ingest.

The available information includes everything you see inside of the data views, as well as a few other options such as NotSent and Impression region tracking. There is a lot of information here that you can only get through the SOAP API objects or that you might not even be able to find anywhere else.

Now that you have all the information and background on automating your email sends, we wanted to share some of our personal experiences and considerations on it. We hope that this information will give some context to allow you to relate this information to your situations and allow you to better utilize it.

# Considerations regarding email automation

In this section, we wanted to share some considerations when using email automation that may help give some insights and context to help you in the future:

- When creating an automation, you should make the email content as dynamic as possible (pulling in via AMPscript or lookups or referencing other blocks) to allow for easy changes, updates, and implementation of new content. Do note that with Journey Emails, Triggered Emails, and Transactional Emails, you will need to pause and republish the trigger in order for it to work.

- Along with the email automation, you should utilize either an import process or SQL queries to update and prepare the sendable data as part of the same automation or prior to entry at the least. Relational data that is used should be updated prior to sending and made sure to be completed beforehand as well to keep it as up to date as possible.

- Creating a journey for drip campaigns or other series of emails can be an amazing asset and help create great customer experience, engagement, and retention, but, along with that, you cannot just *set it and forget it*; you need to constantly monitor it and update or maintain it as necessary. You need to collect as much tracking from each of your automations as you can to help fuel future strategies and ensure your campaigns are optimized.

- Including coupons and discounts inside of automated emails will require careful monitoring to ensure that you do not run out of coupons and that it is giving the correct information to ensure customer satisfaction. This is especially true if you are using the `ClaimRow()` function in AMPscript.

- For sends that are required at a specific time, doing a batch send is optimal. But, when the amount of time that is required between a trigger and message execution is minimal, then you need to utilize a more real-time method.

- The more emails you automate, the more you need to also consider how many times you are contacting your audience. You will want to insert a process to ensure you are not accidentally sending too many emails to your audience, causing them to unsubscribe or send spam complaints about you.

- Ensure the data you collect and use in your automation is clean, accurate, and correctly prepared. If you were to collect data based on user input that was not cleaned or properly validated and use that for your sends, you could be accidentally sending out malformed or incorrect emails with the possibility of even having the whole automation error out. This is aligned with the *garbage in, garbage out* philosophy.

- You will want to have a strong preference and subscription center for your customers to work with to ensure that they can control which publications they feel are appropriate and also to help ensure you engage with them in a pleasing manner and not force them to unsubscribe, removing them from your marketing.

- Automated emails are not just handy for upselling, but also for cross-selling, opt-downs, opt-across, and similar actions. The more flexible and interactive you make your strategy and automations, the more likely you are to find the product or service that the customer wants, thereby enabling better ROI.

- Marketing Cloud is not designed to do heavy tasks. So, when using a higher processing draw and heavier automation, it can lead to slowdowns or time-outs in your instance. You will need to ensure that you keep this in mind as you build this and ensure that you utilize your automated processes efficiently in order to be effective.

There is a lot more that could be written here, but the preceding should help get you to a great place. Much of the best considerations are gathered through personal trial and error. We would highly recommend that you take the previous points as a basis and use that to test and explore the limits of your own automations and strategies.

> **Garbage in, garbage out**
>
> Basically, this phrase means that you receive something of the same quality as the time, effort, and materials you put into it. So, if you throw garbage into a machine, no matter how elegant and awesome that machine is, what comes out will still be low quality.

# Summary

Email automation is one of the core aspects of all Marketing Cloud automation and one of its strongest capabilities. After reading this chapter, you should have a strong knowledge of how email marketing automation works in Salesforce Marketing Cloud, as well as some in-depth information and insights into it.

You should now be able to tell the context of when to use real time instead of a schedule and vice versa, as well as 1:1 versus batch. Now, an aspect that you have also learned, although not explicitly set out as a section, is the difference between real-time messaging and 1:1 messaging, as well as the difference between scheduled messages and batch sends. At times, these can seem synonymous, but as you now know, they are different.

Now, knowing the messaging types and best uses is a huge part of email automation, but the other major aspect is data and analytics. As you have now learned, a campaign without analytics and tracking is like going on a blind date while actually wearing a blindfold, meaning that you might luck out and do well, but since you cannot see anything, it could go terrible very quickly and easily. On top of all that, we also went over some of our personal tips and tricks to keep in mind regarding email automation. These considerations are meant to help to contribute to a strong understanding of email automation in Salesforce Marketing Cloud and the best utilization of the available tools within it.

With the knowledge gained here, you should be able to increase your marketing capabilities with regard to email marketing by quite a bit inside Marketing Cloud. Email marketing automation can be easily applied in many different situations and prove extremely useful, especially in the forward-facing thoughts of building scalable solutions.

In the next chapter, we will be digging into the meat and potatoes of automation: the automation of your ETL and data processes. These processes are key to providing a strong and solid base for all your marketing needs and ensuring that your strategies are possible. Data automation is essentially the bread and butter of what automation is made for. We will be discussing ETL processes via SQL Query Activities, Import Activities, Export Activities, Filter Activities, and more for segmentation, exclusion, and data staging.

# 5
# Automating Your ETL and Data

Emails and other messaging options are cool and all, but without data, it's really nothing more than fancy words and pretty pictures. Data is integral when it comes to marketing. Without data, we do not have an audience to send to nor any idea who or what we should send. Although messaging and email automation may be the more popular aspects, this is mostly because no one thinks about the data part as it is not as fancy or shiny as the cool subject lines, emojis, images, or designs.

To that extent, in this chapter, we will be exploring all things related to automating data in Salesforce Marketing Cloud, with a focus on ETL and Automation Studio. We will dive into topics surrounding data, including introductions into what ETL means as well as specific activities inside Marketing Cloud that can allow us to automate our ETL and data processes. The following is a quick list of the topics that we will discuss:

- *What is ETL?*: An exploration into what ETL is and how it's used in conjunction with automation in Marketing Cloud.

- *Activities for data in Automation Studio*: An exploration into the automation activities available for data manipulation, importing, and suchlike inside Marketing Cloud Automation Studio.

- *SFMC SQL Query activities*: Here, we dive into the activities inside Marketing Cloud that utilize SQL and some best practices regarding their use.

- *Filter activities and data segmentation tools*: We move forward into the UI drag and drop tools and capabilities centered around segmentation that require little to no technical knowledge.

- *Importing data options*: A dive into the options available to bring data inside the Salesforce Marketing Cloud platform.

- *Exporting data options*: An exploration of all the different methods and possibilities in terms of extracting or exporting data from Marketing Cloud.

You will remember that **ETL (Extract, Transform, Load)** was brought up before in *Chapter 2*, *SFMC Automation Tools*, in reference to Automation Studio. This provided a great basic overview of what ETL is and how it's used in Automation Studio, but this chapter will focus on ETL and data in general. We wanted to give a deeper dive into exactly what ETL is with the aim of helping to provide a strong basis in terms of data management, manipulation, and storage inside the Marketing Cloud.

# What is ETL?

ETL has its roots in the rise of central data repositories. With the dawn of data warehouses around the 1990s, tools began being made specifically focused on extracting data from siloed systems, transforming it into the destination format, and then loading it into the new destination (or ETL). Over the years, ETL has grown to become stronger and stronger with the increase in demands during the *data age* of marketing.

ETL tools typically do all three of the steps and are a critical part of ensuring that data is prepped completely and accurately for things such as reporting, analytics, and other data-driven actions, including machine learning. The following is a basic definition of each of the three steps in ETL:

- **Extract**: Retrieving and gathering data from siloed or individual data sources

- **Transform**: Manipulating and altering data to fit inside the proper format/structure

- **Load**: Taking the final data and pushing it into the target system, database, and data mart

Through ETL, you can take data from one environment and transform it to better match the existing formatting and structure of your other data for easier use, reporting, or analysis. ETL also makes it possible to migrate data between a variety of sources, destinations, and analysis tools. This makes it a very critical aspect in producing business intelligence and in the execution of broader data management strategies. Let's go into a little more detail on each of these three steps, starting with extract.

# Extract

The first step is to *extract* or retrieve the data from the source. Although this is certainly not the most glorious or flashy part, it is most definitely the most important aspect of ETL. Why? Well, because without any data, you have nothing to transform or load. So, an improper extract will ruin everything.

Now, a misconception is that the extract will only come from a single source. This is not always the case; usually, you will find that the majority of ETL processes will pull from multiple sources with the idea of combining or otherwise being manipulated into an easier-to-read dataset. This can be from relational data sources or non-relational sources, including many different structures and formats. This leads to the next step, transform, which takes this *big mess of raw data* and makes it meaningful.

# Transform

Now that we have all the data, we need to manipulate and restructure/reformat the raw data we have. The number of possibilities here is really awe-inspiring. Depending on the capabilities of your tool and the data you extracted, the sky is the limit. Refer to the following list of some of the major potential actions in the transform step:

- Aggregation of data (sum, average, and so on)
- Transposing or pivoting of data (columns into rows or rows into columns)
- Splitting or creating delimited lists
- Joining of data
- Filtering, cleansing, and deduplication
- Sorting or ordering
- Calculations of new values
- Translating coded values for easier human reading
- Limiting the columns to be used and removing those that are not necessary for the target
- Data validation and auditing
- Removing, encrypting, or protecting sensitive information
- Adjusting formatting and the structure to match the target's schema

This step is where the magic happens and can take a load of raw material and turn it into an amazing work of art. Depending on the required actions though, this can also be the largest process and time draw, so you need to make sure to keep efficiency and simplicity in mind while planning your transforms. Once you have your beautiful data, you now just need a place to put it.

## Load

In this last step, the data that we have manipulated and transformed is now moved from the staging area where we made our changes and pushed into the end target. This can be any data store, including a flat file or system or a data warehouse. The load can be ingested in different ways, but in general, it is usually one of the following three options:

- **Overwrite**: Completely removes all existing data in the target first, and then loads in new data.

- **Append**: Adds all new data to the target, creating a new record for each row. If there are duplicates with existing records, this can cause an error. It does not require a primary key(s), but without a primary key, this can lead to duplication.

- **Add and update**: Adds all new data to the target, creating a new record for each row, but if there is an existing record, it will update that row with the new data. This requires a primary key(s) to be defined.

As simple as this sounds, depending on the requirements of the organization and the system, this process can vary dramatically. This can include frequency, size limitations, timeout limits, logging, and historical audit trails. In the load, all those matching the schema in the target will be compared to the transformed data, and if they do not match, it could throw an error either for the whole process or for that individual record.

## How is ETL used?

Traditionally, ETL tools are utilized to combine structured and unstructured data from different sources with the goal of loading them into an end target. Through this combination of data into new structures and formats, insights that might have otherwise been hidden can surface through your reporting or analytics. This is also useful for migration from a local system to the cloud, or can even be used to connect partners or vendors in a single system.

ETL can also be used to improve data quality by means of the standardization and automation of processes that move data from a source to a targeted data warehouse. This reduces the likelihood of *dirty* data being passed to the warehouse.

One aspect that is important as regards Salesforce Marketing Cloud is the ability to draw out data and filter and segment this data and reduce columns to create for yourself a sendable audience for each send from a large master list. This capability allows for much better efficiency, customization, and segmentation of your email campaigns.

That being said, SFMC is not designed to be an ETL system and is not to be utilized for major or frequent ETL needs. It is optimized for quick segmentation requirements and more tactical-type manipulations, but once you get to transforming or otherwise interacting with large volumes of data or high-frequency interactions, it tends to fall flat.

To this end, there are limitations that need to be considered for these types of activities within the platform and you should consider doing these actions prior to bringing them into SFMC or inside an external tool that is designed for these actions. This will make your process much more stable and efficient. Now, let's dig into how we can accomplish these ETL actions inside Automation Studio and Salesforce Marketing Cloud.

# Activities for data in Automation Studio

As you may notice, we are exclusively mentioning Automation Studio for ETL capabilities in Salesforce Marketing Cloud. There are some other capabilities in other studios or apps related to it, but they are much more simplified versions with very little power or customization to them.

For instance, some would argue that the filters, measures, and groups inside Email Studio are great examples of ETL and data manipulation, and they would be right … to an extent. Although these are great functionalities, they are better passed in as more support-type functionalities instead of being defined directly as they are not easily automated.

The same is true for some actions and possibilities in Journey Builder, and although those are closer to automation and being powerful, a lot of it is just using a tool in a way it was not intended to be used instead of just using Automation Studio in the first place. So, rather than potentially sharing bad practices and habits, we are going to stick to Automation Studio, which is designed for this type of thing.

Inside Automation Studio, there are very specific activities that are utilized for powerful data manipulation and ETL processes. These activities are unique to Automation Studio and are not easily replicated inside any other place in Marketing Cloud. The following is a quick list of the Automation Studio activities that are related to ETL:

- **SQL Query activity**
- **Import File activity**
- **File Transfer activity**

- **Filter activity**
- **Data Extract activity**
- **Tracking Extract activity**

You may notice that we do not have the **Script activity** listed there. This is deliberate as although the **Script activity** can do some awesome things in the same way as ETL processes, it is done indirectly via a script and not directly via an ETL process. So, think of **Script activity** as ETL-related, but not a direct ETL activity.

As we progress in this chapter, we will be diving deeper into each one of these activities and how they relate to data and ETL automation in the Salesforce Marketing Cloud. This section is a quick introduction to the activities and to ETL in Automation Studio in general. Some of the other activities may also be related to ETL, just not as strongly or directly as these. For instance, a couple of the *refresh* activities that rerun filters on lists are related to ETL, but are very limited in usage and capability.

For the majority, each of these activities only handles some aspects of ETL, whether it's just the extract part or the load part. As we go through each in the sections that follow, we will be sure to mention what steps each one is capable of doing. To start things off, we are going to go with the strongest data manipulation activity in all of Automation Studio and all of Salesforce Marketing Cloud – the **SQL Query** activity.

# SQL Query activities

Now, you may well be thinking, *"Hey, SQL is not ETL, it's a query language … that is structured."* Well, you would be 100% correct and would also have awkwardly explained what the acronym **SQL** stands for (**Structured Query Language**). However, it seems odd to start things off after all the ETL talk with something that is not really directly ETL, right? Maybe a little, but we promise that there is a method to our madness here.

With the background you have in basic ETL, we can now jump right into the possibilities and power of **SQL Query** activities, which are, in our opinion, the most powerful and capable data manipulation option in all of Marketing Cloud. It can be a love/hate relationship, but there is no denying the power these activities bring to you as the end user.

So, why do we want to jump in right away? Why not structure it with all the ETL topics first and then end on SQL? Well, in all honesty, it's because we are excited and wanted to write this section as soon as possible! Oh, and because understanding the different manipulation and querying capabilities of SQL will make for easier understanding in some of the following activities and options.

Also, at least in our opinion, **SQL Query** activities in Marketing Cloud are essentially doing all three steps of ETL each time they are run. Let's take a look at the steps:

1.  Write out SQL that has data sources listed (FROM), or Extract.

2.  Write out the SQL that defines relationships, formats, data types, manipulations, combinations, or Transform.

3.  It then pushes this new data into a custom object, data extension, inside the platform, or Load.

Well, look at all these three steps. Sounds like an ETL process to me! Now, is it the most efficient or powerful way to accomplish this? Nope, not at all. However, it does offer great agile ETL capabilities in a highly customizable way.

Although Marketing Cloud **SQL Query** activities are limited to just utilizing SELECT statements (queries), which takes away a good portion of the language, those query statements have a ton of different functions, utilities, and capabilities that can handle any need you would have that would reasonably be expected from a non-database and non-analytic tool.

## What is a SQL Query activity?

As defined in the official docs, a **SQL Query** is an activity that retrieves data extension or data view information matching your criteria, and then includes that information in a data extension (https://help.salesforce.com/s/articleView?id=mc_as_using_the_query_activity.htm&type=5&language=en_US). Basically, the Marketing Cloud **SQL Query** activity is a way to execute SQL statements inside the platform pulling from data extensions and data views to fill a target data extension. As a note, data views are not targetable or able to be edited by the user.

Marketing Cloud **SQL Query** activities run T-SQL on Microsoft SQL Server 2016, or at least more or less. There are some aspects of SQL Server 2016 that do not work in Marketing Cloud, but it is a good general guideline to establish what functions and capabilities are possible in a **SQL Query** activity.

The following screenshot shows us what this activity looks like inside Marketing Cloud:

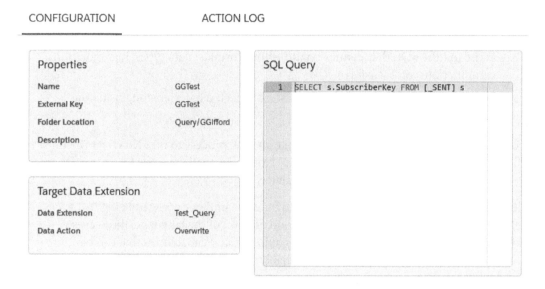

Figure 5.1 – Example of the UI for a Query activity

There are a ton of different considerations, syntax requirements, and known issues related to **SQL Query** activities. Listing them all would probably constitute a book in itself, and it is already pretty well documented on the official docs or on other community blogs or developer forums such as Salesforce Stack Exchange, so we will not be including those here. Instead, we will be concentrating on uses for the **SQL** activity and its relation to data automation in Marketing Cloud.

## Uses of the SQL Query activity in automation

If you go up to the previous *Transform* section and view that list there, that is pretty much everything you can do for the query activity. In our opinion, this can be shortened into three different categories:

- **Data segmentation and preparation for sending**
- **Custom reporting and transforming of data in preparation to export**

These three categories have many different subcategories that fit within them, but we feel that is a pretty good broad definition of the capabilities of the **SQL Query** activity in relation to data automation.

# Data segmentation and preparation for sending

This category is fairly broad as it encompasses all manipulation of data with the intent of preparation and segmentation for sending a message. This could be something as simple as breaking apart a master data extension to specific sendable audiences for your email campaigns, all the way to creating relational data that is used in your emails to properly customize your emails with the most up-to-date information.

Even something as simple as splitting an audience into sendable segments can become astoundingly complex depending on your needs and wants. With the 30-minute timeout, your query has the potential to need to be split into multiple queries with intermediary, or staging, tables due to complexity and volume. This is on top of the potential need for multiple joins and stringent WHERE conditionals, as well as aggregate calculations of information.

Here is a great example of segmentation from a master data extension:

## Email newsletter audience

First, you would need to create a target data extension with the following information:

- **Data Extension Name**: MonthlyNewsletter
- **Data Extension External Key**: MonthlyNewsletter
- **Data Extension Fields and Properties**:

| NAME | DATA TYPE | LENGTH | PRIMARY KEY | NULLABLE | DEFAULT |
|------|-----------|--------|-------------|----------|---------|
| SubscriberKey | Text | 255 | Y | | |
| EmailAddress | EmailAddress | | | | |
| FirstName | Text | 255 | | Y | |
| LastName | Text | 255 | | Y | |
| FavStoreNum | Number | | | Y | |
| NewsSub | Boolean | | | Y | Y |

Table 5.1 – Fields and properties of the MonthlyNewsletter data extension

Then, you would create a **SQL Query** activity in Automation Studio:

- **Query Name**: `MonthlyNewsletter`
- **Query External Key**: `MonthlyNewsletter`
- **Target Data Extension**: `MonthlyNewsletter`
- **Data Action: Overwrite**
- **SQL**:

```
SELECT CustID as SubscriberKey,
Email as EmailAddress,
FName as Firstname,
LName as LastName,
FavStoreNum,
Newsletter_Subscribe as NewsSub
FROM [MyMasterDE]
WHERE FavStoreNum IS NOT NULL
AND Newsletter_Subscribe = 1
AND (Unsub = 0 OR Unsub IS NULL)
```

This will output a new data extension with only the audience that matches the criteria we listed. This criterion is looking to ensure the following:

- That they have a favorite store (`FavStoreNum`) listed
- That they are subscribed to the newsletter (`NewsSub`)
- And that they are not unsubscribed (`Unsub`)

This will reduce our master data down to the specific audience we want to send to, allowing us to prepare and transform the sendable audience easily in the platform. Speaking of transform, you will also note that we are adding aliases to the fields from `MyMasterDE` for the target data extension to allow for an easier-to-understand and more consistent naming convention for our sendable audience. Next up, we will explore preparation for exporting through transformation.

Following are a couple of reference screenshots to help give context inside Marketing Cloud:

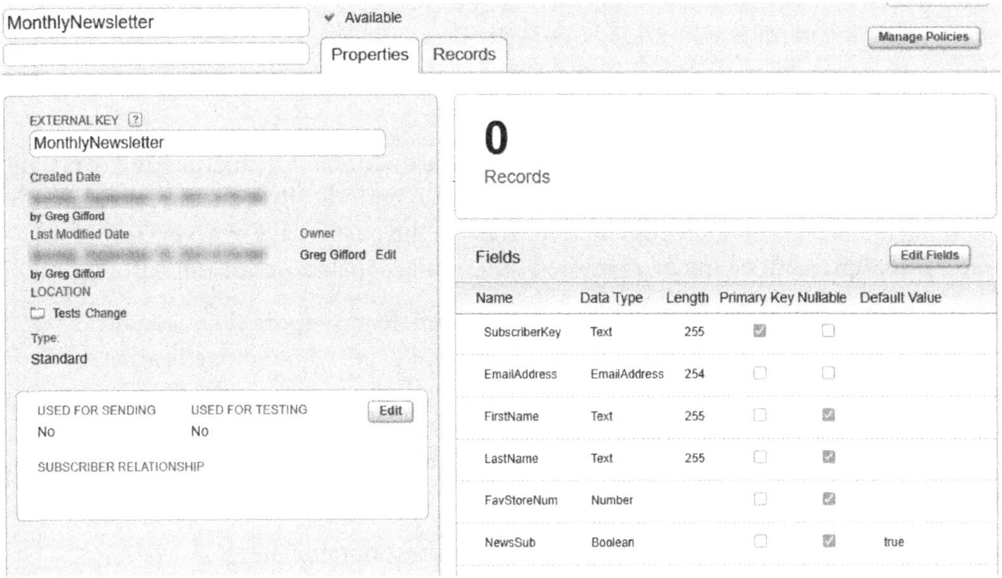

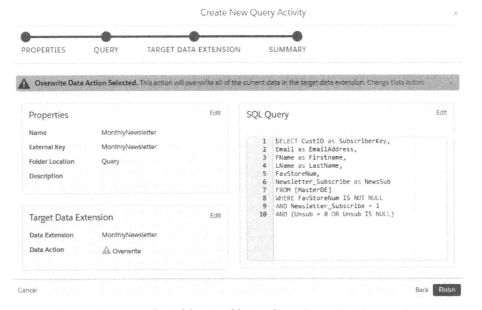

Figure 5.2 – Screenshot of the MonthlyNewsletter data extension

As you can see in the preceding screenshot, all the fields, the external key, and name are filled in the correct locations inside the Marketing Cloud MonthlyNewsletter data extension. Next, let's take a look at the **Query** activity:

Figure 5.3 – Screenshot of the MonthlyNewsletter Query Activity overview

The **Query** activity sample shows the final SQL stored inside the activity along with the correct target, data action, name, and external key. Next up is a look into the options for custom reporting in Marketing Cloud SQL activities.

## Custom reporting

Our definition of custom reporting is a grouping of data for tactical analysis and oversight, usually created and stored in a data extension and run periodically. This can include something like a report on **Recent Click Activity in the past 7 days** or **Overview of all email campaigns sent**, or any of a hundred other things, including custom KPI reports.

Usually, custom reporting is utilized directly in the platform, exported out as a file, or iterated through and displayed in an email or cloud page. As mentioned earlier, these tend to be more focused on tactical analysis and oversight and less on the broader strategy analytics. The higher-level analysis is usually done in a separate analytics tool that views things from an enterprise level instead of just focusing on data available in the Marketing Cloud only.

Following this, we are going to share an example of custom reporting SQL activities to help give further context on what this means.

### Recent click activity in the past 7 days

First, you will need to create a target data extension, with the following information:

**Data Extension Name**: ClickPast7Days

**Data Extension External Key**: ClickPast7Days

**Data Extension Fields and Properties:**

| NAME | DATA TYPE | LENGTH | PRIMARY KEY | NULLABLE | DEFAULT |
|------|-----------|--------|-------------|----------|---------|
| JobID | Number | | Y | | |
| EmailName | Text | 255 | Y | | |
| EmailAddress | EmailAddress | | Y | | |
| SubscriberKey | Text | 255 | Y | | |
| LinkContent | Text | 3000 | Y | | |
| ClickTime | Date | | Y | | |
| LinkName | Text | 1024 | | Y | |
| IsUnique | Boolean | | | Y | |
| SendTime | Date | | | Y | |

Table 5.2 – Fields and properties in the ClickPast7Days data extension

Then you would create a **SQL Query** activity in Automation Studio with the following details:

**Query Name**: ClickPast7Days

**Query External Key**: ClickPast7Days

**Target Data Extension**: ClickPast7Days

**Data Action: Overwrite**

**SQL**:

```
SELECT j.JobID,
j.EmailName,
s.EmailAddress,
c.SubscriberKey,
c.LinkName,
c.LinkContent,
c.IsUnique,
j.DeliveredTime as SendTime,
c.EventDate as ClickTime
FROM [_Job] j
LEFT JOIN [_Click] c
ON j.JobID = c.JobID
LEFT JOIN [_Subscribers] s
ON c.SubscriberKey = s.SubscriberKey
WHERE c.EventDate > dateadd(d,-7,getdate())
```

This will then output a dataset of people who have clicked on an email in the last 7 days. This list will show click information at the Link level, meaning if the person clicked multiple times on the email on multiple links, each one of those clicks will be in this report. Next up, let's take a more in-depth look into data segmentation and send preparation.

In the following screenshot, you can see what a **ClickPast7Days** data extension screen looks like:

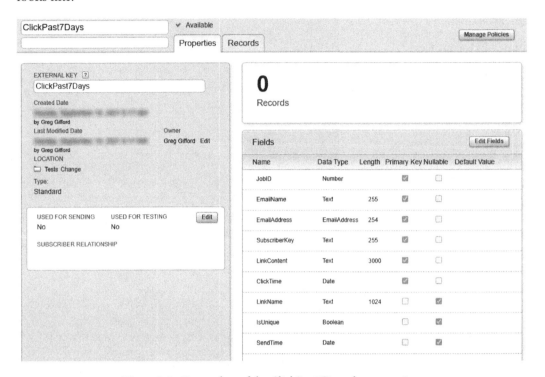

Figure 5.4 – Screenshot of the ClickPast7Days data extension

As you can see, this pulls in the correct fields, names, and external keys, as we listed previously. Now that we have seen an example of the target data extension, we should validate the **Query** activity. This next screenshot shows the completed **SQL Query** activity in Marketing Cloud:

Figure 5.5 – Screenshot of the ClickPost7Days Query activity overview

The **Query** activity sample shows the final SQL stored inside the activity along with the correct target, data action, name, and external key. Once you click **Finish** here, it will finalize this **Query** activity and let it be used in automations or a singular action which is run once. Next, we will be diving into transforming data in preparation to export.

## Transforming data in preparation to export

This final category is focused on exporting data. Now, you may ask, why would there be a category for export? Well, that is because most places will export data to an analytics tool or data lake outside Marketing Cloud where they will take a more enterprise view and not the tactical view we get inside Salesforce Marketing Cloud.

However, the data we have in Marketing Cloud is not always in the same format or structure as the target, so there will need to be a lot of transforming and massaging of data. This is probably one of the most important categories as this is usually vital to your KPI measurements and analytics beyond just email marketing and messaging from Marketing Cloud and, if it is set up incorrectly, can corrupt all of this, leading to massive failures in strategy due to this inaccurate data.

A good portion of this is likely to be focused on the tracking data (Opens, Clicks, and Bounces), which can easily be grabbed via data views or through tracking extracts. So, why would we need a category on SQL queries for something fairly simple? Because, although gathering the info is easy, preparing it for export is not. You may have to do some fancy footwork through joins or apply as well as change the data types and calculations to get the information to a place that fits in your target.

For instance, the following section takes tracking information that we have already gathered and combines this into one giant bulk file with all the most recent tracking dates that can be exported to your data lake.

### Tracking data exports to the data lake

First, you need to create a target data extension with the following information:

- **Data Extension Name**: DataLake_Extract
- **Data Extension External Key**: DataLake_Extract
- **Data Extension Fields and Properties**:

| NAME | DATA TYPE | LENGTH | PRIMARY KEY | NULLABLE | DEFAULT |
|---|---|---|---|---|---|
| AccountID | Number | | Y | | |
| JobID | Number | | Y | | |
| ListID | Number | | Y | | |
| BatchID | Number | | Y | | |
| SubscriberID | Number | | Y | | |
| EmailName | Text | 255 | | Y | |
| SubscriberKey | Text | 255 | | Y | |
| EmailAddress | EmailAddress | | | Y | |
| Status | Text | 25 | | Y | |
| OpenDate | Date | | | Y | |
| ClickDate | Date | | | Y | |
| SendDate | Date | | | Y | |

Table 5.3 – Fields and properties of the DataLake_Extract data extension

Then you create a SQL Query activity in Automation Studio:

**Query Name**: DataLake_Extract

**Query External Key**: DataLake_Extract

**Target Data Extension**: DataLake_Extract

**Data Action**: Overwrite

**SQL**:

```sql
SELECT s.AccountID,
s.JobID,
s.ListID,
s.BatchID,
s.SubscriberID,
j.EmailName,
j.DeliveredTime as SendDate,
sub.EmailAddress,
sub.Status,
s.EventDate as SentDate,
o.OpenDate,
c.ClickDate
FROM [SentDV] s
LEFT JOIN [JobDV] j
ON s.JobID = j.JobID
LEFT JOIN [SubscribersDV] sub
ON s.SubscriberID = sub.SubscriberID
CROSS APPLY(
    SELECT TOP 1 op.JobID,
    op.ListID,
    op.BatchID,
     op.SubscriberID,
    MAX(op.EventDate) as OpenDate
    FROM [OpenDV] op
    WHERE op.JobID = s.JobID
    AND op.ListID = s.ListID
    AND op.BatchID = s.BatchID
```

```
      AND op.SubscriberID = s.SubscriberID
      GROUP BY op.JobID, op.ListID, op.BatchID,
         op.SubscriberID
) o
CROSS APPLY(
      SELECT TOP 1 cl.JobID,
      cl.ListID,
      cl.BatchID,
      cl.SubscriberID,
      MAX(cl.EventDate) as ClickDate
      FROM [ClickDV] cl
      WHERE cl.JobID = s.JobID
      AND cl.ListID = s.ListID
      AND cl.BatchID = s.BatchID
      AND cl.SubscriberID = s.SubscriberID
      GROUP BY cl.JobID, cl.ListID, cl.BatchID,
         cl.SubscriberID
) c
WHERE s.EventDate > DATEADD(day,-7,s.EventDate)
```

This one is a bit of a doozy and can get complicated. There are quite a few different approaches and thoughts on making this type of extract as well as finding the most performant way. As a note, even though this example uses a 7-day period, if you have high volumes of data, then this can time out at the 30-minute runtime max.

> **Did You Know?**
> Using online resources or even a quick Google query on a SQL function can get you detailed information, not just on what the function is, but examples and best practices on how to use it.

After completing this query, you would then do a data extract to push a flat file to the SFTP location of your choice or utilize an API to grab it directly from Marketing Cloud and push it directly into your data lake.

Following are a couple of reference screenshots to help provide context inside Marketing Cloud:

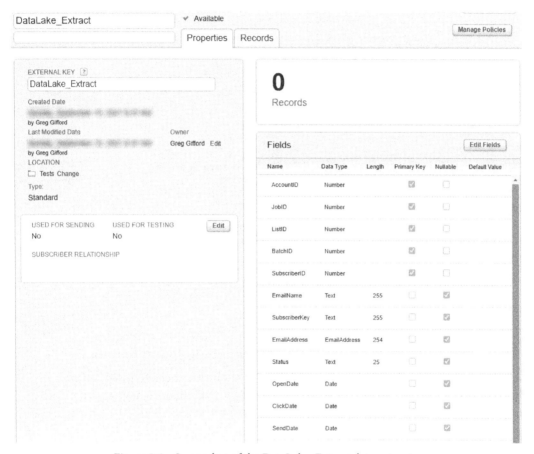

Figure 5.6 – Screenshot of the DataLake_Extract data extension

As you can see in the preceding screenshot, all the fields, external keys, and names are filled in the correct locations inside the Marketing Cloud `DataLake_Extract` data extension. Let's take a look at the **Query** activity next.

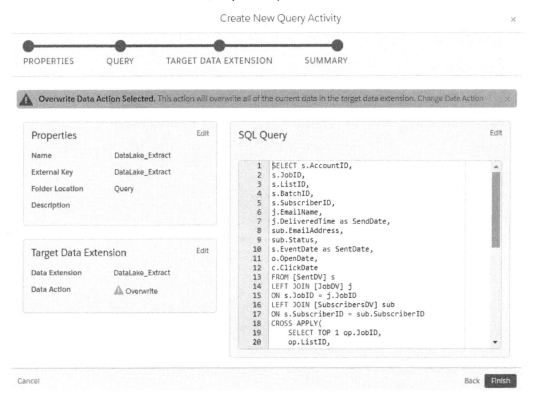

Figure 5.7 – Screenshot of the DataLake_Extract Query activity overview

The **Query** activity sample shows the final SQL stored inside the activity, along with the correct target, data action, name, and external key. Now that we have a pretty solid understanding of SQL, we should take a brief moment to review SQL.

## SQL summary

As you can see from the previous section, there are a lot of uses for SQL and, in all honesty, if you are doing any transforms to data, then 9 out of 10 times, you will wind up using a **SQL Query** activity to do it. It is the most efficient way of transforming data and with the lowest processing requirements of all the available scripts and UI tools available.

**SQL Query** activities are also easily automated as they fit right into Automation Studio and can be used in combination with many of the following activities to make an invaluable automated process. During our discussion on SQL so far, we went over the three major categories of what SQL can accomplish:

- **Custom reporting**
- **Data segmentation and preparation for sending**
- **Transforming data in preparation to export**

These three categories are a good umbrella of the possibilities afforded by SQL, but inside these categories are hundreds of subcategories that can range from simple to astoundingly complex. So, although only three are listed, the usefulness and capabilities of SQL are far beyond this explanation. Feel free to review sites such as W3 Schools (`https://www.w3schools.com/sql/default.asp`) or the official Microsoft docs on T-SQL (`https://docs.microsoft.com/en-us/sql/sql-server/?view=sql-server-ver15`) to get more details and an in-depth understanding of SQL capabilities.

Now, although SQL is pretty darn great in Marketing Cloud, especially regarding automation, there are other options available for us to use. Most of these focus on a specific aspect of ETL, or are not able to be automated, or at least automated easily. For instance, in our next section, we will go over **Filter** activities and other data segmentation, including groups and mobile lists.

# Filter activities and data segmentation

So, not all of us have the development and technical knowledge to write SQL and that is more than OK! Marketing Cloud helps account for that with things such as **Filters**, **Groups**, and **filtered mobile lists**. There also are things called **Measures**, which can be used inside filters and are intended to be *Drag and Drop SQL*, but, in our opinion, they are too unstable and potentially inaccurate to be useful. To that extent, we will not be mentioning much about them here.

As you may or may not know, each of the three options is specific to a data source; for example:

- **Filters**: Data extensions
- **Groups**: Lists (in Email Studio)
- **Filtered mobile lists** (in Mobile Studio)

To that extent, you will notice that the UI tools and options are all specialized and, in some cases, **Groups** and **Mobile Lists**, are not possible in SQL queries. The closest option to SQL queries would be **Filters**, which is where we will start our discussion.

# Filters

This option actually has a few different pieces that make it up. Our focus is going to be on the **Filter** activity, but this will also include things such as **one-time use filters** in UI, **Filter** refreshing options, and the differences between each.

Before getting into the **Filter** activity, we are going to explore the other options first. Let's start with the one-time use filters in the UI.

## One-time use filters

This exists inside Email Studio and can in no way be automated. This can still be useful for automations with its capability for refreshing through an API in scripts. But let's not get ahead of ourselves; more on that later.

So, what the heck is this? A one-time use filter is done when you go to Email Studio and use the **Filter** option, which looks like a funnel on the right side of the row, on the data extension of your choice. From there, you drag and drop the filter criteria you want and then click **Save & Build** to create your new filtered data extension. The following screenshot shows the drag and drop interface for creating filtered data extensions:

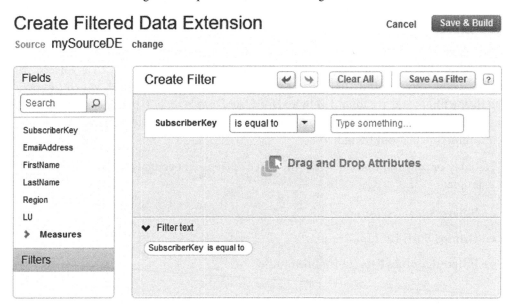

Figure 5.8 – Drag and drop segmentation interface for filtered data extensions

In order to create the filtered data extension, it will require you to automatically create a new data extension. So, after clicking **Save & Build**, you will need to provide a name, external key, description, and folder location where you want the data extension to reside. After all that is completed, you will find your data extension in that folder. It will be very similar to the normal DE, but you will notice on the right-hand side that it now has this weird arrow circle symbol instead of the normal import and filter symbols.

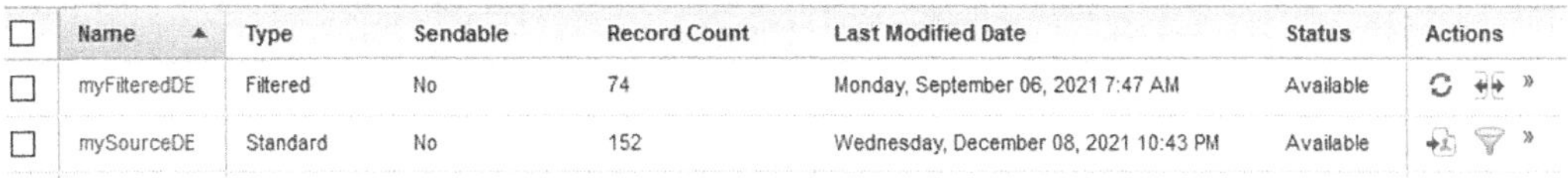

| | Name ▲ | Type | Sendable | Record Count | Last Modified Date | Status | Actions |
| --- | --- | --- | --- | --- | --- | --- | --- |
| ☐ | myFilteredDE | Filtered | No | 74 | Monday, September 06, 2021 7:47 AM | Available | ↻ ↔ » |
| ☐ | mySourceDE | Standard | No | 152 | Wednesday, December 08, 2021 10:43 PM | Available | +↧ ▽ » |

Figure 5.9 – Example of a filtered data extension in UI

So, this arrow circle symbol is actually the symbol to *refresh*. This is how you would be able to rerun the filter criteria on the DE. Now, this is literally the only way to update these data extensions unless you are comfortable with undocumented REST API endpoints (again, more on that later). This makes these great for quickly debugging or troubleshooting, but pretty bad for any automation or repetitive tasks.

So, some of you may have noticed that in *Figure 5.1*, there is a button named **Save As Filter** under the **Save & Build** button. This will actually take your criteria and create something called a **Filter Definition**. This does not execute the filter, but instead saves all the aspects of it inside an object that can be used later. This will be very important when we talk about **Filter** activities later. You can also make **Filter Definitions** under the **Data Filters** folder in the **Subscribers** tab of **Email Studio**.

## Filter refreshing options

As noted in the previous section, this is only related to filtered data extensions and not all filter possibilities in Marketing Cloud. We mention this because there is no activity inside Automation Studio to automatically refresh filtered data extensions like there is for lists and mobile lists. The only way, outside of **Filter** activities, which we will go over next, to automatically refresh these data extensions is through an undocumented REST API endpoint.

> **Undocumented Endpoints**
>
> One important thing to note about undocumented endpoints is that **they are not officially supported or prepared for use by the public**, meaning that there is a risk that things will break or slow down and Marketing Cloud will do nothing to help you resolve this issue as you should not have been touching it in the first place. This means, if you are doing something that is **significant or highly important in production, you likely should not use this method** as there is the risk of failure due to Marketing Cloud deciding to shut it down completely or otherwise change it, thereby breaking your entire process.

Now that we know the risks and understand that this should not really be used in a production environment, let's do a quick exploration of this endpoint:

```
Method: POST
Endpoint: /email/v1/filteredCustomObjects/{{filterDEid}}/
refresh
Host: {{tenantSubDomain}}.rest.marketingcloudapis.com
Authorization: Bearer {{auth_token}}
Content-Type: application/json
```

You will notice here that there are a few pieces that have curly brackets before and after. These are our *placeholders* that you need to enter your values in. Following is a description of what each means:

- `FilterDEid`: This is the object ID of the filtered data extension you are targeting. You can gather this via an API or through some investigation in the UI.

- `TenantSubDomain`: This is your tenant-specific endpoint that you can find in your API package or similar places in the UI.

- `Auth_Token`: This is the OAuth token that is generated via a separate API call to authenticate and provide context for all other API calls.

As noted, this is the only way to refresh it, and the only way inside Salesforce Marketing Cloud that you can do this is via SSJS **Script activity** or the cloud page using *SSJS*. Well, technically, you can use AMPscript as it is a POST call, but we would highly recommend SSJS for all API calls where possible. Now that we have seen that the refresh and automation options for one-time use filters are severely limited, let's move on to **Filter** activities.

# Filter activities

**Filter** activities can be created inside Automation Studio, but they are reliant on **Filter Definitions** being created inside Email Studio. The best part about **Filter** activities is that they are native to Automation Studio, so can easily be inserted into an automation. This is important because the **Filter** activity will not only create a new filtered data extension, but will also refresh the filtered data extension if it already exists! This is the only way to utilize filtered data extensions inside an automation outside of the API, which can be a bit much.

So, what exactly makes up a **Filter** activity? At its core, a **Filter** activity is built upon the filter definition that you create in Email Studio. This defines the data extension you want to use as a source as well as the filter criteria you want to use. From there, you just assign the name, external key, and the other details of the new filtered data extension that is created to house all your data.

> **Note**
>
> We are focusing on **Filter** activities in relation to data extensions for this section, but **Filter** activities can also be used to create new groups by targeting lists instead. This will be discussed more in the *Groups* section following this one.

The following screenshot shows the UI setup wizard around creating a new **Filter** activity and selecting the correct filter definition:

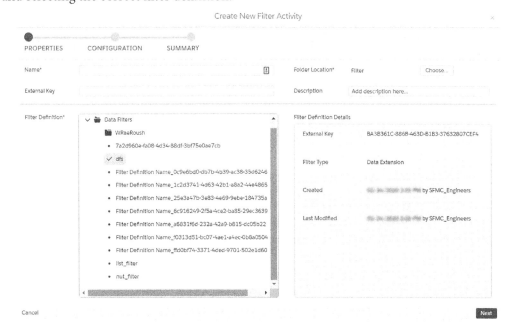

Figure 5.10 – Example of the setup for creating a new filter activity

After this, you then just complete the **Name**, **External Key**, and **Description** fields of the new target data extension you want to create, and then the **Filter** activity is done! Now, one important thing to keep in mind regarding this is that **Filter** activities will only create new data extensions and not target one-time-use filtered data extensions you already created. After the initial build, it will refresh that **Filter** activity-built DE, but that is the only time it will refresh. Next up, let's move on to **Groups**, as they are fairly similar to data extension filters.

## Groups

**Groups** are the list equivalent of filters for data extensions. These can only be created inside **Email Studio** or via a **Filter** activity (described previously). The difference is that for one-time use groupings, there is an **Automation Studio** activity to refresh them automatically. This can be super helpful as you can create it via the UI and still automate the refresh without needing to recreate it in a **Filter** activity and refresh via that activity. The following screenshot shows the UI for creating a filtered group. You will notice that this is very similar to the **Filter Definition** UI.

Figure 5.11 – Example of the setup for creating a new filtered group

The issue here, however, is that lists are no longer the data storage of choice as data extensions tend to be much more customizable, powerful, and performant than lists – so lists are not used beyond subscription status. And things such as publication lists do not allow you to filter them and create groups, so this severely limits the usefulness of groups.

You can use **Groups** on **All Subscribers**, but it does not let you have access to things such as **Subscription Status** or anything like that, which once again limits the capabilities. Long story short, you are not likely to find many people who utilize groups, but if there is a need, this can be pretty well automated. We tend to find that for whatever we would have wanted to try and grab through groups, we can find more, if not better, info from the filtered mobile lists.

# Filtered mobile lists

Although this is taking place in **MobileConnect** (or **Contact Builder**), the capabilities of these lists are not limited to just mobile contacts. The other great thing about this is that mobile lists are technically data extensions, so they are able to be queried in a limited capacity. This can be huge for some use cases. For instance, if you need to delete contacts that have no channels, you can use a filtered mobile list to get this done. There are other ways in which this can be accomplished, such as via a channel address data extract type, but to highlight the power of filtered mobile lists, we will use this method.

The best part about this is that there is an activity in Automation Studio that allows you to refresh these lists at whatever schedule or triggered time period you want. This can be a very powerful tool for keeping your contacts clean and trimmed up. The following screenshot illustrates the UI for filtered mobile lists:

Figure 5.12 – The UI for creating a filtered mobile list

As you can see from the screenshot, the other great thing about filtered mobile lists is that they work based on attribute groups, allowing you to filter based on relational data and not just want is inside that specific object. If you utilize contacts and attribute groups for most of your messaging, then this may be a strong way for you to gather segmented data. The only issue is that the creation of these lists is not able to be automated, just the refreshing part. So, you would have to manually build each and every one of the mobile lists you want to use.

Next, we are going to dive into the **Import Data** options. These options show how to ingest data that has already been extracted and transformed in Marketing Cloud.

# Import data options

For this section, we will be concentrating on just the import options that can be automated and not discussing the UI import options. The main option for this is **Import** activity. **Import** activity requires the use of a *Marketing Cloud File Location* to ingest data, so there will be some considerations when utilizing it. You can create this *File Location* inside the **Administrator** tab in **Email Studio** or inside the **Setup** section.

Essentially, this activity will take a flat file (CSV, TXT, and so on) from the SFTP and then load it inside a data extension or list, separated by a specified delimiter in the file. This process can be automated inside the **Import** activity in Automation Studio and can be completed via a schedule or via a file drop trigger.

There are other options that can be used to ingest data, such as the manual import wizard in the user interface, but these are not capable of being automated. Due to that fact, we are not going to be covering them.

The only other option for ingesting data is by utilizing the Salesforce Marketing Cloud API. There are options to accomplish this in both the SOAP and REST APIs, but the APIs are something we will go into further in the book. For now, we will be moving on to the export data options.

# Export data options

Although things were pretty straightforward and simple as regards importing data, exporting data from Marketing Cloud has tons of options. Even limiting it to just those export options that you can automate, you still have a couple of options:

- **Data Extract**: Exporting data to a flat file from a data extension.
- **Tracking Extract**: Exporting tracking data (open, click, and so on) into a flat file.
- **Other**: There are many other options, including **Convert XML**, **GlobalUnsubImport**, and **Zip Data Extract**.

As a note though, we are not going to be diving too deep into the **Other** section as this is not really relevant to what we are discussing and we have found most of these options to be more niche case uses and not something you see utilized very often. Let's now dive into **data extract** and take a look at how this can be helpful.

# Data extract

This Automation Studio activity extracts information from a data extension and places it in a delimited file. Honestly, it is pretty simple to use with the options you would imagine it would have. There is not much to it, but it can be automated, which is greatly helpful for the ingestion of outside systems.

That being said, there are a ton of different data extract options available to help with your export or file manipulation needs. For the sake of this section, we will limit it to a data extract from a data extension as well as to tracking extracts.

The part that needs to be considered regarding an extract of a data extension is that after the extract is run, the flat file is not created in an accessible place; it is first created inside the Safehouse. You then need to use a **File Transfer** activity to move the file from the Safehouse into the file location you want it to go to. Let's dive a bit deeper into the **File Transfer** activity before moving forward.

# File Transfer activity

**File Transfer** activity has a ton of uses in Marketing Cloud, but for this, we will be focusing on the move from extracting from the Safehouse to the target file location. **File Transfer** activity has two options that show the type of action you are looking to perform with the file transfer. The following screenshot shows the two options in the UI:

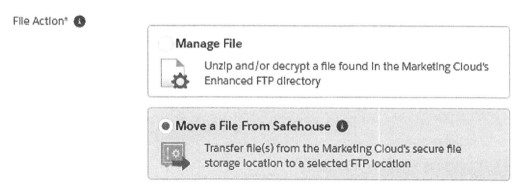

Figure 5.13 – Two action options available for File Transfer

For our needs (data extraction), we will be selecting **Move a File From Safehouse**. From there, we need to enter the filename, or file naming pattern, associated with the exported data. You do this by selecting a destination from your stored file locations in your admin settings.

Next, you will see a few different **transfer settings**. This is essentially used if you want to encrypt the file when you move it from the Safehouse to the target file location. The two options available here are **PGP** and **GPG**, and you can select the desired public key from **Key Storage** in **Admin settings**.

After you run the data extract followed by the **File Transfer**, your file will be sent to the target location and will be available for ingestion by whatever outside service or data warehouse you want. Next, let's look at **Tracking Extract**.

## Tracking extract

Tracking extracts pull data directly from the *backend* of Salesforce Marketing Cloud and get data that users cannot easily access anywhere else other than via the API. This is a great way to get information on interaction and tracking data inside Marketing Cloud and pass it in a raw format to your analytics or reporting system for ingestion.

There are a ton of different options that can be performed in a tracking extract, but the good news is that you can pick and choose which option(s) you want to include. The following is a list of the available outputs from a tracking extract:

- `Attributes`
- `Bounces`
- `ClickImpressions`
- `Clicks`
- `Conversions`
- `ListMembershipChanges`
- `Lists`
- `NotSent`
- `Opens`
- `SendJobImpressions`
- `SendJobs`
- `Sent`
- `SentImpression`

- StatusChanges
- Subscribers
- SurveyResponses
- Unsubs

Now, picking and choosing only what you need is very important as tracking extracts are able to time out. This means that if you try to extract too much data at once, the whole thing will fail. Now, another part of this that needs to be considered in relation to the timeout limit is the date range associated with the extract.

Not only can you select the objects to output, but you can select a range of dates that you want to extract from. The maximum rolling range is 90 days, which means it is a 90-day look back from the current date, or you can set a specific range up to 30 days in length, and that range can go back to account inception and is not limited to 6 months, like **Data Views**. For accounts that have significant data, this can mean that you need to keep the date range low for each extract, or it could time out and fail.

# Summary

With that, you now have a strong understanding of ETL and data manipulation inside Marketing Cloud Automation Studio. Whether you are looking to use SQL queries or import or extract files, you should now have all the information you need to maximize the use of these activities in your automation.

You have dived deep into what exactly ETL is and now have a strong enough understanding of it in general, as well as how it relates in Marketing Cloud, that you can likely impress your friends at the next party with how smart you are. Well, if they are also into nerdy technical things like us, otherwise they might just give you a blank stare as you try to explain it.

We also learned that for **Transform**, the two activities we want to concentrate on are the **SQL Query** activity and **Filter** activities. These offer the best segmentation options, with **SQL Query** activities offering a more versatile capability of transforming outside of just segmentation.

Next, we will take you through one of our favorite topics in Salesforce Marketing Cloud – **Script activities** in Automation Studio. **Script activities** offer you so many options and capabilities through the ability to use in-step scripting capabilities inside of an automation. This includes making API calls and interacting with system objects in Marketing Cloud, such as emails and data extensions.

# 6
# The Magic of Script Activities

**Data** and **extract, transform, load** (**ETL**) are a highly impressive part of the capabilities of Marketing Cloud, but what we feel are the most powerful capabilities all start with the magic of **Script activities**. Script activities are part of Automation Studio activities and allow you to execute **server-side JavaScript** (**SSJS**) within automation. Within this chapter, we will dig into the following topics:

- *Script activities (SSJS and AMPscript)*: What Script activities are in relation to Marketing Cloud and automation, as well as how SSJS and AMPscript are used inside **Script** activities.

- *Overview of SSJS in Marketing Cloud*: SSJS is the proprietary language of Marketing Cloud and is required to be used in a **Script activity.**

- *Oh, the possibilities?! (What you can do in SSJS)*: This takes that base knowledge of SSJS and shows you how you can use it and the possibilities it unleashes.

- *A real-life example implementation*: Now that we know what is possible, let's dig into a real-life example usage of SSJS inside of a **Script activity**.

We must admit that **Script activities** are one of our favorite capabilities of **Salesforce Marketing Cloud** (**SFMC**), so we are very excited to write this and the next couple of chapters. **Script activities** are a great introduction to the proprietary language of SSJS inside of Marketing Cloud, and SSJS and **Script activities** open up so many doors for custom actions, implementations, executions, reporting, analytics, and more!

---

**Development Primer Notice**

As this chapter and the next chapter heavily involve the development languages of SSJS and AMPscript, we wanted to provide some links to help provide some background if needed.

Javascript Overview: `https://developer.mozilla.org/en-US/docs/Web/JavaScript/A_re-introduction_to_JavaScript`

SSJS: `https://developer.salesforce.com/docs/marketing/marketing-cloud/guide/ssjs_serverSideJavaScript.html`

AMPScript: `https://developer.salesforce.com/docs/marketing/marketing-cloud/guide/ampscript.html`

---

Before we get too far ahead of ourselves, let's start out by defining exactly what a **Script activity** is and how to use it.

# Technical requirements

The full code for the chapter can be found in the GitHub repository located here: `https://github.com/PacktPublishing/Automating-Salesforce-Marketing-Cloud/tree/main/Chapter06`.

# Script activities (SSJS and AMPscript)

Inside of Automation Studio, under **Activities**, you will find the most wonderful activity named **Script activity**. Now, what makes this so wonderful? Well, it opens the door to do things beyond what you can do in the **user interface** (**UI**) and allows you to build a scheduled script that can be run with a 30-minute time-out. OK—cool, but what exactly is it?

A **Script activity** in Marketing Cloud is an activity that lets you write a script utilizing SSJS inside of a stored object, the **Script activity** itself, that you can then execute within automation. You can run this as a part of automation or as the whole automation itself, as well as utilize it as both automation types: **Scheduled** or **File Drop**.

> **Note**
> If you do not see this activity inside of Automation Studio, contact Salesforce support or your relationship manager to activate it.

A **Script activity** is one of the most powerful activities in Automation Studio due to its ability to include scripting using *SSJS*. This capability allows you to automate many wonderful things, including preparing content for sends, creating micro-automations inside automation, getting external content, storing/utilizing it in automation, and more. Can we give an example? Sure!

Let's say you have a huge amount of personalized newsletter content that you need to pull from an external resource. For the sake of simplicity, let's say it's all hosted on an endpoint that you can target with a **REpresentational State Transfer** (**REST**) call. Now, you could have all this done inside the email in real time with proper scripting in the email, but that could really bloat the send time to the point that it might make the email unusable, or even time out or error. This is where a **Script activity** comes in.

The **Script activity** would run in the step before you send an email (assuming it is a bulk send through Automation Studio), whereby it will run through each of the **application programming interface** (**API**) calls to collect the content from the external source and then take that returned data and store it inside of a **data extension** (**DE**). You then can just reference the DE on the live email, greatly reducing the time it takes to send each email due to the reduction in processing required.

Now, this is just one of the million uses of a **Script activity**, but we feel it is a great way to show how **Script activities** can make what might be impossible elsewhere in the platform suddenly become possible. Utilizing SSJS inside of a **Script activity** opens many doors that were previously closed.

As you may have noticed in the explanation, we mention it only uses SSJS, and do not mention AMPscript. Yep! That's right—this will only accept SSJS inside of it. But if you do want to use AMPscript inside of a **Script activity**, you have a couple of options available to you.

## AMPscript inside of a Script activity

First is the option of calling in a content block via SSJS that has all your AMPscript in it. The strange thing is that the validator will only allow SSJS, but if you *trick it*, it will run AMPscript perfectly. Now, this may, at face value, seem like: *What is going on? Why would they not just open it to both if it can process both?*

Well, we do not have a definitive answer, but we do have a theory. We think this works because the AMPscript in the content block is being rendered before it enters the **Script activity** environment. This means that the **Script activity** is not processing the AMPscript—it is just receiving the results.

Here is an example of using a content block call to pull in AMPscript:

### Script activity

```
<script runat="server">
  Platform.Function.ContentBlockByKey(
    "ampscriptContentBlock");
</script>
```

In this example, `ampscriptContentBlock` represents a content block from the content builder holding all your AMPscript. We would highly recommend using a **code snippet content block** only for this, as the added **HyperText Markup Language** (HTML) that comes from most other content blocks might cause issues.

So, say—for example—we had a content block with the `ampscriptContentBlock` external key and it had the following AMPscript in it:

### AMPscript content block

```
%%[
SET @sde = "mySourceDE"
SET @tde = "myTargetDE"

SET @rs = LookupRows(@sde, "HasBeenRun", "False")
SET @rc = RowCount(@rs)

FOR @i=1 TO @rc  DO
  SET @row = ROW(@rs,@i)
  SET @pkey = FIELD(@row,"pkey")
  SET @val2 = FIELD(@row,"val2")
  SET @val3 = FIELD(@row,"val3")

  UPSERTDATA(@tde, 1, "pkey",@pkey,"val2",@val2,"val3",@val3)
```

```
NEXT @i




]%%
```

This would then take data from `mySourceDE` and push the specific fields called out (`pkey`, `val2`, and `val3`) into the target (`myTargetDE`) via the `UPSERTDATA` function. This would be run every time the automation runs, allowing for you to automate some scripted updates.

The second option is to do it inline inside of the SSJS. This sounds odd, but it actually works really well, especially when you want to use AMPscript functions that are not replicated in SSJS without creating them yourself. Here is a basic example showing the use of the `ProperCase` function, which does not exist inside of SSJS:

### SSJS inline AMPscript

```
<script runat=server>
Var newStr = Platform.Function.TreatAsContent('\%\%[SET @name
=ProperCase("greg Gifford") OUTPUT(CONCAT(@name)) ]\%\%')
</script>
```

Now, it is definitely not limited to just data interaction or simple functions; there are tons of things you can do with AMPscript inside a **Script activity**, but in all honesty, AMPscript capabilities are not even close to what you can do when utilizing SSJS. To that extent, let's move on to learn more about SSJS inside of SFMC.

# Overview of SSJS in Marketing Cloud

Let's start with an explanation of what SSJS is. SSJS is basically a server-run version of JavaScript to interact with the server and related objects. As it is not run in the browser (client side), it does not have access to the **Document Object Model** (**DOM**) or similar aspects. Before getting too much further into SSJS, we wanted to address the topic itself.

Now, although we are a huge fans and lover a of SSJS, there are many people out there who avoid the topic at all costs or even just refuse to admit it exists. Our thought is that there is a stigma that has been put on this language that causes people to view it as a *dead* language in Marketing Cloud, or at least a less useful one.

This stigma has likely stemmed from the fact that AMPscript is newer, easier to use—especially for email personalization—and can be more efficient. This is what is touted around as the reason SSJS is not so great. Although all those points are true, they are only a small fraction of the story.

SSJS has a significant dominance when it comes to utilizing **CloudPages** and **Script activities**. It has unmatched capabilities there that AMPscript cannot match. This includes many native JavaScript capabilities as well as the ability to interact with **request and response headers**, and other things such as setting or removing cookies. This, on top of the **Core library** (we will be getting to that a bit further along) holding many functions that would only be possible through an API, and also the simplified version of API calls via **WSProxy**, makes SSJS unstoppable.

That being said, though, SSJS does have a place inside of emails as well, but AMPscript is definitely the dominant language there. So, where could we possibly want to use SSJS? Well, in a case where you have a transactional email (let's say a shipping email) that is sent a **JavaScript Object Notation (JSON)** payload that you need to parse out to find the products, the ship date, location, and other details. There is absolutely zero capability in AMPscript to handle JSON, which means it would be a huge mess of substrings and **regular expressions (regexes)** and more that gets complicated and unwieldy very quickly.

The solution is to use SSJS, which can natively interact with **JSON objects** or **arrays** and parse this out. Now, this part is where it takes some thought. Do you write the whole email in SSJS, or do you parse in SSJS and then transition it back to AMPscript? The general best practice says mixing languages is bad, but with how fast AMPscript is in emails, it may make sense to mix languages here. It all depends on what you want to do and what you are most comfortable with. Now that we have a good idea of where SSJS fits inside of Marketing Cloud, let's take a deeper look into what it is.

## What is SFMC SSJS in a nutshell?

In a nutshell, SSJS is an older version of vanilla JavaScript that is processed on the server instead of on the browser, also called the **client side**. SSJS uses **ECMAScript** 3.0 (**ES 3.0**, where **ECMA** stands for **European Computer Manufacturer's Association**), which is a coding standard set for JavaScript. To help give context to this, We believe that modern JavaScript is currently utilizing ES 11. To this extent, we need to keep in mind that a lot of best practices and capabilities in recent and modern JavaScript are not available in SSJS.

As noted earlier, SSJS is processed on the server instead of the browser, which limits a portion of the capabilities of JavaScript. This is due to it not interacting with the DOM or **Browser Object Model** (**BOM**) and not being able to access external libraries. It cannot access external libraries due to security and the way that the code is processed on the server and not in a browser. To its benefit, though, it does offer some extra capabilities that you do not have in JavaScript.

One such benefit is the ability to utilize the `Platform` class and the Core library. These two offer many proprietary functions and capabilities to interact with platform objects and definitions in ways that are not normally possible outside of the API. You also can fake *external* libraries by creating code snippet content blocks to host SSJS code. You can then reference this code into your target content, email, or CloudPage. Next, we will be diving into the different libraries and native capabilities of SSJS in the Marketing Cloud.

## Platform class

The **Platform class** (also referenced as the **Platform library**) is very closely related to AMPscript, containing many of the same functions and uses. There are some differences in syntax and capabilities that can help in making a decision on which language is better for your use case. For instance, the Platform Class includes WSProxy inside of it. This is a built-in SSJS capability to simplify the **Simple Object Access Protocol** (**SOAP**) API and work in JSON instead of **Extensible Markup Language** (**XML**). (More on this in *Chapter 7, The Power of In-Step APIs*.) It also has the ability to interact with the response object to do things such as manipulate cookies, redirect the page, manipulate headers, and more, as well as interact with the request object, pulling post data, form fields, and query parameters from the **Uniform Resource Locator** (**URL**), request headers, and more.

The `Platform` class is included in the default declaration block of SSJS and does not need to be loaded in as the Core library does. You may notice that some AMPscript functions are not present in `Platform`. Things such as `ADD()` or similar math functions in AMPscript that do not exist as SSJS can use the native math capabilities in JavaScript to handle these needs—for example, `ADD(1,2)` would become `1+2` in JavaScript. But there are certain functions in AMPscript that do not have an alternative, such as the math ones referenced, so they are completely unable to be recreated via SSJS. A great example of this is the Salesforce Core-related AMPscript functions. There is nothing in SSJS that can match that capability at all. Next, let's dig into the Core library, which houses many functions completely unmatched by AMPscript.

## Core library

Marketing Cloud Core SSJS is a JavaScript library, which basically just means it is pre-written JavaScript that you can reference for easier development. This is very similar to how client-side JavaScript can reference external libraries, but the main difference is that Core is the only library that can be referenced within Marketing Cloud SSJS. You cannot create your own libraries or reference any other libraries in SSJS.

By utilizing the Core library, you open up quite a few different options that are basically *shortcuts* for SOAP API calls inside of Email Studio. These functions allow you to accomplish many awesome things not possible natively in Platform/AMPscript, including interacting with objects such as DEs, Subscriber, Account, Email, and Triggers. Generally, Core must be used inside of non-sendable environments, but some functions are able to be used in a messaging context as well.

Now, Core—as with most libraries—comes in versions. This means you need to declare which version you want to use when you load the library. Now, this sounds pretty cool, but the issue is that Core only has one specific version that I am aware of, which is version 1.1.1. That being said, when you call the library in, you can just declare it as 1 and it will fill into the most recent version of all non-explicitly set parameters of the version.

To be fair, much of Core can be handled now via WSProxy, but for smaller volumes and certain situations, Core can still be more performant or the more elegant solution. Calling in the Core library alone can affect processing and efficiency, so we would make sure it is necessary before calling it in, instead of including it in each of your developments by default. Now that you have a good idea of what the Core library is, let's explore an overview of the native capabilities of SSJS.

## Native capabilities

Most of the functions and capabilities that are native to JavaScript (and are not browser- or DOM-dependent) are able to be utilized inside of Marketing Cloud, with the caveat being that these capabilities need to be ECMA 3 or before. This includes things such as these:

- **Arrays**—Data storage list-like objects, as exemplified here:

```
[0,1,2,3,4]
```

- **Objects**—Data storage containers for named value and key pairs, as exemplified here:

```
{key1:"value1","key2":"value2"}
```

- **Math**—Properties and methods, as well as shorthand arithmetic operators for calculations, as exemplified here:

```
(1 + 2 / 3 * 4 - 5)
```

- **Functions**—Subprograms that produce callable procedures, calculations, values, or actions, as exemplified here:

```
function sum(a,b) { return a+b }
```

- **Eval**—Ingests a string and evaluates it as JavaScript code, as exemplified here:

```
eval("results = sum(5,5);")
```

- **Switch**—Evaluates expressions matching case statements, similar to CASE in **Structured Query Language (SQL)**. You can see an example here:

```
switch(expr) {
    case 'one':  sum(1,1);  break;
    case 'two': sum(2,2);  break;
    default: 'Not Numbers';
    }
```

- try...catch—Attempts to run a script and then provides the capability to specify a response if an exception is thrown, as exemplified here:

```
try {
    //my script
    } catch(e) {
    //error catching script
    }
```

- And more—multiple loop types; global, scope, and contextual variables; error handling…

These are just some of the capabilities that make SSJS so special and so powerful. Next up, we will be discussing all the possibilities of what you can do in SSJS and going into details about this.

# Oh, the possibilities! (What you can do in SSJS)

Although we are definitely biased in this statement, we still think it is very accurate. SSJS opens up SFMC to the power of custom solutions and development that AMPscript could never dream of doing. Just the capabilities of interaction with API calls and their responses alone puts SSJS beyond the capabilities of AMPscript.

AMPscript is more based on simple personalization, dynamic content, templating, and data lookups to custom objects and manipulations. It is not made for the levels of development and complex solutions you can get with SSJS. Sure, this sounds great and all, but it's all hot air unless we can prove it, right? So, let's prove it. To start, let's discuss arrays and objects.

## Arrays and objects

Arrays and objects are one of the greatest reasons to utilize SSJS inside of the Marketing Cloud. They provide great capabilities around data storage and interaction that are far superior to what is available in AMPscript.

Now, one thing we want to start out with that may seem unimportant but is something that can help give you a stronger understanding when people are discussing arrays and objects is **JSON**.

### What is JSON?

**JSON** (pronounced JAY-SON) is a representation of the data structure; it is *not* an actual array or object itself. So, a JSON array is not a special type of array—it is just describing how the array is structured.

A great example of this would be the different types of milk—for instance, default JavaScript could be cow milk and then JSON would be almond milk. In most ways, it is used in the same way, but they are built/made completely differently.

The other difference is that JSON is universal outside of JavaScript, so it can be used, transmitted, generated, and read from multiple programming environments. JSON is also stored as a string that is then deserialized (converted to a native object) when parsed. Because of this, JSON can actually be stored as its own file, which is just a text file with the extension of `.json`. So, for now, let's take JSON out of the picture and concentrate on finding out exactly what an array is.

## Array...of sunshine?

Arrays in JavaScript are one of our favorite features. We have built so many of our most impressive custom solutions and automations because of the existence and capabilities of arrays. It seems such a tiny thing, but the capability to have robust and indexable data storage natively built into the language is...*powerful*!

OK—that being said, now...what is an array? An array is basically a list-like object that contains data inside indexed locations, starting at the 0 index and going up from there. Due to this indexing nature, you cannot store string descriptors for each index; it is only the numeric index that can be used. An example of an array would be something such as `var fruit = ["Apples","Oranges","Bananas"]`, with the three types of fruit inside of the open and close square brackets being each indexed value. This means that when outputting the information, you would get results such as these:

- `fruit[0] = "Apples"`
- `fruit[1] = "Oranges"`
- `fruit[2] = "Bananas"`

Now, some other neat things can be done to arrays beyond just returning the indexed values. This includes a multitude of capabilities, although some are not available in SSJS due to it being limited to ECMA 3, so we will not be going through this exhaustively.

Natively, you are able to do the following actions in relation to arrays:

- Gather the length of the array (total number of indexed values), as exemplified here:

  ```
  fruit.length //returns 3
  ```

- Turn an array into a delimited string, as exemplified here:

  ```
  fruit.join('|') //returns Apples|Oranges|Bananas
  ```

- Remove the last element of an array, as exemplified here:

  ```
  fruit.pop() //returns ["Apples","Oranges"]
  ```

- Create your own prototypes to use on the `Array()` method, as follows:

  ```
  Array.prototype.myUcase = function() {
      for (i = 0; i < this.length; i++) {
          this[i] = this[i].toUpperCase();
      }
  };
  ```

```
var fruit = ["Banana", "Orange", "Apple", "Mango"];
fruit.myUcase();
//Output: ["BANANA", "ORANGE", "APPLE", "MANGO"]
```

- Sort array values based on a passed function, as follows:

```
var array = [40, 100, 1, 5, 25, 10];

array.sort(function(x, y) {
  if (x < y) {
    return -1;
  }
  if (x > y) {
    return 1;
  }
  return 0;
});
//Output: [1,5,10,25,40,100]
```

- Slice out selected elements in an array as a new array, as follows:

```
var fruits = ["Banana", "Orange", "Lemon", "Apple",
"Mango"];
var citrus = fruits.slice(1, 3);
//Output: ["Orange","Lemon"]
```

Now, we could list a dozen other just as cool features or dive into different ways to utilize the prototype capability to backfill in functionality beyond ECMA 3 into your SSJS in Marketing Cloud, but half the fun of SSJS is finding and solving things in your own unique way. So, we will go over when to use an array.

## When to use an array

Arrays are very much list-based. Think of an array as you would think about a delimited list or an Excel spreadsheet. This is used if you want to have multiple values stored in a single place. It usually works well when you are looking to do something such as execute the same action on multiple different values or want to have multiple outputs slightly altered.

For example, the following code will create three different variable names:

```
<script runat=server>
  Platform.Load("Core","1.1.1");
  var arr = [0,1,2]
  var vName = "myVar"

  for (var i = 0; i < arr.length; i++) {
    Write(vName + arr[i] + '<br>')
  }
</script>
```

The preceding code would output the following result:

```
myVar1
myVar2
myVar3
```

Now that we have a good understanding of when to use an array, let's move on to the next section, which is going to focus on the JavaScript object.

## Object...of my affection?

Objects are basically a combination of the capabilities of arrays and variables. That being said, objects themselves are variables as they must be declared as such, but inside that variable, your object can contain many different values and descriptions assigned to that one variable.

For instance, your variable without an object would equal a single value, like this:

```
var fruit = 'Apple'
```

If you were to store the variable as an object, you could instead store multiple values inside of it, like this:

```
Var fruit = {name: "Apple", type: "Golden Delicious", quantity:
500}
```

As you see in the preceding code, objects use the curly bracket syntax, as opposed to the square bracket syntax of the array. Inside of these curly brackets, each property is stored as a name:value pair (name and value separated by a colon), and each property is separated by a comma.

Then, in order to access the object property, you would use dot notation to iterate through it. To use the previous example, let's try to get the type of apple it is. We would first need to list the object name, and then the dot notation, and then the property name, which would be fruit.type—this would output Golden Delicious. You can also use square brackets to access the object property, like this: fruit["type"]—this would also output Golden Delicious.

The other great thing that objects have is something called **object methods**. Methods are actions that can be performed on objects. They are stored inside properties as function definitions.

Here's an example of this:

```
var fruit = {
  fruitType: "Apple",
  subType: "Golden Delicious",
  fruitId: 123456,
  displayName : function() {
   return this.subType + " " + this.fruitType;
  }
};


//which would lead to being called like:
var display = fruit.displayName()
//Output: Golden Delicious Apple
//to get just the definition, you would remove the ()
var display = fruit.displayName() //Output: function() { return
this.subType + " " + this.fruitType;  }
```

There are a ton of awesome features and great capabilities around objects in JavaScript, but for now, we are going to just touch on how to create or set name:value pairs.

Here is a code example for creating an object or setting a `name:value` pair to an existing object:

```
//create empty object
var obj = {}
//create object with values
var obj = {name:"value"}
//set or update name:value pair to obj
obj.myName = "myValue"   // {name:"value",myName:"myValue"}
//set or update name:value pair to obj square brackets
obj["myName"] = "myValue"
// {name:"value",myName:"myValue"}
```

Now, you also have the ability to delete properties from your object via the `delete` operator, as follows:

```
delete obj.myName
```

As a note on `delete`, it can work outside of just objects but can also fully delete an existing global variable as well. This would mean that after deletion, if you call that variable, it would return undefined or null. Did you know that objects in JavaScript have their own specific `for` loop type?

## When to use an object

Objects are a storage place for you to give properties of a single entity. For instance, instead of just saying a *car*, as you would inside of a normal global variable, an object would say it's a gray 1998 Ford Fusion with 139,990 miles on the clock and that it had its most recent oil change on September 21, 20XX. The object is basically a contextual blob that subsets off from a single **identifier** (**ID**). For example, see the following code sample around the car example we just made:

```
var obj = {
  vehicle: "car",
  make: "Ford",
  model: "Fusion",
  year: 1998,
  color: "grey",
  lastOilChange: "09/21/20XX",
```

```
    milage: 139990
}
```

This is really useful to create a single point of reference rather than have to set individual variables that then need to be passed and used individually each time.

## For...in loop

Now, there is one type of `for` loop that is specifically used for objects—the `for...in` loop. This loop is designed with objects in mind and is optimized for use with it. That being said, though, it is made with the intention of debugging and not really for production or general usage. What the `for...in` loop does is that it iterates through each property inside the object. But, the one thing to keep in mind is that it also will loop over the object prototype methods and properties as well, which can cause issues.

There are other modern-day `for` loop types (for example, `for...of`) that are better suited than the `for...in` loop, but as these are modern, they do not exist in Marketing Cloud SSJS. So, we are stuck with the `for...in` loop when iterating over objects. See the following `for...in` loop example:

```
<script runat=server>
  var obj = {name1:"val1", name2:"val2"}

  for (var x in obj) {
    Write(x + '<br>');  //writes the string value of each
                        //property
  }
</script>
```

Now, you might think this sounds great, and it can be. But as stated previously, we would utilize this only for debugging as there is an inherent risk in this, due to it pulling in prototype methods and properties. The `for...in` loop is also limited to only being useful for objects. It technically can be used for arrays as well, but it is very much not recommended to utilize a `for...in` loop on an array.

There are many major issues and risks in utilizing it this way, including the `for...in` loop returning only as a string, skipping null or undefined values, and more. Let's just say that it is a heck of a lot safer and likely more performant to just use the classic `for` loop for arrays instead. Speaking of arrays and objects, let's next dive into how they work together.

## Arrays and objects together

Arrays and objects are each amazing in their own right and offer so much capability and power, but that doesn't compare to when they work together and you combine them into a single array or object. Nesting arrays in objects or objects in arrays can create unbelievable datasets, creating what is essentially data objects inside of data objects.

Do you have a list of specific subscribers that you want to send to, but need to have all of their details included? Well—you, need an array of objects! Do you have a specific entity that you need to have multiple values listed inside of a property? You need an object with an array. A combination of the two makes so much more possible and increases capability, power, and usability tremendously. OK. Time for show and tell. And as with show and tell, we are going to start with *show*—meaning that we are going to show you examples of an array of objects and an object with arrays. Here is an array of objects:

### Array of objects

```
var arr = [
    {
        id: 1234,
        email: "myName@example.com",
        name: "John Doe"
    },
    {
        id: 2345,
        email: "myName2@example.com",
        name: "Jane Doe"
    },
    {
        id: 3456,
        email: "myName3@example.com",
        name: "Malcolm Doe"
    }
]
```

And here is an object with an array:

**Object with an array**

```
var obj = {
  id: 1234,
  name: "John Doe",
  email: "myName@example.com",
  relatives: [
    "Jane Doe",
    "Malcolm Doe",
    "Mindy Jo Doe"
  ]
}
```

As you can see, this greatly opens up the possibilities of using these for complex data structures and complex logic. This also is a great way to pass data between different contexts or through different API or lookup calls. As we get into the next couple of chapters, we will explore just how powerful arrays and objects are, as well as a combination of both, when dealing with automations in Marketing Cloud.

Next up, we want to go into custom-built **functions** inside of SSJS.

# Functions in SSJS

Have you ever run into the need to repeatedly use a section of code but it can't be run in a loop? Well, Marketing Cloud SSJS has the solution. It's a function! Functions are one of the foundational and fundamental aspects of SSJS and JavaScript in general.

Functions are basically subprograms that can be called by code external or internal (recursion) to the function. As with a program, a function is composed of a sequence of statements. The procedure of a function would be that a value is passed into the function and the function body (sequence of statements) is run against this input, which then returns a value related to the input.

A function is a first-class object, which basically means it's really just like any other variable. This essentially means that the following applies:

- Their returned values may be named as variables.
- They may be passed as arguments to procedures.

- They may be returned as the result of procedures.

- They may be stored in variables as a reference.

---

**First-class object**

This is also known as **First-class function**. A programming language is said to have First-class functions when functions in that language are treated like any other variable. For example, in such a language, a function can be passed as an argument to other functions, can be returned by another function, and can be assigned as a value to a variable.

This definition is sourced from Mozilla official documents. Learn more about first-class objects from: `https://developer.mozilla.org/en-US/docs/Glossary/First-class_Function`.

---

Now, this can be a bit murky, even to someone who is a JavaScript nerd, so to help give some context, we want to share some examples of what each of the preceding points means, as follows:

1. Here is an example of a function's returned values being *named as variables*:

```
Var foo = function() { //my function script }
console.log(foo); //runs function()
```

2. And here's an example of values being *passed as arguments to procedures*:

```
function callback (foo) {
    Foo();
}
Callback(function(){console.log('Successfully passed')})
```

3. Here's an example of values being *returned as the result of procedures*:

```
function(foo) {
    if(foo == 'pass') {
        return function(){ return 'It worked!'};
    } else {
        return function() { return 'It failed!'};
    }
}
```

4.  And here's an example of values being *stored in a variable for reference*:

```
var sum = function (a,b) { return (a+b) }
sum(4,4); //returns 8
```

Now, hopefully, we should all be on the same page with the capabilities and flexibilities of functions. As you can see in some of the preceding samples, functions can be insanely useful not just for the single script you are working on, but can also be used to be shared across multiple scripts. This is basically the definition of a **library**. Utilizing functions not only helps make your code more efficient but also helps when debugging, editing, or modifying.

Instead of having to go into the code and make your update in multiple places, you just make the change in the function, and then it is used in each place it's called out. This allows you to know exactly where to troubleshoot an error and also reduces the risk of missing code and not changing it to the new version.

We usually recommend making a library of functions that you create yourself for reference. We would say to put it into a content block or CloudPage to load in on each of your scripts or CloudPages. This allows you to have your own library of SSJS functions to use at will, greatly reducing the amount of extra coding, but the amount of added and unnecessary code is likely to cause slower processing and reduce efficiencies.

But having this library stored locally as a boilerplate allows you to copy and paste the correct functions across to the script or CloudPage you are working on and will greatly help optimize your workflow while also helping to automate your development, to an extent.

We will go into more detail about how amazing functions are over the next few chapters. They play a huge part in making SSJS a powerful Marketing Cloud automation tool. For now, let's move on to the `try...catch` statement.

# try...catch in SSJS

The `try` statement consists of a `try` block, which contains the script block that you want to try to run, which is encased inside of curly brackets, even if it is just a single statement. Then, after this, we must have either a `catch` block or a `finally` block. This then gives us three possible forms of the `try` statement, as follows:

- `try...catch`
- `try...finally`
- `try...catch...finally`

So, now we know what the `try` statement is and the three forms it can take, let's take a look at what a `catch` block is. A `catch` block contains different scripts or statements used only if an exception is thrown from the script inside the `try` block. Inside the `catch` block, you can add a variable inside the parenthesis to contain the exception that was thrown. If there are no exceptions, though, then everything in this block is skipped over.

A `finally` block contains code that will always be executed after the `try` block and `catch` block have been executed. The `finally` block will always execute regardless of whether there is an exception in your `try` block. This is a great place to put in cleanup code or similar code that must run regardless of the success of the `try` block or if an exception was thrown.

Let's take a look at what a `try...catch` statement looks like, as follows:

```
<script runat=server>
  Platform.Load("Core","1.1.1");

  var ret;
  try {
    var req = new
      Script.Util.HttpGet("https://www.example.com");
    var resp = req.send();
  } catch(e) {
    Write(Stringify(e));
  }
</script>
```

This code will try to do a **HyperText Transfer Protocol** (**HTTP**) GET request to the `https://www.example.com` address, and if it works, it will then store the results in the `resp` variable. If it fails, though, it will instead write a stringified version of the returned exception object to the page (this does not work for **Script activities**). This is a great way to help figure out what is erroring out, as most times on a CloudPage, it will only return a 500 error and give no details as to why it failed.

Another note around `try...catch` statements is that any variables declared and defined inside of them are considered local variables and cannot be used outside of that statement. In order to save the changes made in a `try...catch` statement, you need to set those variables globally prior to the statement, much like you will in a function. Now that we have covered the major native capabilities, let's dig into some of the proprietary libraries inside of Marketing Cloud SSJS.

## More capabilities than we can mention

There are a ton of different capabilities and features native to JavaScript that are part of Marketing Cloud's SSJS that we could discuss, such as `switch` **statements**, **eval**, **error handling**, and more. For now, we want to give a small overview of a platform-specific capability that will be coming up in more detail in the next chapter. For all the other capabilities, we would look at the official JavaScript documents or any of the tons of great blogs and forums out there. For now, let's learn more about WSProxy.

## WSProxy

WSProxy is essentially a JavaScript version of making SOAP API calls within Marketing Cloud that receive and return using JSON objects and arrays. This helps to simplify and optimize API calls to platform objects to get and interact with the data and content stored there. We can tell you that this is one of the best features that have ever been released for Marketing Cloud developers.

Now that we have a strong overview of what SSJS can do, let's dig into an example **Script activity** utilizing SSJS.

# A real-life example implementation

So, now that we have a good understanding of SSJS in Marketing Cloud, let's take a real-life example to run through. Next is a script that you can run inside automation to create a log of the queues inside your triggered sends. Now, to help ensure it only captures those that are relevant, we will be placing a minimum number queued in order for it to be considered a *failure* and be logged.

We are sharing the full file inside of a GitHub repository for easy access here: `https://github.com/PacktPublishing/Automating-Salesforce-Marketing-Cloud/tree/main/Chapter06`. You will notice that this block utilizes arrays, objects, functions, and WSProxy. Because of the length and complexity of the script, we will be breaking it out into sections to explain it.

## Setup

So, basically, you would put the GitHub script inside of a **Script activity** in Automation Studio, set it in automation, and have it run hourly. It will then grab the triggered sends that have a queued value that is above 500 and store it in a DE. Now, as a note, it will not upsert to the DE if there were no *failures*, so it will not bog down the log DE with unnecessary empty entries.

In order to use this inside your SFMC instance, you will need to create a DE to hold the log data. For the sake of the easiest storage possible, we will be just using one field to hold a stringified array listing the *failed* triggered send definitions and their queues. Here's what you need in order to set up this DE:

- **Data Extension Name**: myQueryQueue_LogDE

- **Data Extension External Key**: myQueryQueue_LogDE

- **Data Extension Fields and Properties**: These are listed in the following table:

| NAME | DATA TYPE | LENGTH | PRIMARY KEY (PK) | NULLABLE | DEFAULT |
|------|-----------|--------|------------------|----------|---------|
| MID | Number | | Y | | |
| TimeStamp | Date | | Y | | |
| QueueAlertArrayStr | Text | MAX | | Y | |

Table 6.1 – Fields and properties in myQueryQueue_LogDE DE

Then you can go back and reference this DE periodically to verify time periods where your triggered sends may be queueing up more than they should be or if there are any issues where the trigger starts to fail and queues up instead of erroring.

Now, let's dig into each part, starting with the functions.

# Functions

The functions are a great place to start as they are the workhorse of the script. Now, in this case, we did not need to have these built out as functions as they are only being called once. As stated earlier, though, we like to create functions whenever and wherever we can because of the ability to reuse them easily. The first function we are going to look at is the getTSDKeys function.

## getTSDKeys function

As you can see in the following code snippet taken from the full block of code, the function is actually pretty simple. The function utilizes an input (the midpoint of the **business unit (BU)** you want to look into) to run a WSProxy call to the TriggeredSendDefinition SOAP object to gather CustomerKey (also known as the external key) of each triggered send definition in that account. This being said, in the current state, it will only return up to 2,500 triggered sends, so it is recommended to pass in a filter or create pagination if you have more than 2,500 triggers.

Let's take a look at the code again to remind ourselves:

```
function getTSDKeys(mid) {

    /* Set ClientID */
    if (mid) {

        prox.setClientId({ "ID": mid }); //Impersonates the BU

    }

    var cols = ["CustomerKey", "TriggeredSendStatus"];
    var res = prox.retrieve("TriggeredSendDefinition",
        cols, filter);

    return res;

}
```

As you may have noticed, this function does not set a new WSProxy initiation on each run. This is because it is initiated in the global variables, and to limit processing power and increase efficiency and performance, we keep reusing the same initiation. The rest is pretty straightforward, with `prox.setClientId` setting the correct BU environment (this only works from the parent BU to the child BU) and then the execution of the call.

Next up, we will look into the `getTSDQueue` function, which is a bit more complex than the `getTSDKeys` function.

## getTSDQueue function

The following code snippet will show the `getTSDQueue` function taken from the full code block we shared previously. This code is used to gather the number of queued individuals for that specific triggered send definition. This is handled through WSProxy as well, hitting the `TriggeredSendSummary` SOAP object.

Let's look at the code for this function outside the context of the rest of the **Script activity**, as follows:

```
function getTSDQueue(customerKey) {

  /* Set ClientID */
  if (mid) {

    prox.setClientId({ "ID": mid }); //Impersonates the BU

  }

  var cols = ["CustomerKey","Queued"];
  var filter = {
      Property: "CustomerKey",
      SimpleOperator: "Equals",
      Value: customerKey
  };

  var res = prox.retrieve("TriggeredSendSummary",
    cols, filter);

  var queue = res.Results[0].Queued

  return queue;

}
```

Similar to the getTSDKeys function, this function does not set a new WSProxy initiation on each run to limit processing power and increase efficiency and performance, and also uses prox.setClientId to set the correct BU environment.

The major difference, outside targeting different SOAP objects, is that this one uses a filter. This filter limits the results to a single data object—the one that matches customerkey we gathered from the previous function. This means that to get the queue number for each of the keys returned, you will need to loop and iterate through this function. It is also the reason why the returned variable queue returns a specific part of the results and not the whole thing, unlike the getTSDKeys function.

Now that we have finished with functions, let's take a look at the global variable setting.

# Global variables

This section of the code may be small, but it is highly important as it sets the stage for you to be able to execute the statements you set later inside the code block. Let's take a look at the variables first to refresh our memory:

```
// Global variables
var prox = new Script.Util.WSProxy();

var mid = 123456;
var failures = 0;
var allTriggers = 1; // All triggers in BU, or false (0) if
                     // want specific filters only

var alertArray = []
```

This is where we declare and initiate our WSProxy via the prox variable. It also is where we set the default for our two collection variables, alertArray and failures. This also sets whether we want all triggers from this account or if we want just specific ones. This logic is further down and will be addressed shortly. Each one of these variables is vital to the entire script, and if one were missing or set incorrectly, the whole script would fail.

Let's next take a look at the allTriggers or specific triggers' logic.

# allTriggers logic

This section of code is where we determine whether we will use an array of all the triggered send definitions or whether we only want to use specific ones we listed. This logic is based on the allTriggers global variable. If this is set to 1, or true, then we will use the getTSDKeys function and gather all the keys into an array. If not, then we will use the prepared array we have set in the else statement. By using specific customerkeys only, we also can set custom queue lengths to be included and used to test for *failure*.

Let's dive into the code taken from the full block shared previously to take a look, as follows:

```
if (allTriggers) {

  var tsdArray = getTSDKeys(mid);
  var length = tsdArray.Results.length;

} else {

  var tsdArray =
["TriggerA","TriggerB","TriggerC","TriggerD","TriggerE"]
// External Keys of the Triggers you want to check.

  var length = tsdArray.length;

  var maxQueueArray = [500,500,500,500,500];
// Enter max queue here. Can make an array as well, if
// different maxes per TSD

}

if (!maxQueueArray || maxQueueArray.length == 0) {

  var maxQueueDefault = 500; // Default for if not using
                             // maxQueueArray

}
```

As you may have noticed, there is a section after the `allTriggers` logic that focuses on the `maxQueue` variables. This is because we want to have a default amount set so that if there is no custom array of maximum number before being considered a failure, we still want to have a value to use in our comparison.

Let's move forward and examine the `for` loop that is iterating through and gathering the specific queue information.

# for loop

This is the part where the baker takes all the ingredients and actually makes the pie. Very exciting! As you can see here, the loop iterates through the `tsdArray` array set in the `allTriggers` logic we explored previously, starting at the 0 index and moving up to the total size of the array, all while incrementing by one for each run. There is a ton of information here, so let's review the code before diving in deeper, as follows:

```
for (i=0; i < length; i++) {

    if(allTriggers) {

        var customerKey = tsdArray.Results[i].CustomerKey

    } else {

        var customerKey = tsdArray[i]

    }

    var queued = getTSDQueue(customerKey);

    var queueArrLength = maxQueueArray.length;

// changes maxQueue to array value if exist and equal to i
    if (maxQueueArray.length > 0 &&
        maxQueueArray.length <= i) {

        var maxQueue = maxQueueArray[i];

    } else {

        var maxQueue = maxQueueDefault;

    }

    if (queued > maxQueue) {
```

```
//creates the failure object
var obj = {}
obj.customerkey = customerKey;
obj.queue = queued;

//pushes the failure obj to array
alertArray.push(obj)
failures += 1 //increases failure count

        }

    }
```

As you may have noticed, there is another reference to `allTriggers` here to gather the `customerKey` value. This is because the two arrays are formed differently, so to account for that, we need to specify them differently. After that, we grab the queued number from the function and then examine it against the `maxQueue` value. Now, to get the `maxQueue` value, we need to check whether it is a custom array or the default value; so, with a bit of logic, we determine that and set the correct number.

We will then check whether the queued number we received is higher than the `maxQueue` value, and if so, we then create a `failure` object that contains the `customerKey` value as well as the queue count and then push this into our `alertArray` collection array. This is then followed by increasing the count of `failures` by 1.

Finally, we will explore the last piece of the code—the upsert.

## The upsert

This one, as with the global variable sections, is small, but vital and powerful. Without this section of code, none of the rest would mean anything. This is where we actually take the information we have gathered and push it into a log DE that allows us to view it.

Let's take a look at the code, as follows:

```
if (failures > 0) {

   // Upserts into log DE
   var rows =
     Platform.Function.UpsertData("myQueryQueue_LogDE",
     ["MID","TimeStamp"], [mid,getDate()],
```

```
    ["QueueAlertArrayStr"], [Stringify(alertArray)])


}
```

As said previously, it's simple with a bit of logic and then a `Platform` library function to push the information into a DE. As to why logic is needed, well—if none of the triggers failed, there really is no reason to log this and potentially bog down your DE; instead, it's better to just assume that if there is no entry, then that means it passed. This is why it looks to see whether `failures` is above 0, as that value only increases if something is added to the `alertArray` array, as we saw previously.

We then use the `UpsertData` platform function to take the information we gathered and push a stringified version of the `alertArray` array into the DE. This allows you to view the values as well as to store the array in a JSON format so that you can grab it, parse it, and then use it in another context if needed.

## Summary

Well, that's it for the general overview. That is not to say our journey into **Script activities** and SSJS is done. Far from it. Like, super far from it!

In this chapter, we went over what a **Script activity** is and how it interacts with SSJS and AMPscript, which helped us to understand the basics of syntax on a **Script activity** in the Marketing Cloud. We followed this with an in-depth overview of SSJS in Marketing Cloud, which helped to give us the background inside of SSJS that we needed in order to learn about the capabilities of a **Script activity**. From there, we began to dive into the amazing capabilities that you have when using SSJS in a **Script activity**, such as utilizing Core functions to automate some repeatable tasks via scripts. Then, we ended our chapter with a real-life example of what a **Script activity** can be and how it was built.

In the next chapter, we will be diving into API capabilities in SSJS as well as **Script activities** in general. This is where we will dive into WSProxy, what the SOAP API is, what the REST API is, and how to use each of them. We know we said SSJS was our favorite, but we think SSJS combined with APIs is our real favorite. Are you as excited as we are? Let's move on to the next chapter and see!

# 7

# The Power of In-Step APIs

Now that you've been introduced to the magic of **Script activities**, we wanted to bring you to the next level up – **in-step API execution**. What exactly is in-step **application programming interface** (**API**) execution? For us to define that and how to utilize it to make your Marketing Cloud capabilities so much more powerful, we need to cover the following topics:

- *What are APIs?* A very quick general overview of APIs.

- *The REST and SOAP APIs in Marketing Cloud*: An overview of the two types of API (**REST** and **SOAP**) that are available inside Marketing Cloud.

- *How are the native scripting functions and WSProxy best used in the platform?* Here, we will look at some of the simpler, native functions in the platform around API calls, as well as at utilizing WSProxy, which is one of the easier ways to handle in-platform API calls.

- *How can we utilize the Script.Util functions to make REST API calls?* Here, we will look at ways to go outside the limits of the native functions and utilize all the available methods when you're making your API calls, both internal and external.

- *The capabilities and power of sending API to an external service?* Although there is a ton of internal capabilities that APIs unlock, they also open up the possibility for integrations and external influence on the platform.

- *How does this all come together?* In this section, we will take a deep dive into why all of this is important and powerful.

The APIs in Marketing Cloud open up doors that you may not have even known existed. We can equate the difference in the capability to that of going from AMPscript to **server-side JavaScript (SSJS)**. Sure, AMPscript is powerful and performant, but SSJS can do a ton more. We can see that SSJS is limited compared to what you can retrieve or accomplish with API calls. Even just using WSProxy opens up all kinds of new possibilities.

This is a good segue into our first introductory topic – what are APIs?

# What are APIs?

So, without going into the heavy technical aspects, APIs are a way for applications to exchange data and functionality. A good example is a telephone call. Let's imagine that we have Joe and Judith who are best friends and looking to get together to hang out later today. Now, neither one of them has talked yet to see whether the other is available to play, so the first thing they need to do is get in contact with each other.

For them to communicate and make a plan, they need to talk. To do that, Joe calls Judith on her phone. Judith then picks up the phone, recognizing it is Joe, and says *hi* and waits to hear Joe respond on the other end. After they say their salutations, they work to catch up on how each of them has been doing since the last time they talked. Then, they get to the crux of the call: Joe brings up when Judith will be available to hang out with him at his place. Judith says she is free to come over in 30 minutes. From there, they both say goodbye and hang up.

This was just a perfect example of an API call. How? Let's take a look:

1. The first thing they do is get on the phone. This opens a line of communication between them – think of a server initiating a request to send across.

2. From there, they chat and do a handshake to authenticate they are who they say they are (they recognize their voices, call from a specific number, state their names, and similar indicators). This is the validation and authentication to ensure it is a secure process and the correct service.

3. After this, information is transferred (talking about their day, discussing when to hang out, what they want to play, and so on). This is where the payload of the request is shared with the context of the receiving service.

4. Next, we have the transaction, where the time and location of the meeting are decided. Now that all the necessary information and context have been shared between the services, the action that was requested is returned with a response.

5. Finally, they finish communicating and continue separately. After the response, the services disconnect from each other as the transaction is complete.

At this point, we have a general idea of what it is and how it works, but why would we need to have API calls? API calls allow never-before-seen levels of access across related resources while also retaining things such as security and control. Through this and the speed they offer, APIs have become a very valuable and almost indispensable part of modern business. To understand why we need to have API calls, we want to go over some of the major benefits they offer:

- **Improved connection**: With the massive amounts of cloud applications, servers, and services out there, creating a bridge to connect these allows for better integration so that each disconnected application can seamlessly communicate with each other.

- **Robust data capabilities**: With the strength, speed, and flexibility that is offered by APIs, you can take significant amounts of data and transfer it into new systems or applications at a volume and speed that is not likely to be matched elsewhere. It also takes the data and reduces the number of contexts it has to shift through, including formatting as a data file (CSV, TXT, XLS, and so on) and then transferring that file through a couple of FTP environments and import/transfer processes.

- **Protection and security**: This is probably the biggest selling point of APIs. The level of encryption, protection, authentication, and more that you can utilize in APIs to protect your data is quite astounding. As with all things, this is not irrefutable, but it can provide stronger protection and accurate transfers compared to most of the other available options.

- **Increases the path to innovations**: With the more connections and more paths available, the more options and new architecture and processes we can build. This allows us to explore and innovate to find new best practices and custom solutions.

There are a ton of things surrounding APIs and the technical processes, procedures, and methods, but a good portion of that is not relevant to our discussion around API usage in Salesforce Marketing Cloud. To that extent, we are going to explain the two different types of API that are available in Marketing Cloud.

# The REST and SOAP APIs

Some of the Marketing Cloud developers that have been in the platform for many years may remember that there was a third option for API in Marketing Cloud – XML. Now, rightly so, when we say that, you should shudder with horror as it was not only one of the most antiquated and overly complex API types, but it was, by far, a security nightmare. Thankfully, this option has been retired and is no longer an option.

Now, we are left with just two different types of API in Marketing Cloud – SOAP and REST. Let's take a moment to introduce what each is. Note that we will only be going over how it relates to Marketing Cloud via the HTTP protocol – there is a lot beyond what each type can do:

- **SOAP API**: **SOAP** stands for **Simple Object Access Protocol**, which is a messaging standard protocol system. SOAP utilizes XML to declare its messages and relies on XML schemas and other technologies concerning structure.

- **REST API**: **REST** stands for **REpresentational State Transfer**, which is a set of architectural constraints, not a protocol or standard. This allows for easier implementation and usage.

Inside Marketing Cloud, these are mostly different in terms of their capabilities, with the REST API being the one that interacts with the more current and *new* functions and capabilities, whereas the SOAP API is more in line with the classic `ExactTarget` age stuff. Before we dive too deep into these APIs and how they work inside Marketing Cloud, let's look at the authentication that's required for interacting with Marketing Cloud.

## Authentication

In the past, there were three ways you could authenticate an API call in Marketing Cloud:

- Username/password
- Legacy package OAuth
- OAuth 2.0 enhanced packages

Now, although more options is usually a good thing, in this case, the options were leaving open security risks and causing issues with the scope of permissions and capabilities. Due to these security risks, the first two options have been severely limited or completely turned off. Let's dig into the first option.

## Username and password authentication

The username and password authentication methods were only available in the SOAP API. It was not a possibility for the REST API. This was one of the original authentication methods from many years ago and was based on security protocols and protections from years ago.

This option sounds like it should be secure, right? That is how you log in to most websites, including bank accounts and other highly secure environments. Well, in those cases, this is usually because as the information is being transported over a call to the other secure environments, it is encrypted and obfuscated in a way that makes it hard for anyone to gain access to this information.

However, since the username and password were passed inside the XML body of the SOAP call, a lot of that capability is not possible, which means it is much more vulnerable for malicious people to gain access to it. Not only this, but if someone were to take this, they would not only be able to make API calls but also log in to your Marketing Cloud account and access the UI.

We can see a big risk here, right? As the world has become more and more sophisticated and malicious people have kept getting smarter and more capable, the less secure this has become. This is why the username and password authentication option is no longer allowed to be utilized without special permissions. Next, we will look at the original authentication method for the REST API.

## Legacy package OAuth token

To be fair, when this came out, it was not named Legacy – it was just the **package OAuth token** authentication process. Legacy has been added to differentiate between this process and the new OAuth token process.

This process was much more secure than the username and password process as it utilized a specially made *package* that contained `clientId` and `clientSecret` to act as the username and password for authentication. You would take these values and pass them inside a JSON payload to the authentication endpoint, which then returns an access token that is used for the following calls.

As we mentioned previously, the authentication call is completely separate, so the ID and secret are not passed inside every call. Reducing the number of times it is transmitted reduces the opportunity and risk of a malicious person being able to steal this information. Now, you may be wondering, it stops the ID and secret, but what about that token? Well, to limit the viability of it, they have the token only be valid for a limited window (around 60 minutes). After that, the token is expired and is no longer viable.

Now, this is certainly leaps and bounds above the username and password, but it is now considered a legacy for a reason. There are a few different risks and security holes inside of this that are taken care of with the next option.

## OAuth 2.0 enhanced packages

Over the years, security and protection became a higher priority as the malicious few kept getting more and more sophisticated, and more businesses were moving over to a digital format. This combination opens up more targets with higher values, which makes it more tempting for those talented people to turn to malicious means to get rich quickly.

To help limit some of the new threats and better lower risks, Marketing Cloud introduced a new process for creating OAuth tokens in its packages. This new enhanced package also introduced the concept of **tenant-specific endpoints** for utilizing APIs.

### Tenant-specific endpoints

Before this, you would use a generic API endpoint that was only different based on the stack you were on. A **stack** in Marketing Cloud meant a server stack or the location of the servers that were hosting your instance of Salesforce Marketing Cloud. Now, this is dangerous as it means all those who have an instance in that stack come in at the same place – they just use a different key to open their specific door. This gets someone malicious most of the way to being able to gain access to someone else's stuff.

For example, let's view this like safety deposit boxes inside a bank, but at a place where millions, if not billions, of dollars could be stored inside some of the boxes. You have a box, so you can get through the door and into the room that contains all the boxes. Now, all you need to do is covertly start testing to find the keys for the other boxes. If you do this covertly, this can give you unfettered access to all kinds of important information, as well as the capability to completely demolish or destroy the entire account and be able to do so pretty much undetected. Next, we will go over the **permission scope** capabilities

### Integration type and permission scope

Although technically two separate aspects, they were similar enough to combine into a single section. First, let's look at what an integration type is. The integration options in Marketing Cloud are as follows:

- **Server-to-Server**: This is a direct connection through two secure environments.
- **Web App**: This can be described as a middleware solution that's sitting in a more public setting but still able to store a clientSecret value.
- **Public App**: This is almost completely publicly facing and cannot store anything that can't be viewed by a user.

As you go through this list, the process to get an authentication token becomes harder and more obfuscated. This includes an extra endpoint being required for the web and public app to validate authorization of your application before looking for an access token.

This layer, on top of tenant-specific endpoints, gives many awesome levels of security that bring Marketing Cloud up to a level of protection it should be at. But this isn't done. From there, they also included the capability to set permission scope – not just on the package, but also on the call. So, by doing this, you can have a package with unfettered access, but have the call you are making to get an access token limit that access to just the specific need. This will mean that if someone steals that token, they will only have partial access to do anything until the token times out. Speaking of timeouts, they have shortened this window down to 20 minutes to lessen the timeframe where someone can utilize any ill-gotten tokens.

Now that we have a good understanding of the authentication capabilities, let's explore the SOAP API inside Marketing Cloud.

# The SOAP API in Marketing Cloud

The **SOAP API** in Marketing Cloud only interacts with things you would find inside Automation Studio and Email Studio. The other Studio platforms will require you to use the *REST API*. Now, although it is limited to just these two, this does not mean that the SOAP API is not robust or powerful! Email Studio includes things such as **Triggered Emails**, **Data Extensions**, **All Subscribers**, **Email Sends**, and **Lists**, while Automation Studio includes things such as **Automations**, **SQL Query activities**, and **Filter activities**.

The SOAP API is designed to allow access to not just the capabilities of the UI, but also the capabilities of administration and tracking, as well as data extraction. By using **methods** and **objects**, the SOAP API can interact with and integrate with Marketing Cloud.

## Methods

The first part of exploring what the SOAP API can do in Marketing Cloud is to explore the available methods. Unlike the REST API, SOAP is only sent across the HTTP method of **POST**. To help differentiate this action, methods are passed inside the envelope or header that can show the specified action request.

To be honest, we have not even used half of these methods to perform our SOAP API calls, and we have been working with the API for years. To that extent, do not get overwhelmed by this list of possible methods as only around four or five of them are used regularly:

- `Configure`
- `Create`
- `Delete`
- `Describe`
- `Execute`
- `Extract`
- `GetSystemStatus`
- `Perform`
- `Query`
- `Retrieve`
- `Schedule`
- `Update`
- `VersionInfo`

Out of this list, the ones to pay the most attention to are `Create`, `Delete`, `Describe`, `Retrieve`, and `Update`. Although some of the others, such as `Perform`, `Configure`, and `Execute`, do have capabilities tied to them, they are not utilized very often, so you will not need them as much.

Each method has specific parameters and responses that are included with it. For this API call to be validated, the envelope must meet these required parameters. Next, we will provide a quick overview of the objects in the Marketing Cloud SOAP API.

## Objects

Methods are the action part and the request aspect, while objects are the targets that hold all the information. These objects contain all the information or functionality to complete or return the action or data you need.

There are a plethora of SOAP objects available in Marketing Cloud. We will not bore you by listing every single one as there are legitimately around 262 documented ones and at least a dozen more undocumented ones as well. Instead, we are going to group these objects into *families* and provide a general overview of the possibilities.

## Account

This family is related to the actual account level of your Marketing Cloud environment, meaning you can create users, get business unit names or IDs, and so on.

## Automation

This family is related to the automation processes inside Automation Studio. From here, you can get the overall status, per-run stats, an overview of the automation process, as well as interact, start, pause, edit, and create automation processes.

## Automation activities

This family is related to activities inside Automation Studio (**Extracts**, **File Transfer**, **Filter**, **Imports**, **Query Activity**, and others) and allows you to interact with these capabilities.

## Data extension

This family is related to data extensions, giving you full access to retrieve, create, delete, and more. This includes at a subscriber or row level, field level, or even overall data extension object level.

## Emails

This family is related to all things regarding email messaging. This includes sending and creating send definitions, scheduling, and more.

## Events

This family is related to the tracking events objects. This includes **Click**, **Open**, **Sent**, **NotSent**, **Unsubscribe**, and more. These objects tend to be similar to the data views or tracking extract options.

## Profiles and classifications

This family is related to the definitions of the sender profiles and classifications that are used when sending messages. You can create, edit, delete, or otherwise manipulate these definitions.

## Subscribers and lists

This family is related to the subscriber model in Marketing Cloud. This model includes lists. Through this family, you can interact at a macro or micro (row) level through creation, deletion, updates, and so on.

### Suppression and unsubscribes

This family is related to the suppression and unsubscribing process. This family will give you control over ensuring those that you do not want to send to are not sent to.

### Triggered sends

This family is related to the triggered send capabilities in Marketing Cloud. We have this separate from the email family as this is focused on being utilized by APIs for a 1:1 real-time delivery, while the other is more focused on batch and scheduled sends.

Now that we have a good overview of the SOAP API's methods and objects, we can get a good feeling for what it is capable of. Now, let's move on and explore the REST API's capabilities in Marketing Cloud.

# The REST API in Marketing Cloud

The REST API in Marketing Cloud is very powerful and has been designed to interact with all of the newer Studio platforms. This includes, but is not limited to, Journey Builder, Mobile Studio, Transactional Messaging, and Content Builder. The REST API utilizes a method combined with a specific URL, instead of an object. Although they both use methods, they use different types of methods. Let's take a look at the methods in the REST API.

### Method of REST (API)

Like the SOAP API, REST utilizes different methods to determine the type of action that's performed. The difference is that the REST API utilizes **HTTP methods**, such as the following:

- PATCH: This sends an encrypted payload to interact with the target for the partial update option only.

- POST: This sends an encrypted payload to interact with the target for the new creation option only.

- GET: You can use this to retrieve data or information. No body is passed in the request but it can pass parameters in the URL.

- DELETE: This sends an encrypted payload to interact with the target for the deletion option only.

- PUT: This sends an encrypted payload to interact with the target for overwrite updates, but if that object does not exist, then PUT may create it instead.

As you can see, these methods are very different from the SOAP methods. In general, the actions are the same, just simplified down to the rawest level. Now that we know the methods, let's explore the endpoints that the methods interact with.

## The end(point) of your REST (API)

Similar to how SOAP has a ton of different objects, REST has a ton of different options for **endpoints**. To help make things easier, what we are going to do is provide a list of the different groupings that they have in the official documents and then list each of the endpoint groups, including some undocumented ones for reference. First, let's explore the different endpoint families that are listed in the documentation, starting with Content Builder.

### Content Builder API

The great thing about Content Builder is that it allows you to use content across all different mediums and channels, which means that there is a reduction in duplication or multiple instances of content or **assets**. The term *asset* is what Marketing Cloud uses to refer to all the different types of content stored inside Content Builder.

The reason all of this is relevant is that through this API, you can interact with each of these assets and fully automate your content management inside Marketing Cloud. This API allows you to create, update, delete, retrieve, query, and even publish assets. It is by far one of the most refined and robust API endpoint families available in Marketing Cloud and one of our favorites to work with. Next, we will explore the Journey Builder API endpoint family.

### Journey Builder API

Journey Builder is heralded and lauded as the future of Marketing Cloud and with the vast improvements that have been made over the years, it certainly seems to be true enough. Journey Builder is a strong one-to-one messaging service with a focus on customizing and personalizing messaging across multiple channels.

The API family allows you to interact with Journey Builder in quite amazing ways. You can interact with almost every piece of a journey through the API, including building a journey, firing events, pausing the journey, and accessing analytics and reporting. Although this is not as refined as what is available in Content Builder, it is still a very strong and awesome family of endpoints.

## GroupConnect Chat Messaging API

GroupConnect is something that we have not had a lot of experience with. We know that its capabilities are hugely valuable and we have played with it quite a few times. But since it provides more service-based marketing, it is not something that comes up very often for your average client. GroupConnect is Marketing Cloud's integration with your Facebook Messenger and LINE application. Much like Mobile Studio, there is some setup and connection that needs to be made to integrate this capability.

The API endpoint family here seems to be very useful, with a few known limitations, and from our experience in it, it was pretty easy to use. This API family allows you to automate these messaging channels, similar to email or SMS, by taking data from the system and placing it in a templated message that is then personalized with that information and sent to the user. This is sort of like if a shipment has gone out or a payment has been received.

## MobileConnect API

Now, this family is defined as just MobileConnect in the documentation, but we like to include MobilePush inside of it as well. They are both in the same studio in Marketing Cloud, so it would only make sense to combine them here. MobileConnect is focused around the SMS message channel, whereas MobilePush is focused on app-based push notifications.

The APIs here provide nearly full integration with your Mobile Studio capabilities in both applications. There is even a **software development kit** (**SDK**) for a few languages that are available for these APIs. Although we highly prefer the Content Builder API family, this one is highly robust and refined. It also offers a plethora of capabilities.

## Transaction Messaging API

The Transaction Messaging API family is quite astonishing. It introduces a level of flexibility, speed, and real-time interaction that is unmatched by any other process in the application. Transactional Messaging is essentially a transactional, non-commercial messaging service that strips all the unnecessary processing and procedures, such as suppression or priority level, to ensure as fast and efficient a messaging process as possible.

The other awesome thing this family opens up is the **Event Notification Service** options. This is something that allows an unprecedented level of immediate notifications and alerts around events in Marketing Cloud.

## Event Notification Service

Right now, this service is only applicable to the Transactional Messaging API family, both email and SMS, but it is incredibly powerful and useful for those who need to make real-time decisions to alert and to receive. These alerts are provided via a **webhook**, which is a listening service that is hosted on a web service – this cannot be hosted in a **CloudPage**.

---

**Einstein Recommendations API**

As you may have noticed, we did not mention this endpoint family. This is because these endpoints exist in the `igodigital.com` domain and not the same Marketing Cloud domain as the rest, so we consider it to be an external API. Since we are concentrating on just internal API endpoints, we have not included it here. The **igodigital** API is a very niche group of endpoints, so there is not much general usage that could be shared in this book around it.

---

## Endpoint groups

Now that you have looked through the API families, we are going to share the different endpoint groups that are available at the time of writing. For each, we will specify their names, discovery endpoints, and provide brief descriptions:

- **Address**: `/address/v1/rest` *(mostly documented)* is pretty much used only for validating email and phone numbers in Marketing Cloud.

- **Asset**: `/asset/v1/rest` *(mostly documented)* interacts with Content Builder and all of its assets.

- **Auth v1**: `https://{{subdomain}}.auth.marketingcloudapis.com/v1/rest` *(mostly documented)* groups legacy authentication endpoints.

- **Auth v2**: `https://{{subdomain}}.auth.marketingcloudapis.com/v2/rest` *(mostly documented)* groups new authentication endpoints.

- **Automation**: `/automation/v1/rest` *(undocumented)* groups endpoints related to Automation Studio, including activities and automation objects.

- **Contacts**: `/contacts/v1/rest` *(partially documented)* focuses on Contact Builder capabilities and interactions.

- **Data**: `/data/v1/rest` *(partially documented)* focuses on Salesforce data, data extensions, contacts, attribute groups and more.

- **Email**: `/email/v1/rest` *(partially documented)* concentrates on lists, filters, and subscribers, and not really on emails.

- **Guide**: `/guide/v1/rest` *(partially documented)* focuses on Email Studio capabilities and lets you gain access to some things that normally were only accessible via the SOAP API.

- **Hub**: `/hub/v1/rest` *(partially documented)* is a fairly widespread grouping. It covers areas such as **Campaigns**, **Contacts**, **Attribute Groups**, **Data Extensions**, **Email Previews**, **Tags**, and more.

- **Interaction**: `/interaction/v1/rest` *(mostly documented)* is an endpoint that is completely focused on Journey Builder capabilities.

- **Legacy**: `/legacy/v1/rest` *(undocumented)* is a treasure trove, but we would never look to use any of these in anything related to production. We would list this as high-risk, unstable, and confusing. This group also has some endpoints that require internal authentication to work – so, some of the endpoints are useless to us. That being said, there are so many amazing and useful endpoints in this group to explore.

- **Messaging**: `/messaging/v1/rest` *(partially undocumented)* is tied to the messaging options in Marketing Cloud. It includes capabilities to create, send, and track message definitions, including Email, MobileConnect, MobilePush, and GroupConnect, as well as some RMM interaction.

- **Platform**: `/platform/v1/rest` *(partially undocumented)* is mostly focused on account settings, token and endpoint settings, subscriptions, apps, setup, and Audience Builder.

- **Push**: `/push/v1/rest` *(partially undocumented)* is related to actions and capabilities in MobilePush.

- **SMS**: `/sms/v1/rest` *(partially undocumented)* is related to SMS sends and MobileConnect.

Now, to be fair, there are a couple of other experimental and internal endpoints that we could list, but these will be of no real use for you as they either require authentication beyond what an end user can gather or are so highly unstable that it's a risk to use them for anything at all. With this background, we can see the huge benefit that utilizing these API capabilities directly inside Marketing Cloud through CloudPages or **Script activities**. Now, let's start looking at how we can utilize these API calls inside Marketing Cloud.

# SFMC native functions and WSProxy

Let's look at the functions and capabilities we can use to call these API calls. Now, the good news is that there is capability in both languages to do this. But we would very highly recommend doing most, if not all of your API calls, inside SSJS as the capabilities, functions, error handling, and parsing are so much stronger and more reliable than AMPscript for this. That being said, let's explore the native functions that are built in with an explicit HTTP method.

# AMPscript

In AMPscript, there is a built-in capability to natively handle SOAP API sends (internal). For the REST API, you can use the HTTP functions to make those calls. Outside of that, the API capability is near non-existent as this is not the purpose that AMPscript was built for. For now, let's dig into the functions and get a feel for how they are best utilized.

## SOAP API functions

These functions had to be created because AMPscript has no native way to handle arrays or objects, which is a big part of how the SOAP API is built. These functions can be confusing to jump into, but they are very singular in focus, so once you understand how they work, it is very simple to master them.

This functionality allows you to create objects and arrays, as well as utilize each of the SOAP methods, but it is limited to `Create`, `Delete`, `Execute`, `Perform`, `Retrieve`, and `Update`. One thing to note is that these are very verbose, so what may be a quick couple of lines elsewhere could take 4 or 5 times as many when you're using these functions.

A great example of this is the following script, which is used to send a **Triggered Send Email** using AMPscript and the SOAP API:

```
%%[
SET @emailaddr = "sample@example.com"
SET @subkey = 'Sub123456'
SET @tsObj = CreateObject("TriggeredSend")
SET @tsDefObj = CreateObject("TriggeredSendDefinition")
SET @tsSubObj = CreateObject("Subscriber")
SetObjectProperty(@tsDefObj, "CustomerKey", "MyTriggeredSend")
SetObjectProperty(@tsObj, "TriggeredSendDefinition", @tsDefObj)
SetObjectProperty(@tsSubObj, "EmailAddress", @emailaddr)
```

```
SetObjectProperty(@tsSubObj, "SubscriberKey", @subkey)

AddObjectArrayItem(@tsObj, "Subscribers", @tsSubObj)

SET @tsCode = InvokeCreate(@tsObj, @tsMsg, @error)
]%%
```

This script utilizes the `InvokeCreate` function, along with the `Object` and `Array` functions, to build out a SOAP API call and then execute it inside AMPscript. Next, we will dive into the HTTP functions that are mostly used for the REST API.

## HTTP functions

Now, technically, you could use the `POST` functions for SOAP if you wanted, but it would be a lot of work. In general, the HTTP functions in AMPscript are used for REST API interaction. In general, these are pretty self-explanatory in terms of what they do as the HTTP method they use is part of the function name. So, we won't go into too much detail here on each. Here is a list of the options:

- `HTTPGet`
- `HTTPPost`
- `HTTPPost2`

As you can see, this is pretty self-explanatory, except for `HTTPPost2`. The major difference is that `HTTPPost2` allows you to return a result that is not 200 without throwing an exception, whereas `HTTPPost` does not. It also has a parameter value where you can set a variable to return the status of the HTTP request.

The following is a quick example of using the `HTTPPost2` function to `POST` data to an outside REST API endpoint:

```
%%[
set @payload = '{
"ID":111213,
"FirstName":"Gor",
"LastName":"Tonington",
"TotalAmt":125
}'

set @postrequest = HTTPPost2("https://myAPIURL.
```

```
com","application/json", @payload, true)
]%%
```

Now, we know this seems short, but that is because the native built-in capabilities of AMPscript are very utilitarian and basic. This is not a bad thing – again, this kind of scripting is not what the language was built to do. Concerning most needs around messaging and content, these should allow you to make the necessary calls. Now, let's explore SSJS and see whether that is any different in terms of native capabilities in Marketing Cloud.

# Server-side JavaScript

Note that we are not including special functions, such as WSProxy, as native capabilities and instead concentrating on the Platform and Core capabilities. As we mentioned previously, in SSJS, there are two different libraries with functions inside them. Each has different API capabilities.

## Platform

The platform is the more default type library for SSJS and in that way, it is very similar to AMPscript in native functions. In that vein, the functions are identical for API usage as they are in AMPscript. There are some nuances in how each functions, but in general, they are the same. The major difference is that SSJS does not have an HTTPPost2 function natively. There are some awesome capabilities related to API in Platform, but as stated earlier, they are not what we would define as *native*. To that extent, we are going to move on to Core.

## Core

Core has a couple of capabilities, but it is mostly filled with special made functions to interact with and gather information from SOAP API objects without you having to make the API call. This is the main function of the Core library. Outside that, it does not have any way to interact with the SOAP API outside a completely manually built call that's pushed inside of POST. Core only has two options when it comes to the REST API:

- HTTP.Get
- HTTP.Post

Each is a fairly simple version of the Platform or AMPscript versions. So, rather than going into detail on these, we want to move on to what is, at least in our opinion, the best way to interact with the SOAP API in-platform ... WSProxy!

# WSProxy

WSProxy is a new functionality that was built into SSJS and is much more aligned with the platform and simpler to use than the other SSJS methods. Note that WSProxy is native to SSJS, but we did not include it as a native function because our intended meaning was concerning the libraries, not just the language.

The difference in speed of this function in comparison to most other SOAP-related inline capabilities is astounding. Not only that, but it natively uses JavaScript objects and **JSON** for request and response, allowing for easy parsing and creation.

WSProxy allows you to create the arrays and objects that are needed by the **SOAP XML** through JSON instead, which means that almost any SOAP API can be made using an external service within the platform. The available SOAP actions are Create, Update, Delete, Retrieve, Perform, Configure, Execute, and Describe.

Let's look at an example WSProxy call:

```
//Creates new object(s) inside of the identified SOAP Object
function createGeneric(soapObjName, contentJSON, mid) {
    //example soapObjName: "DataExtension"
    //example contentJSON Object: { "CustomerKey": custkey,
    //"Name": name, "Fields": fields };
    //example contentJSON Array: [{ "CustomerKey": custkey,
    //"Name": name, "Fields": fields },{ "CustomerKey":
    //name, "Name": name, "Fields": fields }]
    //set default date (in a Data Extension) to
    //'Current Date': { FieldType: "Date", Name: "Field2",
    //DefaultValue: "getdate()" }

    if(mid) {
        prox.resetClientIds(); //reset previous settings
        // Set ClientID
        prox.setClientId({ "ID": mid });
    }

    var batch = isArray(contentJSON);

    if(batch) {
        var res = prox.createBatch(sopObjName,contentJSON);
```

```
    } else {
      var res = prox.createItem(sopObjName,contentJSON);
    }

    function isArray(arg) {
      return Object.prototype.toString.call(arg) ===
        '[object Array]';
    };

    return res;
  }
```

This code shows an example execution of WSProxy. Now, this code can be simplified to fewer lines, but what we provided here was a general-use SSJS function to perform a WSProxy create method on any object or input you want to push, including batch creation or impersonation.

Another great thing about WSProxy is that it utilizes your native authentication from your user to make these calls, meaning you do not need to provide any authentication calls or share any sensitive information when you're utilizing this function. Now, some may say, *But what if I want to interact with another business unit?* Well, the good news is that WSProxy allows you to impersonate different client IDs (requires permissions) and even different users, but only from a parent to a child, not lateral or upward.

A good rule of thumb to use is that if you have to use the SOAP API inside Marketing Cloud, then you should use WSProxy. As with all things, there are exceptions to that rule, but most of the time, it is the correct choice to make. Speaking of the best ways to make API calls, next, we will explore the **Script.Util** object.

# Script.Util for the REST API

Now, as some of you may be saying to yourselves (or yelling it at this book), *Hey! WSProxy is based on the Script.Util object!*, and you would be 100% right. That being said, though, as we already went over WSProxy before this section, we will explore the rest of the object as it relates to the REST API.

Even those who may be familiar with SSJS and the Platform library may be scratching their heads and wondering what this crazy person is talking about. But we promise you it is there in the documentation; it is just hidden inside the *Content Syndication* section. Inside this section, three objects ARE listed:

- `Script.Util.HttpResponse`
- `Script.Util.HttpRequest`
- `Script.Util.HttpGet`

As these objects and functions are fairly unknown, we are going to be spending a bit more time explaining them than we did the others. First, we will dig into the `HttpResponse` object.

## HttpResponse

This object is the return that's gathered from the `send()` method that's used in the other two objects. Note that this cannot work independently of either of the other two objects. As shown in the documentation, the following parameters are available for this object:

- **Content**: A string value containing the HTTP response's content
- **ContentType**: A string value indicating the content type that was returned
- **Encoding**: A string value indicating the encoding that was returned
- **Headers**: An object containing the HTTP response header collection that was returned
- **ReturnStatus**: An integer value containing the Marketing Cloud response
- **StatusCode**: An integer value containing the HTTP response status code that was returned

Let's consider a couple of things regarding the parameters we just listed. For instance, the `Content` parameter is returned as a **common language runtime (CLR)** object, which is not compatible with Marketing Cloud SSJS. So, to get that converted, you need to turn it into a string data type and then turn it into JSON format for easier parsing.

Another consideration is that certain business rules can affect your ability to use this object effectively. If you get errors such as `Use of Common Language Runtime (CLR) is not allowed`, then you will want to talk to Salesforce Support and your account representative to turn on any associated business rules related to CLR.

# HttpGet

This object is used to perform GET from the specified URL and interact with HTTP headers. Now, you may be wondering, how is this different from either of the other GET functions in SSJS? Let us tell you: it is a good one. This function will cache content for use in email sends. So, if you have the same content being pulled into an email, using this function will provide the requested content more efficiently because when the second email is processed at the end of the job, it will pull the content from the cache instead of running the method again and hitting the URL.

This call is also set up quite a bit differently than the native functions. This is set up similar to how you would fill any other object in SSJS, but you add properties via dot notation. This is different than utilizing the native functions that add the parameters, similar to JavaScript functions inside parentheses. Due to this type of setup, it does not run when you create the object – you need to utilize the send() method to execute the call. Let's take a quick look at the methods that are available for HttpGet:

- setHeader(): This adds a header to the GET request via name-value pairs. Adding a header will disable content caching.
- removeHeader(): This is a string value that shows the name of the header to remove from the GET request.
- clearHeader(): This removes all the custom headers from the GET request.
- send(): This performs the GET request.

There are also some additional properties that we can use with this object:

- retries: This is an integer that defines the number of times we should retry the call. The default is 1.
- continueOnError: This is a Boolean that's used to indicate whether the call returns an exception or continues. The default is false (it returns an exception).
- emptyContentHandling: This is an integer that defines how the return handles empty content.

Now, let's look at an example of this code:

```
<script runat="server">
Platform.Load("Core","1.1.1")

var url = "https://{{et_subdomain}}.rest.marketingcloudapis.
com/email/v1/rest"
```

```
var req = new Script.Util.HttpGet(url);
var resp = req.send();</script>
```

As you can see, it's a fairly simple call to make. But just because it is simple does not mean there are not some amazing custom things you can do with this call. The next object we are going to discuss is one of our favorite capabilities in SSJS as it allows unparalleled access to API capabilities.

# HttpRequest

`HttpRequest` is our favorite SSJS function, followed closely by WSProxy. Yes, you read that right – we like this more than the legendary WSProxy. This is because this is the gateway for connecting our two favorite things in SFMC – SSJS and the REST API. `HttpRequest` is a powerful method that allows you to make calls inside Marketing Cloud with a plethora of options, including setting the appropriate methods beyond just `GET` and `POST`.

This object and `HttpGet`, to some extent, are similar to the `xmlhttprequest` object in client-side JavaScript. Now, although similar, there are a ton of capabilities in `xmlhttprequest` that are not available inside `HttpRequest`. For instance, a lot of client-side interaction with the call, and using events such as `onclick`, are not allowed.

That aside, the general layout and parameter requirements are similar, so it's a good reference to help if you are having trouble with getting a method or parameter to not function correctly. As we mentioned previously, though, a lot of capabilities are not shared, so if you are looking for things that are not documented on `HttpRequest`, please expect a lot of failures.

As we mentioned earlier, the major drawback to utilizing this method is that it allows you to access methods outside of `GET` or `POST`. This gives you full access to the Marketing Cloud REST API library of endpoints within SSJS, removing the need to push these calls to an outside service. Here is a list of methods that are acceptable to `Script.Util.HttpRequest`:

- `GET`
- `DELETE`
- `HEAD`
- `OPTIONS`
- `PATCH`

- POST

- PUT

As you may have noticed, these are all the available methods, meaning there is no real limit to its capability there. Now, outside the HTTP method, the actual methods of this are identical to those in `HttpGet`, as described earlier, so rather than duplicate, we can just reference that previous section.

Another thing you may notice is that both `HttpRequest` and `WSProxy` seem to stem from the same object – `Script.Util`. To this extent, we like to look at `HttpRequest` as one of the precursors to `WSProxy` that helped pave the way for that amazing capability. Now, that being said, we do feel these are two very different capabilities and are not interchangeable, nor do they affect the effectiveness of each other. We view `HttpRequest` as a way to accomplish REST API calls; `WSProxy` does this for SOAP.

Unfortunately, `HttpRequest` is not as maximized as `WSProxy`, so it is not always as efficient. This means that it can run into issues when you're handling large volumes or frequency due to timeouts or similar errors. But since you should not be doing any heavy processing like this within Marketing Cloud, this should not come into play most of the time.

Now that we have covered the history, let's explore a sample of what it looks like (based on a Marketing Cloud REST call to the Content Builder API):

```
<script runat=server>
Platform.Load("core", "1.1.1");
var accessToken = {{yourToken}};
var url = 'https:// {{et_subdomain}}.rest.marketingcloudapis.
com/asset/v1/content/assets/{{ContentID}}'

var payload = '{{yourPayload}}';
var auth = 'Bearer ' + accessToken;

var req = new Script.Util.HttpRequest(url);
req.emptyContentHandling = 0;
req.retries = 2;
req.timeout = 30
req.continueOnError = true;
req.contentType = "application/json"
req.setHeader("Authorization", auth);
```

```
req.method = "PUT"; /*** You can change the method here ***/
req.postData = payload;


var resp = req.send();
</script>
```

As you can see, a lot is going on and there are a lot of customization options. Although most of them are pretty self-explanatory, let's provide a quick overview to explain what each means:

- `accessToken/auth`: This is the OAuth token you gathered previously from the Marketing Cloud Authentication endpoint.

- `url`: This is the complete URL endpoint of your API call.

- `payload`: This is the *body* of your call. Usually, this will be JSON for the REST API, but it can accept other formats and data types. This is only available for POST, PATCH, PUT, and so on.

- `req`: This object is used to house all the custom parameters and methods.

- `emptyContentHandling`: This is a Boolean that's used to determine whether the call continues without throwing an exception on the error.

- `retries`: This sets the number of retry attempts to make.

- `timeout`: This sets the length of time before the call times out.

- `continueOnError`: This is a Boolean that's used to determine whether the request continues, regardless of `non-fatal` errors.

- `contentType`: This defines the type of content in the payload.

- `setHeader`: This sets the name/value pair of a header in the `Request` call.

- `method`: This sets the HTTP method of the call.

- `postData`: This is where you push the `stringified` payload.

- `send()`: This executes the call on the `req` object.

> **Note on payload/postData**
>
> You must ensure that the payload is a string on submission; otherwise, it will error. This can be accomplished by using the server-side JavaScript `Stringify()` function if the payload is not already a string.

We now have a strong understanding of what options we can utilize inside Marketing Cloud, which is awesome! The question now, though, is why? Why do we need to know this and what is the benefit? Let's find out!

# Why is this important?

Why is the in-step API important to development in Marketing Cloud? Easy. Because they open up possibilities and capabilities that you would not be able to open up natively in scripting. This includes the following:

- Automating UI processes
- Creating, editing, and retrieving data and objects that are unavailable in scripting languages
- Finding innovative ways of self-integration and communication between business units and Enterprise editions
- Automating or scripting administrative or auditing tasks
- Interacting with capabilities and objects that are not normally accessible
- Interacting with external services for integration and interactive purposes

These are pretty huge benefits, right? Well, just making broad statements is easy – let's dive into the details and show you exactly how each is possible. The first step is to explore some thoughts on interacting with and integrating external services. Then, we will go over a few examples to help prove the previous list of benefits.

## External services

Now, most of this chapter and section of this book has been about utilizing the Marketing Cloud APIs inside **Script activities** and CloudPages, but another thing to note is that through `Script.Util.HttpRequest`, you can actually integrate and interact with outside REST API endpoints and collect information internally for use in Marketing Cloud.

Most of this capability is pretty much reliant on the outside service. Since there are a ton of nuances that are different from the internal stuff, this can lead to different approaches, such as the following:

- Authentication requirements
- URL layout
- QueryStrings

- Payload types

- Required headers

- Required content type

- The way the payload is delivered

Each of these differences will change the way you need to build and structure your call. However, the vast majority of the call will remain identical, so with a strong understanding of `Script.Util.HttpRequest`, you will be able to translate the requirements of the outside API call pretty easily into an SSJS call inside Marketing Cloud.

# Example 1

Have you ever had to sit there and repetitively copy and paste the same thing over and over again in Marketing Cloud? It can be a mind-numbing waste of time and skill. Luckily, everyone was right, as most of the time, there is an easier way to do this: through scripting and API calls! Whether it's adding data to a data extension, creating near-identical data extensions, or creating multiple query activities, we've got you covered.

We think the best way to show this is to show you how the REST API can assist with dealing with query activities. Although most of these are undocumented endpoints, they are insanely helpful for times when you need to make one-time bulk updates or create things.

### The create function

First, we will learn how to create a brand-new query activity inside Marketing Cloud via the REST API:

```
function createQuery(tenant,authToken,payload) {


    vvar url =  'https://' + tenant   +  '.rest.
marketingcloudapis.com/automation/v1/queries/';
    var req = new Script.Util.HttpRequest(url);


    req.emptyContentHandling = 0;
    req.retries = 2;
    req.continueOnError = true;
    req.contentType = "application/json"
    req.setHeader("Authorization", authToken);
```

```
    req.method = "POST";
    req.postData = Stringify(payload);

    var resp = req.send();

    var resultStr = String(resp.content);

    var resultJSON =
        Platform.Function.ParseJSON(String(resp.content));

    Write(resultStr);

    return resultJSON;
}
```

By using the preceding script (combined with a prerequisite authentication call to get authToken), you can create a query inside the corresponding business unit that is attached to the authentication token you use. All you would need to include are the following:

- tenant: The tenant subdomain that is provided for your enterprise and package.

- authToken: The token that's collected from the OAuth2 authentication process. You need to ensure it includes *Bearer* before the token itself.

- payload: This is the JSON object or array that contains all the information and details on what you want to create. It should not be ingested by the function as a string, but as an object or array.

To help provide a visual, the following is an example of what payload would look like for this REST API endpoint. This would be passed into the createQuery() function as the payload parameter:

### Example payload

```
{
    "name": "myQuery",
    "key": "myQuery",
    "description": "",
    "queryText": "select *\n FROM [myDE]",
```

```
    "targetName": "myQueryDE",
    "targetKey": "myQueryDE",
    "targetDescription": "",
    "targetUpdateTypeId": 0,
    "targetUpdateTypeName": "Overwrite",
    "categoryId": 123456,
    "isFrozen": false
}
```

As you can see, there is a lot inside the payload to fill out all the fields you would need to inside the WYSIWYG in the UI. The main thing to note is that the `queryText` part should not include any new lines in it. Instead, it should utilize the \n newline character for all the new lines in the SQL.

Using the example payload that aligns the query activity with a SQL query, a target data extension, a folder, or `categoryId` will create your query for you within seconds. Now, you can remove some of these things from the call if you do not have a value you want to use, or if you want it to go to the default, which can help reduce the level of effort. For instance, you can leave out all the parts except for the following:

```
{
    "name": "myQuery",
    "queryText": "select *\n FROM [myDE]",
    "targetKey": "myQueryDE",
    "targetUpdateTypeId": 0,
    "categoryId": 123456
}
```

This is the bare minimum payload that's needed to make the call. The resulting JSON will contain all the detailed information on the object that was created. You can store this elsewhere or parse through it to validate it was entered correctly.

One thing to note is that it is only a 1:1 query creation and that it cannot create in batches using arrays. However, this can introduce your queries being created programmatically via REST, which can help automate your query creation needs.

Now, creation is one thing, but what if, after you make it, you realize you chose the wrong data extension? It looks like you have a lot of queries to go into in the UI to go and make the same small change…right? Wrong!

## The update function

There is also a REST API endpoint that you can use to update your queries. The only thing you would need is `Query Object ID`; then, you can do a `PATCH` call to change whatever attribute or parameter you want:

```
function updateQuery(tenant,authToken,queryID,payload) {
    var url =  'https://' + tenant
  +  '.rest.marketingcloudapis.com/automation/v1/queries/'
  + queryID;

    var req = new Script.Util.HttpRequest(url);
    req.emptyContentHandling = 0;
    req.retries = 2;
    req.continueOnError = true;
    req.contentType = "application/json"
    req.setHeader("Authorization", authToken);
    req.method = "PATCH";
    req.postData = Stringify(payload);

    var resp = req.send();

    var resultStr = String(resp.content);
    var resultJSON =
       Platform.Function.ParseJSON(String(resp.content));

    return resultJSON;
}
```

You may have noticed that this one has an extra parameter in the function – `queryID`. This is because IN ORDER for you to edit your queries, you need to be able to define the one you want to edit. `queryID` is the way you can do this. This ID is the internal, read-only GUID that is created in Marketing Cloud to identify the corresponding SQL query activity object.

This function utilizes the same payload as `create`, so feel free to use that information when you're building this call.

## Example 2

Now, this is a functionality that you cannot get inside the system outside using the API or an **out-of-the-box (OOTB)** preference or subscription center, and that is LogUnsubEvent. This capability will take the information you pass in and create an unsubscribe event, just as if you were to unsubscribe via the one-click unsubscribe button or the default preference or subscription centers.

This means that it will attribute it to the right context based on the data that's input. This can include the following:

- **Job**: Email send event

- **List**: Sending the audience

- **Batch**: Mail batch in the **Mail Transfer Agent**

To do this, you will need to utilize the WSProxy execute method, like so:

```
<script runat="server">
    var prox = new Script.Util.WSProxy();


    /* Set ClientID */
    prox.setClientId({ "ID": mid}); //Impersonates the BU

    var props = [
        { Name: "SubscriberKey", Value: "sample@sample.com" },
        { Name: "EmailAddress", Value: "sample@sample.com" },
        { Name: "JobID", Value: 18099 },
        { Name: "ListID", Value: 8675309 },
        { Name: "BatchID", Value: 0 }
    ];

   var data = prox.execute(props, "LogUnsubEvent");
</script>
```

As you can see, you don't need to do a lot to get this working. Also, you do not need to include every one of those pieces of information. It all *rolls up*, so if you don't know the batch ID, it will still pull via the job and list. Likewise, if you do not know the list, it will still appropriately attach to the job and get the corresponding list. If you do not know the job, it can work off the list, but without the list or the job, it will be logged as an undefined job context as it cannot attach it to an event, but it will still push the unsubscribe through.

This can be insanely useful when you're creating a subscription process or you're on different cloud pages that deal with subscriptions.

# Example 3

This is a small one, but a good one. We have found this to somehow keep winding up in multiple scripts we write around data extensions and reporting. It is a script that clears out the data extension completely! This is done via WSProxy, which utilizes the SOAP API's `perform` method. It is not only amazingly simple to do but lightning quick. Let's take a look at the code:

```
function clearDE(custKey) {
  var prox = new Script.Util.WSProxy();
  var action = "ClearData";
  var props = {
         CustomerKey: custKey
  };

  var data = prox.performItem("DataExtension", props,
    action);

  return data;
}
```

Yes. That's it! Just pop in the `customerkey` or `externalkey` property of the data extension you want to clear out inside this function – it will be emptied within seconds.

We know that you can't contain your excitement for such riveting and awe-inspiring action, but we promise you, it is cool. This allows you to have the same functionality as what is in the UI, but programmatically. For instance, let's say you have sensitive data that you want to use for a specific length of time to run a query on and then want to get rid of it. With this script, you can do this with no issues.

# Example 4

As stated previously, this chapter is not solely dedicated to just the internal Marketing Cloud API, but also interacting with other external services via the REST API. To that extent, we wanted to provide a quick example of this capability.

For instance, if you are looking to get a list of users in an external service to pull in for a Marketing Cloud requirement, you could add a script like this one to ingest that data:

```
function getUser(host,token,userID) {

    var url = host + '/api/users/' + userID;
    var req = new Script.Util.HttpRequest(url);
    req.emptyContentHandling = 0;
    req.retries = 2;
    req.continueOnError = true;
    req.contentType = "application/json"
    req.method = "GET";
    req.setHeader("Authorization", token);


    var resp = req.send();


    var resultStr = String(resp.content);
    var resultJSON
       Platform.Function.ParseJSON(String(resp.content));


    return resultJSON;
}
```

As you can see, the layout, basic structure, and syntax are identical – it is just the authorization and endpoint aspects that are different. So, once you get a handle on the function itself, it opens many large doors for you to integrate and interact with both Marketing Cloud and other external systems you have.

We now have a very strong understanding of not only how to use the in-step API, but why and how to use it. It is one of the strongest things to have in your development toolkit and is also one of the most fun!

# Summary

Although we must say we are sad that we have finished this chapter, which combined our love of server-side JavaScript and Marketing Cloud APIs, we are very happy that we got to share it all with you. As a quick recap, we wanted to go over all the cool things that you should now be able to do after completing this chapter.

After reading this chapter, we have made sure that the next time someone tries to talk to you about SOAP or REST, you will know that they are talking about the APIs and not about their shower this morning. By learning more about the basics of API and the two types of API in Marketing Cloud, we have a stronger understanding of the capabilities and possibilities inside the platform and a beginning of an idea on the capabilities externally.

We have also learned that although the native functions and uses inside AMPscript and SSJS are limited, there are robust capabilities to interact with internal and external APIs inside Marketing Cloud. There are some great built-in capabilities, such as WSProxy and the HTTP functions, that allow you to use `GET` or `POST` to make API calls.

Then, we made a new best friend called `Script.Util` and plan to play with him every day and have fun all the time. We learned just how powerful and versatile this group of functions can be and how they can open up automation and innovation inside Marketing Cloud.

We then learned some cool ways to use this knowledge in the real world and do very powerful and useful things, such as creating and editing queries without logging into the Marketing Cloud UI and using WSProxy to unsubscribe someone and add the context of that unsubscribe to Marketing Cloud.

In the next chapter, you will dive into what we like to call *mini web applications*. These are cool little scripts or cloud pages that have a robust amount of capabilities based on the input of and output to the final destination in Marketing Cloud. These things are not easy to make and are insanely powerful when you do. The hardest part is that most of them need to be customized to the environment, need, and solution, so it's hard to share as a universal solution.

# 8
# Creating Mini Web Apps

Up to this point, most of what we have talked about are journeys and automations and all the things that are possible inside of the tools in Marketing Cloud. These are most definitely the bread and butter of automation in Marketing Cloud, but there is another capability that is fairly overlooked – the ability to augment **Salesforce Marketing Cloud (SFMC)** by creating your own **web app** inside of Marketing Cloud. These web applications are similar to Salesforce Labs products such as **Query Studio** and **Deployment Manager**.

In this chapter, we will cover the following topics:

- *What is a web app?*: A quick overview of what a web app is in regard to Salesforce Marketing Cloud

- *Creating a Marketing Cloud web app*: Provides direction for the different parts required to create a Marketing Cloud web app

- *Setup and administration*: A quick look at permission sets and roles in relation to web applications

- *Installed packages inside Marketing Cloud*: A detailed explanation of how to utilize the installed packages to create your web application

- *CloudPages*: An in-depth look at how to utilize CloudPages to host your web application

- *Example implementation*: A complete example of a web application that has been provided for your use

The goal of this chapter is for you to have a fully implemented web application inside of your business unit and the knowledge and experience to make it better. Throughout the chapter, we will explore each aspect and point you in the direction of how you can best use it or improve the example.

# Technical requirements

As this chapter is based around a significant amount of code, the full code base is stored in a GitHub repository for you to access. This chapter will explain and give an overview of the code base.

The full code for the chapter can be found in the GitHub repository located here: https://github.com/PacktPublishing/Automating-Salesforce-Marketing-Cloud/tree/main/Chapter08

# What is a web app?

So, the first question you might have is *what is a web application or a web app?* A **web app** is basically some sort of software or program that is run through an active network connection instead of being accessed locally through the operating system of the device. You usually need to access a web application through a web browser, and it's programmed using a client-server (user) modeled structure that provides services through a remote server that is hosted externally.

A great example of a web application includes browser-based email services, such as Gmail or Yahoo mail, as well as things such as your online banking services. This may sound like it is essentially just a dynamic web page, and in all honesty, they are strikingly similar. The easiest way to differentiate the two is that the site would have functionality more closely related to that of a software application or a mobile app. Now that we know what a web app is and what it can do, let's start exploring how we can build one inside of Marketing Cloud.

# Creating a Marketing Cloud web app

In order to create one of these applications, you will need a pretty strong understanding of development as well as a strong familiarity with Marketing Cloud.

More specifically, to create a web app in Marketing Cloud, you will need the following skills:

- **HTML**: To create a framework for your frontend.

- **CSS**: To style your HTML to make the user interface a better user experience.

- **JavaScript**: To create client-side capabilities and the functionality of your application. You will also likely want to have strong knowledge of **jQuery** and similar libraries, such as React.js and Node.js.

- **Server-side JavaScript (SSJS)**: To create and use server-side capabilities and functionality to directly interact with servers. AMPscript can also be used, but it is usually much less effective in these situations.

- Knowledge of security headers and defensive validators.

As you may have noticed from the preceding list, the skillset includes both frontend and backend development, which means you will need either a single full stack developer or two developers (frontend developer and backend developer) for this. Most of the backend development will be accomplished via Marketing Cloud proprietary server-side languages, so you can likely pull in a Marketing Cloud developer in place of a backend developer when working on hosting this inside of Marketing Cloud.

This brings us to the point about the need for Marketing Cloud knowledge, requiring a third knowledge set. To be able to appropriately utilize the Marketing Cloud applications and settings to set this up, you will need a fairly strong understanding of the platform. The focus of this knowledge will be on the following:

- **Setup and administration**: Ensuring that the correct user permissions and settings are available and knowing the correct locations and services required.

- **Installed packages**: Knowledge of how to create and build an installed package containing a Marketing Cloud application component and API component.

- **API component permissions and scope**: Knowledge and understanding of how the permissions and scope of the API component work to ensure you only select the permissions you need and help keep this component secure.

- **CloudPages**: Knowledge about creation, editing, and publishing CloudPages. This includes things such as the potential 5-minute server delay on publishing due to server restrictions and that Content Builder blocks will remove JavaScript upon saving.

We will have a look at each of these aspects before we go through an example Marketing Cloud web application. As a note, we will not be going into detail on the syntax and details of the different languages and environments in this chapter. Why? Well, it is because there already exists so many other robust and helpful resources, such as Mozilla MDN docs and W3Schools, that give a broader overview as well as more detailed examples and explanations than anything we could cover in this book. We encourage you to use these resources as well as general Googling to find any help related to those aspects.

First, we will take a quick look at setup and administration.

## Setup and administration

The main focus here will be to make sure that your user has the following capabilities:

- Access to the admin and setup menu
- The ability to set up applications
- The ability to use Content Builder and CloudPages
- Access to all necessary business units
- Correct editing and reading permissions

Usually, as an administrator, you would have no problem with this access. But as not everyone can be an admin, we want to note that if you run into issues with something listed previously not matching or not allowing you to do something, then you should reach out to your admin and have them correct your access. For a listing of permissions and roles and what they do, we recommend referencing the official documentation for assistance.

Next, we will go over setting up the correct package and components inside of Marketing Cloud.

# Installed packages inside Marketing Cloud

Inside Marketing Cloud, there is a section in **Setup** that allows you to create installed packages. This is the same place where we discussed creating an API package and component in *Chapter 7, The Power of In-Step APIs*. This place also has the ability to let you create a *Marketing Cloud App* component from a web page. Now, you will be able to do this via a third-party page as well as via a CloudPage, but as we are concentrating on internal automation in this section, this process will be focused solely on utilizing a CloudPage for this component.

# API component and scope

As we previously went over how to navigate to this place in the setup, we will not go into detail here again (refer to the *Authentication* section of *Chapter 7, The Power of In-Step APIs*, for more details). So, we will instead skip ahead to when you have created your new installed package, but prior to adding any component:

1.  Once you have clicked the **Add Component** button, you will want to select **Marketing Cloud App** instead of **API Integration**, like we did in the previous chapter. See the following screenshot for a visual of this:

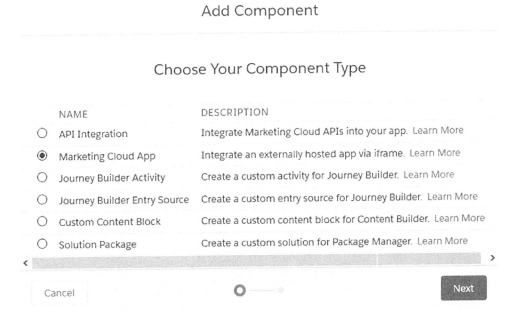

Figure 8.1 – Example of Marketing Cloud App component selection

2.  From there, you will have a screen that asks for the **Name**, **Description**, **Login Endpoint**, and **Logout Endpoint** of your app. Fill in whatever you want for the name and the description is optional, but for **Login Endpoint** and **Logout Endpoint**, you will want to copy in the CloudPage URL from the page you created for this app. Look at the following screenshot for a visual example:

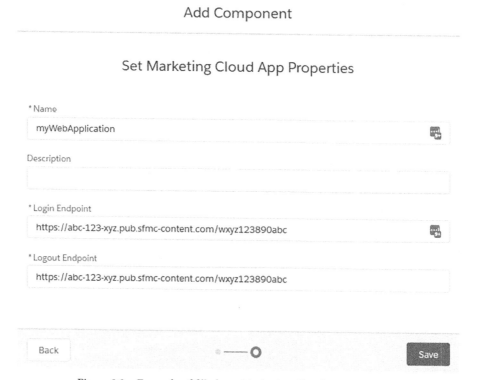

Figure 8.2 – Example of filled out Marketing Cloud app properties

3.  Now we have successfully created the web app! If you have no need for any API connections or anything similar for this application, then you can stop there and be done. But for our example, we are also going to need to add an API component to it.

4.  So, we will once again click the **Add Component** button and this time we will choose **API Integration** as we did in *Chapter 7, The Power of In-Step APIs*. Now, though, when we choose our **Integration Type**, we are going to choose **Web App** instead of **Server-to-Server**. This will provide an added layer of security so that we can ensure it is only used appropriately and only by someone logged into Marketing Cloud.

5.  The section for selecting **Scope and Permissions** is nearly identical, except you will also be required to fill in the **Redirect URIs** section. Inside this section, you will need to copy/paste in the same URL that you put in on the previous **App Properties** section, the CloudPage URL, into this field. Other than that small difference, you will just put in the same scope as you did in *Chapter 7* and then select **Save**.

Now we are set to take a look at the main event, a real-life example of creating a web application inside of Marketing Cloud! In the next section, we will explore CloudPages, hosting our web application inside Marketing Cloud.

## CloudPages

In Web Studio, you will have access to an application called **CloudPages**. This application is where you can create landing pages, microsites, or code resources that are hosted by Marketing Cloud. Also, there are other options such as Mobile Push and Interactive Email pages, but they are not relevant to our purpose.

CloudPages usually comes included with all **Enterprise 2** editions of Marketing Cloud. If you have an edition that does not have CloudPages already included, you will need to talk to your account representative about purchasing it. Another thing to note is that CloudPages costs a Super Message per view, so this will need to be considered as you build your applications.

To navigate to CloudPages, go to the drop-down list of any studio, then go to **Web Studio** and click on **CloudPages** as shown in the following screenshot:

Figure 8.3 – Example showing how to get to the CloudPages application

The part that we will be focusing on inside CloudPages is **creating a landing page**. To get there, follow these steps:

1.  You will need to start by creating a collection. This will be a grouping, similar to a folder, holding your related pages and sites in one place. To create a collection, click on the **Create Collection** button in the top-right corner, as shown in the following screenshot:

Figure 8.4 – Example of creating a new collection inside CloudPages

2.  After setting the name and other details for your new collection, you will want to then click on the newly created collection to open up the **Collection** view. After that, in the top-right corner, you will see a new button called **Add Content**. This button will create a dropdown where you will want to choose a landing page. You will then want to name your page and select **Blank** as the layout, as shown in the following screenshot:

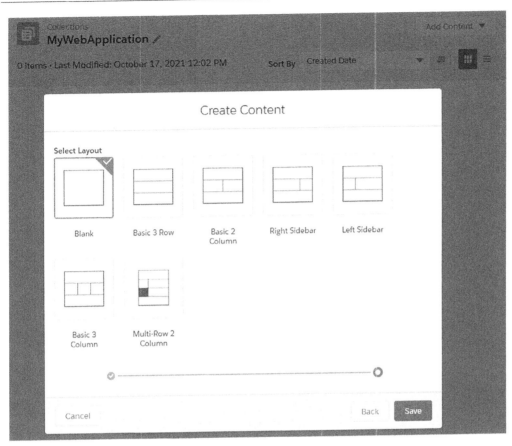

Figure 8.5 – Example of creating a landing page inside of a collection in Marketing Cloud

3.   You can then click **Save**. It will create the page and open up the editor. Sometimes, the editor will open up in **Default** mode, but you will want to click on **Code View** as this will allow you to develop with custom HTML and will also let you remove the default HTML that is created. The following screenshot shows an example of these options:

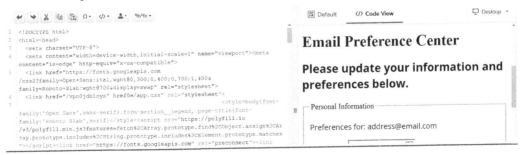

Figure 8.6 – Example of options on editing a landing page inside of CloudPages

After this, you will take the HTML and all relevant coding of your web application that you want to be used inside of Marketing Cloud on the left side editor and then save and publish the page. We will go into more detail about this content in the next section.

# Example implementation

For this example, we wanted to make it relevant, while also simple. We also wanted to make sure it touched on enough aspects to truly give an overview of the capabilities of Marketing Cloud. Without further ado, we want to present you with the real-life example we are planning on creating with you...the *Automation Dashboard*!

# Automation Dashboard

The first thing to address is, what is it? Although similar to the **Overview** page in Marketing Cloud Automation Studio, this app will let you see more details in a much cleaner way as well as provide additional information such as status, next run date, type, the duration of the last run, and the modified date. It also allows for a better overview with a quicker search bar as well as filtering to only allow a view into automations that have been run in the past 6 months.

This also is a stepping stone, a basic model of the possibilities this dashboard offers. You can even offer up the possibility of using this as an overview for all business units, the ability to take snapshots of your automations in a moment in time, and to provide further details and error information. This can include things such as average run time, total errors and successful runs, and more. The following screenshot gives a visual of what the basic Automation Dashboard looks like.

| name | status | ModifiedDate | lastRunDate | NextRun | stepcount | type | lastrunstatus | duration |
|---|---|---|---|---|---|---|---|---|
| Geolocation_Claires_NA_Store_Axis_Test | PausedSchedule | 12/08/2021 12:35 AM | 12/08/2021 12:34 AM | | 1 | scheduled | Complete | 1 mins 33 secs |
| SearchParty | Ready | 12/10/2021 12:09 AM | 12/10/2021 12:08 AM | | 1 | scheduled | Complete | 3 mins 23 secs |
| CCPA_Delete2 | Ready | 10/21/2021 05:08 PM | 10/21/2021 04:58 PM | | 7 | scheduled | Complete | 9 mins 53 secs |
| gg_DELETEME6 | PausedSchedule | 11/14/2021 01:30 PM | | | 2 | scheduled | | |
| AutoSendReport_FULL_2021 | Ready | 11/15/2021 10:36 AM | 11/15/2021 10:33 AM | | 2 | scheduled | Complete | 3 mins 4 secs |
| DE_Inventory | Ready | 11/14/2021 01:30 PM | | | 1 | scheduled | | |
| File-Drop Auto | AwaitingTrigger | 10/19/2021 08:42 AM | | | 2 | triggered | | |
| ImpressionRegions | Ready | 01/06/2022 02:25 PM | 01/06/2022 02:25 PM | | 2 | scheduled | Complete | 21 secs |
| test_Aero | Ready | 11/27/2021 11:21 PM | 11/27/2021 11:21 PM | | 3 | scheduled | Complete | 29 secs |
| CCPA_Itemization | Ready | 10/21/2021 04:29 PM | 10/21/2021 04:21 PM | | 6 | scheduled | Complete | 8 mins 0 secs |
| Combined_NA_Test | Ready | 12/08/2021 12:49 AM | 12/08/2021 12:40 AM | | 1 | scheduled | Complete | 28 secs |

Figure 8.7 – Example view of the Automation Dashboard web application

As you may have noticed, this is a lot different than what you see in **Automation Studio**. This, although a bit less pleasing visually, is a much easier-to-digest data dashboard to help you easily sort or search through to find the overview info you need. The following gives an explanation of what each column represents:

- **name**: The name given to the automation.

- **status**: The overall status of the automation. This is not in relation to the last run status. This will not show an error if the last run was unsuccessful.

- **ModifiedDate**: The last time the automation was edited.

- **LastRunDate**: The last time the automation was run.

- **NextRun**: The next time the automation will run. This will be empty if there is no new run scheduled.

- **Stepcount**: The number of steps inside the automation. This is the number of steps and not the activities in each step. So, if you had 5 activities in 1 step, it would only show a value of 1 here.

- **Type**: This displays the type of automation. The two available values are **Scheduled** and **Triggered**.

- **Lastrunstatus**: This gives the result of the last run. This includes **Error**, **Complete**, and **Stopped**.

- **Duration**: The length of time it took the last time the automation was run.

You may have noticed the names in *Figure 8.7* are blue. This is because they are linked. When you click on a name, it will take you, in a new window, to that automation in Automation Studio. If you want to make any edits, you can just click from this dashboard instead of leaving here and going into Automation Studio and finding that automation again.

As you can see, there can be a lot of useful information in the palm of your hand all within the Marketing Cloud. We like to view this as more of a tracking- and reporting-oriented dashboard for those who want to track automations and view their status without needing to interact with them directly.

As you may have noticed, there is a button at the top left that is labeled **Export Data**. That's right – through some fancy JavaScript, you can click there, and it will download a CSV file of the information used to fill in this dashboard. The CSV file will also contain the **AutomationID** as well as the **ClientId** (Business Unit or MID) of the account.

Now that we have a good overview of what the finished product is going to be, let's start exploring the code.

# The full code

If you follow the preparations from the previous section and add the appropriate URL and application information into this code, you will be able to pretty much copy and paste this into CloudPages and be up and running.

But you are reading this book because you want to learn, not just copy someone else's code. So, we are going to use the next section to go into detail about the code and how it works. The code is split into a few sections, and we shall go through it accordingly. The split is of HTML, SSJS, and client-side JavaScript.

As it is the first part of the code as well as the first part processed on the page, we will start by exploring the SSJS.

# The SSJS

We are going to break this part into different sections. There are four major parts of the SSJS that we will go over. The first is the *validation and security* to ensure that the referrer is actually coming from Marketing Cloud and that the page is secure. Next is the *authorization and authentication* to create an OAuth token for the REST API. After that is the *calling of the REST API* to get the JSON with all automations and then *parse and prepare* it for use in the client-side JavaScript. Lastly, there's the *list of the functions* required to make the other three sections work.

## Security headers and validation

The first section is dedicated to ensuring that the page you make is unable to be used outside the environment you want it to work in. For this reason, we added a few security headers as well as a conditional to check the referrer URL to validate the source of the request. See the following code snippet from the full code hosted on GitHub:

```
//Security headers to secure the page
HTTPHeader.SetValue("Access-Control-Allow-Methods","POST,
    GET");
HTTPHeader.SetValue("Access-Control-Allow-Origin","*");
Platform.Response.SetResponseHeader("Strict-Transport-
    Security","max-age=200");
Platform.Response.SetResponseHeader("X-XSS-
    Protection","1; mode=block");
Platform.Response.SetResponseHeader("X-Content-Type-
    Options","nosniff");
```

```
Platform.Response.SetResponseHeader("Referrer-
  Policy","strict-origin-when-cross-origin");

//Gather the referrer url
var referrer = Platform.Request.ReferrerURL;

//Verifies that this site is being called from within
//SFMC
//Pay attention to this as if they change the domain,
//this will break and toss an error
if (referrer.indexOf('exacttarget.com') < 0) {
  throw error;
}
```

To be honest, most of those headers are not necessarily needed in this case, but it is a best practice to include them every time it is possible as it is usually better to be safe rather than sorry. That being said, if you run into errors that you are not understanding, feel free to explore and investigate whether the issue is stemming from these headers (usually you can see if this is the case inside the console of the browser's dev tools).

The main part that is needed is the validator on the referrer URL. This ensures that if the page gets traffic from anywhere outside of the SFMC UI it throws an error. As you can see, it pulls in the referrer URL via SSJS pulling from the `Request` object. This will return `https://sX.exacttarget.com` with the X being the stack – except for stack 1, which will remove the s subdomain.

After we collect that URL, we then run an `indexOf()` function on it to verify that it has `exacttarget.com` inside of it – used to remove the dynamic stack aspect so it will work across all stacks. Now, at the time of writing this, that was the URL, but we know Marketing Cloud has been working very hard to remove all domains and occurrences of Exact Target still existing in the tool – so in the near future, this may need to be updated to account for this change.

After the comparison we have it throw an error if `exacttarget.com` does not exist in the referrer URL. This will force the page to return a *500 error* and not allow access at all. Next, we will investigate the API authentication portion of the scripting.

## API authentication and OAuth token

In order to utilize the REST API to gather the automations, you need to be able to authenticate your call. Now, you could create a new server-to-server API component and utilize that inside of here instead, but that would limit it to just the MID it is created in. But by utilizing the web app package we created, we can use it across each business unit that it is authorized inside of.

In this example, we have the app information and REST API info, including the ID and Secret hardcoded inside of the page, but for enhanced security you can store it elsewhere and encrypt it accordingly. Prior to that information coming into play though, we first need to validate whether it is authorized by reviewing the `state` parameter:

```
//App information, including REST API info
  var appURL = '{{urlOfCloudPage}}';
  var clientID = '{{clientID}}';
  var clientSecret = '{{clientSecret}}';
  var tenantID = '{{tenantSubDomain}}';


  //Gather state parameter from URL
  var state =
    Platform.Request.GetQueryStringParameter('state');


  //Validate if authorized
  if (state) {
    var code =
      Platform.Request.GetQueryStringParameter('code');
    var payloadObj = {
        grant_type: 'authorization_code',
        code: code,
        client_id: clientID,
        client_secret: clientSecret,
        redirect_uri: appURL
    };


    //Gets Token if already Authorized
    var res = HTTP.Post('https://' + tenantID +
      '.auth.marketingcloudapis.com/v2/token',
```

```
        'application/json', Stringify(payloadObj));

    var resJSON =
        Platform.Function.ParseJSON(res.Response[0]);
    var accessToken = resJSON.access_token;
    var authToken = 'Bearer ' + accessToken;

} else {
    state = GUID();
    Platform.Response.Redirect('https://' + tenantID +
        '.auth.marketingcloudapis.com/v2/authorize
        ?response_type=code&client_id=' + clientID +
        '&redirect_uri=' + appURL + '&state=' + state);
    //Authorizes request if not already authorized
}
```

Basically, the flow of this section is as follows:

1.  Set variables for each of the required data points for authorization.
2.  Validate that there is an existing state in the URL.
3.  If a state exists, then we gather the authorization code and send an API call to get the access token.
4.  If a state does not exist, then create a new random value for the state and redirect to the authorize endpoint.
5.  This redirect will validate if the user is logged into SFMC and authorize and provide a code for use on the token call when it redirects back to the original URL.

The first two parts are fairly self-explanatory and you likely do not need us to go into too much explanation. It is just the setting of variables and then a conditional to check whether a value exists in the state variable we just set. The actions inside of this conditional are where we will need to go into details to ensure understanding. First, we will start with a scenario where state exists, and the condition returns true.

## Validates as true

So, the first thing that happens after validating as true is that we set the variable of code based on the query parameter, also named code, to get this value. This value is very important as it is required for us to make the token call for the OAuth token we need for authorization.

After we have this value set, we then create a new JavaScript Object variable, named `payloadObj`. This object will contain all the correct key and value pairs required for us to use to send to the token endpoint and return an access token.

You will notice that this object is different from those we explored in the previous chapter with the server-to-server API component. This one, `grant_type`, is now an authorization code, and it requires two new keys: `code` and `redirect_uri`. Code is filled from the query parameter that we assigned a variable earlier and `redirect_uri` is the `appURL` variable we defined at the very top of this section. The two remaining keys are `client_id` and `client_secret`, which are used exactly as they are in the server-to-server API call.

Now that we have created the object, we now need to make a `POST` call, utilizing the `HTTP.Post Core` function, to the right endpoint and pass `payloadObj`. Note that the object needs to be stringified, which basically means it needs to be changed from a data type of `Object` to a data type of `String`.

After the call is made, we then parse the response and then grab the `access_token` value from the returned JSON, and then we create a new variable, `authToken`, that then combines the bearer and the space in front of it to create our finalized auth token. This then gets us ready to make any future REST API calls using this token. Next, we will explore what happens if this condition does not validate as true.

## Does not validate as true

Although this section is only two lines of code, there is a lot that goes into it. The first line of code is fairly simple as it just assigns a random **Global Unique Identification (GUID)** to the `state` variable for use in the condition in the next run. This uses the literal `GUID()` function to create it. The next part is the part that requires a bit of extra explanation.

After setting `state`, we then do a `Redirect` server side that sends the browser to a new URL instead of the current one. Now, people might wonder why we would want to do this. Well, that is because, in order to authenticate it, we need to go through the `authorize` endpoint to validate the user is logged into Marketing Cloud and correct code is assigned. So, in order to do this, we need to redirect to that URL and append a few query parameters to the URL to help the endpoint correctly finish its process and redirect back to the page.

As stated, this redirect will actually lead to redirecting back to this page. Once you are logged in and a code has been assigned, the page will be redirected back to the original CloudPage URL you are using, but now with a `state` query parameter as well as a code value. This will then trigger the previous `validates as true` process.

We now have the authentication process down and understood, so let's move on to the retrieval and parsing of the response section of the SSJS code.

## Retrieving and parsing the result

We are going to break this section into three different sections to make it easier to digest. We will first have the retrieval process, where we set up our variables in preparation for the retrieval, followed by the actual function call – the function itself will be gone over in the later sections that go into details on the functions. Next, we will go over the looping through this JSON to iterate appropriately through each dataset. Then, finally, we will go over the actual setting of the values inside this loop to fill a new object that is then pushed into a new array. Let's dig into the retrieval functions and setup!

### Retrieval

This section is actually fairly simple in terms of both the small amount of code and the fact that it is pretty easy to understand. This basically gets a bowl and then goes over and gets the cereal and milk and pours it in. It is a bit more involved than that, but essentially that is what this section is doing. See the following code snippet for
a reference on the block we are discussing:

```
//Sets as global var for final JSON variable
var data = [];


//set Expire value for auto lookback


var expire = new Date()
expire.setMonth(expire.getMonth() - 5)
//5 months subtraction because month is 0 index, meaning
//0 is January in getMonth, but setMonth will see
//Jan as 1.


var autos = getAutomations(tenantID,authToken);
var items = autos.entry;
```

The beginning is setting up the data array global variable to be filled through the iteration of each loop in the following sections – or the bowl that we are going to pour the cereal and milk into. We then also set up the `expire` variable, which is set to be a maximum of 6 months in the past. This is to help us select only those that are relevant in the returned array of automations.

After this, we make the call to the `getAutomations()` function. This function will then run through a script that makes an API to call and retrieve JSON that contains all the automations inside of that specific business unit. This is the milk and cereal part. After that, we then set up the next couple of variables to begin the looping and iteration through the returned object.

## Looping and iteration

Now that we have the data in JSON format, we have each of the automations stored in their own object inside of an array. But how the heck do we get this data out? This is where looping and iteration come into play.

There are multiple types of looping available in SSJS, much more than just the FOR loop that is available inside of AMPscript. The following are some examples of looping available inside of SSJS:

- **For loop**: Repeats until a specified comparison evaluates to false. Here's an example: `for (var i=0; i<arr.length;i++)` – this means the loop will repeat until `i` iterates to the same number as the length of the array (`arr`).

- **For...in loop**: Iterates a specified variable over the enumerable properties of an object. This means that for each distinct property, this loop will run. For example, `for(var in Object)` – this will run for each instance of `var` in the `Object`.

- **Do...while loop**: Repeats until a specified condition evaluates to false. The statement inside this loop is always executed once, but the repetition is determined by the condition set at the bottom. Here's an example: `do { //myStuff }` `while(stuff > 10)` – this will do the statements in the `do` part while the `stuff` variable is greater than `10`.

- **While loop**: Executes the statements as long as the specified condition evaluates as true. A `while` loop is identical to a `do...while` loop but without the guaranteed first execution. For example, `while(n < 3) { n++; }` – this will loop through until n is 3.

For our needs, we are going to be utilizing the `while` loop to loop and iterate through our array of objects to form our output. This part may be confusing though because our output is going to be another array of objects, so why do we need to manipulate this? Simple: because the layout of the original is not something that is easily digested by our `dataTables` plugin for jQuery.

We will go over this more in the section ahead that talks about the client-side scripts and code (Client-side JavaScript). Following is a snippet, removing the setting of variables and iteration parts, that shows the loop and the appropriate loop settings and usage:

```
var c = 0;
while(c < items.length) {
  var a = items[c]


    c++;
}

//Stringify for use in client-side JS
var json = Stringify(data);
```

> **While Loop Variable**
>
> As you can see from this, c is set outside the loop as 0 to make the comparison valid, comparing it to the total size of the array of objects. c is then used to pull a specific object inside that array and then at the end of the loop, we use c++ to increase the value of c by 1.

## Setting appropriate variables

The next part of this that we are going to dig into is setting up the appropriate variables to use when building and parsing out the automation information. Most of this is centered around getting the total runtime from the start and completed times of the automation. See the following snippet of the code for reference:

```
//Auto Object for pushing into data array - resets to
//null on each loop
autoObj = {};

var start = new Date(a.startTime)
var completed = new Date(a.completedTime)
var delta = Math.abs(completed.getTime() -
  start.getTime()) / 1000
```

```
// calculate (and subtract) whole days
var days = Math.floor(delta / 86400);
delta -= days * 86400;

// calculate (and subtract) whole hours
var hours = Math.floor(delta / 3600) % 24;
delta -= hours * 3600;

// calculate (and subtract) whole minutes
var minutes = Math.floor(delta / 60) % 60;
delta -= minutes * 60;

// what's left is seconds
var seconds = Math.floor(delta % 60);
var diff = (hours > 0 ? hours + 'hrs ': '') + (minutes
    > 0 ? minutes + ' mins ' : '') + seconds + ' secs';
```

---

**autoObj Declaration**

Before getting into the calculation for the total runtime, we want to point out, at the top, the variable declaration of autoObj. This is important not only because it sets the data type for this variable, but also because it makes it so that, every loop, it completely clears out the autoObj variable so that there is no accidental duplication across each iteration from data being carried across.

---

For the calculation of duration, we first start by getting the start date and time and the completed date and time from the JavaScript object, a, which was set in the while loop snippet.

From those two, we have to then get the delta, which is the time in milliseconds between when the automation started and when it finished.

From there, we then use math functions to multiply and divide to get the days, hours, minutes, and seconds difference.

Now to ensure each is accurate, we are going to be removing the previous value, days for hours, hours for minutes, and so on from the delta after the calculation. This ensures we get an accurate number at the end.

Now that we have the correct duration, we just need to put it together, which is what we use the `diff` variable for. Essentially, in this, we do an inline conditional that checks to see if each section – hours, minutes, or seconds – has a value and if so, then we add that value plus a label. If it does not have a value, then we do nothing.

## Iteration and manipulation

Now that we are prepped and have the duration ready, we just need to push all the other aspects of the automation into the proper format in this object and push it into the new array. The following snippet shows how we will do that:

```
//Validates if the automation was run in past 6 months
//Or the automation was modified in past 6 months and
//was not run but has schedule type defined.
if ((new Date(a.lastRunTime) > expire) || (new
  Date(a.modifiedDate) > expire && a.lastRunDate ===
  undefined && a.automationType != 'unspecified')) {

  //set each date into a date data type
  var modDate = new Date(a.modifiedDate)
  var lastRunDate = new Date(a.lastRunTime)
  var nextRunDate = new Date(a.scheduledTime)

  //add each key/value pair into autoObj
  autoObj.AutoID = a.id;
  autoObj.ClientID = a.clientId;
  autoObj.Name = a.name;
  autoObj.Status = a.status;
  autoObj.modifiedDate = formatDate(modDate);
  autoObj.LastRunDate = a.lastRunStatus === undefined?
    '' : formatDate(lastRunDate);
  autoObj.StepCount = a.processes ? a.processes.length :
    0;
  autoObj.Type = a.automationType;
  autoObj.LastRunStatus = a.lastRunStatus;
  autoObj.lastRunDuration = diff != '0 secs' ? diff :
    '';
```

```
autoObj.NextRun = formatDate(nextRunDate);


//push autoObj into the data array
data.push(autoObj);
}
```

> **Six-Month Limit Filter**
>
> This section starts with a conditional statement that will validate if the automation has been run in the past 6 months or if it was recently built, in the last 6 months, but not run. This is to help limit the returned automations to only those that are relevant. It also accounts for a limitation in the API that for automation interactions, a separate call to find details on the specific running of that automation is only available via that endpoint for 6 months. Anything beyond that returns an error. Our rationale for this is to display only those automations that are relevant and reduce the noise displayed.

After this, we then utilize the dot notation on the source object set in the prior scripts, the JavaScript object a, to then assign the new key/value property in the new object, autoObj. When using the statement autoObj.AutoId = a.id, we create the parameter key of AutoId inside of the autoObj and then set the value of it to a.id. Or, for a visual, see the following example:

```
AutoObj = {
    AutoId: a.id
}
```

This is then utilized for all the following properties to correctly assign the values to the new properties in autoObj. Then, once we have all these property key/values matched, we use the push() function to take this object and add it into the array, data, which we set previously. This will be the container holding all of the objects of our automations. Next will be a deep dive into the getAutomations() function and how it works.

## The getAutomations() function

This function is the key to the whole page. Without this function, we would have no data for the rest of the code to work with. The function utilizes the undocumented REST API endpoint to bulk retrieve automations. As always, you should be wary of using undocumented endpoints for production or live applications, but as this is for internal reference, it should be no issue.

> **Undocumented REST API Disclaimer**
>
> Salesforce Marketing Cloud's undocumented REST endpoints or SOAP objects are to be used at your own risk. These are unofficial capabilities or access to the platform that at any moment could be altered, removed, or otherwise manipulated, which could break your applications or scripts utilizing them. The other consideration is that as these are not public-facing, the throughput, bandwidth, uptime, and speed may fluctuate or be flimsier than normal, making it an extremely risky solution if used at volume or high frequency. To this extent, it is never recommended to use these endpoints or objects in anything that could have a potential negative impact on your production or live campaigns or processes.

This endpoint exists in the legacy endpoint family. It is actually super-fast considering the significant size of the payload it returns. This endpoint does have a timeout and limitation so if your business unit has an enormous number of automations, it could break and cause this application to error, but we have found this endpoint and scripting to be able to handle all but the most absurd amounts of automations. This is one of the few endpoints that is officially labeled as bulk, and although we have no objective insight into if this is actually a bulk endpoint but, the performance seems to speak for itself.

As a note, the endpoint will return a page size with it, but this page size does not matter as it will always return the full number of automations no matter what value is put in there. The returned array is also formatted differently than most other documented APIs, so it will take a little bit of exploring and experimentation to get the nuances right.

The following is an example of the REST API call to the bulk automation retrieval endpoint:

```
GET /legacy/v1/beta/bulk/automations/automation/definition/
Host: {{tenant_subDomain}}.rest.marketingcloudapis.com
Authorization: Bearer {{authToken}}
Content-Type: application/json
```

As you can see in the preceding snippet, it's a very simple endpoint and it only requires the tenant subdomain and authentication token, like most other REST endpoints. One thing that many find alarming is the part inside of it that says `beta`. We know, this scared us too at first, but this endpoint is utilized inside of the UI of Marketing Cloud, so we think it is fairly safe to assume it is not going to be going anywhere in the immediate future.

To use this endpoint, we are going to be pulling in `Script.Util.HttpRequest()`, which we went over in *Chapter 7, The Power of In-Step APIs*, to handle our API calls. You can see the full function in the following snippet for reference:

```
//gets a JSON of all automations inside of Business Unit
function getAutomations(tenantID,authToken) {

  var url = 'https://' + tenantID +
    '.rest.marketingcloudapis.com/legacy/v1/beta/
    bulk/automations/automation/definition/';

  var req = new Script.Util.HttpRequest(url);
  req.emptyContentHandling = 0;
  req.retries = 2;
  req.continueOnError = true;
  req.contentType = "application/json"
  req.setHeader("Authorization", authToken);
  req.method = "GET";

  var resp = req.send();
  var resultStr = String(resp.content);
  var resultJSON =
    Platform.Function.ParseJSON(String(resp.content));

  return resultJSON;
}
```

This is a pretty boilerplate way of using the `Script.Util.HttpRequest()` function by setting the URL, the method, and other properties, sending it out, and then turning the response into a string first, then parsing it as JSON. This function then just returns `resultJSON` to the variable that is being used to call the function – pretty straightforward.

Now, some of you may have noticed that there is a second function as well. This one is also very important but not as flashy or glamorous as the `getAutomations()` function. It is the `formatDate()` function, which we use to prepare the date for display on the dashboard.

This function basically just takes the date type that is normally used and turns it into a string version that is more readable to the average viewer and appears cleaner. You can check out the script for this function in the following snippet:

```
//prepares the date for display in dashboard
function formatDate(myDate) {
    if(typeof(myDATE) !== null) {
    var month = (myDate.getMonth() + 1),
    day = myDate.getDate(),
    year = myDate.getFullYear(),
    hour = myDate.getHours(),
    mins = myDate.getMinutes(),
    meridiem = '';

    if (hour > 12) {
      hour = Number(hour) - 12;
      meridiem = 'PM'
    } else {
      meridiem = 'AM';
    }

    return ('0' + month).slice(-2)  + '/' + ('0' +
      day).slice(-2)  + '/' + year  + ' ' + ('0'
      hour).slice(-2)   + ':' + ('0' + mins).slice(-2) + '
      ' + meridiem;
    } else { return '';}
}
```

Most of this is pretty straightforward, where we validate that it is a date, then parse it out to get the month, date, year, hour, minutes, and others as their own variable. You might note that `month` has it adding one to the value. This is because `getMonth` is based on a zero index, meaning that January would be returned as `0` and not `1`. So, to make it easy to read, we just add one to it.

After that, we validate the hours to see if it's AM or PM and then adjust accordingly. This is because the datetime object pulled from the source object is in the 24-hour format, and not 12. We then move on to the return value, which is a bit of fancy footwork to create a date such as *11/12/2021 4:51PM*. Now that we have the SSJS part under our belts and we have the data together and ready to be used, let's explore the HTML and CSS framework and styling we set up.

## The HTML and CSS

Admittedly, there is not much HTML or CSS needed here as most of it is pulled in through plugins or libraries. This can be a bit of a bloat and can slow things down, so for sure there are better ways to optimize this, but we have found the following structure and framework to be the easiest to work with while having the least frontend experience needed but still displaying nicely. Following is the snippet of the HTML and CSS needed for this. You will notice at the bottom there is an exorbitant amount of external script libraries, which is what is needed for the framework and `dataTables` plugin:

```
<!DOCTYPE html>
<html lang="en">
  <head>
<!-- Required meta tags and external CSS Style Sheets -->
  </head>
  <body>
    <div style="width:90%; padding:20px 0 20px 0; margin:0
      auto;">
      <button id="exportBtn" onclick="download()">
        Export Data</button>
      <table id="autoTable" class="table table-striped
        table-bordered table-hover">
        <thead class="thead-dark">
          <tr>
            <th style="display:none;">AutoID</th>
            <th style="display:none;">Client</th>
            <th scope="col">name</th>
            <th scope="col">status</th>
            <th scope="col">ModifiedDate</th>
            <th scope="col">lastRunDate</th>
            <th scope="col">NextRun</th>
```

```
                <th scope="col">stepcount</th>
                <th scope="col">type</th>
                <th scope="col">lastrunstatus</th>
                <th scope="col">duration</th>
            </tr>
        </thead>
    </table>
  </div>
  <-- Script/Library blocks and external calls -->
  </body>
</html>
```

As you will notice in the snippet, we removed all the external calls to style sheets or scripts as they are pretty simple to understand, can be viewed in the GitHub repository `https://github.com/PacktPublishing/Automating-Salesforce-Marketing-Cloud/tree/main/Chapter08`, and take up a lot of unnecessary space and can cause clutter. These were replaced by HTML comments showing where they would be placed if displayed.

As previously said, there is not much there. Most of it is dynamically created through the client-side JavaScript we will go over a little later in this chapter. Mostly, you just need to have the `div` container, the export button, and then the table that is going to be holding your data.

The only part of the table that you need to manually set is the head. This is the listing of each of the column names you want to label your data. As you may notice in the code, we have two columns with the style of `display:hidden`. This is to hide them from being displayed as although they are important to have for exporting or if you need them for reference, they are not necessary to be displayed in the visual table. So, by putting this CSS on these columns, we are able to hide this info from being displayed.

As you may notice, we have some inline styling in my HTML, which in almost every way is a no-no for web development, but as the `div` and those `th` tags are the only places we need CSS outside the external style sheets, we just inlined it to have it easier to reference what it is affecting. Feel free to move this to a style sheet, especially if you start to add more custom CSS to your dashboard.

The HTML and CSS parts are pretty easy, considering we are using external libraries and plugins to do most of the work. So, next, we will move to the JavaScript section to discuss utilizing these plugins and libraries.

# Client-side JavaScript

There are a ton of libraries and plugins that we are using, so this actually severely simplifies the JavaScript needed and makes it a much more readable syntax. As stated previously though, using this can lead to page bloat and slow things down, so feel free to adjust it to a more custom and efficient option instead. In fact, if you have the skill to do so, we would highly recommend it. There are a lot of opportunities here.

The first part we are going to go over about the JavaScript used in this page is the creation of the baseline for the automation URL inside of Automation Studio and setting the JavaScript `var` of the JSON coming from the SSJS:

```
let currentUrl = document.referrer;
let autoURL = currentUrl + 'cloud/#app/Automation
   Studio/AutomationStudioFuel3/%23Instance/';

let myJSON = <ctrl:var name=json />;
```

This is pretty simple JavaScript. As this is coming from inside the Marketing Cloud UI, you can use the referrer URL and just add the context for Automation Studio to create the base link for linking to the automation inside. All you would do is append the AutoID of the automation to this link and it will take you to the automation inside of Automation Studio.

The most interesting part is the passing of the JSON from SSJS to JavaScript. In order to do this, you need to use the `<ctrl>` tag that is proprietary to Marketing Cloud, use the `var` aspect, and then provide the name of the variable. Once you do this, it will act similarly to any other personalization or inline call of an AMPscript variable, but with the SSJS variable. This means it will fill in the JSON value on the client side, allowing for the manipulation of it by the JavaScript.

## buildAutoTable()

With the JSON passed from SSJS to JavaScript, we can now begin building our table. To do this, we need to create a function using the `dataTable` plugin. The following function is utilized to build out the table we saw in *Figure 8.7*:

```
function buildAutoTable() {
    let autoTable = $('#autoTable').DataTable( {
        "data": myJSON,
        "paging": true,
        "pageLength": 20,
```

```
"lengthMenu": [ [10, 20, 50, -1], [10, 20, 50,
  "All"] ],
"search": { "caseInsensitive": false },
"columns": [
  {"data": "AutoID",
   "visible":false
  },
  {"data": "ClientID",
   "visible":false
  },
  {"data": "Name",
    "render": function(data, type, row, meta){
        if(type === 'display'){
            data = '<a href="' + autoURL +
                row["AutoID"] + '"
                target="_blank" >' + data +
                '</button>';
        }
        return data;
    }
  },
  {"data": "Status"},
  {"data": "modifiedDate", "type":
    'date-mm-dd-yyyy'},
  {"data": "LastRunDate"},
  {"data": "NextRun",
    "render": function(data, type, row, meta){
        if(type === 'display'){
            data = data == '12/31/1969 06:00
                PM' ? '' : data;
        }
        return data;
    }
  },
  {"data": "StepCount"},
  {"data": "Type"},
```

```
                    {"data": "LastRunStatus"},
                    {"data": "lastRunDuration"}
              ]
         } );
      return autoTable;
   }
   $(document).ready(function() {
      let autoTable = buildAutoTable();
   });
```

Most of this is setting parameters and values to toggle options for the output table of the `dataTables` output. The main point we should focus on is the `columns` section of this JSON config we are pushing to the `DataTable` method. This is where we control what columns are getting output as well as any custom manipulation and attribution of the data in those columns. For instance, you will notice in the `Name` column, we have a function that wraps the data point inside an a tag to link to the **Automation Studio** page for that automation. You will also notice for the first two columns, like in the HTML, we have these as not visible to hide them from being displayed.

Rather than providing a lot of information on how to use `dataTables` and set up the `config` JSON, we instead recommend going to the documentation for more information on how and why this is set up in this manner and other options on what can be done.

Lastly, you will notice a `jQuery` statement, stating that when the page is loaded we should run a function to run the `buildAutoTable()` function. Next, we are going to go over the JavaScript function utilized to allow you to export the Auto Dashboard to a CSV file that you can view in Excel.

## download()

This function takes the JSON data we assigned to the `myJSON` variable coming from the SSJS and then transforms it into a CSV file and then downloads it to your local machine. The major benefit here is that it can allow you to create snapshots in time of what your automations' statuses and runtimes were as well as giving you something that you can view offline, and you do not need to be logged in to Marketing Cloud to view it.

Take a look at the following snippet to see the function we are referencing:

```
//Export CSV JS
function download() {
  let csv = '';
  let items = myJSON;

  // Loop the array of objects
  for(let i = 0; i < items.length; i++){
      let numKeys = Object.keys(items[i]).length
      let counter = 0

      // If this is the first row, generate the
      // headings
      if(i === 0){

          // Loop each property of the object
          for(let key in items[i]){

  // This is to not add a comma at the last cell
  // The '\r\n' adds a new line
              csv += key + (counter+1 < numKeys ? ','
                  : '\r\n' )
              counter++
          }
      }else{
          for(let key in items[i]){
              let data = items[i][key];

              data = data == '12/31/1969 06:00 PM' ?
                  '' : data;

              csv += data + (counter+1 < numKeys ? ','
                  : '\r\n' )

              counter++
          }
```

```
            }


        }


        // Once we are done looping, download the .csv by
        // creating a link
        let link = document.createElement('a')
        link.id = 'download-csv'
        link.setAttribute('href',
          'data:text/csv;charset=utf-8,' +
          encodeURIComponent(csv));
        link.setAttribute('download',
          'AutoDashExport.csv');
        document.body.appendChild(link)
        document.querySelector('#download-csv').click()
    }
```

All in all, it is not really that complex of a function. It utilizes JavaScript to transform the JSON into a rowset that is separated by commas and columns and uses newline characters to separate rows. It then builds out an a tag that has the `href` value set to download the file that we just created and then uses JavaScript to programmatically click this new link and initiate the download.

That is the whole code and explanation, so now all you need to do is copy/paste the code from GitHub into the CloudPages you set up previously, then click **Save and Publish**. Once you do that, you can then go to the top navigation bar and select the **AppExchange** option. See the following screenshot for an example:

Figure 8.8 – Example of where to find the AppExchange option

Once you hover over that, there will be a dropdown that should include the name of the custom application that you created. All you need to do there is just click on the name and it will load in a new iframe in your Marketing Cloud instance. That's it! You now have a fully functional Automation Dashboard inside your account and all the knowledge to build your own custom web applications to be used inside Marketing Cloud.

# The power is yours!

Well, as much as it can be anyway. You have the power and knowledge to customize capabilities, dashboards, reporting, and more through custom-built web applications that are hosted internally on Marketing Cloud and used inside the Marketing Cloud UI. With this power, you could build things such as a NoSQL segmentation tool that can programmatically create often used queries in your account without the user needing to know or understand SQL. Or, build a custom reporting dashboard or tracking log based on data you get via API or other scripts, and so on for your users to easily digest.

There are so many possibilities here that it is hard to list them all. Now, the thing to also keep in mind is that although in our example we did this completely in Marketing Cloud, you are not limited to that.

You can host these applications externally, but you would no longer be able to use SSJS or AMPscript and would instead have to utilize another language to interact with Marketing Cloud via an API. But we will get into this a bit more later in the book.

# Summary

Well, how about that? We got this awesome new Automation Dashboard application that we can add to our Marketing Cloud instances. Not only that, but we have an explanation about what needs to be done to build or customize an application of our own in the Marketing Cloud.

This is the end of our dive into internal automation in Marketing Cloud. We have gone over almost every aspect to optimize your usage of Marketing Cloud without requiring any external services or software.

In the next chapter, we will be diving into automation in Marketing Cloud involving external services. It certainly adds a new layer to what we have already discussed and brings all kinds of new possibilities and capabilities.

# Section 3: Optimizing the Automation of SFMC from External Sources

In this section, you will develop an understanding of common methods and technologies for building custom integrations in Marketing Cloud in order to automate your marketing and business processes. You should feel empowered to begin building external applications and activities following the content in this section.

This section contains the following chapters:

- *Chapter 9, Getting Started with Custom Integrations*
- *Chapter 10, Exploring SFMC as a Piece of the Puzzle*
- *Chapter 11, Exploring SDKs, APIs, and Specs*
- *Chapter 12, Webhooks and Microservices*
- *Chapter 13, Exploring Custom Journey Builder Activities*

# 9
# Getting Started with Custom Integrations

When approaching challenges to core business needs, one of the most important aspects of solutioning is understanding both the feasibility and possible paths that an individual can take to reach their desired outcome. Understanding exactly what you are trying to accomplish, and having a general idea of what possible solutions already exist on the market, will inform you as to whether a custom integration is either a possibility or a requirement for your project.

In this chapter, we will cover how to both understand and identify custom integration capabilities within the existing workflows of your organization. We will cover different integration types, particularly data integration, in depth to understand the different architectures that are commonly used by web services in order to provide automated, cohesive functionality to solve business processes. Finally, we'll examine the concept of limits when considering the feasibility of API integrations and how they should be considered when developing custom solutions. Let's further define what we're talking about and look at the who, what, and why of custom integrations.

In this chapter, the following topics will be covered:

- *The who, what, and why of custom integration*: This goes over what exactly a custom integration entails and why you should use it.
- *Have your cake and eat it too – combining approaches*: This is a look at how to combine custom integrations with out-of-the-box solutions.
- *Building your integrations toolbox*: A dive into the *how* and *what* that is needed for building and maintaining integrations.
- *Point-to-point integrations versus hub-and-spoke integrations*: An overview of the differences between the point-to-point and hub-and-spoke methods.
- *The Paradox of Choice – Finding the Right Tools*: A guide for you to select the right tools to increase the efficiency of the team and lead to a more stable product as the end result.

# The who, what, and why of custom integrations

Whether you are a seasoned developer or just getting started, there is a strong chance that you're at least somewhat familiar with what constitutes an integration. If you've used solutions such as Marketing Cloud Connect, you can easily see the power that integration can provide. Before we contrast these two types of solutions to common marketing automation problems, let's define exactly what we mean by a **custom integration**. The definition for this can be a bit fuzzy, and can largely depend on the context of both your business and your current implementation. But we can largely define it as a software solution that is specific to your exact use case and is wholly configured and maintained within your organization. This could be something as simple as a plugin or webhook to transfer data or something as complex as a full-suite content management system for your organization.

This differs from the out-of-the-box alternative in that, while it might feature a complex set of configurations that can meet your needs, the core solution is both built and maintained by a company or service that is external to your team. Additionally, you have no direct control over the existing functionality provided by the solution. With the generic definitions of each out of the way, let's take a deeper look at both the advantages and disadvantages that come with utilizing out-of-the-box solutions, namely, cost and efficiency when compared to more custom implementations.

# Out-of-the-box solutions

One of the most challenging aspects when considering an out-of-the-box solution is simply knowing the available options on the market that, at least partially, meet the use case that you're presented with. For common use cases, there is likely a multitude to choose from, and the reliability and quality will vary a great deal between them. This is the primary challenge with not only selecting an existing solution that works the best for your organization but also with deciding on a solution at all.

It is important to take great care, and do your due diligence when considering a preexisting solution to meet your use case. Understanding the company's history, its track record for stability and quality, and the roadmap for future upgrades and support against their existing offerings are crucial to examine before even considering the feasibility of either these or custom integrations as the path forward for your project.

## Advantages

When examining out-of-the-box solutions, it can be fairly easy to discern the common advantages and disadvantages associated with their use. By their very nature, they are likely to be generalized and applicable to the widest possible use cases for a given discipline, while sacrificing some of the more niche use cases that developers might encounter. With that in mind, let's generalize a bit and take a look at some of the advantages.

## Cost

This is perhaps the biggest advantage that preexisting solutions maintain over a custom integration. While it certainly might not be cheap, it is likely far more cost-effective to use an existing service than to implement a purely custom integration on a project. Project planning, development, **quality analysis (QA)**, and deployment procedures do not come cheap, and many organizations might find it infeasible to spend resources on a custom integration when an alternative is readily available and can be achieved at a lower cost to the business. Further still is the cost of maintenance and continued support, which might require additional resourcing to accommodate if operating on an otherwise lean team.

## Project duration

Similar to the arguments around cost, implementing your use case on an existing platform saves a considerable amount of time that could otherwise be utilized on other projects. In addition to the speed and efficiency gain realized with an existing solution, you also remove the likely need for iterative development internally to both determine and account for bugs and edge cases that might otherwise be resolved in an existing platform that has spent time honing its system to account for these. When you're in a rush to get a feature into production, this value add can be the deciding factor in your decision regarding implementation.

## Quality and stability

One of the more powerful arguments for using an existing solution is that there are many portions of the development life cycle that are clearly addressed and resolved by the very existence of a widely used solution. Knowing that a process can produce predictable and reliable results that can scale with your needs is a powerful incentive toward choosing an existing solution. Having the confidence that other organizations have battle-tested an existing process is important and ensures that you can spend time being productive rather than on hold while internal development resources work through bugs discovered after the product launch. Never underestimate the value of existing support for an API or service that can save both you and your team valuable time, which could better be spent elsewhere.

Now that we've considered some of the advantages that are inherent in using an existing solution to solve a business case, let's take a look at some of the disadvantages that this approach introduces.

## Disadvantages

As much as there are advantages to this approach, everything comes with caveats or costs. In the next section, we will be exploring the disadvantages that you will need to consider when using an out-of-the-box solution.

## Limited functionality

This is perhaps the most obvious and impactful disadvantage that comes with using out-of-the-box solutions. Because these services must be applicable to a large swath of companies and use cases, in order to be financially viable, the functionality is very likely to be generic in nature. While it's quite likely that a generic solution is applicable to many different scenarios and projects encountered by organizations, since many businesses will face a common set of challenges and needs, there are still more scenarios in which a business need is specific in some way to your organization or existing processes.

## Hidden costs

You've found a quality and well-respected service that accomplishes everything that you need for your project. You've saved your team both the time and effort required to build out their own solution, and now you're the office hero, right? Well, not always. While there are plenty of options that provide quality products in this space, their use should be viewed as an ongoing engagement rather than a one-time expense. Hidden fees, licensing costs, or even existing service rate increases are all things to consider when analyzing the projected cost of your implementation. What looks like a steal now could end up being a costly liability if the circumstances of your partnership change.

## Control

Similar to both of the items listed earlier, at the end of the day, you are not in charge of the solution that you've implemented. Perhaps you're a unique user whose use case depends on a feature in the system that is sparsely used by other organizations. In this scenario, there are no guarantees, other than those explicitly listed in your contract, that the organization operating this solution will continue to service the functionality in the platform that your business relies on. Furthermore, if you're offloading critical processes to external platforms, you've effectively tied the core functionality of your organization to an external company whose financial and product quality you cannot control. While taking extreme care in selecting an offering helps mitigate these issues, they are not ones to toss aside lightly.

Now that we've considered some of the advantages and disadvantages of using a preexisting solution to solve your business case, let's take a look at the pros and cons of custom integration in comparison to this approach.

# Custom integrations

While we've examined some of the benefits and drawbacks associated with out-of-the-box solutions, custom integrations come with their distinct set of challenges and opportunities. The feasibility of this solution is going to depend on many factors, such as your current team structure and use case. That being said, when working in a sufficiently complex marketing organization, the need for flexibility and functionality to meet your specific needs quite quickly becomes apparent.

To begin, let's take a look at some of the advantages that are inherent in using a custom integration rather than an out-of-the-box platform or service.

## Advantages

Custom integrations come with many different advantages compared to out-of-the-box solutions. In the next section, we will be going over all these advantages, in detail, to help you in your decision-making process.

### Flexibility

Similar to how existing integration services are hampered by their inability to accommodate business-specific use cases, this is the strongest argument for custom integrations that an individual can likely make. When using an existing service, it can become frustrating when you encounter some necessary functionality that will be required for your implementation, but it is either not supported or, worse, not even on the product roadmap. By utilizing a purely custom integration, you can define all aspects of your solution in a way that no generalized platform will be able to provide.

These benefits are not just related to the base functionality that you require, but also to all elements of the product life cycle. Enhanced error logging, which fits in with other custom integrations or existing business processes, enhance QA and automation features to keep users more productive and is one of the most powerful impacts that can be seen from using this approach.

### Stability and scalability

Let's say you're using an existing service to automate some marketing tasks within your organization. You set this up ages ago and everything is running smoothly, but now, you're adding additional volume to your processes because you've been so successful (congratulations!). Unfortunately, due to some changes on their end, your existing provider can no longer offer the same level of service to your organization at that scale. Yikes.

Scenarios such as the ones mentioned previously, while admittedly rare, have the potential to derail a successful project and leave teams scrambling to find alternative solutions at what might be very inopportune times. By utilizing a custom integration, you are never caught off guard when it comes to the ability of your solution to handle an emerging scenario. In addition to this, you can scale your integration as your needs evolve, which can both provide the necessary stability for critical processes and save money on hosting so that you're only paying for what you will need.

These are only two benefits of utilizing custom integrations to meet your needs. Of course, the benefits derived and the specific advantages are going to differ depending on your implementation and use case. Needless to say, its ability to meet most, or all, of the challenges you might be facing makes it a tantalizing approach for any new process that you are seeking to implement. Unfortunately, as the saying goes, *nothing in life is free*, and custom integrations are certainly no exception. To that end, let's take a look at some of the disadvantages associated with this approach.

## Disadvantages

As we have seen with out-of-the-box solutions, custom integrations also come with their own caveats and costs. These disadvantages need to be weighed against the benefits to find the best solution for you. In the following section, we will go into detail about these disadvantages to help you with your decision-making process.

## Cost

In the same way that existing solutions can be prohibitive due to their cost, which could be due to hidden fees or just the base contract for the service's use, custom integrations are doubly susceptible to this problem. First, the cost of using a custom integration is going to heavily depend on the existing resources and capabilities that your organization currently possesses. Do you have development, product management, quality assurance, and creative teams on hand in order to complete the product life cycle for your solution? Even if you do, can you afford the opportunity cost of having them occupied while other aspects of your marketing and business efforts go unattended or understaffed?

The single biggest argument against a purely custom integration is that it can be cost-prohibitive, particularly when the effort to develop required features vastly outweighs the immediate benefit that they might have for your team and organization. This isn't to say that the idea is dead-on-arrival, but it's more to highlight how it's an important aspect to consider when you're developing a custom integration. Always ensure that the benefit to reward ratio is considered in tandem with the considerations related to cost based on your organization's current capabilities.

## Time

This is an offshoot of the cost disadvantage, but it's important to also highlight it separately because it's an area where an existing service has a distinct advantage over custom solutions. Simply put, custom development takes time and, sometimes, much more than you might envision when planning out the life cycle for your integration solution. Even the most well-planned and thought-out projects can fall victim to unexpected delays and slowdowns that can challenge your timelines and put the efficacy of the solution in jeopardy. While there are many avenues that could cause delays to your project, here are a few common scenarios that could jeopardize your implementation:

- **Poor planning**: This can be due to a failure to understand the full scope of the project's needs, such as misaligning in terms of resourcing and ensuring everyone who is needed to complete the project has been assigned and time off has been taken into account. Or, it could be any number of other things that revolve around the scoping, resourcing, and cohesive project roadmap that are defined before actual work has begun.

- **Platform limitations**: Unfortunately, while your solution has been well-planned and the necessary functionality has been defined, you might find that your data platforms, or even Marketing Cloud itself, are ill-equipped to handle the functionality that you've outlined. Although this can usually be defined during the project scoping and planning phases, things such as poor documentation or shifting capabilities can arise mid-project and might require more resources than anticipated or even stop your solution dead in its tracks.

- **Changing needs**: In a digital environment, where the rate of change is measured in seconds rather than days, requirements and priorities can change before your solution has had time to adapt. Perhaps your functionality doesn't require further enhancements in order to be legally compliant, or perhaps your implementation no longer makes sense in light of a new business reality. The benefits of flexibility can also bring scope creep and bloat to a project that was otherwise envisioned as lean.

As you can see, there is no easy answer here for what approach should be applicable for your solution. While existing services provide you with a well-tested platform, which is ready to go on activation, they might not be able to accommodate your unique requirements and, thus, might offer a poor solution or none at all. Conversely, while custom integrations can provide us with the greatest degree of flexibility and control, they might be cost-prohibitive or subject to many parts of the development life cycle that have already been solved with an existing solution. If only there were some way we could harness the benefits of both while helping to mitigate some of their distinct disadvantages.

# Have your cake and eat it too – combining approaches

Similar to many things in life, custom integrations and out-of-the-box solutions don't always have to be either/or. Instead, they can be utilized in tandem to take advantage of the strengths implicit in both in order to provide an alternative pathway toward implementing effective solutions in both a cost-effective and timely manner.

One of the many benefits of using a hybrid approach is that it allows you to keep the tools and processes that you love, while still being able to iteratively improve upon them in order to generate more productivity and usefulness from your existing process. For example, perhaps you have a service that you are using for internal communications in your organization. It works great, and collaboration and communication across teams have never been higher, but you often find yourself bouncing back and forth between it and Marketing Cloud to perform mundane tasks such as seeing how your current newsletter is performing, when a new asset has been uploaded by your creative team, or when something goes awry with one of your email programs. While we could build an entirely new messaging service to accommodate these desired changes, that would be time and cost-prohibitive and would interrupt the flow and environment that your team is used to. In this scenario, a smaller and more compartmentalized integration can likely be used to integrate data seamlessly between your messaging service and Marketing Cloud in order to provide the same functionality without the significant drawbacks of using an either/or approach.

Another advantage, which is implicit in our previous example, is that using a hybrid approach to your integrations can force you to think about specific use cases rather than having to envision an entire cohesive structure for your project. This can allow both developers, and non-developers, on your team to hone into and refine use cases to ensure that you are developing solutions that will be both stable and useful to your team. In addition to this benefit, as you keep a more granular focus on both your use case and its desired functionality, additional enhancements and implementations can be uncovered so that you can use the specificity of your specific implementation within a more generalized solution that could be reused across disparate portions of your organization.

As you can see, this is no easy decision, and any implementation, regardless of the approach, will require great care in assessing the capabilities of the organization along with the realities of their financial incentives and overall business goals. Marketers and developers who can easily identify the key capabilities of popular services and combine that acumen with their development skills and considerations in product development can become a powerful force for raising the capabilities and level of efficiency within their organization.

Equipped with the knowledge of the advantages and disadvantages of each approach, let's dive a bit deeper into the different types of integrations and how they can be utilized for different situations.

# Building your integration toolbox

We now have a general idea of what a custom integration entails and how it can fit within our existing services to provide new efficiencies and capabilities to our company. But how do we get started? In addition to the items that we discussed earlier, particularly those in relation to project planning, understanding possible roadblocks, and points of failure in your development process, we need to identify and understand the different types of integrations that are common in the development space.

Before embarking on any integration project, developers need to understand the different types of integration approaches to ensure that the most applicable methodology and implementation technologies are used for a given implementation. The diversity of both integration requirements and capabilities means that a one-size-fits-all approach is likely to fail. Let's take a look at some of the more common methodologies in this space and examine each in turn.

## ETL, ELT, and Reverse ETL

Although we have already covered this type of process in *Chapter 5, Automating Your ETL and Data*, let's take another look at this approach in the context of integrations so that we can identify how it can be applied to any planned integration. ETL is commonly used to populate data warehouses for data migration, data integration, and BI programs. As its name suggests, it consists of three distinct stages known as **extract**, **transform**, and **load**. Let's take a look at each of these processes to identify what's going on within each:

- **Extract**: First, relevant data is discovered and pulled together from multiple data sources and put inside a staging area, which is an intermediary destination before the data warehouse or primary destination for your source data. Since it might not be feasible to extract all the data from all the sources at the same time, a staging area helps bring all the data together at different times without overwhelming the data sources. A staging area is also useful if there is a problem loading data into the final data store, allowing syncs to be rolled back and resumed, as needed, and ensuring there is no loss or corruption to your data within your production environment.

- **Transform**: Transforming the data relates to the manipulation of our existing data in such a way that meets our individual business needs or goals. The data ingested from other services/platforms might not be structured in a manner that is suitable for our tables, so we'll need to clean and filter the dataset in order to make it more compatible with our schema.

- **Load**: Once all of our data has been aggregated and any necessary transformations have been applied, the final piece is to load this data into our data warehouse for storage and future access. A data warehouse will allow users to more easily access valuable data points in a format that is both accessible and one that makes sense for the business use cases of the data stream.

With the basic terminology of each step defined, let's look at the subtle variations of this process, beginning with ETL.

## ETL

ETL is a traditional data integration process whose origins date back many decades. Under the ETL paradigm, data is first extracted from first-party databases and third-party sources, such as Software-as-a-Service tools or cloud applications. Then, it is transformed to meet the needs of the organizations before being loaded into the data warehouse. The following diagram illustrates the ETL process:

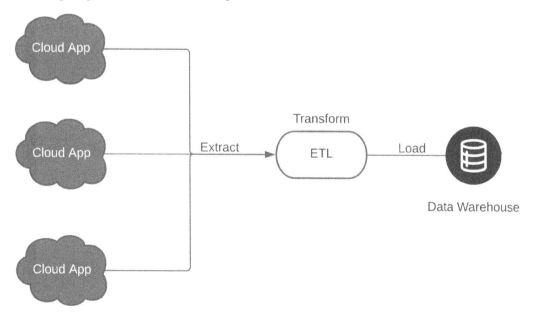

Figure 9.1 – The ETL process

In the preceding diagram, you can see that we are taking data from several different sources, cloud applications in this example, and extracting it into our staging area. In our staging area, we will enrich and transform the data to fit within the data structures that are outlined within our data warehouse. Another advantage of processing our data in this staging environment before loading our data is that it gives us the opportunity to encrypt or remove data that would, otherwise, violate compliance requirements for things such as the **General Data Protection Regulation (GDPR)** or **Health Insurance Portability and Accountability Act (HIPAA)**. Finally, we'll load that data into our data warehouse or application database. Let's take a look at an alternative form of this, known as ELT.

## ELT

ELT, similarly to ETL, involves extraction, transformation, and load processes, but the key difference is the order in which these steps are performed and the consequences that are derived for this organization. The rise of ELT as a modern approach to ETL has been largely fueled by the emergence of cloud data warehouses that are both performant and highly reliable, enabling data transformation and enrichment to occur with the data warehouse itself rather than in an auxiliary staging environment. Let's take a look at a diagram to see how ELT works:

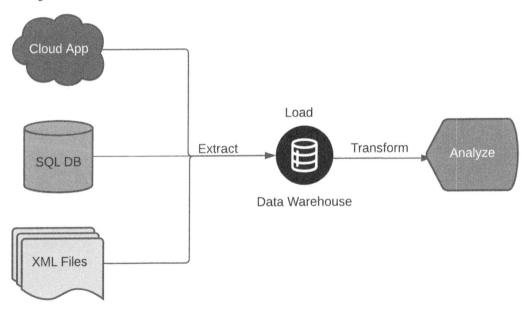

Figure 9.2 – The ELT process

Within the ELT approach, data is extracted directly into the data warehouse in order to be transformed. This process means that ELT uses cloud-based data warehouses to process structured, unstructured, and raw data types. Because of this, ELT works very well with *Data Lakes*. A data lake is a centralized repository that can be used to store both structured and unstructured data, as well as being a method for organizing very large volumes of data from different sources within your integration.

Of course, to derive meaningful insights from the data or for use in BI or CRM platforms, the data must be transformed. But this process allows you to aggregate data across a multitude of sources very quickly and to derive information aggregated across a diverse array of sources. Using this type allows high speed, low maintenance, and flexibility in both the loading and transformation of the data.

## Reverse ETL

As the center of gravity for data processes has shifted into data warehouses, so too has their importance in providing value as a source of record that has the potential to be utilized across a variety of applications and solutions (such as Salesforce). This has led to the emergence of an approach known as **Reverse ETL**:

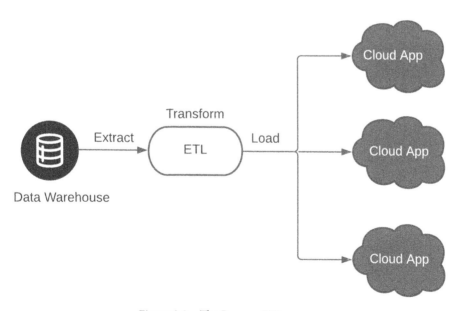

Figure 9.3 – The Reverse ETL process

The power of this approach lies behind the growing centrality of the data warehouse, both as an expansive store of data across various platforms and as a source of data flowing back into these applications in a true analytics operation loop. In the preceding diagram, we can see that we're now operating with the data warehouse as an initial data store that we will use to extract and process our data with a **hub-and-spoke methodology** that takes our centralized data store and allows all of our connected applications and integrations to accept data seamlessly rather than relying on single integrations between our various systems in order to retrieve data in a point-to-point integration. Speaking of point-to-point integrations, let's look at that next.

# Point-to-point integrations versus hub-and-spoke integrations

Now that we've outlined several data integration types, let's take our examination a step further and look at the different architectures that we can utilize to build our custom integrations. In this section, we'll cover both the point-to-point and hub-and-spoke integration types and discuss their structures and costs/benefits in depth. First, let's begin with point-to-point integrations and define what this type entails.

## Point-to-point integrations

We will start by looking at a diagram that illustrates the workflow of a point-to-point integration:

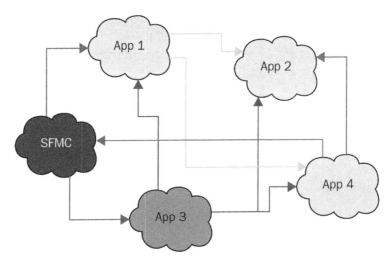

Figure 9.4 – A point-to-point integration

As you can see from the preceding diagram, each system is, essentially, accessing another by direct integration. These services are then further connected with one other through isolated connections. Point-to-point integrations, also known as **one-to-one integrations**, are those that use middleware to enable data sharing between two systems or to serve as an arbiter of some general functionality between two disparate services in a one-way directional flow. The middleware facilitates both the transformation of data and the mechanics of transporting the data. This integration type is among the simplest to set up and, often, can be developed and deployed far more quickly than the other integration types that we've discussed in this section.

Unfortunately, what it gains in initial simplicity comes at a steep cost. Point-to-point integrations are very tightly coupled to the use cases and services for which they were created and cannot be reused for generalized purposes. A simple example might be a gateway that has been constructed to download newly created assets and upload them to an external asset management system. In this scenario, it might be that automation has been constructed to retrieve the assets generated since its last execution, and it calls an external service to authenticate and retrieve those files and post their contents to an existing service. The middleware application is configured to take requests from Marketing Cloud and then makes a direct one-to-one request to the asset management system to maintain the assets. Now, let's suppose we onboard another asset management system that our business team wants to use to validate basic email content that is being generated in Salesforce Marketing Cloud. In this scenario, our existing solution is wholly useless because it can only perform operations against our previous asset management platform. To accommodate this new use case, another automation activity is constructed to call a separate middleware that will then process our data onto the new platform.

In the preceding scenario, with only one expanding use case, we've effectively doubled the number of communications that we need to manage (one for the middleware and one for the destination). This doesn't even account for possible integrations between the asset management systems and Salesforce Marketing Cloud itself, which would further complicate our integration. While we might not need to set up so many different processes related to our asset management, it's easy to see how this integration type can get out of hand quite quickly. With every new integration, we're introducing additional points of failure and security risks. Additionally, we're having to maintain updates and monitoring for each instance of our solution.

As you can see, whatever simplicity we might have gained by adopting this solution for a one-off task quickly spirals out of control as we add additional use cases and integrations into the system. So, are there any scenarios where this integration methodology can be applicable? Sure, but the use cases are limited primarily to those projects with the following considerations:

- **Proof of concept**: Developing point-to-point integrations to determine the feasibility of a production solution or to conceptualize implementations on top of other integration software.

- **Limited use**: When the use case for your integration has short longevity and does not warrant a large investment of resources to develop a more long-lasting and sustainable product. Typically, these use cases are very isolated business needs that have no real use in other parts of your organization or projects.

- **Time-sensitive projects**: Due to their simplicity of setup, and the feasibility of a single developer or small team standing up an integration quickly, these can also serve as a stopgap to provide the required functionality to meet the business needs quickly. This use case should only be used as a last resort since the possibility of these integrations spiraling out of control to become the norm and not the exception is very real.

As noted earlier, while this method can get your functionality launched quickly and with minimal resources, it is less than ideal for enterprise clients who will likely have multiple ongoing integrations. So, if point-to-point integrations aren't desirable for a variety of use cases, what sort of alternative integration method can we rely on? Enter hub-and-spoke integrations.

## Hub-and-spoke integrations

In contrast to the point-to-point integration, the hub-and-spoke methodology uses a fully integrated platform, or **hub**, that manages intra-server communication and data transfer through a centralized service rather than individual routing. Using this methodology, each system that wants to share data across your enterprise applications or integrations has a single connection point that will mediate requests, decoupling senders and receivers of your data. The following is a visualization of the hub-and-spoke methodology:

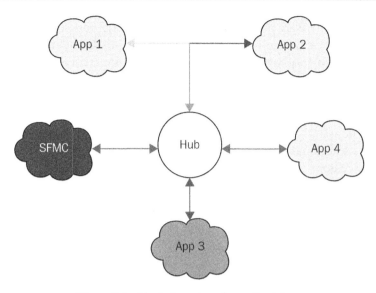

Figure 9.5 – The hub-and-spoke methodology

As you can see in the preceding diagram, the structure of a hub-and-spoke integration differs quite substantially from a point-to-point integration. Rather than disparate services connecting to each other via discrete one-to-one integrations, here, the services are connected through a central source. The services integrate with the central hub through lightweight connectors that facilitate the requests. Using this approach, we can decouple the connector logic from the hub entirely or integrate it as an extension of the platform. This allows us to make significant modifications to our connection logic and architecture without jeopardizing the overall stability of our other services.

One of the primary advantages of this integration type is that it is much simpler, from an architecture perspective, and allows for a more streamlined process in terms of monitoring and security. In addition to this, users of this methodology almost instantly have more control and flexibility in terms of the data and functionality that can be accessed by any other system. Also, we can now track and quantify the requests and transactions being made between various systems to derive even greater insights into how data and the services are operating as a cohesive whole.

Another important aspect of using this approach is the widespread availability of **Integration-Platform-as-a-Service (IPaaS)** offerings, which combine the capabilities of the hub-and-spoke approach in tandem with multi-tenant cloud services. These providers can host applications, servers, and data, provide integration tools and middleware solutions that can accommodate the entire development life cycle, and act as a user-friendly platform that can speed up the integration configuration by using prefabricated connectors and rulesets to quantify how interactions should be handled in a multi-tenant environment.

That's not to say that there are no downsides to using the hub-and-spoke integration approach, as there are certain considerations that must be made to determine its efficacy. In contrast to the point-to-point approach, the initial development and deployment of integrations are likely to be slow, and the processes outlined will need to adhere to the rules you define in the data-sharing model. In addition to this, while IPaaS services do allow for far more efficiencies in terms of the time and difficulty required to enable complex integrations and design, develop, and deploy them, they can come with additional costs. Additionally, they might not fight use cases where the existing integration structure is very custom or niche or those where the data is already mostly centralized and a high degree of flexibility is needed for the details of your integration.

There are other integration methodologies that we have not touched upon in this chapter, but we hope that this provides a general idea of the ways that our services can exchange data and interact with one another. This should help inform the approaches that you take in your integration planning and development processes and what, if any, additional services or solutions might be useful in your use case.

Now, let's turn to a more development-oriented portion of the integration process, and discuss how to select the right development tools and environments to get your project off the ground.

# The paradox of choice – finding the right tools

We've outlined common integration methodologies, their advantages, and disadvantages, and you've got your architecture all buttoned up and ready for execution. So, what now? One of the most challenging scenarios for an intrepid developer or a team that is looking to augment or create a custom solution is to select the right tools that will increase the efficiency of the team and lead to a more stable product as the end result.

The first component is to identify the infrastructure that will necessarily power the great functionality you've envisioned for your use case. Choosing the right data warehouse, ETL tooling, server, and many other aspects of the critical components that will serve your application logic is, of course, key and will greatly depend on a number of factors, from the overall budget of your organization to the capabilities that you are looking to implement. In addition to our infrastructure concerns, we also need to identify the programming languages, APIs, deployment tools, and more that will directly affect the experience of the developers working on your custom integration.

A common approach will be to assess the skillset and familiarity of the different members of the team in order to determine which platforms and languages the majority of the developers feel comfortable with and can use to be productive quickly. This is certainly an effective method that plays into some key considerations when examining the right language and tools for your project. Here are some general guidelines to consider when making your selection:

- **Performance**: How will performance impact your solution? Will your solution require minimal downtime and high-throughput when processing your application logic? Or will this solution experience minimal traffic and serve non-critical infrastructure? It might seem trivial, but the decisions you make around your language and frameworks can dramatically impact the overall performance of your solution if you fail to consider other alternatives. If all you need is a Buick, don't buy a Mercedes.

- **Use in the development community**: This might seem somewhat trivial, but it's important that you think future-forward in terms of the solutions that you are constructing and the tooling you choose. Ask yourself how difficult it would be for the team to hire a new resource with experience in this language/platform, or whether additional resourcing is required for either the new development or the maintenance of your legacy implementation. You might want to develop in either an obscure new language or a dated and ancient one, but never fail to consider that you might need help in a pinch, and it's important to speak a common language with your code.

- **Speed to production**: We've already touched upon this consideration, but it's so important that it bears repeating. Let's say that you picked a language/tool with high usage rates in the development community, and you're at a near-expert level with the same language. The downside is that no one on your team is familiar with it in the slightest. Time is money and getting a solution into production quickly can be the difference between it getting completed or falling into the wastebin of tech projects. Of course, choosing a language that will give you the best performance and productivity in terms of development tools is key. However, spending months just to get everyone up to speed is just as likely to derail the project as quickly as the alternative.

- **APIs**: Because the nature of Salesforce Marketing Cloud automation will inherently feature some level of integration with the API, it's important that you also take the easy approach of interacting with the platform when selecting your language. Is there an existing SDK, which is well-documented, already set up for the language you're considering? If so, does it contain the methods and objects that will predominantly feature in your solution already defined within the code base?

In addition to this, the limitations of the platform and what data can be operated on, and in what way, are important factors to consider for the feasibility of any solution that has at least some integration within Salesforce Marketing Cloud. Understanding commonalities between other API endpoints in terms of data structure and interoperability are also key.

- **Tools and libraries**: When choosing to implement software development tools or libraries into your development process, think carefully about the functionality you are intending to accomplish and streamline by using these items. Too many projects reach an end stage, where developers have added considerable bloat and messiness to their production implementation when only a small sliver of functionality was necessary for the final product. Consider whether the problem you are trying to solve with this library really requires all of the functionality you are importing, or if only a small subset of functions are actually required in your solution.

- **Configuration**: Do all of your team members have the same desktop environment for developing your project? Is your tooling a one-click setup in Linux but a complicated mess of configurations when members are setting up their environments on Windows? It doesn't take long for developers, who've already configured their tools and environments from past projects, to get out of sync and introduce needless delays and confusion into your development life cycle. Consider using containers and tools such as Docker to build your developer environments in a way that is sustainable and easily shareable by the members of your project.

- **Process automation**: It's 4:55 pm and you need to get a new fix into staging before important stakeholders in your company demo your incredible new solution. Easy, right? Well, you just checked and it looks like an errant deployment configuration has actually pulled and promoted code from the wrong environment. Taking care to automate sensitive and repetitive tasks in your development process can be the difference between a smooth code-to-testing process or a code-to-production process being a breeze or a literal nightmare.

Those are only a few of the items that we could touch on in order to aid in the selection of the right tooling and environment for a development project. It's important to understand that, while the actual development is where the rubber meets the road, failing to adequately consider the languages and tooling for your solutions can just as easily derail a project as much as bug-filled code can.

If it's such an important part of the project life cycle, then why are issues with the preceding considerations as common as they are? To some degree, we can develop an affinity for a given language or solution that was either enjoyable to work with or solved a particular use case considerably well. The issue with this is that it can lead us to occasionally always reach for the same tool regardless of the type of issue or use case that we are approaching for the first time. It's been said that *when you have a hammer, everything starts to look like a nail.* Take careful consideration when addressing the aforementioned callouts, and ensure that you're choosing the right tools for your problem and not only those that are the most familiar or enjoyable to work within. It's all too easy to prefer something that will let you start fast and yield rewards more quickly, but it will feel quite the opposite if you're spending all of your time bug-fixing and maintaining a project that is poorly suited for the initial need.

The final point we'll make in terms of choosing the right tools for the job is one that has been touched on numerous times throughout this book. When you do start the planning and development process, *document everything.* Outlining your processes, both development and internal, for developing and maintaining your code base is going to save both future developers and yourself a lot of frustration later on.

We've focused on generic applications and considerations for building custom and hybrid integrations, but let's take a quick look at a specific item in the Salesforce ecosystem that can have an impact as you plan and develop your solutions.

## Know your limits

This will likely not come as a shock to anyone working within the platform, but Salesforce operates on multi-tenant software architecture. This environment is shared by hundreds of organizations across the world, and unfortunately, its resources operate on a finite scale. It should come as no surprise, given that individual tenants will be competing with each other for ever-larger shares of this finite computing resource, that Salesforce has dictated a set of rules and limitations for accessing these resources. We call these sets of rules **governor limits**.

These governor limits help establish defined rules that prevent a single tenant from monopolizing large shares of cloud resources in order to prevent service degradation or disruption of the larger system as a whole. In the core Salesforce CRM, the Apex runtime engine enforces these limits to ensure that Apex code or processes don't exceed an undesired threshold. Due to this, when this limit has been met by a process within Salesforce, the system will return an exception that cannot be handled, and the process will be stopped. Here are the types of governor limits in Salesforce:

- **Per-Transaction Apex Limits**: Here, limits are counted whenever an Apex transaction has been executed. In terms of Batch Apex, these are reset for each execution.

- **Per-Transaction Certified Managed Package Limits**: Certified managed packages—managed packages that have passed the security review for AppExchange—get their own set of limits for most per-transaction limits. The Salesforce ISV partners develop certified managed packages, which are installed in your organization from AppExchange and have unique namespaces.

- **Lightning Platform Apex Limits**: These are limits placed explicitly on the number of requests for resources in relation to the Lightning Platform. These are not particular to standard Apex transactions.

- **Static Apex Limits**: These include generic limits for Apex, such as loop and trigger sizes, payload/callout sizes and times, and more.

- **Size-Specific Apex Limits**: These are size-specific limitations on Apex such as the maximum number of characters in a given class or trigger, the maximum usage size of Apex code in an organization, and more.

- **Miscellaneous Apex Limit**: This refers to the imposed Apex limits that are not encompassed in the other categories, such as SOQL query performance and limits associated with event report size.

- In addition to this report, there are other limits in the platform that can be reached that are not applicable to the previous items (for example, email and push transaction limits), but this should provide a general overview of the types of Apex limits that are enforced within Core CRM.

- While these limits are applicable to Salesforce CRM, Salesforce Marketing Cloud contains a completely different subset of limits and best practices that must be considered when interacting with the API.

- **Time-based limits**: While there is no definitive limit on the number of transactions that can take place within a given minute, hour, or day, it is recommended that you do not use more than 2,000 SOAP calls per minute and no more than 2,500 calls per minute when interacting with the REST API. In addition to this, the yearly allocation of API calls that you are allotted is dependent on your Salesforce Marketing Cloud version and contract, ranging from 0 calls per year all the way to 200M+.

- **General limits**: In addition to the preceding limits, Salesforce reserves the right to rate-limit the API requests in your account if your Marketing Cloud instance is identified as having an overall impact on the system at large. The throttling rate will depend on the rate necessary to stabilize the system. This rate will continue to be enforced until the source of the issue causing the throttling ceases to become a factor. In the SOAP API, this will be returned as an HTTP 500 error, while in the REST API, an error code of `429 - Too Many Requests` will be returned in response to an API call in the platform.

Both the Salesforce CRM and Marketing Cloud API limitations are important to consider when developing your custom integrations or examining the feasibility of your use case. Although they might cause headaches for your development teams, embracing these limitations can allow your organization to develop cleaner, more performant, and stable code bases that will keep the platform up and running smoothly for both other users and yourself.

## Setup and next steps

In this chapter, we've learned more about the definition of what a custom integration is along with some helpful methodologies for planning and envisioning how the systems that we are working with can interact with one another efficiently. In addition to this, we've also examined some considerations and pitfalls to consider when planning your development experience and environment.

To that end, we're now able to start planning and developing our first custom integration for Marketing Cloud. How exciting! In the next chapter, we'll dive into the details of how to build out our integration and how we can use Marketing Cloud in innovative ways to bring productivity and innovation to our business and marketing processes.

# Summary

In this chapter, we reviewed the different methods for understanding and applying custom integrations into our existing business process as well as any items we've identified for automation.

In addition to this, we've gained a greater understanding of the different types of integration, particularly data integrations, and how these architectures can drive the type and method of our implementations. This also gives us a greater understanding of our existing data processes and keeps what we are seeking to accomplish at the front of our minds.

Finally, we examined the concept of limits regarding the Salesforce platform, which helps dictate both the capabilities and types of integrations that might be applicable for our use case. In the next chapter, let's dive a little more deeply into workflows to determine how we can easily refine proper use cases for automation and how Salesforce Marketing Cloud fits into your overall processes.

# 10
# Exploring SFMC as a Piece of the Puzzle

In the last chapter, we covered some key concepts and important considerations when approaching both custom integrations and out-of-the-box solutions, as well as hybrid approaches. *But how can we build on this knowledge in order to start tackling more specific use-cases that we might encounter within a **Salesforce Marketing Cloud (SFMC)** context?* Understanding the differences between things such as **point-to-point** and **hub-and-spoke** integrations gives us insights that we can use during our implementation and solutioning phase. It isn't applicable if we can't find real-world applications for the solutions to begin with.

*So, how can take the leap from a generalized concept to a useful solution?* Unfortunately, again, this will rely on many factors that will be specific to your capabilities and business processes. That being said, we can lay out some helpful rules of the road to find real opportunities for efficiency and automation. These rules can enable you to automate processes within your team and organization to ensure you're getting the most out of your SFMC instance and marketing team more generally.

In this chapter, we'll cover how to identify prospects for automation within your organization's workflow and how to get started creating an automated solution. We'll also look at some common architectures for application development and the importance of **test-driven development** (**TDD**). Let's take a look at the topics we'll be covering here:

- *Knowing about your process flow*: How to examine your current workflows to identify automation opportunities

- *Putting pen to paper*: Getting started with an automated solution through a real-world example

- *Understanding the importance of structure*: Understanding different types of application architectures, along with their benefits and costs

- *Testing, testing, and more testing*: Why testing is so important, and some considerations when developing solutions with a test-driven approach

By the end of this chapter, you should feel more empowered to identify the key points of your workflow that would benefit from automated solutions. In addition, we'll take a look at the Salesforce Lightning Component framework to see a real-world example of how you implement automated solutions in a business context. We'll also talk about application architecture and the benefits of testing. With that, let's take a look at how we can better spot these opportunities for automation.

## Technical requirements

The full code for the chapter can be found in the GitHub repository located here: https://github.com/PacktPublishing/Automating-Salesforce-Marketing-Cloud/tree/main/Chapter10.

## Knowing about your process flow

When seeking opportunities for automation within your business processes or marketing efforts, one of the most important aspects that must be considered is just how well you understand the **end-to-end** (**E2E**) processes occurring both inside and out of SFMC. This sounds obvious, but it can be very easy for developers to become siloed, both in their areas of expertise and with regard to current capabilities or existing solutions being utilized within their organization.

For instance, an SFMC developer may be intimately familiar with their suite of data integrations and custom applications being utilized in the system but fail to understand how these fit within a larger ecosystem of the organization's implementation, particularly around items such as email campaign development or customer life cycles.

That is not to say that we need to have a holistic view of the platform in order to identify any opportunities for innovation or automation. Most developers have probably encountered scenarios in their own development workflow that have proven to be both repetitive and tedious, and are obvious candidates for improvement. Failing to understand how these items even fit within the larger implementation can lead to either less effective solutions or missed opportunities for improving processes.

So, though it feels unnecessary to point out, it's of the highest importance that you first take into account just what your system architecture and process are from a holistic perspective before even thinking about which processes or tasks would benefit the most from automation. Failing to accurately account for this can lead to solutions that automate the wrong part of the process, thus missing opportunities for efficiency or resulting in solutions that are bogged down by trying to understand just what the correct flow is even supposed to be.

If you've got 10 people performing tasks, both within Marketing Cloud and your internal processes, you've likely got more than one different way for these to be accomplished. Obviously, having a well-documented process is important to ensure that teams are following best practices and keeping a consistent approach to issues, but knowing exactly how these are actually being handled in the real world can be another thing entirely.

For instance, consider we have an existing relationship with a vendor that wants to automate the delivery of new campaign-related data for delivery within Marketing Cloud. They have an existing integration that utilizes a **REpresentational State Transfer (REST) application programming interface (API)** to upsert rows through a batched process into a campaign data extension, and this solution has worked reliably for your organization. The vendor assures you that this will be a very similar implementation and that only a modified layout is needed, so you prepare the data extension based on their provided schema, set up the installed package, and *voilà!*—one data integration automated; no problem!

Unfortunately, you quickly find out from your peers working in campaign management that key values that are required to work within their existing template email logic are missing from the schema. Even worse, you find out from the vendor that those data points are not available within their new integration and that both teams will have to go back to the drawing board in order to develop a solution that will resolve these issues.

In this scenario, we had all of the technical *know-how* to provide the vendor with a suitable pathway toward a solution, but we lacked holistic knowledge of how that process interacts across teams in order to develop a solution that actually works to solve the intended problem. This is a simple example, but it highlights the risks of not taking this step seriously and the importance of working to understand how everyone is involved, and the considerations we can draw from that. With this in mind, let's take a look at some subsequent steps and considerations for identifying automation opportunities.

## Identifying owners and key players

This feeds off of the idea that we just illustrated but takes it a step further to focus specifically on identifying and interacting with the key stakeholders and owners of the processes within our workflow. We should not only understand the flow but identify those who own the processes that are being impacted. We should also ensure that they are brought into discussions on both the existing state of the flow and how to garner ideas on common pain points or previously discussed updates to the processes that we are analyzing for possible automation.

Understanding not only the current state but also the evolution of the flow from inception can provide even further insight into the intended use of the processes and what value was sought to be derived from these when they were initially designed.

Some initial questions to ask might be these:

- *How has the workflow/process changed in the recent history of the implementation and what drove those changes?*

- *What was the need for this process in the first place?*

- *What's the E2E process when this flow is operating in a perfect state?*

- *How are exceptions handled currently? If there is a blocker, what is the process for getting that resolved?*

- *Have there been concerns or common issues within the workflow that have been resolved or remain outstanding?*

- *What is the current vision for the future of this process? Is there an expectation that it will continue to be used in the near or mid-term?*

- *How important do you feel this process is toward your capabilities and stated goals?*

Obviously, this is not an exhaustive list of questions to provide to the key players who are close to the process now or have been at some point, but it gives some ideas to get the wheels turning and discussions flowing between the teams to help get an accurate representation of the flow and to possibly find ways to streamline current solutions.

## Creating diagrams for your processes

Once we've met with the key players in the project, the next step is to *diagram* the existing process and how it interacts with each system and team. This diagram should be an extension and a product of the discussions discussed previously. Even if you're utilizing advanced diagram tools or simply creating simple representations in a condensed format and visually highlighting the E2E flow for the process, you are examining for automation, which will bring out insights that might otherwise get missed in the initial step of this process. While it can be difficult to sometimes envision what the diagram should look like, it's sometimes helpful to consider how we envision our documentation or configuration for Journey Builder. We've got a fixed set of steps that are configured in our setup, and, at each point, there is some function to execute and some additional action to take based on the results from the previous step. Perhaps we have a customer welcome journey that encourages conversions after signup. Our first item in the flow is an email sent to the new customer. Now, we could have multiple branch points depending on what the result from the first event is. If the email is not delivered, maybe we want to try a text message, or if the customer converts, we would eject them from the journey. Obviously, this is a simplistic example, but we hope it helps you envision how your diagram overall should flow and what a representation of your processes could look like.

This user's diagram should be completely representative of each given point of the process, the possible paths that can be taken from a given node whenever a certain action is either taken or not, and what possible scenarios could arise from those. In addition, it should illustrate any tools or external solutions that are integrated within the process, even if they perform some trivial action. For instance, understanding whether a process is utilizing Journey Builder or Automation Studio in order to execute some action as a part of the process can dramatically change the type of flow and considerations that must be taken around that node in the process.

Having such a detailed representation of the flow proves to not only serve as a living document that can be used to spot common bottlenecks or opportunities for efficiency, but it also serves as a blueprint you can build a solution from that can more easily understand how functions can be integrated with minimal disruption. This also provides visibility for external resources that might have additional insights or questions to further drive revisions to the process or a realignment of goals.

## Finding opportunities

We've got our process defined with stakeholders, built out a representation of our workflow, and have approval from all parties that it is both sound and well defined. The next step is to find those points within our flow that can be easily removed or rearranged to provide efficiency and stability without yet resorting to thinking directly about how processes can be automated.

It is much better to consider how the process itself can be altered to be more streamlined before we look at efficiency or productivity gains so that we can be sure that the solutions we implement will work within a well-oiled machine and have the maximum impact rather than being a small improvement on a process that could be better designed.

Once we've confirmed that our process is configured in such a way to maximally promote efficiency and productivity, we can start to look for points in our flow that are apt candidates for automation. Let's look at some key considerations when examining a process to determine if it's a valid candidate for automation, as follows:

- **Continuity**: *How often does this process change or suffer from a lack of stability to handle circumstances that you can't mitigate easily with an automated solution?* If you're examining a key component of your workflow that you find is changing what it produces or consumes either in its function or data **inputs/outputs** (**I/Os**), then this is likely not an ideal candidate for an automated solution.

    If, however, you identify that a portion of your flow is very repetitive and is reliant on fixed or limited variability among data points, then this might be an item for further consideration.

- **Time**: Being a key component when examining opportunities, this is more of a function of the type of flow you are seeking to automate than continuity. Examining the level of human effort and time lost to a specific part of the flow is particularly relevant for those tasks that are within some internal business process in your organization.

    The point here is to define those tasks that take up some significant percentage of effort or time to complete. While there might be plenty of opportunities to reconfigure a portion of your flow to decrease the amount of effort needed to complete some tasks, if it only takes a few minutes to complete infrequently, then it's obviously not worth the effort to flag as a candidate for automation.

Another consideration with regard to time, rather than how much it's consumed by your organization performing a given task, is what the external experience is like for your customers and what their expectations are with regard to a response after a given action. For instance, on password-reset requests, an immediate response is expected by most users, and even a short length of time between the request and the follow-up is enough to frustrate even the most patient customers.

- **Importance**: Another criterion for finding a suitable process for workflow automation is its importance to both your flow's goals and its place within the flow as a whole. While it might make sense to automate a given task in your flow that you feel is repetitive and universally hated by your team, also consider just how critical a given item is in regard to the overall workflow. Anything that can bottleneck or—worse—derail the ideal path of your flow is worthy of consideration from the start—something that, while annoying, might be relatively unimportant to the overall process and might not be the best candidate for automation, even considering that it meets some of the other criteria highlighted previously.

- **Capabilities**: Let's say we've identified a task that's critical to our workflow that is repetitive, rule-based, and accepts a defined range of inputs in order to function. That sounds like a great candidate for automation! Unfortunately, it's all for naught if the process to automate the task is not supported within either the tools we are using within the flow or the capabilities of the system as a whole.

  For example, let's say we've identified that a large amount of our team's effort is related to tracking the amount of time spent on various tasks within Marketing Cloud and then logging this data in a **time management system** (**TMS**). While we can access the audit information around the platform, it's certainly not all-encompassing, and the nature of the work being performed can lend itself poorly to encompassing effort and time for a given task. We could obviously use various browser extensions or tools to help improve the efficiency of this process, and in this case that is a great idea, but the opportunity to completely automate or make significant gains in this task is limited by the capabilities of the system and the nature of the issue itself.

The inverse of this plays into another consideration in regard to capabilities. We've touched on this several times in this book, but it bears repeating in this context. If there is some functionality within SFMC (or any other tool/solution that makes up a portion of your flow) that can help automate the process you've identified, then don't reinvent the wheel. While custom integrations and solutions external to the system can be powerful multipliers on the platform's capabilities, it's always preferable to keep your solutions within that framework rather than moving off-platform just for the sake of doing so.

While these are important items for consideration when identifying opportunities for automation within your workflow, they're certainly not exhaustive. As you can see, rule-based, repetitive, or time-consuming processes are obvious candidates for finding a suitable use case, but there are clearly more things that must be considered before landing on the right candidate. In general, when approaching this for the first time, also look for quick wins or low-level efforts for automation when you've identified multiple applicable situations for improvement within your processes. This can help drive more buy-in and understanding as to how this can be a powerful multiplier in driving success within your workflows.

We've examined some helpful considerations when identifying opportunities for automation within your workflow or processes. So, let's move forward and take a look at an example solution that automates some functionality within Marketing Cloud in order to illustrate how we can actually put pen to paper after identifying a process that we want to automate or enhance.

# Putting pen to paper

We've spent time documenting our current flow, speaking with key stakeholders to find points well suited for automation, and we've got a process selected that we can automate. Now, we need to start thinking through the possible mechanisms and design patterns that will power the automation solution behind our selected process. This can be a tricky undertaking, as every solution comes with a different set of circumstances and challenges.

Often, just the concept of getting started or knowing where to begin can be overwhelming and might discourage some developers from continuing their efforts, particularly if the solution primarily benefits their development processes or if the team working on the solution is small. To that end, let's create a sample solution that shows how we can leverage Marketing Cloud in order to automate some functionality in an effort to both build confidence and get those creative wheels turning!

## Defining a use case

For our purposes here, let's assume we work within an organization that is utilizing both Sales Cloud and Marketing Cloud to meet all of their **customer relationship management** (**CRM**) needs. While Sales Cloud is the system of record, there is data that exists in Marketing Cloud that does not necessarily flow back with regularity into Sales Cloud. One such example is a data extension maintained in Marketing Cloud that houses the journey history for a given contact in the platform. This data extension contains an aggregate of data from several sources, including **Journey Builder Update Contact** activity events and engagement data retrieved from **Data Views**.

While we could create a custom object in Sales Cloud that is then populated utilizing Marketing Cloud data, the records don't fit well within our existing data model. Also, the nature of the sources and complexity in aggregating the data means that it's not a likely candidate for complete data integration in the near future. Making matters worse, the key users of this data will be non-technical representatives working within Salesforce.

During the representative's work day, they routinely touch base with customers around their recent purchases with the company, upcoming engagements, and document delivery and signing, among other things. Being strong proponents for marketing automation, we've wisely automated most of our communication tasks with customers by using Journey Builder and Salesforce data entry events in order to automatically send document completion reminders and follow-up tasks, among others.

While everything usually goes off without a hitch, our representatives occasionally need to have the capability to troubleshoot and validate what the customer experience has been when receiving complaints in regard to messaging, document generation, or even service request reminders. Given the volume of items to track down and the number of individuals who would need access, simply providing a flat file or having the representative log in to Marketing Cloud would be neither ideal nor feasible.

So, we've got a process that has a defined set of inputs, is a bottleneck for moving forward with a given part of our organization's workflow, and has a clear and defined definition of the type of problem we are aiming to solve (that is, visibility of existing data on demand). After examining our capabilities, we've discovered that there are API endpoints capable of retrieving data from Marketing Cloud, as well as the lightning component framework, that will allow us to make those calls and take user input, all from within our existing CRM tools.

This sounds like a great candidate for automation and one we can use to provide our representatives with the auditing ability needed to quickly respond to these requests without needing Marketing Cloud resources. To begin, let's first understand what a lightning component is and what it does.

## Understanding the lightning component framework

The lightning component framework is a Salesforce-native **user interface** (**UI**) process for creating dynamic applications and widgets for the Salesforce platform. It is used to build responsive and dynamic **single-page applications** (**SPAs**) within the core CRM platform. In lightning components, a component is a bundle of code. The bundle contains all the resources related to a component, such as the controller, helper, and markup.

A basic lightning component contains the design of a page in **HyperText Markup Language (HTML)** with some lightning tags. The component uses JavaScript on the client side and Apex on the server side. We can utilize this framework in order to create custom solutions, or leverage existing integrations within Salesforce in order to extend the functionality of the platform and provide enhanced mechanisms of integrating Marketing Cloud into the core platform.

## Prerequisites for creating a component

In order for our lightning component to function, we'll need to ensure that we have configured our data source and installed the package on the Marketing Cloud side.

First, let's define the structure of our data extension. It should look like this:

| PersonContactID | ActivityType | ActivityDate | ActivityResult |
|---|---|---|---|

Table 10.1 – Structure of the data extension

We'll now describe the structure of the preceding extension:

- `PersonContactID`: This column should contain the **unique identifier (UID)** we'll use to map our activities. The naming here comes from the `PersonContactID` field on the `Account` object within Salesforce.

- `ActivityType`: The values here should reflect the various types of activities within our data, such as email/**Short Message Service (SMS)** sends, tasks, and more.

- `ActivityDate`: This should contain the date for which the instance of an activity was generated.

- `ActivityResult`: This identifies the status of execution on the event. This can define whether an email was sent or bounced, a text message was undelivered, or any other status that can be applied from the type of activity generated.

This data extension will contain a log of each event that occurs for a given account record, such as email engagement, journey tasks/cases created, signing document sent, among others. We will populate this through Journey Builder, API events, and **Structured Query Language (SQL)** queries that unify this data from separate staging tables.

In addition to setting up our Send Logging data extension, we'll also need to create an installed package so that we can authenticate and make API calls to Marketing Cloud from an external system. The process for doing this is outside the scope of this book, but you can find more information in the Salesforce documentation (`https://developer.salesforce.com/docs/marketing/marketing-cloud/guide/install-packages.html`).

Now that we have everything configured on the Marketing Cloud side, let's start developing our lightning component.

# Building our lightning component

So, we've created our data extension schema and an installed package, and we've configured our data sources in order to pull the necessary data for our component. This setup will provide the backend service that we can utilize in order to aggregate and compile everything into a readable format for our lightning component. Now, let's take a look at each of our necessary files in order to get a better idea of how this application will function.

## Apex class

This is our custom controller Apex class that will be responsible for making our API calls in Marketing Cloud and returning the data we want to display in our component. An **Apex class** is a set of procedures or methods, defined in Apex, that enables users to attach a set of logic in response to some event within the system. These classes can contain variables and other classes, in addition to handling exceptions or executing static methods.

We can utilize Apex classes in order to execute the backend logic of our solution, based on events that occur from our user (such as creating input and searching the data extension). The structure of this class follows these syntax and definition requirements:

```
private | public | global
[virtual | abstract | with sharing | without sharing]
class ClassName [implements InterfaceNameList] [extends
ClassName]
{
// The body of the class
}
```

In addition to this, we must define our Apex class with the following:

- **Access modifiers**: Access modifiers, such as `public` or `private`, define the accessibility of your methods within your Apex class. These access modifiers are not required when defining an inner class. The `class` keyword, followed by the name of the class, is an absolute requirement.

- Optional extensions and/or implementation.

For our solution, our Apex class should be quite simple. We'll need functionality that can take and accept data from the frontend of our component and then make an API call to Marketing Cloud in order to retrieve the filtered dataset from our `Activity` data extension.

Then, it should return that data to the frontend of our component so that we can display this to the end user. Here's a generic idea of what some of our methods in the Apex controller should look like:

```
@AuraEnabled
public static String getMarketingCloudToken(){
    String responseBody = makeJSONPostCall(
    MARKETING_CLOUD_AUTH_URL,
    JSON.serialize( new Map<String, String>{
        <grant_type': 'client_credentials'
            <clientId' => ClientID,
                <clientSecret' => ClientSecret
                    <account_id': YOURMID
            } ), NULL
    );
    return ((Map<String, String>) JSON.deserialize(
    responseBody, Map<String, String>.class))
    .get( ACCESS_TOKEN );
}


@AuraEnabled
public static String searchDataExtension(String Email) {
        String authToken = getMarketingCloudToken();
        Http h = new Http();
        HttpRequest webReq = new HttpRequest();
        webReq.setMethod('GET');
        webReq.setHeader('Authorization',
            <Bearer <+ authToken);
        webReq.setEndpoint(searchDEURL);
        HttpResponse res = h.send(webReq);
        String response = res.getbody();
        return response;
}
```

In the preceding snippet, you can see that we're doing the following two things:

- First, we're making a REST API call to Marketing Cloud in order to generate our access token. Then, we're returning that token as the result of our method so that we can call it in a subsequent method in order to authenticate into Marketing Cloud.

- Then, you can see that in our `searchDataExtension` method, we're first authenticating into Marketing Cloud and assigning that value to the `authToken` variable. Finally, we're making a `GET` request to Marketing Cloud in order to retrieve a **JavaScript Object Notation (JSON)** representation of the filtered data derived from user input.

Again, this is only a sample of the full class structure, but it's enough to see how this fits together.

## Component markup

Component resources will contain the markup of your component, along with any relevant variable declarations or event handlers that can be utilized within your lightning component.

This should be considered as the *frontend* of our component and is used to control the UI display of our search form, declare component variables that we'll use to programmatically get and set our component data, and declare the types of pages that our component can be displayed on, among others. Let's look at some sample component markup for our solution here:

```
<aura:component implements="flexipage:availableForAllPageTypes"
access="global">
  <aura:attribute name="searchId" type="String"
    default=»» />
  <aura:attribute name="searchResults" type="String[]" />
```

Notice here that we're doing a few things, as follows:

- First, we define where our component can be executed using the `implements` attribute on our primary element. In this example, we've specified that this can be executed globally across all page types, but we could make it more granular if needed.

- In addition to this, we've instantiated two variables, `searchId` and `searchResults`, and have assigned `String` and string array data types to them, respectively.

This will allow us to get and set these values within our component, as follows:

```
<div class=»table-search»>
<lightning:input
  type=»text»
  name=»email-search»
  placeholder=»Enter A PersonContactId To Search
    Data Extension»
  value=»{!v.searchId}"
  />
<div class=»search-icon» onclick=»{!c.searchSubmit}">
  <lightning:icon
    iconName="utility:search"
    alternativeText="Search"
    size=»small»
    />
</div>
<aura:if isTrue="{!not(empty(v.searchResults))}">
  <table>
    <thead>
      <tr>
        <th>PersonContactId</th>
        <th>Activity Type</th>
        <th>ActivityDate</th>
        <th>ActivityResult</th>
      </tr>
    </thead>
    <tbody>
      <aura:iteration items="{!v.searchResults}"
        var=»row»>
        <tr>
          <td>{!row.personcontactid}</td>
          <td>{!row.activitytype}</td>
          <td>{!row.activitydate}</td>
          <td>{!row.activityresult}</td>
        </tr>
```

```
      </aura:iteration>
    </tbody>
  </table>
</aura:if>
</aura:component>
```

Here, we have some simple markup to enable our user to set the value for `searchId` within a simple input and a simple search icon that will execute an event when clicked. Notice we've attached an event called `searchSubmit` to this icon—this will be triggered from our client-side controller whenever it is clicked. Finally, we've added a table to display our data extension results whenever our `searchResults` array becomes populated with data.

## Client-side controller

Our client-side controller will contain functions related to events that occur within the component, such as when the user enters the desired `PersonContactId` object field and clicks our search icon. Client-side controllers are meant to be lean and only serve as a handler to pass event data from our component markup file to our helper methods. As such, this file will only contain an event handler for when the icon is clicked in our component, as illustrated in the following code snippet:

```
({
    searchSubmit: function (component, event, helper) {
    helper.getSearchResults(component, event, helper);
    }
});
```

As you can see, we've defined a `searchSubmit` function that we tied an event to in our component markup, so clicking on the search icon will now call this event, which will pass the information to our helper file for further processing.

## Client-side helper

This file contains our utility functions for the component. In order to maintain code readability and testability, you should keep your client-side controller as lean as possible and include any functions that do complex processing within the helper.

For our purposes, we need to create a function that is triggered by the event in our client-side controller that will take our user input from the component file and pass that data to our Apex class, where the actual process of getting Marketing Cloud data extension data is performed. Then, it will take the returned input, assign the values to our searchResults array defined in our component markup file, and show the data extension rows to the end user. Here's the code required to achieve this:

```
({
    getSearchResults: function (component, event, helper) {
        var action = component.get ("c.searchDataExtension");
        var searchId = component.get ("v.searchId");
        action.setParams ({ SearchParam: searchId });
        action.setCallback (this, function (response) {
            var temp = response.getReturnValue ();
            var json = JSON.parse (temp.toString ());
            var primNode = json.items;
            var resultsArr = [];
            for (var i in primNode) {
                var arrVals = primNode [i] .values;
                resultsArr.push (arrVals);
            }
            component.set ("v.searchResults", resultsArr);
        });
        $A.enqueueAction (action);
    }
});
```

Notice here that we're defining the Apex method that we want to call—searchDataExtension, in this example—and then passing in the value for searchId that the user defined in the component markup. Finally, we're taking the response and assigning it to the string array variable we've set up to be displayed in our UI.

We're done! We defined a gap in functionality that existed in our organization and met our criteria for a process that could be automated. Then, we utilized the existing capabilities in our current platform in order to extend the base functionality and provide our representatives with visibility into our Marketing Cloud data to prevent a bottleneck from occurring.

Obviously, the solution that we've developed here is specific to the Salesforce ecosystem, and the same code structure and organization is not going to be entirely applicable in other contexts (though we can apply similar principles). This is obviously a very specific use case, and we could have illustrated many other capabilities here that also provide valuable additions to your processes. Some examples for further consideration might be something like these (or something else entirely):

- CMS utilizing the Content Builder REST API

- Custom Journey Builder activities that retrieve data from external sources during the customer life cycle

- Version control and **continuous integration/continuous delivery (CI/CD)** solutions for your journeys and assets

The point here is that the possibilities are only limited by the platform capabilities and your imagination! We hope that this was helpful in highlighting an example where a project has clear goals, a straightforward structure with minimal resources needed, and a direct connection to work going on in Marketing Cloud.

# Understanding the importance of structure

Speaking of structure, after seeing how we were able to structure our lightning component solution in a component-based architecture, it's important that we also highlight different solution structures in order to more easily understand how your project might fit together as individual pieces interlaid with the generalized functionality. We'll take a look at some common design patterns for solutions, as an alternative to the component design pattern we used previously, but first, let's define a few key terms.

## Model

The **Model** means data that is required to display in the view. This is a representation of the critical information used within your architecture. Unlike the other components of this architecture, the Model is not dependent on either the Controller or View and can further define rules and meaning for the data being utilized in your application.

# View

The **View** represents UI components such as **Extensible Markup Language (XML)**, HTML, and so on. The View displays data from the Model and sends events, such as clicks and input submissions, from the user to the Controller for further processing. In the **Model-View-Controller (MVC)** pattern, the View will be updated whenever the state of an element has been modified within the model.

# Controller

**Controllers** are an intermediary between the Model and View components, providing Model data to the View and processing user events. When some event takes place within the View, the Controller will process the event based on business logic and will either return a response directly to the View or will update/retrieve data from the Model to update the data presented in the View.

## MVC

The MVC framework is a design pattern that separates the components of an application into three buckets: Model, View, and Controller. Each of these components is built to handle specific aspects of an application. MVC separates the business logic and presentation layer from each other. As a helpful tool, let's take a look at a visualization of the MVC architecture in order to better visualize how each piece fits together:

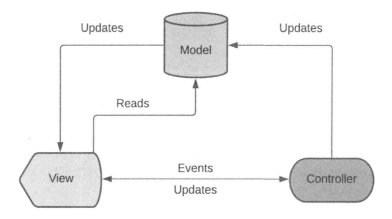

Figure 10.1 – MVC architecture

Let's walk through the flow represented in *Figure 10.1*. A user interacts with the View of our application, such as clicking the search icon in our previous example, and due to this action, an event is triggered to the Controller, which can either update the View directly or will structure and pass on the details of the event to the Model to let it know that some change within the View has occurred. The Model then takes that event and takes some action, such as adding a row to a database or returning data extension rows, and then passes this change back to the View in order to display to the user (as with our search results in the previous solution).

This is a very common design pattern and one that developers will likely already be familiar with in some capacity. It comes with several advantages, such as these:

- **Separation of concerns** (**SoC**) within an application.

- MVC responsibilities are divided between the client and server, compatible with web application architecture.

- Each component can be tested separately.

- Utilized by popular frameworks such as Rails and Spring.

That being said, there are some disadvantages to using MVC design patterns as well. The independent nature in which each component can be developed can sometimes lead to portions of the application falling behind in the development life cycle compared to others. Also, it's very easy to experience code bloat within your controller, leading to an architecture that can be difficult to both maintain and effectively understand how its components and functions are working together. Finally, this architecture can be ill-suited to smaller, complex, and large applications. A simple set of functions that don't require much UI input would be ill-suited for this, but so would a complex set of business rules with multiple layers of abstraction.

## Model-View-ViewModel

The **Model-View-ViewModel** (**MVVM**) pattern is similar to what we saw with MVC, but with some clear and obvious distinctions. The key difference here is the replacement of the controller in the MVC architecture with the ViewModel. The **ViewModel** is a representation of all the data you want to display on the page and is, as the name suggests, a model for the view. Let's take a look at a representation of this pattern to get a better idea of the overall flow:

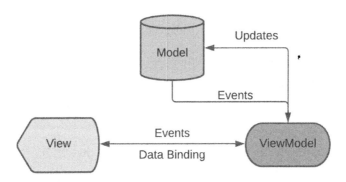

Figure 10.2 – MVVM architecture

As you can see here, the View uses data binding with the ViewModel in order to serve as a representation of the state of the ViewModel. It can also receive events or notifications from the ViewModel. The ViewModel, in turn, can receive events from the View as well as send events to the Model. Finally, we have the Model, which can receive updates from the ViewModel as well as send a notification back to the ViewModel. In a traditional MVC pattern, anytime the user wants to manipulate some data in the View, even temporarily, they must invoke some functionality within the Controller itself to perform the change. By using MVVM however, the View and the ViewModel communicate via data binding, method calls, properties, events, and messages.

Here, the ViewModel exposes not only models but other properties (such as state information) and commands, whereas the MVC format is specifically designed to create an SoC between the Model and View. The existence of the ViewModel within MVVM allows both the Model and View to update when some change to the existing Model has occurred. In this scenario, there is two-way data binding.

This is not to say that MVVM completely eliminates the use of a Controller. In fact, that are patterns such as **Model-View-Controller-ViewModel (MVCVM)** that continue to use the Controller to process logic while the ViewModel becomes extremely simplistic, making them ideal for low maintenance, and ongoing testing or stability concerns.

There are obviously many other development patterns out there, and each will have its strengths and weakness in relation to the type of solution that you are seeking to implement. Certainly, for microservices and Webhooks, you may not need a design pattern per se. The main takeaway, which we hope was illustrated in our lightning component solution example, is that understanding how your components in your solutions interact and share concerns with one another can help you identify how to structure your application as well as provide a deeper understanding as to what is happening *under the hood* and to anticipate issues before they occur.

# Testing, testing, and more testing

In past chapters, we've stressed the importance of testing your code, but an equally important consideration is to structure your development processes around the ideas of testing in order to provide stable products that are **user experience** (**UX**)-friendly and can handle edge cases.

In our previous example, we conveniently left out the importance of testing in order to illustrate the core functionality of the platform, but it should not be ignored. Before we end this chapter, let's take a look at the TDD process just so we can ensure we're keeping this key component *top of mind* while we develop our automated solutions.

## Creating specific tests

Developers should create specific unit tests to verify the functionality of individual features and pieces of functionality. We must first ensure that the test is valid and compiles before we can successfully execute the test. During initial development, and even outside of it, the unit test is likely to have a failure due to either some bug in the code or a misunderstanding of requirements. This type of failure is informative as it either reflects a misunderstanding of the requirements or some defect within the expected functionality that can further illustrate changes that need to be made in either the design or the implementation process.

## Correcting the code

When a unit test fails, we will obviously need to make revisions to our existing solution until the requirements have been further defined or our solution is executing as intended. Depending on the type of failure that we have, either in design or implementation, the type of correction that must be applied can differ significantly. A change in requirements or desired user behavior could require more thorough documenting of the user flow, while bugs within the implementation may require rework of existing code or even the development of further tests.

## Refactoring the code

Once you are finished with your changes and can confirm that the test executes successfully, look for any optimizations or efficiencies that can be added to increase the stability and performance of the functionality you are testing. Obviously, any changes that are made to the functionality should be retested after updating.

This is a simple concept, but it's a powerful one that can affect the performance, overall usability, and success of your project. Test coverage with this methodology is much higher compared to the conventional development models because this process focuses on creating tests for each functionality right from the beginning. It also helps developers hone in on the requirements from key stakeholders since it requires a thoughtful and considerate approach to each component within the solution. It will not only ease the addition of testing later in your application but also ensure that you have sufficient code coverage and that the developers are staying productive and not working on issues that were thought to have been resolved long ago.

# Summary

We've covered a lot in this chapter, but we hope that you feel you have a stronger grasp of how to identify items within your organization that could be good candidates for automation. Also, as we've discussed, sometimes, the hardest part of implementing a solution is to put pen to paper and get started on designing and implementing a solution. To aid in this, we've covered a simple solution that automates some functionality for members of our team using Salesforce and hopefully provides some helpful ideas and inspiration to identify similar aspects in your own workflow that can be enhanced within the Salesforce ecosystem as a whole.

Finally, we've discussed some common architectures that are widespread in their use across the web development ecosystem. While this can seem a bit theoretical at face value, we should now be able to see how these patterns are put into use by defining the meaning of their components and viewing their functionality in relation to the sample use case we covered in this chapter. We've also briefly touched on the importance of testing and the concept of using TDD in order to refine both the design and the solutions within our application.

Now that the importance of placing testing at the forefront at all times has been highlighted, in our next chapter, we'll dive deeper into Marketing Cloud more granularly. We'll also examine **software development kits** (**SDKs**), APIs, and everything in between.

# 11
# Exploring SDKs, APIs, and Specs

In the previous chapter, we went through a sample solution to extend our business capabilities, as well as to highlight the importance of structure and **test-driven development** (**TDD**).

Now, let's focus on two other aspects of development that form the core functionality that will become the backbone of any integration into Marketing Cloud: **application programming interfaces** (**APIs**) and **software development kits** (**SDKs**). It goes without saying, but external solutions to automate certain processes within your flow aren't exactly useful if they don't have some mechanism for actioning on data across systems. Knowing how and what capabilities or support your platforms have is going to dictate the exact nature of the integration and what method you choose to adopt in your solution.

We've covered substantial ground in understanding exactly what APIs are and how they can be utilized in *Chapter 7*, *The Power of the In-Step APIs*, but let's remember that we can define APIs as a way for applications to exchange data and functionality. They allow us to exchange information across disparate systems to automate individual pieces of a larger solution or to provide some means of information retrieval, transfer, alteration, or deletion.

In this chapter, we will cover the following topics:

- **Understanding APIs**: In this section, we will go over not just the REST and SOAP APIs, as we did in *Chapter 7, The Power of In-Step APIs*, but look into other aspects and uses of APIs beyond just the context of Marketing Cloud.

- **Requests and protocols – a deep dive**: Along with new types come new ways of making the requests. This section will dive deeper into the raw details of making an API call in REST and SOAP.

- **To SDK or not to SDK**: Now that we know the basics of the raw material, we can look at the pre-made code wrappers that use it and explore how useful they can be.

While we've spoken about both types of APIs in Marketing Cloud, **SOAP** and **REST**, other items around API architecture are perhaps not directly applicable to Marketing Cloud but are helpful to know when you're integrating services across platforms that are external to Salesforce. To begin, let's recap and then dig into some of the different types of web APIs that are being utilized by developers and organizations today.

# Understanding APIs

Previously in this book, we noted that there are some key protocols and specifications for APIs that define how systems can interact with one another, as well as in what format or structure the requests between them need to be configured.

In this section, we'll expand on those protocols and add some alternatives to those two approaches that have been common in the past or are currently growing in popularity. We'll also dig into SDKs to understand what they are, how they differ from APIs, and what sort of advantages and disadvantages may come from using them in your project. To begin, let's take a look at the different types of APIs to gain a more general understanding of how they operate.

## Open APIs... what does that mean?

Very similar to its name, **open APIs** are generally available to all. They are also known by names such as *external* or *public*, which means they have much more relaxed security measures. This allows developers and external users to easily access this data.

> **Not OpenAPI**
>
> One important clarification to be made is that open APIs are not related to the OpenAPI specification, which is a guideline, not a type of API. The OpenAPI specification is a guideline for how to structure and document an API.

With these more relaxed security measures, open APIs typically only require a moderate level of authentication to gain access. It is similar to someone that just has a lock on the handle, but not a deadbolt. It will work most of the time, but if someone wanted to get in, they could probably break it down. This feature makes open APIs an excellent option to streamline communication with third-party services and allows software developers to quickly implement components without restrictions.

An open API has many advantages, including the ability to rapidly innovate on an existing solution without having to write code to derive some core piece of functionality, such as data aggregation and formatting, communication or payment processing, and detailed search, among many others. Providers of open APIs can dramatically expand their user base and notoriety while providing third-party developers with the capability to create proprietary solutions that rely on their service and draw in additional users.

There are some obvious downsides of using an open API, many of which will depend on the quality of the service being provided by the API. There are many highly regarded open APIs in the market, including those offered by companies such as Apple and Google, but there are also many less reputable providers that may provide services rife with bugs, security flaws, or performance limitations.

Another disadvantage of using an open API is that your functionality is at the whims of those operating the API. Sudden changes to the terms of service could lead to rate limiting, incurred costs, or even a change in the core capabilities that your organization relies on. Most large companies that operate popular open APIs will often provide more support, legacy features in the event of a new product roadmap, and more bandwidth than some of their smaller competitors. Ensure that you are taking these items into account when you're utilizing an open API to prevent any future headaches in your solutions.

Next, we will make things a bit more secure and exclusive by looking at partner APIs.

## Partner APIs... a little closer to the vest

Although very useful, an open API is... well... wide open. Sometimes, you need something a bit more exclusive. This is where you use a **partner API**. A partner API is only available to specifically authorized developers or organizations that will consume the API. A partner API is used mostly for business-to-business (or partnership) communication or another similar company-to-company activity.

For example, let's say that business A wants to share customer data with their marketing agency, business B, which is wholly separate from business A. By using a partner API, business A can provide a method for business B to consume this data in a fast and secure way.

As such, partners that utilize these services have clear rights, and likely a contractual agreement that allows them to utilize these APIs. Due to this, there is a particular need for stronger authentication, authorization, and security mechanisms than we would see implemented with an open API. We see this sort of implementation when we work within Marketing Cloud since our API calls with the platform require more advanced security methods than a public method would provide. In addition to this, though the routes that can be retrieved are for public consumption, access to any individual route or data is self-contained to the individual partnership an organization has with Salesforce Marketing Cloud.

The advantages of partner APIs lie primarily in their ability to provide a more tailored, and likely stable, degree of services to an organization and a level of direct support to the individual partner than you would find in an open API (which has likely no direct support). In Marketing Cloud, we can see this directly regarding Salesforce Support and in the multi-tenant environment, which allows us to easily access subsets of data within our organization's instance. Existing relationships with the API provider can also streamline requests for additional functionality and provide more guidance toward accomplishing a project's goals. This is because the publisher is likely very familiar with both the API service and a partner's individual needs and business model.

Unfortunately, these partnerships may not come cheap and, while partners will have direct engagement with the API publisher and possibly some means of influencing their offerings, they still have no direct influence or control over the system at large. Smaller clients may find little recourse when their API publisher changes capabilities, particularly if they are using a more niche functionality that is not widely consumed across the publisher's partner base.

Although partner APIs are pretty great, let's look at an even more secure type of API call… internal APIs!

## Internal APIs… all in the family

Sometimes, no matter how good of a friend someone is, you need to keep things inside the family only. This saying is the equivalent of an **internal API**. An internal API is an API that opens up the backend data and application functionality for developers to use and manipulate. However, it only allows this data and functionality to be accessed by those within the company or organization. This differs from the previous two approaches in that the routes are completely private to the internal users and creators of the API specification. Though these internal APIs may be used by developers to create public-facing interfaces or applications, their use is wholly prohibited to access any resource that's external to the API publisher.

We can see these types of internal APIs in use within the Marketing Cloud ecosystem. Most developers will have found some activities that, while directly or programmatically accessible within the general UI, are not exposed through an API service, neither documented nor undocumented.

Sometimes, you have different tools or sections of business that need to collaborate or otherwise share data or information regularly, and it's just too difficult to do without an API. This is where internal APIs come in as they can allow other internal, completely vetted developers to create these connections to ensure the data is shared quickly and securely. If this is all internal, no sensitive or critical information will be able to be seen by anyone it should not be seen by. The best part of all this is that internal APIs usually include an audit trail of system access, meaning that you will be able to track down actions to users for added accountability.

The primary disadvantage of internal APIs is that additional development and project management time is needed to map out the internal solutions and develop and test them. Where the open and partner APIs allow users to take advantage of existing offerings, sometimes at a cost, internal solutions must be built from the ground up and might be beyond the technical skill or resources that are available for a given team. Still, they can be a powerful force when developed smartly.

## Composite APIs... with our powers combined

As that old gum commercial said, two things can be better than one. That is the theory behind **composite APIs**. These APIs generally combine two or more separate APIs to create a sequence or series of events based on the input. These can be related events or completely interdependent operations.

**Composite APIs** shine when you need to handle multiple, complex, or very tightly related API events. By using a composite API, you can sometimes even increase speed and/or performance in comparison to using each call individually. This is especially helpful when we want to create some chain of functions where the input of a subsequent step is determined by the output from a request in a previous step.

A good example of this is the composite request type that exists within Salesforce CRM. Using this request type, you can execute chained API requests in a single call, which will return a single response and only execute a single call within the platform. For reference, let's take a look at a scenario that illustrates how this functionality works:

```
{"compositeRequest" : [{
   "method" : "POST",
```

```
"url" : "/services/data/v53.0/sobjects/Account",
"referenceId" : "myReferencedAccountID",
"body" : { "Name" : "My cool Account" }
}, {
"method" : "POST",
"url" : "/services/data/v53.0/sobjects/Contact",
"referenceId" : "mySuperCoolContactID",
"body" : {
  "LastName" : "Soup-herman",
  "AccountId" : "@{myReferencedAccountID.id}"
  }
}]
}
```

In this example, we are chaining two events together: one to create an account object record within CRM and another to create a contact that is linked to that account record on its `id` field. We do this with our initial `POST` request to the `Account` API route, which is assigned to the `referenceId` property. We can use this to access the response for subsequent requests.

There is a lot of power in this API type when you're developing for situations where several API calls are needed to perform sequentially. Now that we have a good grasp on what types of APIs are out there and their general uses, let's learn how to use them via requests.

# Requests and protocols – a deep dive

We've walked through the various API types that are commonly used in web application development, so we should now have a deeper understanding of what each is used for. In this section, we will dive into the world of requests and protocols. However, before we begin, it might be helpful to clarify what we mean by a "protocol" in regards to what we've discussed in this chapter.

In essence, protocols are defined rules that are agreed upon by all parties to define the way a service can communicate with other services on the web. As Marketing Cloud developers, we are likely very familiar with the **File Transfer Protocol** (**FTP**), which is a protocol that defines how we can send files between machines on the internet. Another might be the **Simple Mail Transport Protocol** (**SMTP**), which defines how we can send emails to a given customer or defined audience. Within the context of this chapter, we will largely use the term "protocol" to refer to the HTTPS protocol. HTTPS simply defines the set of rules that allows a service to communicate with a web server to send and receive data in an encrypted way.

Now that we have clarified our definition of protocols and set the stage for our discussion in this section, let's dive into requests, such as SOAP and REST, to gain insight into what each is and how they are structured.

## SOAP – not the kind you use in the shower

As we discussed in *Chapter 7, The Power of In-Step APIs*, **SOAP** is a messaging standard protocol system. SOAP utilizes XML to declare its messages and relies on the XML schema and other technologies regarding its structure.

Working with SOAP requests and responses can, unfortunately, become very complex – especially when they're used in their raw XML form. Fortunately, several languages help make more efficient use of SOAP via shortcuts to reduce the level of complexity. For example, the .NET platform hides the XML to a large extent, making utilization less reliant on understanding XML.

The capability to utilize these shortcuts comes from the **Web Service Definition Language** (**WSDL**). The WSDL is pretty much like a contract that is signed between the provider and the recipient of the service (sort of like a cell phone service contract). This contract, or method signature for us programming nerds, allows the process to publish a machine-readable document that helps define endpoints and all the corresponding procedure details.

One of the major differences that helps set SOAP apart from other services is that it does not require a specific transport protocol; it can be used over HTTP, SMTP, TCP, or others as needed. Being protocol-agnostic allows SOAP to work in a wider variety of contexts, which allows for a degree of flexibility in communication types compared to other approaches.

Let's take a look at the general structure of a SOAP request, along with some examples, so that we can understand what's going on:

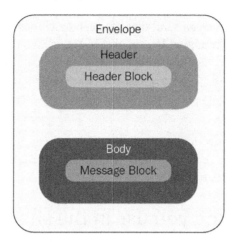

Figure 11.1 – Visualization of a SOAP API envelope

Notice that the structure of the SOAP message contains the following components (including a fault component):

- Envelope
- Header
- Body
- Fault

When visualized in XML, our preceding diagram will look as follows:

```
<?xml version = "1.0"?>
<SOAP-ENV:Envelope xmlns:SOAP-ENV = "http://www.w3.org/2001/12/
soap-envelope" >

  <SOAP-ENV:Header>
      {{your header content here}}
  </SOAP-ENV:Header>
  <SOAP-ENV:Body>
      {{your body content here}}
      <SOAP-ENV:Fault>
          {{your fault content here}}
      </SOAP-ENV:Fault>    </SOAP-ENV:Body>
```

```
</SOAP_ENV:Envelope>
```

Let's take a look at some of the components that make up this message to determine their purpose within the context of a SOAP message that intends to deploy a triggered send in the platform.

## Envelope

The SOAP envelope is the alpha and omega of SOAP calls. It is the main wrapper, sort of like an envelope that holds a letter in the mail, that needs to be opened before the other contents and then closed once the rest of the content has been entered.

The envelope is required in every SOAP message and must be the root element that encapsulates all of the components within the message. The envelope for our triggered send, as well as most or all the requests that we will make to Marketing Cloud, will have a structure similar to the following:

```
<?xml version="1.0" encoding="UTF-8"?>
<s:Envelope xmlns:s="http://www.w3.org/2003/05/soap-envelope"
xmlns:a="http://schemas.xmlsoap.org/ws/2004/08/addressing"
xmlns:u="http://docs.oasis-open.org/wss/2004/01/oasis-200401-
wss-wssecurity-utility-1.0.xsd">
</s:Envelope>
```

Notice the use of the xmlns attribute within the envelope's syntax. This is referred to as an XML namespace. Every element within a SOAP message belongs to a namespace and provides us with a way of qualifying the data to identify which source we are referring to in our message when we're referencing XML. For instance, if we had two data sources that utilized the values with the same attribute name, such as id, then we can use these namespaces to differentiate which value I'm referring to, to remove any ambiguity from the message.

Here's a simple example based on the aforementioned scenario:

```
<s:Envelope xmlns:account="https://example.com/xml/account"
xmlns:lead="https://example.com/xml/lead">
<account:id>Account1</account:id>
<lead:id>Lead1</lead:id>
</s:Envelope>
```

Now that we have the envelope, let's explore the header!

## Header

The header element in a SOAP message is a child element of the envelope and, unless stated otherwise in the WSDL, it's an optional element in the request. The header contains application-specific information, such as security or encryption information, that is associated with the request.

If a header element is specific, then it must be the first child in the message. One important attribute, though there are several that can be defined, on the header element is encodingStyle. The encodingStyle attribute identifies the rules that are used to encode the SOAP message. This attribute determines the serialization rules and can be applied to any element within the SOAP message. It's important to note that, unless otherwise indicated, this attribute will apply to the contents and all the children of the specified attribute.

In the context of our trigger example, we'll use the header element to define the action we want to invoke with our request (Create), our tenant-specific SOAP API service endpoint, and an auth token that we can use to authenticate into Marketing Cloud for our request. Let's take a look at how that header would be structured:

```
<s:Header>
 <a:Action s:mustUnderstand="1">Create</a:Action>
 <a:To s:mustUnderstand="1">{{myTenantSubDomain}}.soap.
marketingcloudapis.com/Service.asmx</a:To>
 <fueloauth>{{myAuthToken}}</fueloauth>
</s:Header>
```

We've defined the action to be invoked in our request, Create, where the message will be routed (notice the a namespace variable that's being referenced here), as well as our authentication token, which we will generate before this request is sent.

## Body

The body of a SOAP call is similar to the body in a letter – it is the part that contains the main purpose and the majority of the relevant content of our message. The body sits within the envelope and contains application-defined XML data that will be used within the message.

Although the body contains most of the content, there is one element that sits above it as the first element in a SOAP envelope – the header. If there is a header within the message, then the body element would need to immediately follow the header, but if there isn't, then the body will be the first element within the envelope.

Let's take a look at our body element for the triggered send request and look at the important items that are present within this portion of our message:

```xml
<s:Body
    xmlns:xsd="http://www.w3.org/2001/XMLSchema"
    xmlns:xsi="http://www.w3.org/2001/XMLSchema-instance">
    <CreateRequest
        xmlns="http://exacttarget.com/wsdl/partnerAPI">
        <Options>
            <Client>
                <ClientID>{{MID}}</ClientID>
            </Client>
        </Options>
        <Objects xsi:type="TriggeredSend">
            <Client>
                <ClientID>{{MID}}</ClientID>
            </Client>
            <PartnerKey xsi:nil="true" />
            <ObjectID xsi:nil="true" />
            <TriggeredSendDefinition>
                <PartnerKey xsi:nil="true" />
                <ObjectID xsi:nil="true" />
                <CustomerKey>{{MyTrigger_ExternalKey}}
                </CustomerKey>
            </TriggeredSendDefinition>
            <Subscribers><SubscriberKey>test@example.com
              </SubscriberKey>
            <EmailAddress>test@example.com
              </EmailAddress>
              <Attributes>
                  <Name>FirstName</Name>
                  <Value>Wiley</Value>
              </Attributes>
            </Subscribers>
        </Objects>
    </CreateRequest>
</s:Body>
```

Here, we'll define the namespace for `CreateRequest` to generate from the Marketing Cloud WSDL. Then, we'll declare the MID that we wish to execute this triggered send request within. Next, we must declare our object type from the `xsi` namespace and set the object that we want to perform `CreateRequest` on to be of the `TriggeredSend` type.

Finally, we must define the associated triggered send definition for the triggered send that we wish to deploy and dictate the values for the `Subscriber` object type, as well as an additional attribute – `FirstName`, in this instance – that we want to pass in the trigger request so that our email can utilize this value at send time.

This makes up the overall structure of our triggered send SOAP API request, which will generate an email send to a subscriber within the Marketing Cloud platform. Let's take a look at one more element of our SOAP request that we could also include within our message.

## Fault

A fault element is fairly self-explanatory. It is the element that will convey errors and status information within the SOAP message – almost like that tattle-tale kid we all knew in school, always telling the teacher who was at fault for all the bad things.

Although tattle-tale has a bad connotation, it is useful here as we can utilize the fault element to construct error handling and provide more meaningful details of an exception when one occurs. The fault element sits within the body element, as a child element, and is wholly optional – there is no requirement to include it in your SOAP call. If the fault element is declared, however, both the child `faultcode` and `faultfactor` elements are required. Here's a breakdown of the sub-elements that are available for the fault element:

- `faultcode`: A string value that is returned to identify the fault. The available values are `VersionMismatch`, `MustUnderstand`, `Client`, and `Server`.

- `faultstring`: This is a long-form description of the cause of the fault.

- `faultactor` (optional): This is a long-form string on the assumed entity that may have caused the fault.

- `detail` (optional): This contains the app-specific error information concerning the `Body` element.

Here's a sample containing a fault where there is a version mismatch with the defined namespace on the envelope:

```
<soap:Fault>
    <faultcode>soap:VersionMismatch</faultcode>
```

```
    <faultstring, xml:lang='en">
        Message was not SOAP 1.1 compliant
    </faultstring>
    <faultactor>
        http://sample.org.ocm/jws/authnticator
    </faultactor>
  </soap:Fault>
```

Now that we've covered how SOAP requests are structured and function, let's take a deeper look into REST to identify its key components and request makeup.

# REST – but not a nap

RESTful APIs represent the state of a given resource. When the RESTful API/service is called, it will return the representation of the resource's state back to the client in the form of JSON, XML, or some other format. For instance, when we call the Content Builder API to return an asset, I'm requesting Marketing Cloud to return the state of a given resource, such as its last modified date, folder name, or `publishedURL`.

Unlike SOAP messages, the request and response sizes for REST are much less verbose, so they can process requests much quicker than SOAP in most scenarios. In addition, the structure, function, and REST services are quite different. Here are some core principles that define an architecture that's considered to be RESTful:

- **Client-Server**: This should be split in two: the **client side** and **server side**. Each of these applications must be fully independent of each other. This will allow for improved scalability and management due to the varying levels of security concerns between the two.

- **Cache**: The platform should be able to temporarily retain, or cache, responses or data points to allow for increased performance. This provides a better user experience. You should explicitly state if data is cacheable or non-cacheable.

- **Layered**: The REST API architecture should be like an onion and consist of a multitude of layers. These layers should then operate together to build a hierarchy that will in turn create a more scalable and flexible application. This layering can also offer more stability due to it restricting component performance access outside the immediate layer.

- **Stateless**: This means that all the data is stored on the server, which offers much greater security. However, this requires every call to include every single piece of information that's necessary to make the call work.

- **Uniform Interface**: By using various data formats, a uniform interface can improve information sharing. It also simplifies the architecture since all the components will follow the same rules when they speak to each other. This makes it easier to understand the interactions between the different components.

Before we dive into the core components of a REST request, let's look at a visualization of the request structure, similar to what we outlined for SOAP:

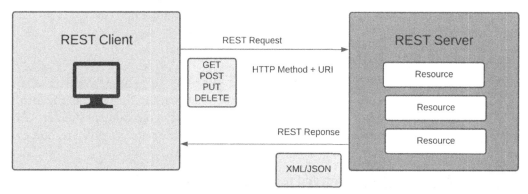

Figure 11.2 – Visualization of the request structure of a REST request

In the preceding diagram, we've outlined the general structure of a REST API request. The client, or software that runs on a user's computing device, initiates a request to the server, which can be any service we are using that offers an API to access its resources.

This request from the client specifies the type of action we'd like to take on the given resource, using verbs such as GET, POST, PUT and DELETE on the Marketing Cloud REST API, along with the endpoint of the resource that we intend to access. This request is then processed by the server, which will return a response to the client that contains information about the status of the request. This can include metadata about the request itself, any errors that may have occurred on the server processing the request, or the resource that we've requested.

Now that we have a basic idea of the flow, let's look at the key components that make up a REST API request.

## Request URL

The request URL defines both what service you are making a request to, as well as the type of resource or functionality that you are attempting to access. The request URL consists of a few basic pieces:

- **Base URL**: This is the root domain, or subdomain, that you are making your call to receive a response from the server.

- **Resource/Path**: This is the route that you are calling on the service and lets it know exactly what resource you are attempting to access. An example would be the Content Builder REST API resource path. When we attempt to access the asset model, we can use the `/asset/v1/content/assets/{id}`resource path within our request URL to specify the resource we are looking to return data about.

- **Path parameter**: These are required by the API call and act as part of the REST endpoint. It's a further specifier concerning the resource that you are seeking to access. Using the Content Builder example we discussed earlier, an example of a path parameter would be `categories` in the `/asset/v1/content/categories` path.

- **Query string parameter**: These parameters can be specified after the path parameter and refine the subset of the data to be returned when certain method types are used. These parameters are initialized with the `?` character following the endpoint and each argument is separated with an ampersand, `&`. An example of this can be found in the Content Builder API asset simple query endpoint. Query string parameters are passed to the end of the endpoint to limit the result set to only include assets that have not been excluded by the filtering logic. An example is `/asset/v1/content/assets?$filter=Name%20like%20'hello%20 world'`.

As with SOAP, there is a request header that is necessary for REST. We will dive into this in the next section.

## Request headers

**Request headers** are used to pass additional information in the request using name/value pairs. These set the context of the call that you are trying to process and provide the required information for the call to take place. This can include the format of the response, authentication, and many other settings that are critical to the request. Let's look at some of the more common request header properties that you might use in a standard request:

- **Authorization**: This contains the credentials, usually a token of some sort, to be used to authenticate the call.

- **WWW-Authenticate**: This property simply defines the type of authentication that's necessary to access a given resource. Often, this is sent along with a 401 response code, which means *unauthorized*.

- **Accept-Charset**: This property contains the charset information around what is acceptable by the client.

- **Content-Type**: This property will include the media type of the content (for example, text/HTML) inside the response to help the client process the content correctly.

- **Cache-Control**: This property contains the server cache policy, which means it can define if this content can be cached and reused or if it needs to be pulled every time.

## Request body

The request body is used to send and receive data for our request. When we use the POST or PUT methods within our request, we should include all the resource information within the body of our request as these methods work on the entire resource. In these scenarios, we shouldn't use either query string or path parameters to identify the resources that we wish to request.

## HTTP methods

These methods were discussed previously in this book. They are versions that comprise the portion of our uniform interface criteria we said was a requirement for an API to be RESTful. This allows us to take some defined action on a given resource. Let's take another look at some common methods and what functionality they perform in a request.

## POST method

The POST method is most commonly used to create a new resource, to further refine the result that's returned when a GET request with a query string parameter is too verbose, or to ensure the nested logic can easily be processed by the server. A successful POST request should create and associate the new resource with some parent element and assign a unique identifier to the system that this resource can be retrieved with in another API call. Upon successfully processing the POST request, the server should return an HTTP status of 201, followed by metadata concerning the newly created resource.

## GET method

Unlike the POST method, the GET method is used to retrieve a representation of a resource rather than creating a new one on the server being requested. Using this method, while a request body can be included, it will likely be ignored and will not be considered to have semantic value to the overall request. Worse, for some API services, it may cause the call to return an error response. Any further refinement of the resource you are seeking to read should come from path and query string parameters within the request endpoint.

Upon a successful request, a 200 response should be returned to the client, along with a representation of the resource in its current state. If the request is malformed, a 400 (Bad Request) error may also be returned, indicating that there was an error with the nature of the request for a resource. To reiterate, GET methods are generally considered safe in that they do not mutate or alter a resource on the server and only return a representational state of a resource. By safe, we mean that concurrent requests will not change the representation of the data and it will be returned identically in each request, without risk of modification or corruption.

## PUT method

The PUT method is commonly used to provide an update action on a server resource. Using this method, you can specify an updated representation of an asset within the request body and, targeting the specific resource URI, update the representation of the resource on the server. In addition to this scenario, the PUT method can also be used to create a resource where the client specifies a resource URI that does not currently exist on the REST server. Because there can occasionally be some ambiguity on the client side concerning the existence of a resource, this method shouldn't be utilized to create new resources as the POST method is the preferred alternative to the create method.

When an update is successful, a 200 HTTP response is returned (or 204 if it's not returning any content in the body). If you are using the PUT method to create a new resource, a 201 HTTP status will be returned if the creation request was successful. A body in the response is optional as having the call provide one consumes more bandwidth.

## PATCH method

The PATCH method is similar to the PUT method in that it is used to modify an existing resource on the server. Unlike the PUT method, though, the body of a PATCH request holds a set of instructions that are used to describe how a specific resource on the server should be changed to create a new version of it.

So, when using PUT, we need to provide the complete representation of the resource, along with the modifications that we want to apply, rather than just including those portions of the resource representation that we would like to update. To that end, when you use the PATCH method to update a portion of the resource, it is recommended to use the **JSON Patch** data format in most instances to represent only those updates that you want to make on a resource. For example, let's say we have the following resource:

```
{
    "prop1": "someVal",
    "prop2": "anotherVal"
}
```

Now, we want to update the value for prop1 to some other value and remove the prop2 property while replacing it with a string array. By using JSON Patch, we're able to represent these changes in a concise format that can be understood by the server so that it only updates the resource where those items have been updated. Let's take a look at what this patch looks like:

```
[
    { "op": "replace", "path": "/prop1",
      "value": "newProp1Val" },
    { "op": "add", "path": "/newProp",
      "value": ["hello world"] },
    { "op": "remove", "path": "/prop2" }
]
```

This results in our resource having the following structure:

```
{
    "prop1": "newProp1Val",
    "newProp": ["hello world"]
}
```

This a simple example of using JSON Patch, which you would specify as the content type of your request within the request header. This should give you some idea of a few of the available operations (`add`, `replace`, and `remove`), as well as the basic syntax that you can use to perform this.

Now, this is not to say that JSON Patch is required to make PATCH requests to all systems. Many developers will likely have performed the PATCH method on resources within Marketing Cloud by using the standard JSON content type and request body. This is just to provide an alternative that may be required or be more powerful when you're working with some external services. Finally, the PATCH method is similar to PUT concerning the status that's returned when some resource representation has been modified.

## The DELETE method

This method is self-explanatory and is used to delete some resources on the server where the request is being made. Like GET requests, this method *can* use a request body, but it should generally be avoided to prevent confusion and issues in the request that may be difficult to pin down.

The requests resource identifier, for either an individual resource or a group collection, should be passed in the URI as a path or query string parameter. Successfully deleting a resource should return a 200 response to confirm that the resource has been deleted. This response will return metadata about the resource that was deleted and can sometimes contain sufficient volume as to be impractical, depending on the service. In such scenarios, the server should return a 204 response, which indicates that the deletion was successful but returns an empty response body with no additional information about the deleted asset.

In addition to these two HTTP response codes, a 202 response is also common and indicates that the resource has been identified and is queued for a deletion process to occur. This may be supplemented with a unique request identifier that can be used to call other services to confirm the final status of the deletion request. Finally, once the resource has been deleted from the server, further GET requests to retrieve the representation of this resource should either return an HTTP 404 (Not found) or HTTP 410 (Gone) response, indicating that the resource can no longer be retrieved from the server.

Now that we have more in-depth knowledge of the various components of a REST request, let's put this all together and look at an example REST API POST request that will return a filtered set of assets and data points from Content Builder:

```
POST /asset/v1/content/assets/query HTTP/1.1
Host: YOURENDPOINT}}.rest.marketingcloudapis.com
Authorization: Bearer TOKEN


{
    "page":{
        "page":1,
        "pageSize":50
    },
    "query":{
        "leftOperand":{
            "property":"createdDate",
            "simpleOperator":"greaterThan",
            "value":"2021-07-04"
        },
        "logicalOperator":"AND",
        "rightOperand":{
            "property":"assetType.name",
            "simpleOperator":"equal",
            "value":"png"
        }
    }
}
```

Here, we defined our request to use the POST method on the /asset/v1/content/assets/query resource path. Then, we specified a header, Authorization, that gives the server further information about the request so that it can authenticate that the call is coming from a valid source. Then, we defined the request body as a JSON blob that defines both the size of the request that we wish to return, as well as the filter criteria that we want to use to winnow the result set.

In this section, we covered both the SOAP and REST requests in detail. Now, let's take a quick look at another growing architecture for designing and consuming APIs that has been growing in popularity in recent years: GraphQL.

# GraphQL – making data easier

**GraphQL** is a query language that is used for interacting with APIs. In GraphQL, a set of information is interpreted within the context of a graph. Within this information is nodes, which are used to represent objects and are defined within the GraphQL scheme system, and edges, which represent the connections between the nodes within the graph structure. This allows for a clear relationship to be made between queries and increases the level of connectivity between different objects.

This approach differs from the traditional REST approach, which relies on rigid server-defined endpoints to process requests, in that you can use GraphQL to send queries to get all of the data that you require within a single request. To visualize how this differs from a traditional REST approach, let's consider the following endpoint and resource:

```
// GET /person/1
{
    "name":"John Doe",
    "lastlogindate": "07/04/2021"
}
```

Here, we're requesting a specific resource path on the server and requesting the representational state of the `person` object, where the identifier for this person is `1`. Now, let's say we have another resource path that also returns data about this person's employer and relevant details about their role within that company.

*How can we retrieve that data in addition to the data that we have on the* `person` *resource path?* Well, we *could* make another (a secondary) request to retrieve that information from the employer resource path and use scripting to combine the responses into a single representative object containing our data. If we were the creators of the API, we could join that data into a single API point to combine both pieces of data into a single resource that could be accessed at once.

Unfortunately, in both scenarios, this solution leaves a lot to be desired. In our first solution, we doubled the number of requests that are required to retrieve a unified dataset; it's not difficult to see how this would cause problems with scaling for more complex approaches.

In the second solution, we're coalescing the response from these resource paths into a single location, which increases the overall size of the response that's returned and may lead to slower response times and bloated request sizes (or even muddy data relationships). Let's see how this might be defined using GraphQL:

1.  First, we must define the schema of the objects that represent our `Person` and `Employer` types:

```
type Person {
    id: ID
    name: String
    lastlogindate: Date
    employer: Employer
}

type Employer {
    id: ID
    name: String
    role: String
    manager: String
    person: Person
}
```

2.  You may have noticed that we have not defined how these objects are fetched from the client. One of the primary differentiators between REST and GraphQL is that the resource you are attempting to access is not defined explicitly to a particular route that contains only state representations for that asset type. This is the `Query` type in our schema:

```
type Query {
    person(id: ID!): Person
    employer(id: ID!): Employer
}
```

3.  Great! We have our first query. If we want to look at accessing the person's name along with, let's say, their manager's name, we could execute our query to retrieve only those values that we need:

```
// GET /graphql?query={ person(id: "1") { name, employer
{ manager } } }
```

```
{
    "name":"John Doe",
    "employer":{
        "manager":"Jane Doe"
    }
}
```

From the preceding code, you can see that we've resolved the issues that we had contemplated in our REST approach to retrieve this data.

Using this approach, we can define exactly what data we need to retrieve to the client and simplify the process so that we can return all the data, in a single request, without over-fetching or under-fetching the necessary data that we want. In GraphQL, we can traverse from a single entry point to its related data by following all of the relationships defined in the schema within a single request.

In REST, multiple endpoints, or bloated responses, would be needed to retrieve the same result set. Another advantage of GraphQL is that, if you are constructing an API for a service, your API performs self-documentation by using the schema/type system. We can easily iterate on future developments using this structure. In GraphQL, the identity of an object is separated from how a developer fetches it. In REST, the endpoint is the identity of an object.

That is not to say that GraphQL is better than REST in every respect as there are several advantages to using REST over GraphQL. For instance, when we're using GraphQL, there is no way to get a unique identifier for a given object because we use the same URL for all the requests. To cache with GraphQL, you will need to construct a caching mechanism.

Also, REST offers significantly more capabilities concerning error handling and monitoring. For instance, as we described in the *REST – but not a nap* section, malformed requests or errors with resource representation are returned with HTTP errors that provide some meaningful context as to the nature of the error. In GraphQL, a 200 response is always returned, regardless of whether there was an exception within the request. This makes it more difficult to isolate individual failures within an API request and can lead to lost time troubleshooting that wouldn't be as intensive if you were using the REST API.

Now that we've discussed SOAP, REST, and GraphQL, and we understand the structure of each architecture and how requests are composed, let's look at another topic that is important for developers: SDKs.

# To SDK or not to SDK

So, you might be asking yourself: *what is an SDK anyway?* **SDK** stands for **software development kit**, and it's a set of tools, programs, or guidelines that are used to develop applications for a specific platform (such as Marketing Cloud). SDKs can include APIs, developer environments, documentation, code samples, libraries, and many other resources that can reduce the complexity and time necessary to construct applications for a given platform or service.

A good way to visualize the utility of an SDK is to think of a piece of furniture being shipped to your home from a retail outlet online. When it arrives, the pieces are neatly assembled and grouped by their functionality or position and will likely be easily marked. In addition to this, you may receive a set of simple tools that are specific to the piece of furniture and allow you to construct the product much faster than you otherwise would.

Now, compare that with having to go purchase or chop wood, purchase each piece that's necessary for the furniture, take measurements and determine the optimal places to bind different pieces, and so on. In this example, the former is the SDK, while the latter would be creating an application from scratch.

SDKs allow developers to get started in a platform quickly because they abstract away a lot of the base-level components that are needed for common functionality. They commonly provide well-documented resources that can provide more clear insight into how the platform functions than traditional documentation can sometimes convey (due to the overwhelming nature of learning every bit of minutia of the platform to develop).

## APIs versus SDKs

It can be easy to confuse these two items for those unfamiliar with using SDKs or APIs, so let's provide some clear differences to eliminate any confusion. What makes this particularly confusing is that SDKs commonly contain APIs.

When a developer uses an SDK to create a piece of functionality or an application, those applications need to make requests to extend that functionality with other platforms. In this scenario, an SDK will include an API to facilitate that communication, but it should be understood that APIs cannot be used to construct brand-new specifications or an application. Simply put, *SDKs usually contain APIs, but APIs do not contain SDKs.*

That being said, envisioning APIs as components of SDKs isn't quite right either since you can use an API without an SDK. In business scenarios where this capability is limited in scope or functionality, you may find that there is a legitimate choice between using an SDK and simple API integration to handle data transfer between two services.

On one hand, it's much easier and faster to develop integration using an SDK because many methods and common utilities are already defined and ready for use. On the other hand, an API is much more efficient in that it does not come packed with utilities that may not be particularly useful for your task at hand.

Let's wrap this up in a table so that we can see a side-by-side comparison of the high-level differences between APIs and SDKs:

| Category | API | SDK |
|---|---|---|
| Purpose | Connects and integrates software and services. | Contains a variety of development tools that are used to streamline development. |
| Characteristics | Lightweight, efficient, and specialized for the purpose at hand. | Includes many utilities and tools that provide more comprehensive functionality beyond singular use cases. |
| Use Case | Adding specific functionality to an application or service. | Used to create new applications or services that have a multitude of functionalities or requirements. |

Table 11.1 – API and SDK comparison

As you can see, each option has utilities and places in a developer's toolkit, but the use case for each will largely depend on what you wish to implement. Understanding the purpose of each option will help you make stronger decisions as to whether an API or an SDK is suitable for your project's use case.

## Advantages and disadvantages of using an SDK

Now that we've highlighted some key differences between SDKs and APIs, it's a little clearer as to where each of them has its place within the development life cycle. If we've got a project limited in scope that uses a well-supported API for integration, we don't have a strong case for an SDK.

Alternatively, if we're building a full-suite application that integrates with a platform such as Marketing Cloud, then an SDK seems to make sense to save us quite a bit of time and frustration. But the scope of the functionality isn't all there is to it. Let's take a look at some of the advantages and disadvantages that come with using an SDK.

Here are the advantages:

- **Simplified integration**: Simply put, starting an application or project with a suite of built-in tools, including authentication, preformatted requests to the platform, data sanitization, and other utilities, makes our lives *a lot* easier. In addition, the SDK can reduce a lot of overhead by simplifying the way that our code is both compiled and understood by providing developers with a structure to interact with an application that they are familiar with. Most SDKs will feature common build tools, documentation, and sample code that provides a very solid base for developers to hit the ground running, where they may get hung up on individual platform quirks and inconsistencies without the SDK.

- **Stronger security**: When you use an SDK from a reputable platform, a lot of security measures and features have likely been implemented for the developer, requiring them to spend less time worrying about the scoping and user permissions, which can bring stability and reassurance to the final application being developed.

- **Cost savings**: Depending on your organization and resourcing, this might be the single biggest argument for using an SDK. Simply put, time is money, and using an SDK can provide powerful cost savings as development time for critical infrastructure is dramatically reduced.

- **Reliability**: As we all know, with new development comes bugs. Not only would we incur additional development time implementing new features that the SDK may already include, but we also can expect that we'll have to work through various rounds of QA and revisions before we can have a reasonably stable suite of features. When you use an SDK from a large platform, you can take advantage of the fact that most or all of the utilities and tools within it have been tested thoroughly and are production-level quality right out of the box, thus providing another huge metric that can save both time and money.

Now, let's look at the disadvantages:

- **Dependency**: You've found a great SDK for the platform that you're integrating with, and you've built a full suite of functionalities using the utilities and tools included within it. *Set it and forget it, right?* Well, maybe not. An API is only as good as the support it receives. It can constantly update in an ever-changing landscape of development, which can leave a previously solid SDK in shambles as antiquated coding practices, unmaintained libraries, and deprecated functionality begin to pile up and threaten the stability of your application. If you utilize an SDK as the critical backbone of your project, make sure you understand whether there is an intention to maintain it and keep up to date on changes or updates that you may need to make to keep your application or service running smoothly.

- **Overhead**: We've already touched on this to some degree in our analysis of the differences between APIs and SDKs, but it's worth reiterating. Even if our application or service is somewhat complex in terms of its functionality, and requires only minimal integrations to function, this doesn't necessarily mean that SDKs are a good fit. There are many circumstances where the sheer size of the tools and functions that are provided in an SDK dwarfs the amount that's needed to construct a viable solution for your use case. If you want to pick a piece of fruit from a tree, you wouldn't use a crane, so ensure that, while you're not reinventing the wheel by building everything from scratch, you also aren't bogging down your development processes with more tools than you need.

- **Patchwork functionality**: We'd all love for an SDK to solve all the development scenarios that we are undertaking, but the case is that most will not have a complete toolkit for all development scenarios within the platform. By their nature, they will be somewhat generic to anticipate the most common development cases and will likely focus on applying them to a wider audience than catering to niche functionality or requests. Doing a thorough analysis of the capabilities of the SDK can prevent issues where you discover you need to build a substantial portion of the application yourself halfway through a project.

These are only a few of the advantages and disadvantages that come with using SDKs, and you'll see that a lot of these callouts we also made in our discussions around external libraries and third-party tools in *Chapter 9, Getting Started with Custom Integrations*. The main takeaway is that SDKs are not a *one-size-fits-all approach* and you need to consider your options carefully before determining whether using one makes the most sense for your project. Next, let's look at the SDKs that are offered by Marketing Cloud to see what offerings are provided by the platform.

# Marketing Cloud platform SDKs

While other SDKs are offered by Marketing Cloud, such as the Content Builder Block and Mobile Push SDKs, for our purposes, let's provide a brief overview of the wider platform SDKs as they serve a more general purpose that fits within the scope of our content within this chapter.

The Marketing Cloud platform SDKs offer a framework for structuring and managing requests and functionality through both the SOAP and REST API services provided by the platform. It also provides utilities around token management, pagination and recurring requests, object instantiation, and definition, among other utilities that can remove some of the more tedious pieces of integration for Marketing Cloud developers.

Because of the nature of Marketing Cloud's services and current capabilities, this essentially serves to automate the structure of the requests and responses of API calls in the platform with a method that works within the set programming language that the SDK was created to understand. At the time of writing, there are six platform SDKs currently being offered by Marketing Cloud:

- C# SDK
- Java SDK
- Node SDK
- PHP SDK
- Ruby SDK
- Python SDK

While each SDK offers services that fit within the specific language that you are developing with, they support built-in methods on a similar subset of objects out of the box. It should be noted that this list is not all-encompassing for every SDK. For instance, the support that's built into some – in particular, the Java SDK – offers a wider range of object support than others, but this is meant to serve as a list that is more or less common among the different SDKs. These objects are as follows:

- Campaign
- Campaign Asset
- Content Area
- Data Extension
- Data Extension Column
- Data Extension Row
- Email
- Folder
- List
- List Subscriber
- Subscriber
- Triggered Send
- Bounce Event
- Click Event

- Open Event
- Sent Event
- Unsub Event

What likely jumps off the page for anyone with experience developing API requests for the preceding scenarios is that the available objects in the Marketing Cloud SOAP and REST reference greatly outnumbers the availability of the objects that are supported within the official SDKs (at the time of writing). It should come as no surprise that, while these SDKs do support REST methods for items such as authentication, the overwhelming value in their utility is concerned with working with SOAP objects.

Now, you should have some appreciation for how much more complex it can be to structure and execute a SOAP call in comparison to REST. In fact, since all the new Marketing Cloud API services are transitioning over to a RESTful API architecture, relying on the SOAP protocol as a key component of integration becomes less and less of a necessity.

Now, this is not to say that it's not currently a critical component – far from it. Many pieces of the platform do not have exposed REST routes for performing basic **create, read, update, and delete** (**CRUD**) actions on their elements in the platform. It's just to highlight the efficacy of using the SDK will likely become diminished with time as most common programming languages already feature lightweight libraries for handling REST requests that can be easily imported and utilized, as well as offering a much smaller package than the current SDKs offered by the platform.

For instance, let's take a look at two calls we can make to authenticate with the `v1/token` endpoint in Marketing Cloud. One will use the Ruby SDK methods, while the other will use the standard Ruby HTTP client, `Net::HTTP`. First, here is the SDK authentication:

```
def getSDKToken()
  authClient = MarketingCloudSDK::Client.new({'client' =>
    {'id' => CLIENTID,'secret' => CLIENTSECRET}})
  return authClient
end
```

The following is a simple implementation that uses the `Net::HTTP` client API:

```
def getRestToken()
  uri =
    URI('https://auth.exacttargetapis.com/v1/requestToken')
  Net::HTTP.start(uri.host, uri.port, :use_ssl =>
```

```
        uri.scheme == 'https') do |http|
    req = Net::HTTP::Post.new(uri)
    req['Content-Type'] = 'application/json'
    req.set_form_data('clientId' => CLIENTID, 'clientSecret'
      => CLIENTSECRET)
    response = http.request req # Net::HTTPResponse object
    responseObj = JSON.parse(response.body)
    token = responseObj["accessToken"]
    return token
    end
  end
```

As you can see, the SDK version is less verbose and its method can be configured with only a few lines, but it's also not overly complex to implement a similar method ourselves with a standard library. Moreover, we can now use this generic API library to construct additional requests for Journey Builder, Content Builder, or any other portion of the platform.

This becomes more difficult when you're attempting to retrieve information via the SOAP API, but it's still not difficult to implement using standard libraries that have wide use in whatever language you've chosen to implement your project in. You'll find that the SDK itself often utilizes these same libraries to build the necessary utilities and functionality for use within the SDK.

While it may require longer initial development to construct methods for REST and SOAP calls yourself within the platform, doing so can provide greater levels of visibility into the functionality you are providing. It also allows you to extend the base object support to accomplish use cases that are not suitable with the stock capabilities of the API.

For instance, let's take a look at what a Ruby implementation that extends object support to the Send SOAP object would look like:

```
et_client = Savon.client(
    wsdl: wsdl,
    endpoint: endpoint,
    wsse_auth: [username, password],
    raise_errors: false,
    log: false,
    open_timeout:180,
    read_timeout: 180
```

```
)
```

First, we need to initialize our SOAP client utilizing the Ruby gem Savon. This allows us to make simplified SOAP calls to Marketing Cloud. This is the gem that the standard SDK utilizes to perform these requests as well. We'll define some important pieces, such as the endpoint for our instance, WSDL, and the `auth` and `timeout` parameters. Now that we have configured the general client, we're all set to structure the SOAP requests that will return data from Marketing Cloud:

```
rqst = {}
rqst['ObjectType'] = 'Send'
rqst['Properties'] = ['ID',
'EmailName','SendDate','NumberSent',
'UniqueClicks','UniqueOpens','Unsubscribes','HardBounces',
'Subject']
filter = {'@xsi:type' => 'tns:SimpleFilterPart'}
filter['Property'] = 'SendDate'
filter['SimpleOperator'] = 'greaterThan'
filter['Value'] = '2020-12-17'
rqst['Filter'] = filter
```

Here, we're creating an empty request and setting some properties that will define the type of data we want to return, as well as the source object that it should be retrieved from. First, we initialize our request and specify the object type to be the `Send` object in Marketing Cloud. Then, we define the columns that we want to retrieve in our request to process the data. Finally, because we want to return a more refined and relevant dataset, we can use `SimpleFilterParts` to only return those that have a `sendDate` value greater than or equal to December 20, 2017. This ensures that we do not have a bloated request and can improve performance and efficiency by only returning the data that we need.

With our SOAP client configured and the basic properties of our call set, we can perform our API call to retrieve the data:

```
rqstmsg = {'RetrieveRequest' => rqst}
response = et_client.call(:retrieve, :message => rqstmsg)
if !response.nil? then
    envelope = response.hash[:envelope]
```

```
    retrieveresponse =
      envelope[:body][:retrieve_response_msg]
        if retrieveresponse[:overall_status] == "OK"
        p 'Success'
        results = retrieveresponse[:results]
        if !results.kind_of?(Array)
          results = [results]
        end
        @send_results = results.to_json
        #results.each {|list| p "ListID: #{list[:id]}
        #{list[:email_name]} #{list[:send_date]}
        #{list[:number_sent]} #{list[:unique_opens]}
        #{list[:unique_clicks]}"}
    end
```

Here, we specified this call as a `RetrieveRequest` and assigned the properties that we configured in the previous snippet to form the structure of our call. Then, we used our Savon configuration, which has been assigned to the `et_client` variable, to perform the retrieval. From there, we checked the state of our `RetrieveRequest` to ensure the request was valid, and then printed the data we retrieved from Marketing Cloud to the console.

In this example, we extended support to this object using the Ruby Savon library, which is utilized by the SDK for requests and specifies the data that we wish to return, along with `SimpleFilterPart`. This limits our result to only those that are sent after a certain date. Once we've done this, we can take this data and expose it to the frontend of our application or write its results to the command line for easy validation and reference.

The point of this is not to discourage the use of Platform SDKs. The goal is far from this as they can be simple methods for prototyping and creating limited functionality in a much quicker way than constructing and testing these yourself. There is more to highlight in that (in some cases) you can easily construct your base functionality using lightweight libraries or standard language capabilities to meet your use case. There are several advantages to doing this. Ensure that you have a more lightweight solution that can be extended to meet your use cases, which may or may not be standard capabilities of the platform SDKs.

# Summary

This was a highly complex and technical topic – congratulations on making it through! We did not mention how this would be useful for automation, but you need to think back to all the cool stuff we did in the first eight chapters while discussing internal automation. With all these new options and cool things that we just went over added to that, can you see all the new awesome possibilities lining up? We can!

As a refresher, in this chapter, we looked at the different types of APIs beyond just a simple explanation of SOAP and REST. We also examined the different ways to run requests and the protocols and structures that enable these capabilities. Finally, we took a deep dive into SDKs to see where they can help or hurt your developer environments.

We now have a solid grasp of these technical fundamentals and are much stronger technical resources ourselves. Now, let's turn our attention to webhooks and microservices to see how we can start putting these ideas into action.

# 12
# Webhooks and Microservices

In the previous chapter, we dove into the wonderful world of APIs and SDKs to determine how they could be utilized to implement custom solutions and what the costs or benefits that could be associated with each type are. We learned about the different types of requests that are common in both Marketing Cloud and web development generally. Then, we really honed in on each request type and the overall structure that allows us to communicate with services across the web.

In this chapter, we're going to expand on our API knowledge to understand the concept of using an event-driven framework that lets us act on data in real time rather than with user-driven requests. This is a powerful tool for a variety of reasons, particularly how it allows us to automate functionality, both within Marketing Cloud and external to the platform, which isn't really possible to do efficiently with traditional APIs as defined in our last chapter.

Also, we'll go back to a conversation on application design and structure and introduce the concept of microservices. You will see how this concept differs from traditional application development and architecture we might be more familiar with. This will help inform us on how to best structure the overall application in order to provide the most benefit to us as developers working on a system and ensuring we build services in an efficient, easy-to-maintain, and sustainable fashion. As an overview, in this chapter we will be covering the following:

- Webhooks versus APIs

- An event-based example

- Microservices…assemble!

While examining the aforementioned topics, you may find it difficult to form a connection between the theory and the work we do within Marketing Cloud. We'll show an example for webhooks that should help clarify how some of these ideas are relevant to our work as Marketing Cloud developers. We also hope that you consider each item carefully and consider possible similarities to the work you do on a daily basis. While it's true that the last few chapters of this book contain quite a bit of theory, each item has a direct correlation to the work that we do within Marketing Cloud even outside the scope of custom application development. With some careful consideration, we think you will see the connections and feel more empowered to view your work both in Marketing Cloud and external to it in a new, and hopefully more informed, light. Now, without further ado, let's take a look at the first topic of our chapter, **webhooks**.

# Technical requirements

The full code for the chapter can be found in the GitHub repository located here: `https://github.com/PacktPublishing/Automating-Salesforce-Marketing-Cloud/tree/main/Chapter12`.

# Webhooks versus APIs

So, before we get started comparing these two, let's define what webhooks are and how they can be utilized within an application. Webhooks, also referred to as **web callbacks** or **reverse APIs**, are a method that allows an app or service to send real-time data to another application or service when some given event has occurred. Whenever an event is triggered, the webhook registers the event and aggregates all of the data for the request. The request is then sent to a URL, specified in a configuration within the service registering the event, in the form of an HTTP request.

Webhooks allow us to process logic efficiently when an event occurs within the service providing the webhook. The information structure passed from the webhook is decided by the service provider passing the event. Webhooks can also be utilized to connect events and functionality on two disparate services so that some event on one platform triggers another event on a separate platform without any user delegation or input. An example of this might be where we configure webhooks within both GitHub and Slack and utilize them together such that a message is posted on a Slack channel whenever a new commit has been made and merged into our master branch. By using webhooks, we can allow services to talk to each other in an automated way, which allows us to construct functionality that may not be possible using the standard API approaches discussed in the previous chapter.

It's quite easy to confuse webhooks with APIs, especially given that they both communicate utilizing the same methods. Also, the responses for webhooks can feature a very similar structure as that of a traditional API request. We can even see how they could be utilized separately to construct similar functionality in a given scenario. In the previous chapter, we examined APIs in depth and saw that we could utilize requests to return the state of a given resource. If the primary use case for webhooks is event-driven requests, couldn't we also just use an API call to determine the status of an event? Sure, we could do that. Utilizing this method would be an implementation of a concept known as **continuous polling**. The following diagram illustrates the continuous polling concept:

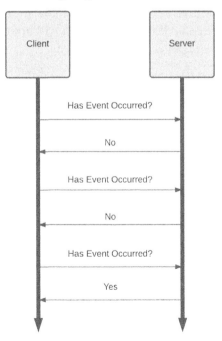

Figure 12.1 – Continuous polling visualization

Using continuous polling, we configure our client to make regular requests to the server to determine whether anything has changed with a given resource. We can execute these calls in either an automated or manual fashion. But the primary thing to note is that we request the server at some interval to return a status of a resource and run this process continuously. We make an arbitrary number of requests that will tell us whether an event has occurred, and to send data about the event when it has, even though most of our requests to the server will return a status that no change has occurred. As you can see in *Figure 12.1*, our client makes a total of three requests to the server for the resource status but is only returned meaningful information that a change has happened on the third request. You could visualize this approach as a parent and child on a long car ride, with the child continuously asking, *Are we there yet?*. Of course, at *some* point, the answer will be *yes* but it will only come after many *nos* and noticeable frustration from the parent.

Obviously, this is not an ideal approach. We're essentially wasting resources on both ends making requests to the server when the result of the request will probably not provide any meaningful information on the resource we are seeking information about. While we're still able to detect changes, this comes with several disadvantages, such as the following:

- Resources on both the client and server sides are expended for every request. This leads to inherent inefficiencies in how our application will function.

- We could overwhelm the server if our data is needed in real time. Thousands of requests per minute could lead to overages in API limit allotment such that our calls would fail even if an event has occurred.

- The data returned when the polling *does* detect an event has occurred is inherently *stale*. If your polling frequency is a few minutes, or hours, then the data returned is indicative of the state of a resource at that specific instance and may become invalid at any interval between your polling cycles.

That's not to say that there is no use for polling generally, but it is by its very nature an inefficient process. If the event data is not time-sensitive, and our schedule is on the order of a day or more, then a simple automated poll to check status is not likely to provide significant risk or impact to resources. Still, this provides little gain but with only slimmer risks. So, how do webhooks compare to continuous polling in terms of functionality and efficiency? The following is a visualization of a webhook:

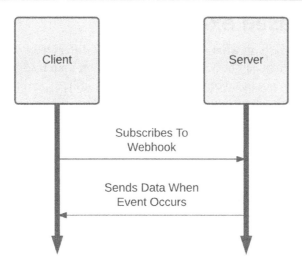

Figure 12.2 – Webhook visualization

As you can see in the preceding diagram, webhooks have a simple overall structure. Rather than initiating requests from the client to the server to determine the current state of a resource, we instead subscribe to a webhook that will notify us when the event has occurred by posting data to an endpoint that we define within the service where the event occurs.

It's not hard to see the benefits of utilizing webhooks over continuous polling in order to retrieve data when a given event occurs. Unlike polling, we can ensure that our data is updated in real time since our application will receive data corresponding to an event as soon as that event has occurred. This ensures that we don't suffer from the stale data problem that is present with polling. In addition to this, we don't overwhelm resources since we're not making continuous requests to return the resource states. Only a single request is needed and is executed by the server, to your configured endpoint, only when a specified event has occurred. There's no need to worry about governor limits or scaling your polling procedures.

In review, the primary difference between the two is that, with an API, a user makes a request to retrieve data from an endpoint and then receives a response. Webhooks are simply HTTP messages that are sent as the result of some event on a third-party service. Webhooks and APIs are closely related, with webhooks even being referred to as reverse APIs by developers. Now that we know the nomenclature and definitions, let's dig a little deeper with a practical example for demonstration.

# An event-based example

We now have a solid grasp on what a webhook is, how it differs from an API, and the types of scenarios where it can be a more effective solution than traditional API requests or polling. What might not be so obvious is how we can utilize them to extend our capabilities within Marketing Cloud to improve our current processes. To that end, it might be helpful for us to look at a simple webhook implementation that works with Marketing Cloud to automate an internal process common to many organizations.

For our example, let's say that we are currently using Content Builder to create and manage our email campaigns within Marketing Cloud. Furthermore, we are also utilizing content blocks within Content Builder to modularize our development processes and keep things compartmentalized and easy to maintain. Unfortunately, we've identified issues with version control when working on content as a team and want to minimize impact when multiple people are working on an individual campaign. To allow for more efficient backups, we're also utilizing GitHub to version-control our code and to keep backup repositories of our production content to prevent an untimely deletion.

This process works well, but it's still cumbersome to sync the data from our repository and Marketing Cloud and the updates are still manual and prone to user error. It sure would be great if we could just automatically add content to Content Builder whenever we've pushed new content to our repository. That's where webhooks come in!

By utilizing a webhook with GitHub, we can automatically post-commit data whenever a push event is triggered for our repository. Even better, we can configure an endpoint that our webhook can post to. This endpoint can contain logic to process the new files and create them within Marketing Cloud automatically.

First, let's outline exactly what we are trying to implement. When a file is created and pushed to our GitHub repository, we want to trigger an event in Marketing Cloud that will grab the raw data from the file and create a code snippet content block containing that data within Content Builder. While we could also selectively update or remove content based on the event in GitHub, we'll stick to just creating new content now for ease of demonstration.

We'll also assume that we will structure our repository such that our code snippet content blocks are nested in individual folders whose names correspond to a category ID in Content Builder. So, an example of our repository might look like this:

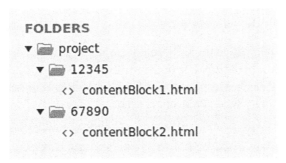

Figure 12.3 – Webhook example project structure

Finally, let's also call out that our example won't be applicable for pulling larger files (>1 MB) from the GitHub REST API. Although it is possible by utilizing additional API routes, it is beyond the scope of this example. Before we can implement our new webhook functionality, we're going to need a few things so we can get started setting everything up:

- An account within GitHub
- A repository to manage content
- A JSON Code Resource page in Marketing Cloud to serve as our webhook endpoint

That's all that we need to get started building our solution. With these items set up, let's take a look at configuring the webhook for our GitHub events.

## Configuring the GitHub webhook

There are certain steps required to begin the configuration of the GitHub webhook. Please follow these listed steps to begin the configuration:

1. First, we'll need to configure the webhook and application token on the GitHub website in order to set up our integration.

2. To create a webhook for a specific repository, navigate to that repository's landing page and select **Settings** from the page's menu.

3. Then, we'll navigate to the **Webhooks** section in the **Settings** menu and select **Add Webhook**.

4. This will bring up a **Configuration** menu that we can use to define where the webhook should post data, the structure of the data to be sent, and what event type should trigger a request.

In this menu, we'll define the following items:

- **Payload URL**: This will be the URL that we want to post the event to whenever it is triggered within GitHub. For our purposes, we will configure a JSON Code Resource CloudPage to accept requests from GitHub and to perform our content creation functionality when an event is fired.

- **Content Type**: The type of data that the webhook will post to our endpoint. Available options are `application/json` and `application/x-www-form-urlencoded`. The appropriate choice will depend on your system and preference, but for ease of use, let's go with `application/json` for this example.

- **Secret**: This is an optional input that allows you to specify a secret token that can then be utilized to secure your webhook and ensure that only events from GitHub are processed by the endpoint's logic as valid events. We certainly wouldn't want to execute functionality when the request is made from a random source, so implementing some security protocols such as the secret token is important for production implementations. While we could implement other protocols, such as checking the referrer or other request information, this provides us with a simple mechanism of securely authenticating that a given request originated from GitHub. Since our example is purely for demonstration, we'll skip this step and just focus on the functionality for now.

After we've configured the primary information about our webhook, listed previously, we'll then want to configure what types of events will trigger a request. While there are many different event types that we could target, from the forking of the repository to the creation of new issues, we will select **Just the push event**. Since we only want to create content once some new content has been pushed to our repository, only firing the webhook for push events should be sufficient. Then, we simply set our webhook as active and save. Now our webhook is live and will automatically send data when a push event has occurred for our repository!

Our webhook has been configured and we are all set to post events to our new endpoint, but we've still got one more configuration to take care of within GitHub. While we are ready to receive event data from our webhook, we need to set up a new access token in order to retrieve the raw content data from our repository to generate the content block in Marketing Cloud.

To do this, navigate to the **User Settings** menu and select **Developer Settings**. From there, we'll select **Personal Access Tokens** and create a new access token. In this configuration, we'll want to provide it with a helpful name that identifies the webhook service that we have constructed. We'll also need to set an expiration date for the token or configure it to never expire. Finally, let's select the token to allow the repository scope to read content that has been pushed to our repository. After saving your configuration, you will be presented with your access token. This token will not be visible again, so ensure you store the token for your application before navigating away from the page.

That's all we need for our example service in order to receive events from GitHub and authenticate them into our repository and retrieve the raw content from our push event. Now, we'll head over to Marketing Cloud to configure the endpoint we specified for our webhook.

## Setting up the endpoint

With our webhook set up on the GitHub side, which will send data to our endpoint when an event occurs, now it's time to configure our endpoint to execute our content creation logic when data has been posted to it. As stated previously, we can utilize a JSON Code Resource page to serve as our endpoint, but we could just as easily construct this to be hosted on any server and utilize an array of technologies. Since our purpose here is to demonstrate an example scenario, and given that most of you will be familiar with Code Resource, we'll select this option to process our logic. So, how do we begin? Well, first, we'll need to highlight the relevant pieces of data from the GitHub request that we can key off of to retrieve the relevant data and create our newly pushed content within Marketing Cloud:

```
{
    "repository":{
      "contents_url":"https://api.github.com/repositorys/
        {username}/{repositoryname}/contents/{+path}"
    },
    "commits":[
      {
          "added":[
            "12345/contentBlock1.html",
            "67890/contentBlock2.html"
          ],
```

```
      }
   ]
}
```

While there is much more data returned in the event request from our webhook, this is the overall structure that contains the relevant pieces that we will utilize for our example solution. First, note that there is a property called `contents_url` within our JSON payload. This value provides us with the base URL of our repository that can be utilized to make API calls to find files with a specific path within our repository. In addition, we have the `added` array under the `commits` property, which will house any files that have been newly added as a result of our push event within GitHub.

With our generalized payload structure in hand, let's define the individual pieces of functionality that we'll want our webhook to execute in order to create our code snippet content block within Content Builder:

1.  Retrieve the payload from GitHub and grab JSON for further processing.

2.  Parse the `added` array within the payload in order to determine the files that have been created in our latest push event.

3.  Retrieve the category ID, filename, and raw file contents of each item in the `added` array.

4.  Create all-new code snippet content blocks within the specified folders within Content Builder.

## Step 1 – retrieving the payload

First, we'll need to set up the script to retrieve the payload data and allow us to further process the JSON data being posted from the webhook. To do this, we'll utilize both the `GetPostData()` and `ParseJSON()` SSJS functions, which will retrieve the data and parse the JSON object:

```
<script runat=server>
Platform.Load("core", "1.1.1");
var postData = Platform.Request.GetPostData();
var json = Platform.Function.ParseJSON(postData);
</script>
```

Now that we've pulled in the JSON data and have it ready for processing, we need to assign the relevant data points we highlighted in the payload to variables that we can utilize for further processing.

## Steps 2 and 3 – parsing the added array and retrieving the contents

Now, we'll grab the `contents_url` parameter from the payload. Notice, in our example, the value in the payload is appended with the `{+path}` substring. We'll want to remove this portion from our variable as it's not relevant for pulling the final path to the files that we wish to retrieve. Finally, we'll also grab the added array from the `commits` property so that we can iterate through each added file and retrieve its contents:

```
var baseContentsURL = json.repository.contents_url;
baseContentsURL = baseContentsURL.slice(0, baseContentsURL.
lastIndexOf('/') + 1);
var addedFilesInCommit = json.commits[0].added;
```

That's all we need in order to accomplish the aforementioned items, and we now have our variables assigned for the base content path URL as well as our added array. With that in hand, we need to write our function to call the GitHub REST API to return the raw contents of our newly pushed files. Let's take a look at what that script looks like and then break down its components a little further:

```
function getRawGithubData(assetPath, contentURL) {
    var accessToke = "YOUR GITHUB ACCESS TOKEN";
    var auth = 'token ' + accessToken;
    var url = contentURL + assetPath;
    var req = new Script.Util.HttpRequest(url);
    req.emptyContentHandling = 0;
    req.retries = 2;
    req.continueOnError = true;
    req.contentType = "application/json"
    req.setHeader("Authorization", auth);
    req.setHeader("user-agent", "marketing-cloud");
    req.setHeader("Accept",
      "application/vnd.github.VERSION.raw");
    req.method = "GET";
    var resp = req.send();
    var resultString = String(resp.content);
    return resultString;
}
```

As you can see here, we are using `Script.Util` in order to make a GET API request to GitHub to retrieve our file content. To make this request, we'll need our function to accept parameters for `contentURL`, which we assigned to a variable and formatted in the previous step, and the path of the file that we'll pull from our added array assigned previously as well. Before we can complete our API call, we'll need to further define the following items in our request:

- **Authorization header**: This allows us to authenticate our call into the GitHub API to confirm that only we can retrieve the data relevant to an individual file. For this header, we'll simply need to concatenate `token` followed by the GitHub personal access token that we created and saved in the GitHub configuration portion of this example.

- **User-agent header**: A user-agent header is a requirement on GitHub REST API calls, so we'll have to pass a value for this header in our API call for it to function. The exact value doesn't matter, but it should be reflective of the platform/purpose of the call with which we are planning to execute. For our purposes here, we'll set this value to `marketing-cloud`.

- **Accept header**: We will specify this header to let GitHub know that we want to return the raw data of the file in the request-response. This allows us to utilize the exact contents of the file without any further processing or decoding on our end.

That's all that we need to define to make our request in GitHub in order to retrieve the file contents of whatever asset path we pass into this function. We'll make our request and return the content of that request as an output of the function so that we are able to retrieve the file contents and upload the asset to Marketing Cloud. With our function set up to retrieve the contents of the files added during the commit, we'll now need to write our function that writes this content to Marketing Cloud.

## Step 4 – creating new content

While we could utilize several methods in order to create this content, such as the Content Builder REST API, for ease of use (and to save us from setting up packages and authenticating into Marketing Cloud), we'll use a platform function approach to creating this content. Before we dive in, it's important to note that the documentation outlining the possible routes and functionality within Content Builder can be found in the official documentation located here: `https://developer.salesforce.com/docs/marketing/marketing-cloud/guide/content-api.html`.

Let's take a look at what that function looks like before outlining what's going on:

```
function createAsset(assetName, assetContent, assetId,
assetCategoryId) {
    var asset = Platform.Function.CreateObject("Asset");
    var nameIdReference =
      Platform.Function.CreateObject("nameIdReference");
    Platform.Function.SetObjectProperty(nameIdReference,
      "Id", assetId);
    Platform.Function.SetObjectProperty(asset, "AssetType",
      nameIdReference);
    var categoryNameIdReference = Platform.Function
      .CreateObject("categoryNameIdReference");
    Platform.Function.SetObjectProperty(
      categoryNameIdReference, "Id", assetCategoryId);
    Platform.Function.SetObjectProperty(asset, "Category",
      categoryNameIdReference);
    Platform.Function.SetObjectProperty(asset, "Name",
      assetName);
    Platform.Function.SetObjectProperty(asset, "Content",
      assetContent);
    Platform.Function.SetObjectProperty(asset,
      "ContentType", "application/json");
    var statusAndRequest = [0, 0];
    var response = Platform.Function.InvokeCreate(asset,
      statusAndRequest, null);
    return response;
}
```

Here, we are outlining a function called `createAsset` that will take some parameters and utilize them to actually create our code snippet content block within Marketing Cloud. Our function should accept parameters for the following properties of our Content Builder asset:

- Asset type ID
- Category/folder ID

- Name

- Content

First, we'll need to define the asset type that our content belongs to. While we have written our function to make this process generic, we could also hardcode it directly if we are only utilizing this webhook to process data for a given type. Here, we'll let the function take it as a parameter and assign the type ID according to that. Next, we'll need to retrieve the `categoryId` parameter and define that value for the `Category ID` property of our asset initialization. This ID will specify exactly what folder we wish to insert this asset into. Finally, we'll grab both the asset name and content parameters and then assign them accordingly to our `asset` object. Then, our function will create the asset with the values defined previously and insert this content into the specified folder within Content Builder. Now, all that we need to do is iterate through the added items in the GitHub JSON payload and invoke the preceding two functions to retrieve the content and create it in Marketing Cloud:

```
for (var i in addedFilesInCommit) {
    var assetPath = addedFilesInCommit[i];
    var categoryId = assetPath.substring(0,
      assetPath.indexOf("/"));
    var contentName =
      assetPath.split("/").pop().replace(".html", "");
    var contentData = getRawGithubData(assetPath,
      baseContentsURL);
    createAsset(contentName, contentData, 220, categoryId);
}
```

Notice here, we are iterating through each item in the array and then assigning an `assetPath` parameter that will equal the path of the file that has been pushed to our GitHub repository. Because this path contains both the name of the file and the category ID, as defined in the naming convention we discussed at the start of this example, we'll want to parse out each of those values separately from the added array item within each iteration. Finally, we'll invoke our GitHub REST API call function and assign it to a variable that will now contain the raw content of the file we've retrieved. After that, it's as simple as calling our `createAsset` function, noting that we are passing in a value of `220` for our asset type ID as this corresponds to code snippet content blocks within the Content Builder API asset model. For a complete list of asset type IDs, please refer to the Content Builder Asset Type documentation, located at `https://developer.salesforce.com/docs/marketing/marketing-cloud/guide/base-asset-types.html`.

That's it! With the preceding code saved and published to the endpoint that we defined within the GitHub webhook configurations, we are now all set in order to start syncing our push event file data with Content Builder. Whenever we've added, committed, and pushed an event to our repository, this endpoint and logic will automatically be processed and the new content will be created within Marketing Cloud from the data we've pushed to the repository.

This was a somewhat simplistic example, but we hope that it helps highlight the different ways that we can utilize webhooks to create an event-driven set of functionality within Marketing Cloud that automates our processes or provides some new degree of efficiency. Utilizing the aforementioned solution, we could easily scale it to more comprehensively handle our assets or even define our own schema for mass creating any set of Marketing Cloud objects that are accessible either through platform functions or API routes defined within the documentation.

In addition to using external services in order to generate event-driven functionality, there are webhook services within the Marketing Cloud ecosystem that allow the user to subscribe to certain events and then receive automated requests posted to a defined endpoint whenever an activity has occurred. One such method is Event Notification Service, which provides a webhook functionality that allows developers to receive relevant deliverability and engagement metrics on an email or text deployment automatically. This allows us to further automate processes in order to provide an immediate response or insight following some user engagement with our content. So, say we have an order confirmation email that contains a link for support or further information. We could set up a webhook that receives a request when the link is clicked and then takes some further immediate action (such as emailing a more detailed order receipt to the user).

The core concepts for utilizing the GitHub integration and Event Notification Service remain largely the same. Though the steps to accomplish both will differ in their configuration or endpoint, the basic premise is that we utilize the following steps to create our integration:

1. Configure an endpoint to receive requests.

2. Register and verify that our endpoint is able to securely authenticate and process calls from the webhook.

3. Create the webhook subscription event such that an event will be fired to our provided endpoint whenever a defined action has occurred.

With Event Notification Service, these steps are largely generated through API requests to defined routes within the Marketing Cloud REST API. In our GitHub example, these are done through simple **User Interface** (**UI**) configurations made within the repository settings, but the overall flow necessary for constructing these solutions is essentially the same.

Understanding the importance of event-driven requests, and how they can be utilized both within Marketing Cloud and externally in order to generate real-time functionality, is key. Familiarity with the distinction between webhooks and APIs allows us to choose the appropriate tools for a given use case and allows developers to select the appropriate tool for a given task and ensure that we're keeping efficiency and maintainability at the forefront of our application development. Now that we have introduced the concept of webhooks, let's move on to another concept that can aid us in building solutions that are both efficient and can scale.

# Microservices, assemble!

It's no secret to any of you that business requirements or existing flows can change, sometimes on a daily or weekly basis. As such, development teams are compelled to adapt to changing circumstances by extending new functionality into a given service or by altering its capabilities to meet both existing and new challenges. Unfortunately, it's not always so simple to extend functionality or revise existing solutions within our applications. We may have portions of our code base that are generic but intertwined and dependent on the execution of some other component.

When starting a project, when the focus is narrow, the code base can be very manageable and somewhat self-contained since it should encapsulate all of the base functionality outlined in the discovery process. Over time, additional functionality and components are added such that the code base and build, integration, and test processes can become cumbersome to manage or decouple. With more and more code being utilized in a central location, best practices were developed for ways to modularize the functionality of the application to make the code more maintainable and generalized (that is, they can be used by other parts of your application). Unfortunately, all of these individual modules must still be compiled together into a single code base in order to deploy the application. So, regardless of how the improved modularity of the application has impacted the developers working on it, at the end of the day, it still needs to come together in a single deployment for the entire code base to go to production. Enter **microservices**.

Microservices are an architectural pattern that differ from a monolithic approach in both the structure of the development process, as well as that of deployments. In a microservice architecture, we break down individual pieces of functionality into discreet, loosely coupled entities that have their own code base and can be deployed and managed independently from the rest of the application. So, when we have a simple update or new service addition, we can both develop and deploy the individual piece of functionality as a separate code base rather than worry about app-wide testing and deployments or integrations. Before we clarify this topic any further, let's take a look at the monolithic approach for building applications and then compare that with a microservices architecture so that we can see the pros and cons of each:

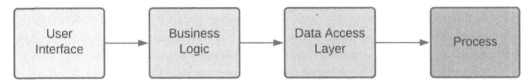

Figure 12.4 – Monolithic architecture diagram

A monolithic architecture is used for traditional server-side applications where the entire functionality or service is based on a single application. The entire functionality of the site is coded and deployed as a single entity and all dependencies are intertwined together. As you can see in *Figure 12.4*, a monolithic architecture comprises a UI, a server-side application (**Business Logic** and **Data Access Layer** in the preceding figure), and a database that contains relevant information that we can read and write with our application. Now that we have a base definition of what a monolithic architecture comprises, let's take a look at some advantages and disadvantages of this architecture.

## Advantages of monolithic architecture

This is the architecture that most developers in Marketing Cloud will be familiar with concerning application development. A single suite of tools or technologies is selected to solve a given range of use cases, and the development process will more or less flow through a common build and deployment process that will be global in its management of the code base. Not only is this process intuitive, particularly when coming from a hobbyist or more isolated developer experience, but it can also allow developers to get started on a project quickly.

First, let's look at some of its advantages:

- **Simple to develop**: Because this is the traditional method of developing applications, it's quite likely that your development team feels comfortable utilizing this architectural pattern for your application. In addition, when fleshing out your workflow and desired functionality for the application in the planning stages, it is much simpler to structure and build your application from the ground up in a monolithic architecture that allows for code reuse and shared datasets. Separating your code logically into components that are still related within a single application can introduce the concept of modularity without having to build individually separate services.

- **Simple to deploy**: This might be the most obvious benefit of utilizing a monolithic architecture. Simply put, it's much easier to stage and deploy a single code base than to manage multiple directories or files. Rather than worrying about varying build processes or service quirks, it's all rolled into one package that you can put into production at once.

- **End-to-end testing**: It should come as no surprise that end-to-end testing of your application or service is much easier when the entire suite of functionality is hosted within a single code base. There are many tools out there that can automate our testing procedures much more easily when our application is unified within a single code base.

## Disadvantages of monolithic architecture

As you can see, some of the most key advantages of utilizing this architecture are related to its simplicity to develop, test, and deploy. Most developers will be familiar with this workflow and easily understand the efficiencies that it can provide, particularly during the initial build and deployment process. That being said, this is not without a few disadvantages as well. Let's take a look at a few key costs when implementing this approach:

- **Changes can be complex**: Utilizing a single code base to provide all of the features of your application or service can become very difficult to manage when the overall size and complexity of your code are significant. If we have an individual feature or component to develop or extend, we are unable to isolate that code individually from the other components in our code base and we must test and deploy the entire application as a single entity just to accommodate this change.

- **Scalability**: Let's say we have developed a suite of services that will automate business tasks in our organizations in addition to providing some functionality related to customer experience (an API gateway for email data, for example). Some of the functionality is used quite rarely, while others are much more in demand and receive lots of traffic each day. We could implement elastic scaling of our services so that the servers can process spikes in traffic and allocate more resources when many requests are being made simultaneously. Unfortunately, with a monolithic architecture, we can't selectively scale the individual portions that may receive the most traffic since the entire code base is effectively a single, coupled entity. This means we have to scale the entire application, even though only a small handful of components might require it. This can lead to poor user experiences or costly resource use that could be avoided with a more decoupled architecture.

- **New technology barrier**: When we use a monolithic architecture, decisions about the technologies to utilize need to be made as part of the overall discovery process. As requirements change, and new languages, tools, or services are created to more efficiently handle common development issues, we may want to implement or utilize these new technologies to more efficiently deliver our features or to provide some capability that isn't supported in our current implementation. Utilizing a monolithic approach, we may have to rewrite large portions of our application to support this new technology, which might not be feasible from a time management or financial cost perspective.

As you can see, there are some obvious advantages and costs associated with utilizing a monolithic architecture when building applications or services. While it may be more intuitive to use this approach, and even desired when the level of complexity in the application is known to remain small, these advantages come at the cost of maintainability and scalability, which may be substantial barriers when considering your implementation.

Let's now take a look at an alternative approach that was created to address some of these concerns:

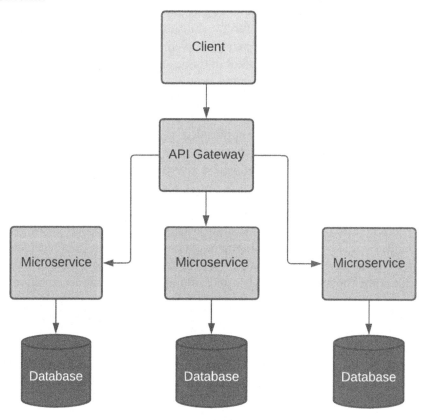

Figure 12.5 – Microservice architecture diagram

As you can see from the preceding figure, the structure of this architecture differs substantially from a monolithic approach. Instead of the more linear flow that we outlined with a monolithic approach, here we've decoupled our services and routed them through an API gateway. This allows us to route the appropriate request to individual microservices, providing a level of service decoupling that is not possible in the other architecture. For clarity's sake, let's define what each of these pieces does at a high level:

- **Client**: The client can be any type, including a mobile application, single-page app, or integration services. It's essentially how a user or service interacts with your application.

- **API gateway**: An API gateway is a sort of reverse proxy that sits between the client and your application microservices. It routes requests from the client to the appropriate microservice needed to perform some action. This is not a required entity for a microservices architecture as your client *could* call the necessary microservices directly, but it can sometimes be more efficient to utilize one (or multiple) API gateways that can route requests more efficiently or offer additional features, such as authentication and caching, that might not be easily implemented in a direct communication pattern.

- **Microservice**: As the name implies, microservices are small, independent pieces of functionality that are maintained in their own separate code base and are deployed individually from other microservices and features of an application. They will generally be grouped by the domain that they fall within (such as order management, shipping information, and cart functionality) and are accessed utilizing simple requests.

- **Database**: This is the actual datastore for the microservice, and it is the database for the information processed by the service.

As you can see, microservices differ from a monolithic approach in some distinct and important ways. First, it decouples functionality by their domain or purpose into entirely separate code bases, languages, deployments, and build processes. From an end user perspective, the functionality of a monolithic and microservice application is essentially the same but the method with which that functionality is built is quite different. In the monolithic approach, we're taking all our disparate features and services and rolling them up in a single application that a user interacts with. With microservices, however, we separate our application into a subset of smaller applications that interact with our application in such a way that the overall suite of services mirrors what our single application could do but in a much more efficient and manageable structure for developers. To illustrate this difference a bit more, let's list some characteristics of a microservice that define its purpose and how it can be managed:

- Microservices should be small, loosely coupled, and managed independently of other services in the application. Each service should use a separate code base.

- Each service can be created, managed, and deployed independently of any other service within the application.

- Services should communicate with other services utilizing well-defined APIs, though the internal implementation details of a given service are hidden from other services.

- For the most part, each microservice will have its own private database that it maintains separately from other services.

The key takeaway from these points is that each service is its own self-contained entity that can be managed wholly separate from the other services comprising an application. This lends itself well to extending the functionality of your application as you can have disparate teams contributing to the same overall functionality while still retaining the overall architecture of your implementation. Whether you are using completely different technologies or languages, hosting platforms, or any other differing item in the development process, as long as you have a common set of instructions for accessing and processing data from the service, they can be implemented within the same architecture to drive the functionality of an application.

Now that we have examined some of the advantages and disadvantages of a monolithic architecture, let's take a look at the microservices model in order to determine the pros and cons of its implementation.

## Advantages of microservices architecture

Here are the advantages:

- **Loose coupling**: Since each microservice is essentially its own mini-application, the risk that a change in one portion of the application will cause unanticipated changes in another is minimized greatly. Not only does this allow us to more easily maintain, test, and troubleshoot individual pieces of functionality of our application, but it also prevents a single errant piece of code in one part of our application from causing a widespread outage. This also allows us to provide more granular monitoring for individual components of our application rather than a more global service.

- **Technology flexibility**: We've highlighted this previously, but it's an important advantage when using this architecture. Because each of our services is maintained and deployed individually, no individual component is tied to the overall technology stack of any other service. This allows us to more easily upgrade or implement functionality utilizing the most up-to-date tools and technologies, which may provide a substantial benefit when compared to the initial implementation decisions during project discovery. Additionally, it widens the scope of the teams that can work on functionality for an application since it allows developers to work on their own piece of functionality in isolation from the application in whatever technology stack they feel most comfortable with.

- **Encourages refactoring**: When you've got an application that has become highly complex, and where functionality for different items can have interdependent relationships with the same sets of code, it can be discouraging to rewrite or refactor your code base. The adage *if it isn't broke, don't fix it* is commonly used in this context as the benefits that we might derive from improving our code can sometimes conflict with the costs of testing, maintenance, and downtime if the code in question is shared across the application. Microservices allow us to more granularly improve specific, self-contained sets of functionality without as much worry that our refactoring will have unintended consequences. This encourages developers to continuously refine their implementation to make it more understandable, efficient, and maintainable.

## Disadvantages of microservices architecture

These are the disadvantages:

- **Lack of governance**: We shared that technology flexibility and loose coupling are key advantages of utilizing this architecture, but they also can become an issue as well. While having the freedom to implement new technologies or languages for each individual service in our application allows us to expand the scope of people who can contribute and ensures that we can apply more efficient technologies more easily, it can come at a cost if done too frequently. Since there is no centralized framework with which each service is developed (though there can be a business requirement), you may end up with so many different languages and frameworks being used that some services become unmaintainable. Implementing the flavor-of-the-month framework for a given service might seem great at the time, but could be a niche item or unmaintained tool before you know it.

- **Complexity**: While it's true that we have offloaded a lot of the complexity of each individual service into its self-contained code base, we've also introduced quite a bit more complexity into the system as a whole. More complex integration and routing can introduce complexities that are implicitly handled by the likely more simplified routing present within traditional monolithic applications.

- **Data consistency**: With each microservice using a private datastore and responsible for its own data persistence, it can be difficult to derive data consistency across your application. While there are services that can help manage this, and even different application patterns specific to this issue, it's a common concern when utilizing microservices in data-heavy applications.

- **Latency and congestion**: Because our services need to communicate directly with the application or other services, we can introduce congestion or latency in our network if the methods within our services are highly dependent or poorly structured. For instance, if we have a service A, which calls service B, which then calls service C, and so on, we can incur significant latency that will affect the overall user experience or even the general functionality of our application.

Each implementation comes with its own set of benefits and challenges, and the type that you choose to implement will be based on a multitude of factors, such as the complexity of your application, the expected roadmap for functionality, and the scope of development resources available. Though the benefits of microservices are clear, it is often recommended that, unless constructing complicated enterprise applications, you utilize a monolithic approach to begin with. This is so that you can more quickly get an idea into production and determine whether the future needs of your application merit the implementation of a microservices architecture. Segmenting your code into more modular components, simplifying build and deployment processes, and keeping the data model more self-contained are all ways that you can build within a monolithic structure while still keeping your application flexible enough for an eventual pivot to microservices if the move seems warranted. Finally, microservices are not necessarily better. If making simple changes to your application requires you to update and deploy 5-10 different services, then it defeats the purpose of using this architecture. It's simply a method for managing complex functionality within an application when the logic can be easily decoupled and managed by multiple teams using their preferred technologies.

Outside of understanding these two approaches concerning application development, there is a benefit in considering these architectures and their cost/benefit even among constructing simple functionality within Marketing Cloud. For instance, let's consider we have a simple automation that contains some simple scripts that will create data extensions, queries, or journeys. We *could* write a single script that reads some input, from a data extension perhaps, and then uses that data to determine which function in the script to execute (create a data extension or create a query, for example), but that doesn't feel like an efficient method for implementing this solution. For one, we now have multiple, unrelated pieces of functionality being housed within the same code base, which makes it more difficult to maintain and could lead to a small error in one piece effectively derailing the entire script. A more efficient solution would be to have each script separated to only handle the domain that is relevant for its functionality. In this instance, we might have a script for creating data extensions, one for creating queries and another for creating journeys.

By compartmentalizing the individual pieces into their own, distinct **Script activities**, we've created a system where single errors in one script have little to no impact on our other scripts and allow us to make updates more selectively to individual pieces of functionality rather than constantly tweaking a single **Script activity** to manage all pieces. Now, you might be hard-pressed to consider this implementation a true example of a microservices architecture as it is traditionally understood within web application development but a lot of the same benefits can be derived by utilizing this system as with microservices. Obviously, the understanding of this in the web application space is hugely beneficial for us as Marketing Cloud developers as well as when we are building complex applications that interact across services to automate some functionality within Marketing Cloud. That being said, we hope that the takeaway from this chapter for you has been that you can utilize these generic concepts, with regard to both microservices and the other topics we've discussed so far in the book, in order to start thinking differently about how your work in the platform itself is done. While you may not always find a quick correlation with the work you're doing on a daily basis, understanding these architecture patterns will inform how you operate within Marketing Cloud and can allow you to approach problems from a more knowledgeable perspective that will drive efficiency and maintainability in your solutions.

## Summary

We've covered several different key ideas within this chapter that we hope you found both informative and enlightening for how you consider the work that you do as a Marketing Cloud developer. The differences between webhooks and APIs, and how we can utilize webhooks to create an event-driven, real-time solution, are so important in taking your integration with Marketing Cloud to the next level. As we have seen the rise of many platforms and services that implement webhooks, such as GitHub, Discord, and Slack, there have arisen numerous opportunities for automation across disparate systems to allow functionality that would otherwise be either impossible or wildly inefficient.

In addition to discussing webhooks, we also went through an example that creates content whenever a push event has occurred within GitHub. Obviously, our example was somewhat simplistic with many assumptions made for ease of demonstration, but it should provide a strong springboard for you to take this functionality to the next level. As Git has become an indispensable tool for teams across all development spaces, integrating this technology with Marketing Cloud through automated services can be a powerful multiplier that will increase the efficiency and happiness of developers or marketers working within the platform.

Finally, we reviewed what microservices are and how this architectural pattern differs from the traditional monolithic approach to application development. We highlighted some of the advantages and disadvantages of each approach and carefully considered how different factors, such as application complexity, team capabilities, or modularity, can affect our decision in regard to the optimal solution for our given use case. We also took a step back to consider how these ideas could be envisioned in the context of Marketing Cloud automation, and how automation itself can be thought of as a microservice architecture.

After reading this chapter, you should feel inspired to create event-driven functionality that can create value for your organization or developer experience. You should also be able to more clearly see how to apply the concepts in this book to the work that you do in Marketing Cloud, even outside of the context of custom application development.

In our next chapter, we're going to tackle custom Journey Builder activities, specifically an activity that can greatly expand both the utility and capabilities of Journey Builder within Salesforce Marketing Cloud.

# 13

# Exploring Custom Journey Builder Activities

In the last chapter, we highlighted some of the possible use cases and advantages of using event-based architecture. In addition to covering the concept of webhooks, including how they differ from a traditional API, we also outlined a sample use case that allows users to set up a GitHub webhook in order to automatically sync content between a repository and Content Builder in Marketing Cloud. Utilizing event-based architectures such as what we just described is important to allow us to create real-time functionality rather than having to utilize concepts such as continuous polling to ensure that data or the resource state is synced between two systems.

In this chapter, we're going to examine another concept around event-based functionality that is specific to Marketing Cloud, known as **Journey Builder custom activities**. You are likely familiar with the standard suite of activities available within Journey Builder for building functionality that can action on individual user data in real time, and indeed, we've outlined some of that functionality and activity here in an earlier part of the book. Similar to this, Journey Builder also offers us a framework for building our own functionality and integrating our services directly within the Journey Builder framework.

In this chapter, we're going to learn about the following topics:

- **An overview of the required files and structure for Journey Builder**: In this section, we'll dive into the requirements and basic needs for our custom activity.

- **Setting up your package and environment**: We dive deeper to set up and build our environment for the custom activity.

- **Exploring configuration and activity UI**: This is the setup of the structured logic and interactivity aspects of the custom activity.

- **Using the postmonger events and payloads**: This is where we deal with payloads, requests, and responses for our custom activity.

- **Implementing handlers and authentication**: These are the final touches to secure our custom activity and to utilize the logic and scripting that is needed for our intended results.

Through these topics, we will be able to build our very own example custom Journey Builder activity and will add some very powerful capabilities to your automation capabilities in relation to Marketing Cloud. However, before we get onto these topics, first, let's take a look at the technical requirements that you will need to follow along with this chapter.

# Technical requirements

While we will go through important aspects of the code base in this example, it is expected that you have some rudimentary knowledge of the Node.js environment in order to understand the content of this chapter. In addition to this, it is recommended that you have some knowledge of jQuery, which we will also utilize within our activity, along with a basic familiarity of how to utilize the GitHub **Command-Line Interface** (**CLI**) for management and deployment. In addition to this, we will be utilizing the hosting service, Heroku, to host and serve our application that integrates with Journey Builder. Heroku is a **Platform-as-a-Service** (**PaaS**) cloud that allows us to build, host, scale, and deploy our application, which will interact with Journey Builder to deliver end-to-end functionality. Before getting started, let's take a high-level view of how the overall flow will work in our example.

Figure 13.1 – The custom activity flow

As you can see from the preceding diagram, Journey Builder will broadcast events to our custom activity, which will then process the data sent in the event data and make a POST request to a **Code Resource** page in order to log the relevant data into a data extension. These events will fire when any kind of activity occurs in Journey Builder, such as editing the activity configuration or a contact reaching the activity within a running journey. In those events that involve the initialization or configuration of our activity, the custom activity will process the logic we have defined for those events and then send a response back to Journey Builder containing details of the configuration. However, when an actual record reaches this activity in a running journey, the custom activity will process encrypted production data from Journey Builder and then request the code resource page to execute the logic on that page driven by the data posted from our activity. From there, the code resource will post a response back to the activity (such as 200 *OK*), and then our activity will return a status of the execution back to Journey Builder, and the record will either proceed in the journey or not. With that high-level overview out of the way, let's dive into the required files and structures of the activity.

# An overview of the required files and structures for Journey Builder

When a contact enters this custom activity at a given juncture in the journey, we're able to access their data programmatically and take some action, as defined by the structure of our application integrating with Marketing Cloud. Let's imagine that we have a complex customer journey that contains several touchpoints within our journey that interacts with customers utilizing email, text, or push communications.

We've got a great direct mail service that we've been using in our ad hoc campaigns, and we'd like to utilize that service to automate our mailers whenever someone has reached a specific point in our journey (say, after a recent purchase). While we could build an automation or scheduled service to do this, these services do not operate in real-time and might not be adequate for reaching our customers as quickly as possible in order to generate conversions.

Here, we could configure an application external to Marketing Cloud that is set to receive data from our journey entry source and utilize this to automatically create our mailer, utilizing our direct mailing service API. Then, we can integrate that custom service directly into Journey Builder. This is so that it becomes a configurable activity on the canvas, and we can easily add to any part of the journey that we'd like.

This is only a sample scenario, but it's easy to envision the myriad of ways that you could implement this kind of system to accomplish real-time activities that reach a customer in an automated fashion exactly when you want them to. Aside from a mail service, we could create custom decision splits that action on data external to Marketing Cloud, coupon lookup and claiming services, query internal data stores for further customer personalization, and many other possible services and integrations that meet your organization's needs.

So, we've got a basic idea of what a Journey Builder custom activity is, *but how can we get started building our own?* In this chapter, we will create a custom activity that will post a simple payload to a CloudPage as a proof of concept in order to become more familiar with how we can extend Journey Builder to provide enhanced functionality with custom activities.

We'll utilize an existing repository as the base for our application in this example, but we could construct our functionality in many different ways depending on our experience, capabilities, and familiarity with various languages or technologies. Although there is some degree of flexibility in how your application can be constructed, it must contain the following items in order to function within Marketing Cloud:

- `index.html`: This will serve as the frontend of your application and will be the user interface that users see whenever they configure an instance of your application within Marketing Cloud. This page will be *iframed* as the configuration menu and should contain any relevant user inputs or configuration settings that you want to expose to Journey Builder users. This file must live in the root directory of your application.

- `config.js`: The configuration file will provide Journey Builder with metadata about your application, such as the size of the configuration window, data that you want to pass from the journey to your application, the general flow of your configuration menus, and more.

- `postmonger.js`: This is a JavaScript utility that allows us to enable cross-domain messages for our application. This allows our application and Journey Builder to communicate through a set of predefined events that allows our app to programmatically access and trigger the functionality that is necessary for our application to function.

- `require.js`: This is used to manage dependencies between different JavaScript files within our application and will help to load items such as our `postmonger` file.

- `customActivity.js`: This file will house the `Postmonger` events that we want to initiate within our application or Journey Builder, as well as the primary store of functionality for our frontend.

Now we have some idea of the critical files that are necessary for our application, *but how does it function, on a base level, within Journey Builder?* Let's examine the overall flow of how a custom activity will function within our journey. First, when our application has been integrated with Journey Builder and is available as a configurable activity on the canvas, our `config.js` file will be read by Marketing Cloud to determine the name of our application, the icon to display in the activities menu, and other metadata about our application to allow the user to interact with it.

When a user drags our activity onto the canvas and opens the configuration menu, Journey Builder will `iframe` in our frontend, which will contain the user input necessary for any custom configurations that are needed to accomplish our functionality (in our example, this is the CloudPage URL). When this item is being loaded, the `Postmonger` events are triggered to execute certain pieces of functionality, such as retrieving the existing configuration for an instance of an activity, and any relevant functionality that is related to our load functions is processed.

Conversely, when the user has completed the configuration for an instance of the activity and has clicked on the **Save** button to save the configuration, the data relating to that instance of an activity is stored within the `inArguments` part of our payload and is accessible by our application anytime that activity is executed.

So, with our activity initialized and configured, a user enters the journey and reaches our custom activity. When this occurs, Marketing Cloud will send contextual data about the configuration of the activity, along with any relevant user data that we have elected to capture from our customer, as encoded JSON in a `POST` request to our application. The application then decodes the JSON by utilizing a **JSON Web Token** (**JWT**) signing secret, which is provided in your Marketing Cloud app configuration. This is able to parse the data for further processing of the functionality. Following this, the application sends a response back to Journey Builder, letting it know the status of its execution, and then custom proceeds along the journey to the remaining activities in the flow.

That is a high-level overview of the required files and overall structure being utilized by Journey Builder and our application in order to communicate and provide enhanced functionality as defined by our application. So, with that information in hand, let's dive in and start setting up our application!

# Setting up your package and environment

Before we can begin building our sample application, we'll need to configure some items upfront to ensure that we have a solid base with which we can build. First, we'll need to select a method for hosting our application, along with the types of technologies that we will utilize to construct our application. For this example, we're going to utilize Heroku to host and scale our application. **Heroku** is a PaaS cloud that can enable us to host, deploy, and monitor our application in an intuitive way that ensures we can get started quickly and easily troubleshoot our application.

Also, while we could utilize any number of programming languages or frameworks to build our activity with, for this example, we will be creating a Node.js application to serve as our custom Journey Builder activity.

With those caveats out of the way, first, let's take a look at how to create your application within Heroku and link it to a GitHub repository that we will use to manage our code base.

## Setting up your application in Heroku

We'll execute the following steps to get this setup going:

1.  First, navigate to the Heroku application menu, and select **Create new app** to create our application.

Figure 13.2 – The Heroku app creation menu

2.  Then, we'll simply give our application a unique name and create our application in Heroku.

3.  Now, we need to configure our application to pull its source for a central Git repository and utilize this as the deployment pipeline for our application. Note, in the preceding screenshot, that we can also utilize the Heroku CLI to manage our deployments and code base, but for the purpose of this example, we will utilize GitHub. Whenever we commit and push a new change to the master branch of our GitHub repository, our application should automatically update and publish the new changes for Journey Builder to reference.

4. To do this, first, we'll need to initialize a repository that contains all of the necessary code to run our custom Journey Builder activity application. For ease of demonstration, let's clone the sample GitHub project repository for custom activities available within the `Chapter13` subfolder of the following repository: `https://github.com/PacktPublishing/Automating-Salesforce-Marketing-Cloud`. This will give us a solid base to work from and ensure that we can demonstrate the functionality of our custom activity much more quickly.

5. With our sample project structure cloned to local storage, we should now create a new repository for our application within GitHub, and set our origin for this application to the new remote URL of our repository by utilizing the following:

```
git remote set-url origin new.git.url/here
```

6. Now, all we need to do is push our local repository to GitHub with Git push and we're in business! We've got our repository configured and a boilerplate template ready. So, let's go back to Heroku to integrate our new Git repository into our application. Under the deploy section of the Heroku interface, navigate to the **Deployment method** section of the menu and select **Connect to GitHub** to link our newly created GitHub repository to our Heroku application.

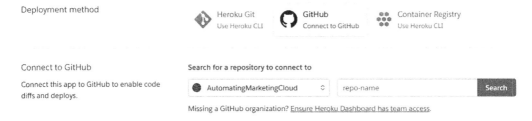

Figure 13.3 – The GitHub connection menu

7. We can utilize a simple search feature to find our repository, after authenticating it into GitHub from Heroku, and then select **connect**. Now our application source is linked to our repository!

8.  From here, we can then choose to deploy our code base automatically whenever a new commit has been pushed to an individual branch. As you can see in the following screenshot, we'll set our configuration to automatically deploy our code from GitHub to our application whenever a commit has been pushed to the master branch of our repository. This ensures that our application is always up to date with the newest source from our repository.

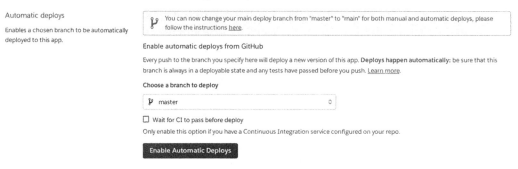

Figure 13.4 – The automated deployment menu

9.  Now, with the automated deploys enabled, all that we have to do is push any changes, and our application is updated. To see our application in action, scroll down a bit further and select **Deploy Branch** from the manual deploy menu to start a manual build of our application for Heroku. Once our build and deployment have been completed successfully, navigate to the top of the page and select **Open app** to see our application. Here is the screenshot of the UI of our application:

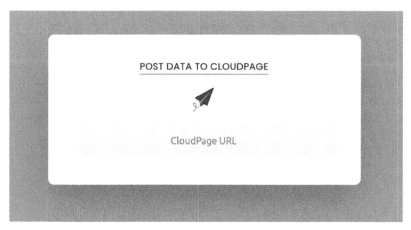

Figure 13.5 – The application UI

Now that we have configured and confirmed that our application UI is loading as intended, let's configure our Marketing Cloud Journey Builder integration so that we can ensure our activity is integrated and now loading on the Journey Builder canvas.

# The Marketing Cloud custom activity configuration

With our Heroku application configured and deployed to production, we now need to configure the integration on the Marketing Cloud side to ensure that our custom activity is available as a configurable item on the canvas. To do this, follow these steps:

1.  We need to navigate to **Setup menu** within Marketing Cloud and then to the **Installed Packages** submenu underneath the **Apps** section on the page.

2.  From there, we'll select **New** from the button in the upper-right corner in the **Installed Packages** menu.

3.  Now, we'll give our package a name and description so that we can more easily identify it when accessing the list of installed packages from the menu screen.

4.  Then, once we're inside the configuration of our newly created package, we'll select **Add Component** to add the custom activity integration to this package. From there, we'll select the **Journey Builder Custom Activity** option as the type of component that we'd like to create. Then we will fill out the relevant details for our custom activity integration.

## Add Component

* Name

automating-mc-jbca

Description

Example custom activity for Journey Builder

* Category

Custom ▼

* Endpoint URL

https://automating-mc-jbca.herokuapp.com/

Back ●——O Save

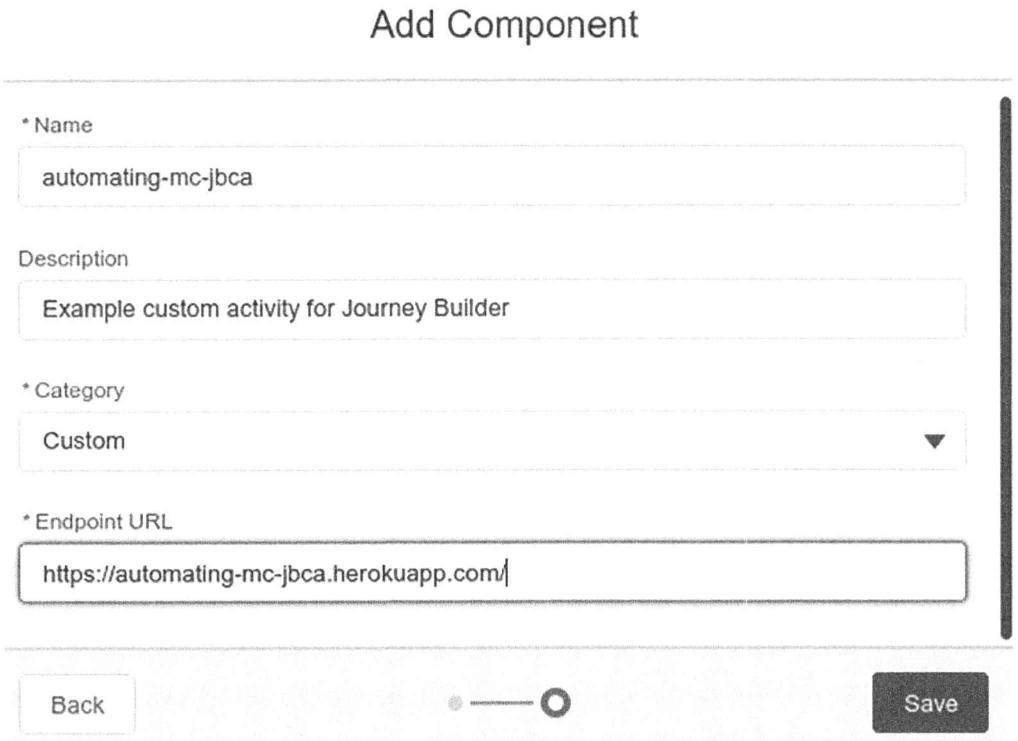

Figure 13.6 – The custom activity configuration menu

5.  In addition to **Name** and **Description**, there are two other inputs for both **Category** and **Endpoint URL**. **Category** will define what section of the activities menu our application will reside within. For this example, we'll just set that value to **Custom** since it's simply a demonstration of functionality. If we were developing a messaging service or decision split, then we would utilize the messages and flow control categories, respectively.

6.  Finally, we need to provide the URL of our application where the index.html file will be served. Simply copy the URL of the application that we tested in our Heroku configuration step and click on **Save**.

7.  Now, let's navigate to Journey Builder and create a simple flow to see whether our application is available and ready to be utilized within Journey Builder.

8.  Next, we'll need to create the CloudPage that our activity will post to. Additionally, let's create a data extension that our CloudPage will upsert a payload to, just so we can more easily confirm that our application is working end to end. First, navigate to CloudPages and create a JSON Code Resource page that will house the following script:

```
<script runat=server>
Platform.Load("Core","1");
var postData = Platform.Request.GetPostData();
Platform.Function.InsertData("CustomActivityTest",["ac-
tivityData"],[postData]);
</script>
```

9.  As you can see, the only functionality that our CloudPage is responsible for is inserting the payload being sent from our custom activity into a data extension, called CustomActivityTest. To that end, we'll also need to create a data extension with this name, along with a field called activityData with the maximum text value set to empty. Now, when our custom activity posts a request to our CloudPage, we're able to log the contextual data from Journey Builder and our application into this data extension. The related visualization is shown in the following screenshot:

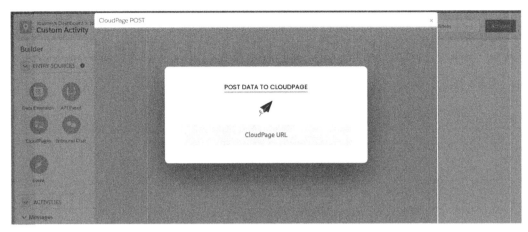

Figure 13.7 – A custom activity in Journey Builder

10. That's it! After navigating to Journey Builder, we can now see that our custom activity is both available as a draggable activity within the **Custom** activities section as well as configurable on the canvas. Now, users can configure and save the activity within their journey flow. The only necessary input will be for our users to enter the CloudPage URL, as created in the preceding step, into the input provided within our custom activity.

So, we've identified how we can host and deploy our custom application and how we can integrate it with Journey Builder to appear as a configurable activity on the canvas. *But how is it working? Further still, how can we configure this to actually do something when a user initiates an activity for execution within the journey?* Well, we've covered the basic implementation of getting our custom activity onto the canvas, so now it's time to really dive in to see what's going on and how our application will function in production.

# Exploring configuration and activity UI

Before we do a deep dive into our application and see how we will configure each item to create our custom activity, first, let's take an overview of the overall code structure and call out the key files that we will be reviewing as the key components for creating our custom activity.

Note that this doesn't mean there is no other utility to the other files in our code base, but rather the ones we will highlight will affect the overall configuration and unique implementation of our application. So, let's take a look at the overall project structure.

Figure 13.8 – The custom activity project structure

As you can see, we have quite a lot of files in this directory that all serve a specific function. Let's highlight the important ones that we'll be reviewing within our demonstration and describe what each does at a high level:

- `config.json`: This file houses the metadata of our application, and it is utilized by Journey Builder to determine what data we want to accept as `inArguments` for our application among other items in our activity configuration.

- `index.html`: As discussed previously, this will serve as the user interface that our users see when they configure an instance of our activity.

- `customActivity.js`: We've already covered this at a high level, but this file will serve to process the logic from our frontend and fire our `Postmonger` events, both to and from Journey Builder, to generate the necessary configuration for our activity. Additionally, we'll also use this to capture the user input within the activity and create the payload that we'll use to process on the server-side part of our application.

- `activity.js`: This is the file that will contain our logic to execute when a given route has been called from Journey Builder. Here, we can decode our JWT and execute logic when our *Edit*, *Save*, *Validate*, *Publish*, and *Execute* routes are called for our application.

Now that we have highlighted the important files that we will be configuring for our demonstration, with the understanding that these files do not encompass *all* the important functionalities and key components of our application, we can move forward and examine each in more detail. To begin, we'll start with one of the most important pieces of the custom activity, our `config.json` file.

## The config.json file

For this file, we'll break down our `.json` file into a few separate sections and analyze each one. This ensures that we can keep things logically consistent and discuss the purpose for individual properties without presenting them in an overwhelming context. We'll examine this file in more depth than other parts of this application because it is so central to how your application is configured and processed by Marketing Cloud. Let's take a look at the first part of our file and provide some additional context for our configuration:

```
"workflowApiVersion": "1.1",
"metaData": {
    "icon": "images/iconMedium.png",
    "iconSmall": "images/iconSmall.png",
    "category": "custom"
},
"type": "REST",
"lang": {
    "en-US": {
        "name": "CloudPage POST",
        "description":
```

```
                "Sample Journey Builder Custom Activity",
            "step1Label": "Configure Activity"
        }
    },
```

As you can see, in this section, we're going to define some metadata about our application that Journey Builder will use to place it on the canvas, add a label to our *iframed* configuration window, and provide the name of our custom activity as it appears on the canvas. Additionally, we're configuring our icon files, located in the `images` folder within our project directory, to define what icon our activity should utilize when it is placed on the journey canvas. The properties to further refine, largely due to the ambiguity of their values, are `type` and `category`. Let's define both and show the possible values for each here, for further reference:

- `category`: This value determines which part of the **Journey Builder** activity menu your application will reside within. Although we also can set this value within our installed package, as you saw earlier in our configuration steps, our setting in this file will override that value if we should choose to set it here. The list of accepted values here are as follows:

  - Message (messaging activities)

  - Customer (customer update)

  - Flow (decision splits)

  If the value that you provide for this property does not match any of these options, then Journey Builder will default the `category` selection to `custom`. In this scenario, your activity will appear within the custom activities menu of Journey Builder.

- `type`: This is a property that maps to the type of activity you are using to create. It is similar to a category but more granular, and its value must be representative of an approved activity type that is represented within the Journey Builder JSON data structure. Valid options for this configuration are as follows:

  - `MultiCriteriaDecision`

  - `DataExtensionUpdate`

  - `EMAILV2`

  - `EngagementDecision`

  - `randomSplit`

- `Wait`

- `Rest`

These values should be somewhat self-explanatory and map to already existing activities that you will find on the **Journey Builder** activity menu, such as EMAILV2, which corresponds to an **Email** activity, and `Wait`, which corresponds to **Wait** activity within Journey Builder. For generic custom activities that do not easily confirm an existing type, utilize the `Rest` value to accommodate these use cases.

Now, let's take a look at the next part of our `config` file to see what additional items we are configuring for our activity:

```
"arguments": {
    "execute": {
        "inArguments":[
                {"subscriberKey":"{{Contact.Key}}"}
        ],
        "outArguments": [],
        "url": "https://automating-mc-jbca.herokuapp.com/
            journeybuilder/execute",
        "verb": "POST",
        "body": "",
        "header": "",
        "format": "json",
        "useJwt": true,
        "timeout": 10000,
        "retryCount": 5,
        "retryDelay": 100
    }
},
```

In this part of our `config` file, we define both the route and information that will be sent every time an instance of our custom activity is executed within Journey Builder.

First, let's examine the `inArguments` object. This specifies the data that will be sent to our application whenever a subscriber enters our activity. While we can set this data during the configuration event of our activity instance, we can also define values here that will be passed.

In our preceding example, we want to pass an attribute called `subscriberKey` that will equal the value of `ContactKey` for the subscriber that has reached our activity in the journey. Notice that we are using a data binding syntax to programmatically populate that value for our payload depending on the subscriber's data rather than some global configuration.

There are numerous options for pulling data here, such as from our Journey Builder default email/phone values or an attribute from our entry source event. But for the purpose of our example, we'll keep it simple and only pass `ContactKey` to our application.

> **Tip**
>
> For further information on the capabilities of data binding, please refer to the Salesforce documentation located at `https://developer.salesforce.com/docs/marketing/marketing-cloud/guide/how-data-binding-works.html`.

In addition to this, we could also capture some responses from our application and return these values for further processing by other activities within Journey Builder by using the `outArguments` property in our `config` file. This is beyond the scope of our book, but it's an important concept to note for scenarios where the returned data is needed for further processing by an activity. For the remainder of this section, we're defining further parameters for Journey Builder to process when executing the activity. Let's briefly look at a few, as follows:

- `Url`: This is the route that Journey Builder will call when running the `execute` method inside our activity instance. With our project set up, this will equate to the URL of our application that the `journeybuilder/execute` route appended to the primary URL.

- `useJwt`: We can use this setting in any of our routes to let Marketing Cloud know that we wish to receive a JWT to validate that the call is coming from Journey Builder. For our `execute` method here, we'll set this value to `true`.

- `timeout`: *How long (in milliseconds) do we want to allow our application to continue processing until it times out?* The default value for this is `60,000` ms.

- `retryCount`: *How many times would we like to retry the execution of our activity after it has timed out, in accordance with the window we have set in the previously defined property?* The default value for this property is `0`.

- `retryDelay`: *How long would we like to wait (in milliseconds) before we retry our execute method?*

The remainder of our `config` file primarily consists of setting the configuration arguments for the remaining routes, apart from `execute`, for our application: `Edit`, `Publish`, `Stop`, and `Validate`. For our example, we will not further define these properties as extensively as our `execute` method. The only route that must be defined here is Publish. Finally, let's take a look at the final part of our `config` file that we wish to highlight:

```
"wizardSteps": [
    { "label": "Configure Activity", "key": "step1" }
],
"userInterfaces": {
    "configModal": {
        "height": 640,
        "width": 900,
        "fullscreen": false
    }
},
```

Here, we are defining some basic properties regarding the configuration frame of our activity as it appears on the Journey Builder canvas. The `wizardSteps` property is an object array that defines the possible steps to navigate through our configuration of the activity.

Here, we might define the different labels and steps of a multi-step activity on the canvas. However, for our example, we only need the primary configuration. So, we'll keep our configuration short and simple. Finally, there is the `userInterfaces` property. This is a required element for the UI and defines the overall `height` and `width` values of our configuration menu. As you can see in our preceding example, we've elected to show our custom activity configuration modal at 640 x 900, and we don't want our modal to appear as a fullscreen configuration window in Journey Builder. Now, let's take a very quick glance at the application UI just to make some quick notes.

## The index.html file

As we defined earlier, this file is the UI of our custom activity and must live in the root of the project directory. For this file, we could load in any number of CSS of `.js` files in order to dynamically render our frontend or even use templating engines to modularize our UI and deliver a more templated content delivery system.

Our use case is simple; we only need to provide input for our users to enter in a CloudPage URL that our activity can make a POST request to. The only important thing to note here is that we want to use require.js to load our customActivity.js file, which is located in the js folder, as a dependency so that we can utilize the functionality within that file to make our UI interact with Journey Builder and perform its intended purpose. To do this, we'll simply include the following script within our index.html file:

```
<script type="text/javascript"
    src="js/require.js"></script>
<script type="text/javascript">
    (function() {
        var config = {
            baseUrl: 'js'
        };
        var dependencies = [
            'customActivity'
        ];
        require(config, dependencies);
    })();
</script>
```

Then, we'll create a simple input that will capture our CloudPage URL, which our customActivity.js file will pull to pass to our server-side scripts for further processing:

```
<input type="text" id="cpURL" class="fadeIn second"
name="cpURL" placeholder="CloudPage URL">
```

That's all we need to configure in our config file and frontend in order to make our application recognizable to Journey Builder and to provide our users with an opportunity to configure an instance of an activity. Now, let's take a look at the Postmonger events and payloads that will interact with Marketing Cloud in order to process data to and from our application.

# Using the Postmonger events and payloads

We've highlighted the important items in our `config` file, along with the `config.json` and `index.html` files for our frontend. Now, we'll turn our attention to the `customActivity.js` file and go through it in parts, in the same way as the previous section, to identify what is happening within our application.

First, we'll initialize a new `Postmonger` session in order to utilize events defined by Marketing Cloud that allows you to interact with Journey Builder:

```
var connection = new Postmonger.Session();
var payload = {};
$(window).ready(onRender);
connection.on('initActivity', initialize);
connection.on('clickedNext', save);
```

Here, we'll call a function, named `onRender`, that will execute once the **Document Object Model (DOM)** is ready and we can begin processing our JavaScript functions. By utilizing our `onRender` function, in the initial configuration of our activity, this event will call the `initActivity` Postmonger event, which will initialize our activity and pass any of our `inArguments` objects defined within our `config` file to our application. Once we have configured our activity, it will broadcast the configured payload that we will further define in another function implemented in this file. This is so that we can retain our saved configuration input even after we've closed and reopened our activity configuration.

Next, we will tell `Postmonger` that, upon execution of the `initActivity` event, we would like to execute a custom function, called `initialize`. Let's take a look at how our `initialize` function is constructed:

```
function initialize(data) {
    if (data) {
        payload = data;
        var setcpURL = payload['arguments']
            .execute.inArguments[0].cloudpageURL;
        $('#cpURL').val(setcpURL);
    }
}
```

In this function, we are passing in a parameter called data that is equal to the inArguments object array, which we will define within our customActivity.js file. If our activity has been configured previously, meaning a user has added an input for the CloudPage URL in our UI, we will pull that value from the payload and pre-populate that data as the value for our input of the UI for this instance of our activity. This ensures that, when users return to the configuration of our activity before activating the journey, then their previous configuration will be retained and they will not have to reinput a value to process the activity successfully.

Finally, we'll execute a custom function, called save, whenever the clickedNext Postmonger event has been fired within Journey Builder. This event is triggered when a user clicks on the **Next** button within the configuration modal of the activity configuration modal in Journey Builder. Normally, we could use this event to display multi-event configuration menus by serving different menus to our users whenever this event has been triggered.

For the purposes of our example, and since our configuration consists solely of a single menu, this event is triggered whenever the user clicks on **Done**. This is because there are no other configuration steps to complete. Now, let's take a look at our save function:

```
function save() {
    var cpURL = $('#cpURL').val();
    payload['arguments'].execute.inArguments = [{
        "subscriberKey": "{{Contact.Key}}",
        "cloudpageURL": cpURL
    }];
    payload['metaData'].isConfigured = true;
    connection.trigger('updateActivity', payload);
}
```

As you can see, in our save function, the first thing we want to do is capture the CloudPage URL input for our activity since this is the primary driver of functionality and is the only configurable property within our activity. Then, we'll redefine our inArguments object array to contain both the ContactKey of the subscriber that is entering our activity in the journey and the input that our Journey Builder user has specified for the CloudPage URL.

Finally, we'll set the `isConfigured` property for the `metaData` object in our payload to be equal to `true`. This is a key step because it is necessary for Journey Builder to fully recognize our activity as having been configured and ready for activation. Without setting this value to `true` before attempting to publish a journey containing your activity, the journey will fail to publish, and you will be required to reconfigure the activity until this value has been set.

Finally, we'll execute the `updateActivity Postmonger` event. This event takes the configured payload as a parameter, and executing this event will close the configuration window within Journey Builder for your custom activity and save the payload information that you have passed to it in the canvas. From there, we can reopen the configuration of our activity and retain the payload data that we have defined within our `save` function in order to pre-populate the CloudPage URL data in the same way that we did for the `initialize` function earlier.

That's the only configurations we need to process within our `customActivity.js` file for our application to process events within Journey Builder and create a payload that we can then utilize on the server side of our application to perform the actual `POST` request to our CloudPage that will save our user data to a data extension.

It should be noted that this is a very simple representation of all the possible events and functionalities that can be utilized within this file in order to accomplish your use cases within Journey Builder. We could programmatically access the `eventDefinitionKey` journey to dynamically retrieve data extension attributes at configuration time for our payload, access tokens for further API processing, along with many other types of functionalities that can provide enhanced integrations and event services between our application and Journey Builder. With our client-side scripting, configuration, and UI ready to go, let's take a look at how we can authenticate our token from Marketing Cloud and perform the final set of functionalities required for our application.

# Implementing handlers and authentication

So, we're now able to add our application to Journey Builder, load our application UI, and both save and initialize our activity data within Journey Builder for further processing and configuration. Now, we need to actually do something on the application side with the payloads configured from Journey Builder. To do this, we'll examine some of the contents of our `activity.js` file in order to determine how to create the final pieces of functionality.

Before we can begin, we need to complete one final piece of configuration for our application. Since we only want our `execute` method to process if we've identified that the request is coming from Journey Builder, we'll need to decode and authenticate the JSON Web Token posted to our execute route. To accomplish this, first, we'll navigate back to our installed package within Marketing Cloud.

In the primary package details, we'll want to copy the value of the **JWT Signing Secret**. This will allow us to decode the JWT and confirm that the request origin is Journey Builder. To do this, we'll use the following steps:

1.  With the signing secret in hand, navigate back to the Heroku application menu and select the **Settings** tab from our primary application configuration page.

2.  From there, scroll down to find the **Config Vars** section. **Config Vars** allow us to securely set and store environment variables that can then be called throughout our application programmatically and will allow us to both safely store our signing secret and utilize it in our code base in order to decode the JWT.

    So, let's create a config var, called `jwtSecret`, and assign it a value that is equal to the signing secret that we copied from our Marketing Cloud package.

Figure 13.9 – Heroku Config Vars

3.  While we won't examine it in depth, in our code base, we have defined a JavaScript file in our `lib` directory that contains a simple function for decoding the JWT by taking both the JWT passed from Marketing Cloud and the signing secret in order to validate whether the request has been successfully authenticated. We'll just need to ensure that our `activity.js` file has access to this function by requiring it within our file. We can do this by utilizing the following:

```
const JWT = require(Path.join(__dirname, '..', 'lib',
'jwtDecoder.js'));
```

Now, we're all set to code the functionality that will execute whenever Journey Builder calls a given route within our application. For all routes, other than our `execute` route, which is triggered when a contact enters our activity in a running journey, we'll simply log some request data to the console and then send a `200` response back to Marketing Cloud to let it know that the `POST` request to our route was handled successfully. No actual functionality will be processed when these routes are called other than logging, and the general structure for each of these handlers will look like the following:

```
exports.route = function(req, res) {
  logData(req);
  res.send(200, 'someRoute');
};
```

However, for our `execute` route, we'll want to authenticate the request and then process the payload data before setting up our `POST` request to whatever CloudPage the user has specified. Let's dive into this route and see how we can implement this functionality:

1.  First, we'll define our `execute` handler and then run our JWT decode function against our signing secret:

    ```
    exports.execute = function(req, res) {
      JWT(req.body, process.env.jwtSecret, (err, decoded)
        => {
        if (err) {
          return res.status(401).end();
        } else {
    ```

    Here, notice that we utilize the `process.env.jwtSecret` syntax as the parameter for our signing secret. We can utilize the `process.env.configVarName` syntax to access any environment variable that we have configured within our settings menu in the application configuration screen.

    Then, we'll run a check to see whether an error was returned during the decoding of our JWT. If one was returned, we'll return a `401` Unauthorized status and end the processing of our `execute` method. If no errors were returned, our logic will continue processing and our decoded payload values will now be accessible within the `decoded` JSON object output as a result of our `decode` function.

2. Now that we have authenticated our request and have a `decoded` payload to work with, we'll further check to ensure that `inArguments` are available for us to process:

```
if (decoded && decoded.inArguments &&
    decoded.inArguments.length > 0) {
    var decodedArgs = decoded.inArguments[0];
    var cpURL = decodedArgs.cloudpageURL;
    var subKey = decodedArgs.subscriberKey;
else {
    console.error('inArguments invalid.');
    return res.status(400).end();
}
```

Since our `inArguments` data contains all the relevant data that is needed for our application to function, such as `ContactKey` and the CloudPage URL, we'll only process our `execute` method further if this object array is available and has data to process. If the data is not available in the `decoded` payload, we'll return a `400` Bad Request status from our `execute` handler and end any further processing. Assuming that our `decoded` payload does contain this data, we'll then grab the root node from our `inArguments` object array and assign variables to our CloudPage URL and `ContactKey` data, which we will then process to our CloudPage.

3. Finally, we'll construct the last piece of our custom activity that will take our CloudPage URL and `ContactKey` data and form a `POST` request that our CloudPage will receive and upsert directly into our data extension:

```
var cpPostBody = JSON.stringify({
    "activityData": {
        "SubscriberKey": subKey,
        "CloudPageURL": cpURL
    }
});
request.post({
    headers: {
        "Content-Type": "application/json"
    },
    url: cpURL,
    body: cpPostBody
```

```
    }, function(error, response, body) {
        if (error) {
            console.log(error);
        };
    });
    logData(req);
    res.send(200, 'Execute');
```

First, we'll create our request body, which will consist of our `ContactKey` data and the CloudPage URL in JSON format for our request. Then, we'll utilize the requests library in order to make a simple `POST` request to the URL defined in our activity configuration. If an error occurs during our request, we'll log that data to the console, but we'll return a `200` status back to Journey Builder regardless of the processing of our logic at this point of our activity (though we certainly could provide additional error handling or retries).

That's it! We've now fully configured and deployed our custom activity to Heroku, and it is ready to implement within Journey Builder across journeys and points within our flow. Now, whenever a user drags our activity onto the canvas, configures a CloudPage URL, and activates our journey, any contact who enters our activity will have their contact key data logged to the data extension that we configured earlier.

Before we wrap up, there's one more topic that we can touch on briefly that you might find particularly useful during the development, testing, and deployment of your custom activity.

# Utilizing logging

While it's always nice when things go smoothly, you might run into errors or unidentified issues as you go through the tutorial in this chapter whose underlying causes can be difficult to determine. To that end, do not hesitate to utilize logging within your application to determine points of failure or to output sample data from your payload in order to aid you in your investigations or development.

Heroku offers a simple method for accessing the logs of your application. From your application configuration and settings screen, simply click on the **More** drop-down menu on the right-hand side of the page and select **View Logs**. On this screen, you will see all of the logged events from your application. This will include deployment statuses, requests from Journey Builder for applications resources such as the `config.json` file, whenever a route is posted from Journey Builder, and any custom logging within your application. Let's take a look at what a sample log for an application might look like when starting up following a new deployment with Git:

Figure 13.10 – The Heroku logs

As you can see here, we are able to retrieve the logs of individual events related to our deployment, including the status of our application's state. In addition to this information, which can help find errors related to the application's state or deploy status, we are also able to view any relevant information logged from our application.

The amount of data returned here is somewhat limited, particularly if you are testing heavily, but you can also process these directly from the command line by tailing your logs with the Heroku CLI. Setting this up is outside the scope of this chapter, but you should be able to find numerous resources on Heroku's website and across the internet for accessing this data with ease.

If you're finding yourself stuck, or just want an idea of what your configured payload looks like before writing your execute logic, never hesitate to write to the console in order to more easily determine where things are going wrong and how you can resolve them.

# Summary

We covered a lot in this chapter and, although our sample activity was simplistic and not entirely indicative of a production use case, we hope that it helped empower you to create new functionalities within Journey Builder that automate your use cases and extend the capabilities of your Marketing Cloud account.

After reading this chapter, you should have the ability to build and deploy an application through Heroku and be able to integrate the application directly within the Journey Builder UI in order to provide enhanced functionality to both technical and non-technical resources alike. With even just a few simple tweaks to our CloudPage, we could extend platform functions as real-time events within Journey Builder.

In the next chapter, we'll take a reflective tour of the journey in terms of what we have learned within this book and the lessons and tools that we can take away from this resource in order to become more competent, powerful, and efficient developers within our organizations and in the Marketing Cloud community as a whole.

# Section 4:
# Conclusion

This section is a wrap-up of the book, giving a few quick recaps and last-minute tips and tricks. This section contains the following chapter:

- *Chapter 14, Carpe Omnia*

# 14
# Carpe Omnia

You did it! You read the whole book! We are very proud of you and happy that you liked our book enough to read it from cover to cover. Well, we hope you did at least. *Automation for Marketing Cloud* can be a daunting topic and is certainly one that takes a bit of effort to learn about, so we want to congratulate you on all your efforts!

You may be asking yourself, *What does this fancy chapter title mean? Is it just some attempt to make the authors feel smart?* Well, maybe a little bit but it also has a great meaning, albeit a bit greedy. *Carpe omnia* means *seize everything* in Latin. This, we feel, is something marketers, developers, professionals, and everyone in general should take to heart. If you see an opportunity, whether noon, night, or break of dawn, seize it! We feel like, if there is one way to end this book, it is with words about moving forward and getting the best out of life that you can.

Our goal with this last chapter is to go over everything you just learned and make sure you did not miss anything or to discover whether you want to go back to something for a refresher. There were a ton of topics in this book, ranging from theory to practical examples to development outside of Marketing Cloud. With all these topics, it can certainly be easy to have missed things or for things to have gotten confused in some way. Hopefully, with this last chapter, we can help you discover anything you might want to go back and reread.

As this is goodbye, for now, we are also going to give a few last-minute words of advice and tips and tricks to help you with automation in Marketing Cloud. Not every bit of knowledge, best practice, or hack could make it into the book, so there are a ton more for us to share here.

Then, we will give a final farewell and wish you the best of luck for your adventures in Marketing Cloud and hope to meet again! For now, let's take a look at what you have learned over the last 13 chapters.

This chapter is divided into the following sections:

- *Lessons we've learned so far*: A brief look back over the last 13 chapters and all that we have learned to this point

- *Final lessons and examples*: Our last two quick lessons and examples to share for you to use in your future endeavors in Marketing Cloud

- *Last-minute tips and tricks*: A few last-minute words of advice from us to share with you in the hope it will help guide you to further success

# Lessons we've learned so far

The first thing we want to do in our closing chapter is to make sure we covered everything we wanted to. Throughout this book, we have explored many different things in many different ways. Some of it was more theoretical than other parts – but all of it was very useful and very relevant. Our goal in this section is to ensure you absorbed what we were hoping you did and that when we leave you, we leave you best prepared for the future.

We went from learning the basics of automation and its uses and then went all the way to building your own custom activities and microservices to interact with Marketing Cloud. Quite a journey to go on all in a single book!

With that being said, our journey began with a bit of theory upfront where the first few chapters were completely focused on the setup and practical definitions of key philosophies, thoughts, and other highly important factors and related items. This setup was hugely important to help not only to pave the way forward for the rest of the topics we discussed but also because understanding these aspects allows you greater insight and innovation in your day-to-day activities, both inside and outside of Marketing Cloud – helping to lead you toward further growth.

We then concentrated on automation possibilities and capabilities within Salesforce Marketing Cloud. Through exploring the proprietary languages (such as AMPscript and SSJS), the native tools (such as Journey Builder and Automation Studio), and other less obvious possibilities, we were able to get a strong grip on not only what works but to build a strong base to better figure out what is possible for future automations from within Marketing Cloud.

After we dove deep inside of Marketing Cloud, we started our adventure into the possibility of automating Marketing Cloud from outside of Marketing Cloud. By exploring custom API interactions and integrations, SDKs, webhooks, and microservices, we were able to find ways to do so many tasks in Marketing Cloud without ever opening the user interface at all. We also found many ways to use those as well as custom Journey Builder activities to further supplement and integrate with Marketing Cloud to greatly increase capabilities and performance. That catches us up on all that we went over. That was a lot, wasn't it? The main aspect that we hope was gathered from this book is the ability to take what was written here and grow something of your own, instead of just copying what is shared. The information here is powerful, but with a growth mindset, someone can take this power and make it stronger. The possibilities in Marketing Cloud are boundless. This whole book was just centered around automation inside Marketing Cloud, which is only a single part of the platform's capabilities. Imagine the series of books that would be needed to cover every aspect. We think it would be too much for one person to read and fully understand!

We are very glad to have shared this with you, but we aren't finished just yet. Next, we are going to give a couple of extra insights into automation for Marketing Cloud that we could not fit into the other chapters.

## Final lessons and examples

Now that we have gone over everything you should have picked up from our book, we wanted to give a few words of advice and some further places to investigate Marketing Cloud automation. Unfortunately, trying to document every single aspect of automation for Marketing Cloud is a task that would require an encyclopedic-type book series, which is a bit much for this book.

For that reason, we wanted to promote two more important things to consider when working with automation in Marketing Cloud. First, we will investigate another way for an automation to be triggered – from another automation!

## Calling an automation from another automation

The cool thing about this method is that it can string automations together without having to rely on syncing schedules or dropping files. This will allow you to utilize a **Script** activity in Automation Studio to call the next automation you want to run.

## How does this work?

Well, the **Script** activity would use WSProxy or other functionality to interact with the SOAP or REST API. From there, you would just use the corresponding object or endpoint to start your automation. As a note, many people stick with the WSProxy version as it does not require the application and component `clientId` and secret in order to work – reducing security risks.

Here is a quick example script using WSProxy to start another automation:

```
<script runat=server>
    Platform.Load("Core","1.1.1");


    var prox= new Script.Util.WSProxy();
    var objId = {{autoObjectID}}
    var props = {
            ObjectID: objId
    };


    var opts = {};


    var request = prox.performItem("Automation", props,
        'start', opts);
</script>
```

Using the preceding code, replacing `{{autoObjectID}}` with the ID of your automation, will start the next automation immediately. Now, you may wonder, how am I supposed to get the automation object ID? Well, the good news is we can use another WSProxy call to get that, no problem. Here's the next sample call to get an automation object ID:

```
<script runat=server>
    Platform.Load("Core","1.1.1");
    var prox = new Script.Util.WSProxy();

    var name = "My Automation";
    var request = prox.retrieve("Automation",
        ["ProgramID"], {
        Property: "Name",
        SimpleOperator: "equals",
```

```
        Value: name
    });

    var objId = request.Results[0].ObjectID;
</script>
```

Now we just take that ID that is returned and plug it into the first example script, and we will then start that corresponding automation. Pretty darn cool, right? Well, this opens up even more possibilities too, such as continuous automations!

## Continuous automations

Ever had something that you wanted continuously monitored or looped through constantly for an extended period? By having two automations that call themselves via the previous method, you can! See the following visualization of what a continuous automation looks like:

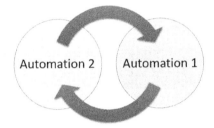

Figure 14.1 – Visualization of a continuous automation

Now this is a huge draw on processing and can open you up to risk if one of the calls fails or there is some other error, so you need to take caution when implementing something like this. Prior to creating any of these automation types, you should take a deep dive into reviewing the drawbacks and costs and compare those to the benefits.

> **Drawbacks to Looping Automations**
>
> Keep in mind that looping an automation can mean that once Salesforce starts charging or limiting the number of automations you can run, you will be burning through those pretty quickly.
>
> Secondly, you open up the risk that there could be an error that will break the loop, which means you might need another automation to monitor it, further increasing the process draw.
>
> And finally, this draw on processing will slow down all other processes and your instance, and if it is significant, Salesforce may throttle or cancel some of your processes without warning.

This can open you up to having something like a triggered send monitor script to measure whether the queue goes above a certain level or a continuous comparison on a data extension to watch for new records and perform an action on them. But with great power comes great responsibility as the platform is not designed nor built to do this for the native user. You are essentially using the capabilities in a way that falls well outside of best practice, meaning you are taking on a great amount of risk and danger when implementing it.

## Script activity continuous automation

If you are using script activities for an action, you have another option, which is one we prefer, continuous automation. This one uses the hourly schedule, which is a native function, but then uses a built-in timer, a reference data extension, and two instances of the same script activity in the automation.

Basically, what this does is make an automation that runs every hour and then makes the automation run for around an hour. This way, once run one ends, run two begins – making the automation run near continuously. See the following illustration for a visual example of this process:

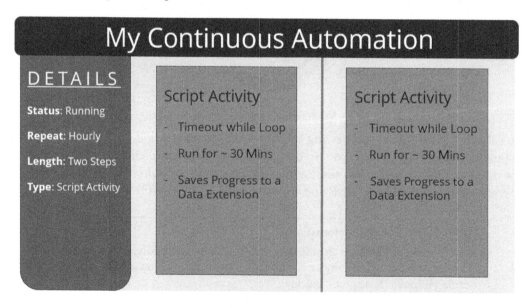

Figure 14.2 – Visualization of continuous automation with Script activities

To help expound on this process, we are going to utilize the same script that we used in *Chapter 6, The Magic Script of Activities*, for the triggered send queue checkup (`https://github.com/PacktPublishing/Automating-Salesforce-Marketing-Cloud/tree/main/Chapter06`). This time we are going to modify it to run repeatedly for a set amount of time using a `do...while()` loop to set a time limit:

```
var date = new Date(),
startTime = now.getTime(),
timeOut = 1620000; //27 minutes
//60000 milliseconds in a minute


do {


  //your JS code


} while((new Date().getTime() - startTime) < timeOut)
```

As you can see from the preceding code, we would be setting a time limit via the `timeOut` variable that would wrap around the entire script. You would wrap this around your `for` loop from the triggered send queue checkup script. This would then have the script run repeatedly for around 27 minutes each time – with around a 1-minute runtime, this gives enough buffer to allow for server slowdowns to ensure it does not time out and stop the automation. You can see a full implementation of a very similar script to this one as well as a full walkthrough of it on Greg's blog (`https://gortonington.com/alert-for-your-triggered-send-queue-limits-in-sfmc/`).

Now, with this script running at roughly 30 minutes each time regardless, we just put the same exact script in two steps, making the runtime roughly 1 hour. This then, combined with the 1-hour repeating schedule, will make the automation run pretty much continuously.

On a semi-related note, we could also envision the concept of a scheduled automation that doesn't actually live within Marketing Cloud at all. Let's take a look at how we can create the concept of an automation utilizing tools external to Salesforce Marketing Cloud.

# Creating automated scripts with Heroku Scheduler

Let's say that we have a very useful script that we've written in our favorite programming language, perhaps one that automates the deletion of old assets in Content Builder. We're all set up and running it locally, but it's a bit cumbersome to remember to do it on a regular basis in order to keep things nice and tidy within our asset paths. Perhaps we could convert it to an SSJS script and execute it in an automation, but an alternative approach might be to utilize cron job tools such as **Heroku Scheduler** in order to execute our script on a defined schedule.

## What is Heroku Scheduler?

We discussed how to create and configure an application utilizing Heroku in the last chapter, but there are some benefits of the platform that we didn't discuss. One of the benefits of utilizing Heroku as your hosting service, in addition to the Git deployments and enhanced logging covered previously, is the availability of Heroku add-ons that can enhance your application. Heroku add-ons are cloud services that are available as extensions to your application on the platform in order to easily integrate different pieces of functionality to support your application without any additional coding or solutioning.

These add-ons can range from provisioned databases, monitoring, and analytics, among others. One such add-on that is commonly used by applications hosted on the platform is Heroku Scheduler. Heroku Scheduler is an add-on that allows us to schedule a given task to run at a specific interval continuously, ranging from every 10 minutes to once daily. Utilizing this add-on, we can specify the command that we want to execute during the specified interval, and it will execute following the schedule set. Granted, we could write our own application job scheduler that would provide us with much more flexibility and reliability, but not every production use case requires this solution, particularly those that are not tied to complex or critical tasks.

So, it's not difficult to see how we could construct similar functionality to scheduled automations utilizing this add-on. We could set it to execute a command that runs a set of corollary operations that essentially has the same effect as executing a subset of functions within an automation in Marketing Cloud. Now that we know what Heroku Scheduler is, let's take a look into how to use it and why.

# How and why to use Heroku Scheduler

In order to utilize this add-on, follow the steps for application creation and initial deployment that we outlined in the last chapter. With your application configured and a script deployed, simply navigate to the **Resources** tab of your application configuration screen and select the **Find More Addons** option and search for the Heroku Scheduler add-on in order to provision it for your application. Though this service can run on a free tier, you might be required to have a payment method on file for your account just in case your usage of this service exceeds the usage limits on your Heroku account.

So, let's envision that we have a simple Python script that calls the Content Builder REST API for all assets in a given folder, aggregates the collected assets, and then performs a REST delete request in Marketing Cloud to remove the assets found in our script. We can keep all of our logic self-contained in a single file that can be executed with a simple command such as python contentDeletion.py, which will execute our script logic whenever it is invoked. With our Heroku app configured, and our script deployed, we can then provision the Scheduler add-on and then apply a configuration similar to the one next:

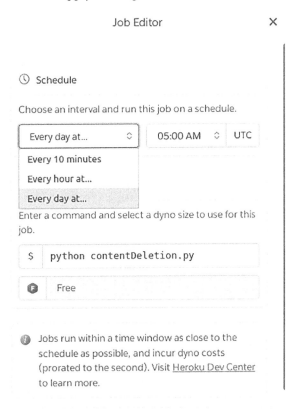

Figure 14.3 – Heroku Scheduler configuration modal

As you can see from the preceding screenshot, we're setting our scheduler to execute our Python scripts utilizing `python contentDeletion.py` at a daily interval starting at 5 A.M. UTC. Now, without any manual intervention on our end, we're able to aggregate and delete assets within Marketing Cloud automatically every day with our simple Python script.

So, we understand the how in relation to Heroku Scheduler, but why should we utilize this over automations within Salesforce Marketing Cloud? Well, it largely depends on your use case and the complexity of the functionality that you are trying to perform. For our scenario above, we could run simple **Script** activities within an automation that pulls our assets and performs the delete function without having to develop and deploy an application.

That being said, suppose our functionality was sufficiently complex and had complex data integration or aggregation logic. Not only would we be adding bloat to our Marketing Cloud instance and bogging down the system while we executed our automation, but also we're unable to utilize helpful libraries or programming language features that can make things much more efficient and debuggable when compared to a custom script.

In addition to Heroku Scheduler, there are several other scheduling add-ons available in the store that can execute logic at intervals as short as 60 seconds. This provides us with even more possibilities than we could realistically execute within Marketing Cloud automations, though the range of applications for such short intervals might be somewhat limited. This is not to say that this should be a preferred method of building scheduled, automated solutions. There are complexity and concerns with this method that are not present in Automation Studio, and in fact, most will find that the majority of use cases are better suited to execution within automations. In addition, automations in Marketing Cloud give us access to a suite of platform functions and capabilities that would be much more complex to develop from scratch. That being said, for functionality that is sufficiently complex or resource-intensive, a Heroku app using Heroku Scheduler is a great alternative. We can build our solutions in our favorite tools, easily integrate version control into our solutions, and worry less that we're bogging down Marketing Cloud with our custom functionality.

Now, let's take a look at some final tips and tricks that you mind find helpful when developing for Marketing Cloud.

# Last-minute tips and tricks

As Marketing Cloud experts, we wanted to share a few more quick tips that you can use when building your automations or other solutions using Marketing Cloud. These are some things that we have picked up or learned along the way, usually the hard way, and want to share them to help spread the knowledge and make the path forward a little bit easier each time.

Starting off is a very solid piece of advice that we still have to remind ourselves of every single morning:

- *Marketing Cloud is the Wild West. This means you can do almost anything you want in it, but the bad side is that it is unpredictable at times and a script or automation that worked before may not work for your new solution.*

  By keeping this in mind, you can make sure not to let assumptions or best practices limit you from doing amazing custom work, but you will also need to account for many unexpected issues and problems that you have never run into in the past.

  Next up is another strong piece of advice that should be followed every day when working in Marketing Cloud. This one concentrates on preparation and discovery.

- *Before doing anything in Marketing Cloud, you will need to do your research. Marketing Cloud allows you to do amazing things in many customizable ways – but because of this, it allows you to set up things in ways that are not scalable or efficient. You need to know what to do before you do it or you could be completely rebuilding all your hard work every couple of months.*

  Knowing the capabilities and impact related to each aspect of your needs from Marketing Cloud will allow you to build smartly and create an elegant solution. This will increase the scalability and longevity of your solution, reducing the duct taping and rebuilding of less researched solutions.

  This next one is pretty obvious to most, but to anyone that is just starting out or coming from one of Salesforce's other clouds, it is extremely important and highly relevant.

- *Salesforce Marketing Cloud is a completely unique experience compared to many of the CRM and core platforms, utilizing completely different interfaces, structures, development experiences, native languages, and APIs. You cannot easily translate from SFDC to Marketing Cloud or vice versa.*

One thing that many that work in Salesforce Core or similar clouds don't realize is that Marketing Cloud is built in a completely unique way compared to most of the other available clouds. Marketing Cloud is essentially a completely different skill than core clouds due to this and there is no real major translation of skill from one to the other.

For instance, as an MVP focused nearly exclusively on Marketing Cloud, the author's high level of skill and expertise in this area would be nearly meaningless if he were to try and work in Sales Cloud or Service Cloud. These are completely different platforms that require different skills.

This next one is a favorite and one that we try to live by every day of our lives. It is a mantra that we strongly believe is the most important part of achieving success within Marketing Cloud.

- *To succeed in Marketing Cloud, you need to be engaged in the community. By sharing your knowledge, skills, and expertise with others, you gain further knowledge, understanding, and insights you cannot get any other way. Plus, there is no better support group for when you get stuck or just need to vent.*

One of the most important factors we have found in a person's success in Marketing Cloud is how active and engaged they are in the community. This can include places such as blogs or forums as well as Salesforce Community Groups and Salesforce Trailblazer Community forums.

Whether official or unofficial, there are a ton of different places out there to interact, communicate, and learn. We highly recommend going out and doing so if for no other reason than to get a different viewpoint and context on solutions in Marketing Cloud to help you think outside your current box.

- *When developing solutions for Marketing Cloud, you may feel that you're developing for a closed system and that common web standards or tools are of limited use or consideration.*

To some extent that is true, and you may often find that the best solution is to leverage existing functionality on the platform. This shouldn't discourage you from considering how you can integrate third-party services or build custom enhancements for your solutions on the platform. In fact, doing this can both allow for a much larger suite of capabilities in addition to encouraging a new way of thinking about how you develop on the platform.

- *Obtaining and nurturing your knowledge about modern web application development is an important practice and one that can ensure you're staying informed about current trends and web capabilities.*

As you gather that knowledge base, you will start to see more possibilities through Marketing Cloud integrations that can ensure you are getting the absolute most out of your solutions. Salesforce Marketing Cloud is a powerful platform, and one that provides you with the possibilities to meet a near-endless number of use cases, but we can only extend it fully when we see it as a larger player within the cloud services space.

So, stay curious and never hesitate to consider the work you're doing in Marketing Cloud in the light of some other field or perspective. It will open doors to automation that you hadn't previously thought possible and will expand your own capabilities for automation and efficiencies on the platform.

Hopefully, all these last-minute tips and tricks will help you reach new levels inside of Marketing Cloud. Alas, we have reached the end and must bid you a good day and start our goodbyes.

# Summary (adieu and auf wiedersehen)

It has been our pleasure writing this book and we hope that you have enjoyed it even half as much as we enjoyed writing it! As with nearly everything in Marketing Cloud, there are a million different ways to accomplish the action of saying goodbye. There are multiple words in multiple languages that all mean essentially the same thing…but are slightly different.

If we were to sum up Marketing Cloud, we would say that this is an apt description. In a certain situation, *adieu* might be the perfect thing to say and be highly appropriate and acceptable, but in others, it might make more sense to use *auf wiedersehen*, *goodbye*, or *ciao*. Although these words each mean almost the exact same thing, they each have their own context and their own best place. For someone in the United States, if they said *adieu* to their friends, their friends might not understand what that word means and be confused, but if they said *goodbye*, it would be easily understood. The reverse is true as well. In France, *adieu* would be easily understood, but using *auf wiedersehen* might cause confused looks. Similarly, in Marketing Cloud, where some scripts may accomplish the same things, the value of each is dependent on the context and desired output. This is due to the minor differences in how they are run or what language they use. For example, using an SSJS Core function instead of an AMPscript lookup will allow you to use simple or complex filters outside of just *key equals value*, allowing for more flexibility.

Now, this may seem like a bit of a long way to just say goodbye in other languages and explain why we are doing it, but we hope that this example will help emphasize the meaning behind this book. Although this book gives you a ton of great example solutions and great information, the goal was not to provide something to just copy and paste from, but to instead inform you to make your own decisions and find all the unique and appropriate solutions for your automation needs.

On that note, we must leave you, but first, we want to give another heartfelt thank you for reading our book and we greatly hope you enjoyed what we created. Good luck in your future automations and solutioning and always remember to explore and innovate – you never know what new process or hidden gem you will find!

# Index

# O

Packt.com

Subscribe to our online digital library for full access to over 7,000 books and videos, as well as industry leading tools to help you plan your personal development and advance your career. For more information, please visit our website.

## Why subscribe?

- Spend less time learning and more time coding with practical eBooks and Videos from over 4,000 industry professionals

- Improve your learning with Skill Plans built especially for you

- Get a free eBook or video every month

- Fully searchable for easy access to vital information

- Copy and paste, print, and bookmark content

Did you know that Packt offers eBook versions of every book published, with PDF and ePub files available? You can upgrade to the eBook version at packt.com and as a print book customer, you are entitled to a discount on the eBook copy. Get in touch with us at customercare@packtpub.com for more details.

At www.packt.com, you can also read a collection of free technical articles, sign up for a range of free newsletters, and receive exclusive discounts and offers on Packt books and eBooks.

# Other Books You May Enjoy

If you enjoyed this book, you may be interested in these other books by Packt:

**Becoming a Salesforce Certified Technical Architect**

Tameem Bahri

ISBN: 9781800568754

- Explore data lifecycle management and apply it effectively in the Salesforce ecosystem

- Design appropriate enterprise integration interfaces to build your connected solution

- Understand the essential concepts of identity and access management

- Develop scalable Salesforce data and system architecture

- Design the project environment and release strategy for your solution

- Articulate the benefits, limitations, and design considerations relating to your solution

- Discover tips, tricks, and strategies to prepare for the Salesforce CTA review board exam

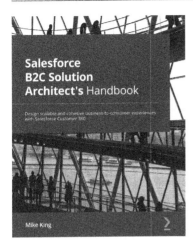

**Salesforce B2C Solution Architect's Handbook**

Mike King

ISBN: 9781801817035

- Explore key Customer 360 products and their integration options
- Choose the optimum integration architecture to unify data and experiences
- Architect a single view of the customer to support service, marketing, and commerce
- Plan for critical requirements, design decisions, and implementation sequences to avoid sub-optimal solutions
- Integrate Customer 360 solutions into a single-source-of-truth solution such as a master data model
- Support business needs that require functionality from more than one component by orchestrating data and user flows

# Packt is searching for authors like you

If you're interested in becoming an author for Packt, please visit `authors.packtpub.com` and apply today. We have worked with thousands of developers and tech professionals, just like you, to help them share their insight with the global tech community. You can make a general application, apply for a specific hot topic that we are recruiting an author for, or submit your own idea.

# Share Your Thoughts

Now you've finished *Automating Salesforce Marketing Cloud*, we'd love to hear your thoughts! Scan the QR code below to go straight to the Amazon review page for this book and share your feedback or leave a review on the site that you purchased it from.

https://packt.link/r/1803237198

Your review is important to us and the tech community and will help us make sure we're delivering excellent quality content.

Made in the USA
Las Vegas, NV
23 July 2022

52056796R00254